VOICES
OF A
BLACK NATION

VOICES
OF A
BLACK NATION

POLITICAL JOURNALISM
IN THE
HARLEM RENAISSANCE

Edited by
Theodore G. Vincent

Foreword by
Robert Chrisman

Africa World Press, Inc.

P.O. Box 1892
Trenton, New Jersey 08607

AFRICA WORLD PRESS, INC.
P.O. Box 1892
Trenton, NJ 08607

First published in 1973 by Ramparts Press, Inc.

Cover design by Ife Nii-Owoo

Library of Congress Catalog Card Number: 90-64142

ISBN: 0-86543-202-3 Cloth
       0-86543-203-1 Paper

The completion of this study was made possible by a grant from the Center for Afro-American Studies at the University of California at Los Angeles.

Credit is due the Hon. Thomas W. Harvey of Philadelphia, present head of the Universal Negro Improvement Association, who made available over half a hundred long-lost issues of the *Negro World* and an issue of Garvey's daily *Negro Times*. Mrs. Amy Jacques Garvey generously provided copies of her early editorial in the Garvey weekly. Bill Taylor of Los Angeles made available copies of the *Crusader* from the Cyril Briggs papers. Robert Paul Kaufman of Berkeley provided copies of the Chicago *Whip*. Mildred Balima of the Library of Congress traced down early issues of the *Negro World* and *Emancipator* which had been retained in a Justice Department file. Miriam Knight of Berkeley provided copies of the *Africa and Orient Review* from the British Museum collection. Librarian Dorothy Porter of Howard University made available fourteen issues of the *Crusader* and copies of the *New Negro* and *Challenge*. Jean Hudson of the Schomburg Library in New York deserves commendation for providing a myriad of copying machines for the many time-pressed researchers using that invaluable collection. The Black American newspaper collection amassed by Ann Reed of the library at the University of California, Berkeley, was also extremely useful for this study. Acknowledgement is also in order for Professors Arthur Smith and Stanley Coben of UCLA, H. Viscount Nelson of Dartmouth, and Emory Tolbert of San Diego, for their help in the gathering and assembling of material.

Contents

II.
QUESTIONS OF IDEOLOGY

III.
ECONOMIC ISSUES

IV.
THE BLACK AMERICAN AND THE THIRD WORLD

V.
THE HARLEM RENAISSANCE

VI.
TOWARD THE FUTURE

Foreword

The political reality of the black press has always been acknowledged, but seldom explored and rarely in political terms. While it is a truism that the press is a political instrument, the nature and the quality of its political effect is rarely comprehended. We too often tend to regard the press's sphere of political activity as being confined to positions taken on the editorial page, to the omission, diminution and bowdlerization of significant news. While such observations are correct in and of themselves, they do not identify the basic political reality of the press.

First and foremost, the press is an organizing device. It orders, shapes and directs the consciousness of its readers. V. I. Lenin's observations on the press are of significance here. In one context he remarked, "Revolution is a little review and a little screw"—that is, agitation and propaganda plus the organizing activity of revolutionary cadre. On another occasion he stated, "As long as I have my *Pravda* [which he founded and edited] I do not need an organizer." The newspaper or periodical is not only a collection of facts and attitudes, it is a social experience, and its continuing publication is itself a political process.

For, the individual reading a newspaper or periodical is not only being exposed to a collection of facts and attitudes, he is undergoing a collective experience; he is part of a community of fellow readers who share the same experience with him. In this respect a newspaper or journal is an organizing device, one which shapes the collective consciousness of all its readers. It further creates a community among that readership, who are all simultaneously exposed to the same experience its pages provide. One could accurately regard a newspaper as a printed rally.

But the press is not only an organizing vehicle, it is also a major instrument of propaganda. Although the term "propaganda" has a negative connotation in this society, we must recognize that this derogation itself derives from propaganda, from the bourgeois myths of "impartial facts," "both sides of the story," "objective view," etc., with which we are indoctrinated and pacified. To propagandize means, literally, to propagate one's own vision of reality, to disperse it among a community of readers, viewers and listeners. As such, the press not only reaches a collective audience which is already responsive to its message, it also creates a new audience. With proper sensitivity and receptiveness to the needs, the desires, the dreams, the realities of its audience, it articulates and defines for its readership what that community has dimly felt, sensed or observed in privacy, declaring that collective consciousness in clear, cold, black type.

So the press functions as a continuous political process, one which organizes, propagates views and defines new directions, new problems and new solutions for its community. A given publication must not only find a particular chord of interest among its readership to give it an audience in the first place, it should also create new levels of consciousness based upon its first entry into the reading community's collective mind. Very often, whether a publication's circulaton expands, stays fixed or dies depends upon its ability to understand correctly the consciousness of its readership, to respond to that consciousness and shape it further, and to anticipate the direction of the community's consciousness as social, economic and political conditions change. Furthermore, the press itself becomes an instrument of that change.

It is thus with considerable satisfaction that I have read Theodore Vincent's *Voices of a Black Nation.* This collection of writings from the black movement press of the twenties and on through the thirties provides valuable insight into the major political and ideological currents among black groups of that time, as well as the means of persuasion employed by black journalists during this significant era.

As Afro-Americans, we have always understood the importance of the word as a vehicle for shaping political consciousness. We have understood this not only through our magnificent tradition of oratory, from David Walker and Frederick Douglass on through Martin Luther King and Stokely Carmichael, and our recognition of its impact in political terms; we have also understood the significance of speech and the written word if only through the systematic efforts of the white power structure in the United States to suppress their development among black people.

Literacy for black Americans during our three hundred years of bondage has always been a strategic weapon, a resource to be denied to us by any means necessary. We are aware of course of the universal ban against teaching blacks the fundamentals of reading and writing which prevailed through the Emancipation Proclamation and which exists now in subtler but equally damaging forms.

We are also aware of the powerful impact that black literacy itself had and still has upon the political shape of Afro-Americans. In his *Autobiography,* Frederick Douglass outlines the development of his literacy and the extraordinary hardship and danger involved in its acquisition. It was symbolically fitting that Douglass learned of the antislavery movement in the North through reading an abolitionist newspaper while still enslaved. It is further fitting that he founded and edited the powerful black movement newspaper, the *North Star,* upon his escape to a dubious freedom.

Nor is it surprising that the mass black nationalist leader, Marcus Garvey, saw it essential to found and edit the *Negro World,* which became the ideological arm of the UNIA; nor that W. E. B. DuBois founded and edited *The Crisis,* which performed a similar function for the NAACP. In contemporary times, we find *Muhammad Speaks, The Black Panther Intercommunal News Service, Freedomways* and *The African World* as black periodicals which assume their historic function of organizing collective black consciousness, educating that consciousness and providing it with ideology and program for action.

Voices of a Black Nation is a valuable collection of historical documents which tells us where the black press and black movements have been and, by extension, provides us with insight into the black liberation movement today. For perhaps the most important function of the black press is to record the black struggle as it happens, not through the retrospective survey of documents, which is the historian's method, but in registering the immediate, contemporary and timely political realities as they existed then and as they still live among us now.

Robert Chrisman
Editor,
The Black Scholar

Preface

In the last five years there has been a phenomenal growth in the radical black American press. In 1972 the most widely read of all the black newspapers are the five-year-old *Black Panther* and the ten-year-old *Muhammad Speaks,* each claiming over a half million in weekly paid circulation. Other newspapers in the liberation movement include the *New African* of the Republic of New Africa; *Babylon,* the organ of the Eldridge Cleaver faction of the Black Panther party; the internationally distributed *Black Times;* and the *Garvey Voice,* the organ of a resurgent Universal Negro Improvement Association. Politically radical magazines abound, almost all of them created in the past five years. There are *Black Scholar, African Opinion, Black Politics, Global Views, Soulbook, Sobu News, Black Creation, Black Poetry, Black Dialogue, Freedomways* and more. Johnson Publications, long the leader in the magazine field, has taken note of the competition now offered by radical and revolutionary journals; and Johnson has recently undergone a major shakeup of its editorial department, turning *Ebony* militant and changing the name of *Negro Digest* to the more pertinent *Black World.* Well-established black newspapers had suffered a long period of decline and many of them had become little more than free "throw-away" advertising sheets for supermarkets. Now some of these older papers are under "new management"—young radicals who are bringing these journals back to life by making them a tool for transforming and liberating black society.

The new radicalization of black journalism is long overdue. If the present boom in radical journals continues, the fourth estate can become once again a major adjunct of the liberation struggle. But it is doubtful that the newspapers and magazines will ever again hold the unique power that was theirs during the prime of the black press, when in 1926 it was termed "the greatest single power in the Negro race."[1]

The year 1926 was the height of the Harlem Renaissance. Dramatic social and economic changes were transforming Black America. Adventurous and optimistic "New Negroes" created a wide assortment of radical and revolutionary organizations. The "New Negroes" of the Renaissance seized the opportunity to transform the black press from an institution for the cultured elite into a mass-media organ for all black people. And then as now it was the more militant journalists who attracted readers to the black press.

The radical Renaissance press was marked by a fierce journalism of defiance, a defiance seen most spectacularly in the leading weekly of the period, Marcus Garvey's *Negro World*. Garvey transferred to the printed page the dynamism of his oratory, bellowing that the African colonies belong to blacks and "by God we are going to have them now or some time later, even if all the world is to waste itself in blood." A magazine called the *New Negro* summed up the attitude of the Renaissance black toward white violence. It was an attitude similar to that taken by Malcolm X and the Panthers: "It takes this form: if white men are to kill unoffending Negroes, Negroes must kill white men in defense of their lives and property." The militancy showed itself in calls for race awareness, as in a *Negro World* editorial stating: "In a world of wolves one should go armed, and one of the most powerful defensive weapons within the reach of Negroes is the practice of race first in all parts of the world." The radicals of the Black Renaissance faced the question of national loyalties in much the same way black power spokesmen do today. From a 1919 issue of the *Messenger* came the statement, "Intelligent Negroes have all reached the point where their loyalty to this country is conditional." The *Challenge* declared an oath that "By eternal heaven—I swear never to love any flag simply for its color, nor any country for its name. . . . The country of my patriotism must be above color distinction, must be . . . of liberty and not of bondage, of privilege to all, not special privilege to some." [2]

Traditional articles of faith and loyalty were everywhere attacked by Renaissance radicals. Said the *Messenger* of Thanksgiving, "We do not thank God for anything. Our deity is the toiling masses of the world, and the things for which we thank are their achievements." The terms of political dialogue were broadened to include options outside the

American system. The *Crusader* described "the two most likely proposi-
tions" for the salvation of black people to be "the establishment of a
strong, stable, independent Negro State . . . in Africa or elsewhere" and
"the establishment of a Universal Socialist Co-operative Common-
wealth." The *Crusader* concluded, "To us it seems that one working for
the first proposition would also be working for the second
proposition." [3]

The political outlooks, organizational forms, and factions of the
present were originally produced in the Harlem Renaissance of
1917-1934. The Pan-Africanist movement, so strongly promoted
by the *Black Scholar,* dates effectively from the First Pan-African Congress of 1919. Modern black nationalism dates from the emergence of
the massive Garvey movement of the Renaissance. The initial cadres of
black communists developed alongside the Garvey movement. Today,
the argument between separatists and civil rights integrationists is but
an updated version of positions laid down by Garvey's Universal Negro
Improvement Association on the one hand, and the then-ten-year-old
National Association for the Advancement of Colored People on the
other. The terms of the present split between nationalists and the political left also date from the period 1917-1934.

The ties between radical politics of the Renaissance and the present
are but vaguely understood. No doubt there is some awareness in the
Republic of New Africa that their "separate state" ideas were formulated by black communists of the Renaissance. There are rather well-
known personal connections, such as that Elijah Muhammad of the
Nation of Islam was initially a Garveyite, as was the father of Malcolm
X. And a few Panthers are aware of the debt their party owes to the
aged Renaissance radicals Harry Haywood and Cyril V. Briggs, who
proffered their advice to the formulators of the original Panther program. However, little has been done in the way of systematic study to
reveal the similarities and differences between the ideas and programs
of the Renaissance and those of the present. Such a study can be made,
and the radical press of the Harlem Renaissance is a rich source of
information.

This anthology of Renaissance social and political commentary is
compiled exclusively from the black press, the great majority of excerpts being taken from the bluntly radical periodicals, from the writers

who called themselves "New Negroes." Their outlook and their achievement can better be understood with some knowledge of the period and
of the role of the black press as a whole during those years.

*   *   *

The prime of the black American press covered the years of the U.S.
involvement in World War I and the height of the Great Depression of
the 1930s. In the number of newspapers and magazines on the news-
stands, and in the percentage of blacks reading them, the Renaissance
press outstripped any other in American history. The size of the press
mushroomed as journalists capitalized on the dramatic story of the
World War, on the mass migration of blacks from the rural South to
northern cities, and on the rediscovery of black culture. Essays, poems,
short stories and serialized novels were published, not only in black
magazines but in black newspapers as well. Historical articles, literary
criticism, and, to a lesser degree, theatre and art criticism were regular
features in the Renaissance press. News reporting was embellished with
countless unsolicited firsthand accounts of the black struggle sent in by
those who appreciated the work being done by the press and recognized
it as "The Voice of the Negro"—as Robert Kerlin aptly titled his 1919
press study.[4]

In many respects this Renaissance "New Negro" era produced the
greatest display of mass media talent ever produced by black people in
this country. Today the great power in the media is television, where
blacks are occasionally employed but almost never in control of program content. The social and political power wielded today by television was in the Renaissance era largely in the domain of the press.
Significantly, this period was also the prime time for the American
press in general, for the great metropolitan dailies, and for a vibrant
ethnic American foreign language press as well. Of course, true freedom
of the press has been restricted by backers and advertisers, and the
distribution of black papers and magazines has been restricted by
government actions and mob violence. But during the turbulent Renaissance era "New Negroes" were able to rush into print before the
censors could react; and radicals were able to make their journals some
of the most widely read black newspapers and magazines in the
country.

If the spokesmen for the 1970s are going to match the power of the black radical media of the Renaissance, then groups like the Black Panthers, the Black Muslims, and the Republic of New Africa will have to liberate some radio and television stations. Unfortunately, freedom of the press has not been extended to television and radio; one can hardly imagine the FCC granting a broadcast license to an even vaguely revolutionary black organization.

There were reasons black journalism was the most liberated of black institutions involved in political expression. The press, like the comparatively nonpolitical church and fraternal orders, was created by blacks to serve black society. The black press, from its inception in the 1820s, had avoided competition with white newspapers and magazines by concentrating on issues affecting black people. The product offered by the press was ideas about the black situation; and to a large extent, the judge of what was "fit to print" was the black editor. During the Renaissance virtually every prominent black involved in the social or political struggle of black people contributed articles to black newspapers and magazines.

The New Negro press was enhanced with the writing of numerous renegades from the American intellectual establishment. Black sociologists, economists and historians sought the platform of the press as an escape from the white-controlled intellectual world of black colleges and universities. Black colleges were obliged to cater to racially ignorant but prestigious groups like the American Association of University Professors, whose friendship was needed to keep the black colleges in good standing with white philanthropic foundations that kept the colleges alive with well-measured handouts. Of course, the black press had its share of white financial backers; but if the backers wanted a return on their investment they had to grant the black editor some leeway in attracting readers with provocative journalism.

At the turn of the century there were roughly two hundred organs of the black press, both newspapers and magazines. In the early 1920s there were close to five hundred. Today, even with the radical press revival, there are no more than two hundred. In 1912 there were four black newspapers in Chicago; in 1921 there were nine; today there are four. In New York in 1912 there were four black newspapers, in 1921 eight, and today there are three. During the New Negro era there was a massive infusion of new leadership in the field of journalism. Fewer than half of thirty-eight leading newspapers of the New Negro period had been in existence prior to World War I; and only two of the period's two dozen news magazines predated the war. The impact of the black press on its public was ably described in a 1919 dispatch of the newly founded Associated Negro Press news service.

> Fifteen years ago, it was the exceptional home that received its race newspaper each week; five years ago it was the average home; today, the average home receives not only one race periodical, but usually two or more, and the exceptional home, office, store, the schools and churches and libraries, receive from six to more than a score. This is PROGRESS; this is SUCCESS. But we have a long way to go. True, in thousands of instances, the remotest cabins in the distant hills receive their newspapers now, and the occupants read them religiously. Through the magnificent advantages of the Associated Negro Press, all important happenings of the race are known regularly in every section of the nation, and by all classes. . . . [5]

The press blossomed as part of a major social change in black society, the transformation from a predominantly rural population to an urban one, a change that would bring people to look to the media for information. Blacks in the new urban setting needed newspapers to learn of their new environment, and those in the rural hamlets of the South wanted to know of the life their relatives were living in the cities.

It was the World War that brought about the urbanization of the black American. When the war cut off the flow of European immigrants to the industrial centers of the North, the industrialists turned to the South and the black man—and woman—for a continuing supply of labor. The First World War also brought the tide of protest upon which the press rose in importance and militancy. As Gunnar Myrdal noted in *An American Dilemma*, "It was largely the Negro newspapers that made the Negroes fully conscious of the inconsistency between America's war aims to 'make the world safe for democracy' and her treatment of this minority at home."[6] Declared the black weekly Indianapolis *Freeman* of October 18, 1919, "The Negro press was never more militant nor more wide awake for race progress than it is today. Our press is the people's natural spokesman, and its voice rings true. It is sane without being timid—radical without being a firebrand." A 1922 analysis of sixty-four black newspapers found nearly 40 percent of the news items and 50 percent of the editorials in these papers devoted to racial wrongs and what could be done about them.[7]

It was during the World War that one first heard the distinction between "New Negroes" and "Old Negroes," generally a drawing of lines between young militants and accommodationist black leaders held over from the past. The distinction was initially drawn on the question of whether or not black Americans should support the U.S. entry into the war. New Negroes condemned the hypocrisy of fighting abroad for what was denied at home, while many established black leaders took a conservative stand endorsing the effort. Government-inspired pro-war hysteria had made opposition difficult; it was in seeking a platform for opposition that many a key New Negro was drawn into journalism. Such was the case with Carl Murphy, who in 1918 joined the editorial staff of his father's Baltimore *Afro-American* in order to disseminate some of the pacifist and socialist philosophy he had learned in college. From 1922 on Murphy would be editor-in-chief of the influential weekly. There emerged during the war expressly New Negro publications, the first being Hubert H. Harrison's *Negro Voice,* the organ of his pacifist Afro-American Liberty League, and A. Philip Randolph and Chandler Owen's socialist *Messenger.* Cyril V. Briggs founded his revolutionary *Crusader* monthly in 1918, after having been fired as editorial writer for the weekly *Amsterdam News* because of his antiwar editorials, such as the one headlined "Security of Life for Poles and Serbs— Why Not for Colored Nations?"

There were dramatic aspects of the war that needed no editorializing. Some 387,000 black troops were mustered for the war effort and nearly 200,000 of them went to Europe. Front-page photographs of black soldiers sold newspapers and gave the readers a sense of impending change in race relations. Here were black men sanctioned by the United States government to carry arms at a time when there were hardly a handful of black policemen in any major city in the U.S.

The return of black fighting men from Europe at war's end provided issues that further stimulated the growth of the press. Numerous newspapers and magazines expressed the view that "the BLACK MAN FOUGHT TO MAKE THE WORLD SAFE FOR DEMOCRACY, he now demands that AMERICA BE MADE AND MAINTAINED SAFE FOR BLACK AMERICANS," as stated by C. V. Richardson in his Houston *Informer* (which he was just then beginning to build into the most prominent black weekly in Texas). Enterprising weeklies like the Norfolk, Virginia, *Journal and Guide* and the Baltimore *Afro-American* ran exposés of black troops being mustered out of service without severance pay, and of others who were disarmed and then detained in military camps without being discharged. Tensions developed in the cities as white troops returned and sought employment. Finding jobs hard to get, whites demanded that black migrants from the South be removed to make job openings for themselves. The tensions erupted in bloody race riots that swept twenty-six cities in the "Red Summer" of 1919. As dutifully reported in the black press, most of these riots may have started like lynching bees of the old South, but this time murdered blacks took whites along with them to the grave. A memorable sub-headline on one postwar riot report in the black weekly Washington *Bee* ran, "Colored Rioters Poorly Armed: But Casualty List Favorable Despite Handicap."

During the war the press had played a key role in promoting the "great migration" of rural blacks to northern cities; however, by the early 1920s it was apparent that the North was failing to live up to its billing as the promised land. For the black public the move north had evoked images of acceptance into the mainstream of American life. Prior to the war, when there were few blacks in the North, they had indeed been treated better than in the South. But once the population in northern centers began to approach the proportions of blacks in the South, the blacks found themselves battling to keep the North from adopting southern customs of racial segregation. The black press of the early 1920s chronicled countless desperate civil rights struggles, such as the one detailed under this heading in the weekly Chicago *Searchlight:* "Jim-Crow School Scheme Exposes Attempt to Inaugurate Separate Schools in Chicago—Discovered and Opposed."

The mood of the New Negro press was expressed in the naming of its journals: *Crusader, Emancipator, Challenge, Competitor, Advocate, Whip, Protest, Hornet, Harlem Liberator.* It could also be noted in the mottos chosen: the *Negro World*'s "The Voice of the Awakened Negro"; the *Messenger*'s "A Journal of Scientific Radicalism"; the *Challenge*'s "It Fears Only God"; and the Baltimore *Afro-American*'s and the Raleigh *Independent*'s "Independent in All Things, Neutral in Nothing." The militancy was foretold in the titles chosen by columnists: "Shafts and Darts" and "Under the Lash of the Whip." A number of papers carried platforms, printed regularly on the editorial page. The tone of these is typified by one in the Los Angeles *California Eagle* of Charlotta A. Bass:

1. The hiring of Negroes as a matter of right, rather than as a concession, in those institutions where their patronage creates a demand for labor;

2. The increased participation of Negroes in municipal, state, and national government;

3. The abolition of enforced segregation and all other artificial barriers to the recognition of true merit;

4. The patronizing of Negroes by Negroes as a matter of principle;

5. More rapid development of those communities in which Negroes live by co-operation between citizens and those who have business investments in such communities; and

6. An enthusiastic support for a greater degree of service at the hands of all social, civic, charitable, and religious institutions.

It was in promoting organizations and the ideologies that went with them that many New Negro journalists were drawn into the profession. Actually, few of the leading New Negro journalists had had journalism as their first calling. There were trade union organizers like A. Philip Randolph and Chandler Owen of the *Messenger;* and Hubert H. Harrison of the *Negro Voice,* who had played a key role in organizing black workers for the memorable Industrial Workers of the World strike at Paterson, New Jersey, in 1913. W. E. B. DuBois left a professorship at Atlanta University to edit the NAACP organ the *Crisis,* and sociologist Charles S. Johnson left a college post in 1922 to edit the Urban League's *Opportunity.* There had long been professional politicians in the black press, but they had almost all been functionaries of the Republican party, which did next to nothing for the black struggle. The New Negro era brought a new breed of politician-journalist: socialist W. A. Domingo of the *Negro World* and New York *Emancipator*; communist George Padmore of the *Negro Worker*; Charlotta A. Bass of the *California Eagle* and the California Progressive party; and William Bridges, of *Challenge,* who headed the Black Nationalist Liberty party until he was expelled for his ties to Tammany Democrats.

The black newspapers of the Renaissance were in a position somewhat analogous to that of the underground press today; that is, they were providing information and opinion for an oppressed social and political minority. Their readers were engaged in a day-to-day struggle and the newspapers and magazines had to reflect that effort. The New Negro era was also the prime of the American ethnic and foreign language press, in which the top papers were those emphasizing the struggles of recent immigrants to obtain their share of American prosperity.

There have been, however, countertendencies in the black press. During the Renaissance there were attempts to copy the style of the white dailies in appealing to readers with the yellow journalism of crime and sensationalism. One study found that the black papers featuring sensationalism were generally in the same cities in which the white press emphasized this type of journalism—in Chicago, for instance, one black weekly, the *Whip,* featured a gangland gossip columnist, "Nosy Knows," and the leading black weekly, the *Defender,* was prone to juxtapose stories of southern white atrocities against blacks with black crimes news, as in "Boils Wife in Oil, Grins While She Burns." One Pittsburgh paper carried a comic strip about a fellow obsessed with numbers—i.e., a weekly tip on the numbers racket.

The editors and publishers of black weeklies were always mindful that its black readers were also buying the white dailies. Featuring news and analysis of black protest was but one method for distinguishing the black from the white paper. Another tactic for attracting readers was to play up the social world of "black society"—the black bourgeoisie being most likely to have the extra cash to purchase black papers. A number of smaller weeklies subsisted almost entirely on the readership of the local bourgeoisie, who would scan each issue to see if their names had achieved the honor of notation on the printed page. The typical society page of a black paper offered diversion and escape from the real world and pandered to the middle-class values of conspicuous consumption and hedonistic self-indulgence. This catering to the middle class has been severely criticized and ridiculed by scholars, particularly E. Franklin Frazier in his influential *Black Bourgeoisie.* But this criticism should not obscure the radical side of the press and the special problems facing blacks in producing *any* type of journal.

Almost all black newspapers, even in the heyday of the New Negro press, were in constant and serious financial difficulties. The turnover among the smaller ones was enormous. The 1966 *Negro Handbook* listed only thirty-three black weekly newspapers having a continuous existence from the New Negro period. As noted by Myrdal, "The main observation about the advertising in the Negro press is that there is so little of it. The paucity of advertising, of course, makes the economy of the Negro newspapers precarious. It cannot keep the copy price too high, either, if it wants a substantial circulation."[8] (The usual price in the New Negro era was five cents locally, ten cents out of town.) Many papers received financial aid from political parties, and in the North there developed the phenomenon of new newspapers springing up just before an important election—and disappearing shortly thereafter. There were other forms of financial aid: as listed in the 1925–26 *Negro Yearbook* there were seventeen newspapers connected with religious groups, half a dozen with fraternal orders, and four with black colleges. During the New Negro years a dozen or more attempts were made at starting black daily newspapers, but Black America did not have the finances for this effort. The only daily to survive was the *Atlanta World,* which was launched in 1928. (Since 1956 the *Chicago Defender* has put out a daily edition.) The ideal format for the black newspaper proved to be the weekly. The leading weeklies of the Renaissance hired large staffs of reporters, editorial writers and office personnel, and purchased their own printing plants, and became among the most formidable business enterprises in Black America.

Of the newspapers of the Renaissance a dominant role was played by Marcus Garvey's weekly *Negro World,* the organ of the Universal Negro Improvement Association, his worldwide black nationalist organization. The internationally distributed *Negro World* became in the early 1920s the first black paper to top two hundred thousand in circulation. Significantly, whereas the leading white newspapers have usually been politically conservative, the paper that led the way in the rise of the black press was the organ of a militant black power organization. There were three newspapers rivaling, and by the late 1920s surpassing, the *Negro World:* Robert S. Abbott's Chicago *Defender;* Robert L. Vann's Pittsburgh *Courier;* and Carl Murphy's Baltimore *Afro-American.* These papers developed national editions, making them, like Garvey's, weekly news magazines. The *Afro-American* also inaugurated in the 1930s a chain of newspapers in four eastern cities. The editors of the *Defender,* the *Courier* and the *Afro-American* were uncompromising in their demands for political, social and economic equality and hired some of the most outspoken columnists.

There were more than a dozen regionally distributed news weeklies.

In four of these—William Monroe Trotter's Boston *Guardian,* Roscoe Dunjee's Oklahoma City *Black Dispatch,* T. Thomas Fortune's New York *Interstate-Tattler,* and Charlotta A. Bass's Los Angeles *California Eagle*—there was substantial support for causes connected with the political left and/or black nationalism.

The vast majority of black newspapers were small-town operations in the South where freedom of the press was minimal and where it was dangerous to endorse even the NAACP, much less trade unionism, socialism, or black nationalism. The small-town papers were most often gossip sheets for the local bourgeoisie; and the vibrancy of the Renaissance was rarely recorded. When these papers did carry controversial news it was usually a report from one of a half dozen black news services. The provocative columnists of big-city papers might have enlivened the small southern weeklies, but only one of these writers was syndicated—Dean William Pickens. By jealously hoarding their columnists the major papers helped to sell their national and regional editions.

To evaluate the political side of the black newspapers one has to look to the big cities, especially those outside the South. There it was safe to present strong support for civil rights movements and give substantial coverage to the activities of the more radical organizations, a journalistic approach that won readers. The rise of the Pittsburgh *Courier* in the mid-1920s can be attributed to editor Vann's adoption of a more militant editorial policy and his hiring of two columnists from the staff of the socialist *Messenger* magazine. The Philadelphia *Tribune,* Indianapolis *Freeman,* and New York *Age,* three of the leading black papers in circulation prior to World War I, failed to capitalize on the growth of the press in the postwar era, and significantly they had played down news of black radicals. The New York *Amsterdam News,* today the leading black paper in that city, did not rise in prominence until the 1930s, when it enlivened its staff with a number of young writers of strong left-wing opinions.

Black American magazines followed the pattern of black newspapers: the leading journals were those with militant editorial policies. The leader in the field of general news monthlies, with a circulation of nearly one hundred thousand copies, was the NAACP organ *Crisis,* founded in 1910 and edited by Dr. W. E. B. DuBois. A. Philip Randolph and Chandler Owen's *Messenger,* founded in 1917, developed a circulation of well over fifty thousand. Cyril V. Briggs's *Crusader,* launched in 1918, reached a circulation of thirty-seven thousand. The National Urban League's *Opportunity,* founded in 1922, built a circulation near fifty thousand. Like *Crisis* and *Opportunity,* the *Messenger* and the *Crusader* also had organizational backing. The *Messenger* received aid from the Socialist party, and for its first years had ample advertising from SP-led trade unions. The *Crusader* was the official organ of the small revolutionary group, the African Blood Brotherhood. More important for its circulation, the *Crusader* was sold extensively in the widespread Garvey movement.

Significantly, at the end of the First World War there were more general news monthlies than at any other time in Afro-American history (including the present revival). This was the comparatively flush time for the black economy, brought about by war industry employment. Most of these magazines were started during or immediately after the war. During the short boom period, magazines geared to social protest, in addition to those mentioned, included the *Challenge* of William Bridges, Duse Mohamed Ali's *Africa and Orient Review,* the *Negro Voice* of Hubert Harrison, the *New Negro* of A. V. Bernier, and the *Promoter* and the *Veteran.* There were others appealing to black high society: *Favorite,* edited by Fenton Johnson, the *Competitor* of Robert L. Vann, and Anthony Overton's *Half-Century Magazine,* the title of which connoted a half century of freedom from slavery. Garveyite Willis N. Huggins produced a magazine directed to black social workers, *Up-Reach.* And there were magazines with a regional circulation, including the Rhode Island *Triangle* and the Memphis *Negro Outlook.*

Unfortunately, of the more than two dozen general interest magazines published during the early Renaissance, only *Crisis* and *Opportunity* survived the period. Very few outlasted the economic recession of 1921–22. The *Crusader* was reduced in 1922 to the *Crusader Bulletin,* and went out of existence entirely in 1923. *Half-Century* survived until 1925 primarily because its owner, Anthony Ovington, was one of the wealthiest blacks in the United States. In 1928 the *Messenger* went out of existence as a mass circulation magazine and was replaced by the *Black Worker,* the trade union organ of the Brotherhood of Sleeping Car Porters. There probably would have been numerous successful black monthlies had the cost of producing and distributing them not been so much higher than that of newspapers.

In the late 1920s and early '30s there was a short resurgence in the magazine field. Robert S. Abbott took profits from his *Defender* to produce for three years a general news periodical, *Abbott's Monthly.* The Garvey movement inaugurated *Black Man,* a monthly published irregularly until 1940. The Communist party founded the internationally distributed *Negro Worker.* And in the academic field, the *Journal of Negro Education* was founded in 1932. The difficulties for black Americans in the magazine field are evidenced by the fact that despite a tremendous interest in the scholarly study of black life generated in the Harlem Renaissance of the 1920s, there was but one scholarly journal to publish continuously through the Renaissance period, Carter G. Woodson's *Journal of Negro History.*

As blacks lost their wartime employment, and were then hit with a recession, the publishing of both magazines and newspapers suffered; and the ability of newspapers to hold their own was in no small part attributable to their editors' having the foresight to make their weeklies double as magazines as well as newspapers. The Chicago *Defender,* Pittsburgh *Courier* and Baltimore *Afro-American* even serialized novels.

The failure of literary magazines in a period of prodigious literary output followed the pattern which saw blacks driven out of the record business at the start of the financial boom in jazz recording. The prime example in the music field is Harry Pace, who inaugurated his Black Swan record company shortly after the World War; in one year he had introduced to the public a number of top stars of the coming "Jazz Age." But as fast as he introduced them they were pirated away with fat contracts offered by the larger white recording companies. Pace was forced to sell out to Paramount (which didn't get many of his artists since most of them had already gone over to Columbia). In this period, 1919–22, it was the black magazine that was introducing the poetry and short stories and novels of the Black Renaissance. The wholesale failure of the magazines coincided with the "discovery" of black writers by white liberals and leftists. Harlem was raided by white literary impresarios who came away with poems, novels and stories, and in some cases took the writers as well—poet-novelist Claude McKay becoming an editor of Max Eastman's *Liberator,* and short story writer Eric Walrond an editor of *New Masses.*

The Renaissance writer Langston Hughes has sketched in his autobiography the tragic story of the publication of the one issue of *Fire.* In the summer of 1926, Hughes and six other artists pooled their meager resources to bring out a beautifully printed glossy magazine that would be "worthy of the first Negro art quarterly." They had no organizational backing, only one of them even had a job. They had to go one thousand dollars in debt to publish, and once *Fire* was printed, they had no way to distribute it. According to Hughes, the failure of *Fire* "taught me a lesson about little magazines. But since white folks had them, we Negroes thought we could have one, too. But we didn't have the money."⁹

The problems of founding a quality literary magazine can be contrasted with the task of launching a newspaper. The thirty-two-page Chicago *Defender* was initially four pages of newsprint peddled on streetcorners by editor Abbott. The Chicago *Broad Ax* likewise started as a small sheet peddled on streetcorners by editor Julius Taylor and his wife. Robert L. Vann launched the Pittsburgh *Courier* by pooling with a factory worker the savings from their wages.

Financial problems were by no means the only ones confronting the black press. Although there was nominal freedom of the press, there were special problems for black journalism in distribution. The importation of northern papers into the Deep South was a risky business; and there was no chance for publishing a genuinely radical periodical there. During the World War, agents peddling the Chicago *Defender* in the South had been beaten, run out of town, and had their papers confiscated. A letter to the editor printed in the July 1920 issue of the *Crusader* tells of the problems of distribution:

> [Somewhere in the South. Names are deleted for safety of the writer.]
> Dear Sir: We here in the South are not allowed to sell Northern newspapers. We have to slip the paper into the hands of our friends, and I am trying to induce my friends to subscribe by the year for the *Crusader*. Every public school teacher is closely watched, also the Negro preacher. I give you this and you can read between the lines. You will please send me the magazines as I notify you. I will be responsible for every one sent to me for my friends.

In addition to the extralegal threat of the lynch mob, the distribution of the New Negro periodicals was hurt by government threats and outright prohibitions. The *Messenger* lost its second-class mailing privileges for three years, after a 1918 issue which carried a satirical article,

"Pro-Germanism Among Negroes." The May-June 1919 issue of the *Messenger* was denied the use of the mails entirely, because of its radical content. And during the war an issue of the weekly Richmond *Planet* was denied use of the mails because of its allegedly seditious antiwar content. In 1923, on the pretext of gathering information for a mail fraud indictment against Marcus Garvey, a raiding party of government agents confiscated the entire subscriber mailing list of Garvey's *Negro World*. Garvey had to obtain a court order to retrieve his list and keep his paper going. In 1920 an attempt was made in Congress to pass a law prohibiting the use of the U.S. mail to any "Negro publication" that was deemed to advocate "racial violence." As noted by Harlem Renaissance poet and novelist James Weldon Johnson in one of his New York *Age* editorials, the passage of such a law could have been interpreted to exclude almost any black publication from the mails, were the government interpreters typical Southerners. Though the law did not pass Congress, the press reaction to its very proposal showed that many papers felt threatened, for it seemed to fit a pattern. Reports issued by the U.S. Justice Department* in 1919 and by a New York State Legislative Committee in 1920 condemned allegedly seditious editorials and news stories in more than two dozen black newspapers and magazines, including the *Messenger, Crusader, Challenge, New Negro, Promoter, Crisis, Negro World, Veteran,* and *Emancipator.* The folding of many of these journals may have been in part attributable to a loss of advertising and other financial backing scared away by these reports.[10]

The Depression decade of the 1930s was a disaster for the black press. At the time of the stock market crash there had been one hundred thirty black periodicals in the fifty largest U.S. cities; less than half of these were in existence by 1935. These failures marked the end of an era of political introspection in the black press that had been noted in its extreme by a variety of forms of black nationalism.

Nineteen thirty-three ushered in the integrationist New Deal of Franklin D. Roosevelt, and it would give the black struggle a new

---

* The compiler of the U.S. Justice Department report was the future head of the FBI, J. Edgar Hoover. The report rings with racial prejudice, as when it refers to "the better behaved" black publications; when it condemns the "insolent, offensive" *Messenger;* and when it degrades the Madagascar poet Andy Razafkeriefo with the query "if that is a name."

direction. The slogan "Black and White Unite and Fight" replaced the New Negro slogan "Black Unity." The struggle of economic classes pushed racial battles into the background. Economic conditions dictated a cooperative effort of black and white poor, and the threatening growth of worldwide fascism further helped to generate a "United Front." The leading black weeklies—the *Defender, Courier, Afro-American* and *Amsterdam News*—would build ever-larger circulations by promoting economic equality and fighting fascism. But there was something about this New Deal struggle that would undermine the vitality of the black press. The overall objective of the struggle had shifted from that of blacks trying to become free blacks, to that of black Americans seeking to enter the American mainstream. During the New Deal the black press was doing itself in, in much the same way that the ethnic-American foreign language press was running itself out of business by encouraging the assimilation of its readers into the American "melting pot."

During the Renaissance, black nationalist, black socialist and black communist organs had all proposed various applications of Black Power. The New Deal offered consensus politics. As applied in the black press this type of politics meant that radical programs were echoes of those devised by the white left, moderate programs echoes of those of white liberals.

The shifts in political style during the 1930s could be discerned in the list of black periodicals that failed. With the change in black voting preference from Republican to Democrat there were failures among the GOP-backed black weeklies. But more significant were the failures of papers that had been favorable to the black nationalist Garvey movement. Garvey's *Negro World* itself folded in the summer of 1933; and it is worth noting that the *Negro World* had endorsed Democrats consistently since 1928. Many papers that had been favorable to Garvey folded, including the New York *Interstate-Tattler,* the Chicago *Whip,* the Buffalo *American,* the Omaha *Monitor,* and the Cleveland *Advocate.*

A remarkable development of the reputed left-wing New Deal period was the virtual elimination of the black socialist and black communist press. Whereas the black leftists of the New Negro era had proudly published periodicals expressly for the black struggle, the leftists of the New Deal saw little need for such organs. The folding of the *Messenger* in 1928 had closed out the last mass circulation socialist organ for blacks. And the black communist press was eliminated when its *Harlem Liberator* was discontinued in 1934 and the international monthly *Negro Worker* in 1937.

A hallmark of the New Negro press had been its variety of political expression. What made this possible was the presence of nationalist, socialist and communist organs that were distributed to a general mass readership. Black journalism was a risky business and espousing radical social and political movements could cost a fearful loss of advertising; the existence of militant periodicals was essential for pushing the more run-of-the-mill periodical to deal with radical ideas. The Garveyite black nationalist *Negro World,* for instance, reached every corner of the United States. The existence of the *Negro World* put pressure on other papers to take note of the ideas and activities of black nationalists; and where one paper in a city would continue to avoid the issues presented by the Garveyites, another would step in and try to corner the local nationalist market, the existence of which had been proven by the success of the *Negro World.*

The radical periodicals published by and for blacks were essential for developing a black political perspective. The establishment of identifiable positions of political ideology are essential for political development and struggle--an oppressed group must have programs and ideologies through which to conduct the struggle. These were provided in the Renaissance press. They were lost in the New Deal press.

The shift from independent to interracial political struggle was severely criticized by Dr. DuBois in his *Crisis.* Always the political gadfly and critic, DuBois had earlier opposed the nationalism of the New Negro period because he feared it was too insular, too divorced from the need to cooperate with whites for common goals. The political shifts of the early 1930s disturbed DuBois for the opposite reasons—he feared that the group power of the black American would be submerged and lost in coalitions with white liberals and radicals. In the *Crisis,* Du Bois began pushing for black separatism, independent black trade unions, independent black political organizations, black control of black colleges, etc. Then in 1934 he resigned from the *Crisis* due to severe criticism of his nationalist stand hurled at him by his NAACP associates.

W. E. B. DuBois and Marcus Garvey were but the two most prominent black journalists pushed out with the changing times. Across the political spectrum, key journalists whose politics had been nurtured in the New Negro era were eliminated from the field. Cyril V. Briggs was relieved of his editorship of the communist *Harlem Liberator* by a man more in tune with the United Front politics of the New Deal than was Briggs, who in the early 1920s had headed the nationalist African Blood Brotherhood. George Padmore resigned as editor of the *Negro Worker* and angrily renounced his affiliation with communism upon learning that the new United Front policy entailed the curtailing of aid to revolutionary movements in colonial Africa. Out of journalism in the early 1930s were the left-wing columnists Frank Crosswaith of the *Messenger* and later the *Defender,* and Floyd Calvin of the *Messenger* and then the *Courier.* Garveyite columnists eased out included Ulysses S. Poston of the *Negro World, Negro Times, Tattler, Courier* and *Contender;* Arthur S. Gray of the *Negro World* and numerous West Coast weeklies; and Bennie Butler of the *Negro Times, Tattler* and other New York papers. Lost from the scene in the early 1930s were prominent Harlem Renaissance writers and poets who had played a role in journalism, including Eric Walrond of the Garvey Press, *Opportunity* and *New Masses*; Jessie Fauset, assistant editor of *Crisis*; Wallace Thurman, managing editor of the *Messenger*; and Claude McKay of the *Liberator*. (Significantly, of the above-mentioned individuals, it could hardly be said they were eliminated because of age, since only DuBois and Gray were over fifty.)

The actual top circulation of black newspapers—the backbone of the black press—came in 1950, with 2,440,000, compared to a top in the New Negro era of 1,600,000 in the late 1920s. (In 1910 the newspaper circulation had been somewhat between 300,000 and 500,000.) But the 1950 figure does not reflect the shallowness of the press at that time. It lacked a single nationalist, socialist or communist periodical. The newspapers of 1950 had lost not only political variety but quantity as well, being consolidated into 187 papers, with half the circulation held by the top two dozen publishers. And there were sizable cities with large black populations that had no local black press, including Hartford, Connecticut; Wilmington, Delaware; Lexington, Kentucky; and Austin, Texas.

After 1950, financial pressures, not unlike those confronting the declining white dailies, drastically curtailed the black press. By 1966 the number of newspapers was down to 124; the circulation had been cut to 1,580,000, and a growing portion of this was in papers that were becoming free distribution throw-aways. While the essential newspaper side of the press was collapsing, there developed a boom in the magazine business. However, as listed in the 1966 *Negro Handbook,* the magazine field was a political wasteland. There was a half million circulation in such publications as *Bronze Thrills, Hep,* and *Jive,* the likes of which were nonexistent in the New Negro era. Another million in circulation was held by the only slightly more socially conscious journals *Ebony, Sepia* and *Elegant.*

In 1966 *Muhammad Speaks* was but three years old and just beginning to build its massive circulation. The *Black Panther* and most of the other radical black periodicals had yet to appear.

1. Edwin Mims, *The Advancing South, Stories of Progress and Reaction* (Garden City: Doubleday, Page & Co., 1926), p. 268.
2. *Negro World,* October 16, 1918, quoted in W. F. Elkins, "Suppression of the *Negro World* in the British West Indies," from *Science and Society; New Negro,* September 1919; *Negro World,* July 26, 1919; *The Messenger,* August 1919; *The Challenge,* August 1919.
3. *The Messenger,* December 1919; *The Crusader,* April 1921.
4. Robert T. Kerlin, *The Voice of the Negro 1919* (New York: E. P. Dutton & Co., 1920).
5. Quoted in Kerlin, *op. cit.,* p. 1.
6. Gunnar Myrdal, *An American Dilemma* (New York: Harper & Brothers, 1944), p. 914.
7. *See* Frederick G. Detweiler, *The Negro Press in the United States* (Chicago: University of Chicago Press, 1922).
8. Myrdal, *op. cit.,* p. 922.
9. Langston Hughes, *The Big Sea* (New York: Hill and Wang, 1940), p. 238.
10. *See* A. Mitchell Palmer, "Radicalism and Sedition Among the Negroes as Reflected in Their Publications," report of the U.S. Department of Justice, vol. 12 of Senate Documents, no. 153, 66th Congress, 1st Session, 1919, pp. 161-187. *See also* the Lusk Committee Report, "Revolutionary Radicalism, A Report of the Joint Legislative Committee of New York Investigating Seditious Activities," vol. 2.

VOICES
OF A
BLACK NATION

Note to the Reader:

In the interests of authenticity, the original articles which follow are reproduced precisely as they were first printed, including any aberrations of spelling or punctuation. Only those misspellings which were clearly typographical errors, or unusual punctuation which might confuse the meaning, have been changed. All omissions are indicated by ellipses.—Ed.

I.

The
Emerging
New Negro

1.
General Trends
and Issues

World War I cut off the flow of white immigrant laborers from Europe and created a labor shortage in the growing northern industrial centers, which brought about a "great migration" of rural blacks to northern cities. The black press took a key role in promoting the migration; and one paper did more than any other to promote the move out of the South, the Chicago *Defender* of Robert S. Abbott. Subsidized with employment advertising from northern industry, Abbott launched a national edition of his paper in 1917. The style of the *Defender* appeal to southern blacks is shown in selection (b), an editorial by columnist W. Allison Sweeney, whose professed specialty was "breaking southerners and 'white Folks' niggers on the wheel." (Sweeney broke into journalism at the turn of the century with a massive pictorial article on black history that was widely published in white as well as black publications. He joined the *Defender* shortly before the World War. His death in 1921 was reported in black papers across the country, a testimony to the wide popularity of his *Defender* column.)

The U.S. government whipped up a prowar hysteria after the American entry into the conflict. Traditional black leaders generally accepted the war as a legitimate fight for democracy; in so doing they alienated themselves from an emerging group of young radicals. To these self-proclaimed "New Negroes," it was rank hypocrisy for blacks to fight abroad for what was denied at home. However, making this argument in a censored wartime press proved difficult. The *Messenger,* one of the first expressly "New Negro" journals, smuggled in the anti-war message through satire, as in "Pro-Germanism Among Negroes"; and injected it in the form of an afterthought in "The Failure of the Negro Leaders." The latter article, by Chandler Owen, is selection (c).

43

(Owen and A. Philip Randolph were co-editors of the *Messenger*. They had been brought together through trade union and Socialist party work in New York. Owen was a renegade from the black upper class in North Carolina and a graduate of Virginia Union University.) Selection (a), from the pen of Randolph and Owen in the *Messenger*, presents their "Thanksgiving" homily to revolution, which exemplifies the way they saw the black struggle tied in with the worldwide revolutionary surge of the immediate postwar period.

There were some four dozen major race riots between 1916 and 1921, twenty-six alone in the "Red Summer" of 1919, when city after city was bathed in blood. Almost all of these confrontations occurred in border or northern states; if there was any pattern here it was the attempt of white mobs to terrorize blacks and reduce them in the cities to the position they had long held in the rural South. However, in many instances the white mobs were met with well-placed gunfire. The black press applauded this fighting spirit, as shown in selection (d), a report on the Tulsa riot of 1921 in the Washington *Bee* of Calvin Chase. (Chase was one of black journalism's senior editors, having founded the *Bee* in 1879. He was involved in the Niagara movement of Dr. DuBois and later supported DuBois in the building of the Pan-African Congress movement. Chase died in 1921 and his paper folded shortly thereafter.)

With the riots there came a wave of lynchings. Selection (e) from the Washington *Eagle* describes the roasting alive of a lynch victim—a not uncommon form of the barbaric ritual. (The *Eagle*, one of the weeklies launched during the World War, was the organ of J. Finley Wilson, Grand Exalted Leader of the Elks fraternal order and, during the 1930s, one of the most influential civil rights fighters in the country.)

The white mobs of lynchers have been gradually replaced with the legal lynchers of the American police and court system. The connection between the lawless mob and the licensed lyncher is discussed in selection (f) from Carl Murphy in his Baltimore *Afro-American*. (Murphy was in his late twenties when he became involved with the Socialist party while teaching at Howard University during the First World War. In 1922 he took over editorship of the Baltimore weekly founded by his father and built it into one of the top three black papers in the country.)

Black urbanization brought to the forefront many new problems of race relations, one of the more important being residential segregation—ghettoization. In southern cities this was accomplished through zoning ordinances expressly designed to separate the races. In the North the same thing was accomplished through the restrictive covenant. As shown in selection (g), from Julius Taylor in his Chicago *Broad Ax*, these secret agreements of realtors and "homeowners' associations" were bitterly opposed by blacks from the start. (Taylor founded the *Broad Ax* in Salt Lake City in the 1890s as an organ for black miners. At the turn of the century he moved it to Chicago, where his paper became a noted source of anti–Booker T. Washington sentiment.)

Selection (h) is an exposé of Ku Klux Klan activity in Watts, California, run in the Los Angeles *California Eagle*. The initial influx of black people into the Watts area of Los Angeles came in the early 1920s. In 1925 the KKK engaged in a concerted effort to discourage the growth of the black community. The Klan design was to pit the sizable Italian-American community against the blacks, with the help of paid Uncle Tom blacks. The editors of the Eagle, Charlotta and Joseph Bass, obtained a secret letter of Klan plans. The publishing of the letter brought a libel suit from the KKK. The *Eagle* editors won the court case. (The key figure on the *Eagle* was Mrs. Bass, who became editor in 1912. When later married she shared the editorship with her husband, but remained the decision-maker. In the early 1920s she was co-president of the Los Angeles branch of the Garvey movement, and also developed a close friendship with A. Philip Randolph and Chandler Owen of the *Messenger*. Editorially she was severely critical of the left-nationalist split that developed in the East. In 1952 Mrs. Bass was the Progressive party candidate for vice-president of the United States.)

In the great economic depression of the 1930s, the "last hired, first fired"–usually black–suffered a disaster double that of the white American. A lament over the declining fortunes of black institutions is presented by Professor Kelly Miller of Howard University in selection (i), from the New York *Amsterdam News*. (Miller was a regular contributor to this paper and many others. In the radical period after World War I, Miller had been pegged as one of the more prominent "old crowd Negroes." With the coming of the New Deal he became an outspoken red-baiter, and was a friendly witness for the McCarthyite witch-hunters of the late 1940s.)

Eviction for non-payment of rent was one of the more common tragedies of the Depression. To halt evictions, Communists organized "anti-eviction militias"–actually any group of people around who would carry household belongings back in as fast as the sheriff and his men carried them out. A number of these contests ended in violence. The worst case occurred in Chicago: three blacks were shot dead by police while attempting to stop the eviction of a seventy-two-year-old woman. In selection (j), editor Joseph D. Bibb of the Chicago *Whip*, in his "Under the Lash of the Whip" column, comments on the unfair criticism of the Communists in the so-called "eviction riot." Selection (k) presents two short articles by Cyril V. Briggs in his weekly communist *Harlem Liberator* describing the phenomenon of the rent strike, which by the mid-1930s had become a widespread protest action in New York.*

* For background information on Bibb *see* page 244; on Briggs *see* page 123.

[a]
A THANKSGIVING HOMILY
TO REVOLUTION
A. PHILIP RANDOLPH and CHANDLER OWEN
Messenger/December 1919

... First, we are especially thankful for the Russian Revolution—the greatest achievement of the twentieth century.

Second, we are thankful for the German Revolution, the Austrian Revolution, the Hungarian Revolution and the Bulgarian Revolution.

Third, we are thankful for the world unrest, which has manifested itself in the titanic strikes which are sweeping and have been sweeping Great Britain, France, Italy, the United States, Japan, and in fact every country in the world.

Fourth, we are thankful for the solidarity of labor, for the growth of industrial unionism, for the relegation of trade unionism, for the triple alliances of the railway, transport, and mine workers in England and America.

Fifth, we are especially thankful that radicalism has permeated America, giving rise to many of the greatest strikes in history, such as our present steel strike, mine strike, and our impending railroad strike.

Sixth, we are thankful for the first successful general strike, in America, which lifted its awful head (awful to capital) in Seattle, Washington.

Seventh, we are thankful for the New Crowd Negro, who has made his influence felt in every field—economic, political, social, educational and physical force. The New Negro has been in the front ranks of strikes. He has taken his place in Socialist politics. He is an integral part of nearly every great social movement. In the field of education, The Messenger Magazine and The Crusader have become fixed parts in the life of Negro Americans, while The Messenger interprets the Negro's new point of view to nearly eighteen thousand white readers every month. On the field of physical force, the Negro has been right on the job for the protection of his home, his life and his loved ones. The Washington, Chicago, Longview [Texas], Knoxville, Elaine [Arkansas] and Omaha riots are bright spots in the New Negroes' attitude toward American lawlessness and anarchy. They represent the New Negro upholding the dignity of the law against both the white hoodlums and the government—the latter of whom should have seen that law was upheld.

Eighth, we are thankful for the waning influence of the Old Crowd Negro and white leaders, and especially pleased to see the accelerated rate by which their power and influence are declining every day, while the new type of leadership of the New Crowd Negro has become popular with the masses in every nook and corner of the world.

Lastly, we are thankful for the speedy oncoming of the new order of society in which Thanksgiving will be relieved of its cynicism and hypocrisy—when people may be thankful every day of the year instead of as now upon one day, which is more lip thanks than real thanks. The sleeping giant—Labor—has awakened, and for this there should be thanks and rejoicing indeed.

From an editorial entitled "Thanksgiving." The article was unsigned; Randolph and Owen were the editors of *The Messenger*.

[b]
URGING BLACKS TO MOVE NORTH
W. ALLISON SWEENEY
Chicago Defender/June 23, 1917

A white folks nigger . . . has recently been called to my attention, and for the same reason that an unchecked rat has been known to jeopardize the life of a great ship, a mouse's nibble of a match to set a mansion aflame, I've concluded to carve a
"Slice of Liver or two"
from that bellowing ass, who, at this very moment no doubt, somewhere in the South, is going up and down the land, telling the natives *why* they should be content, as the *Tribune* puts it, to become "Russianized," to remain in that land—to them—of *blight;* of *murdered* kin, *deflowered* womanhood, *wrecked* homes, *strangled* ambitions, *make-believe* schools, *roving* "gun parties," *midnight arrests, rifled* virginity, *trumped up* charges, *lonely* graves, where owls hoot, and where friends dare not go! Do you wonder at the thousands leaving the land where every foot of ground marks a tragedy, leaving the grave of their fathers and all that is dear, to seek their fortunes in the North? And you who say that their going is to seek better wages are insulting

truth, dethroning reason, and consoling yourself with a groundless allegation.

This article bore the headline "A Chicago 'Nigger' Preacher, A 'Feeder,' of the 'Little Hells,' Springs Up to Hinder Our Brethren Coming North."

[c]
THE FAILURE OF THE NEGRO LEADERS
CHANDLER OWEN
Messenger/January 1918

The Negro leaders have failed. It is hard to admit. Race-pride revolts against it. But the remedy lies in recognizing the condition and setting out to remedy it.

Negro leaders like Dr. W. E. B. DuBois, Kelly Miller, William Pickens, Archibald Grimke, James W. Johnson, Robert Russa Moton, Fred R. Moore, Wm. H. Lewis and Chas. W. Anderson are a discredit to Negroes and the laughing stock among whites.

We have no ill-feeling toward these men. Many of them have held out the best light (or the least poor) for the race during the last ten or twenty years. We have admired them and we recognize their full merit and worth. We do not now impugn the motives of most of them. We impeach their methods. We do not hold that reality actuates them. But we bring against them the worst indictment of the modern world—ignorance—ignorance of the methods by which to achieve the ends aimed at.

Let us take Dr. DuBois, for example. He has done some good work in stimulating the formation of the National Association for the Advancement of Colored People. He has persistently and consistently stood for the abolition of disfranchisement, discrimination and Jim Crowism. He has fought to secure larger measure of support for institutions of higher education and to increase public and high school facilities for Negroes. As a general principle he has opposed segregation. Lynch law he has condemned directly. He fortunately supported woman suffrage though his reasons therefor were not sound and sufficient.

Still Dr. DuBois has frequently urged the adoption of many measures which defeat his very purposes and aims. To illustrate: He opposes, we believe sincerely, segregation. Yet he was among the first to advocate a Jim Crow training camp for Negroes and he has been a repeated supporter of Jim Crow Y.M.C.A.'s. Some shadow of practicality might be urged in support of the Y.M.C.A. measure as the lesser of two evils, but the Jim Crow camp is indefensible—military duty not being a benefit, but a burden, shunned and rejected from early history by those who could escape from its hideous clutches and its grim tentacles.

Lynch law, Dr. DuBois condemns directly, but he has seldom, if ever, shown a grasp of its true causes and the probable remedy. One has not seen where the Doctor ever recognized the necessity of the Negroes getting into labor unions in the South as a means of eliminating the Negro as a scab, allaying thereby the ill-feeling against him by the working white man, while at the same time, limiting and controlling the supply of labor, which would increase the demand for labor both white and black. Moreover, this would be the strongest blow which peonage could be dealt.

Instead, however, we see Dr. DuBois and all the other Negro editors and leaders herald in big headlines, "Negroes Break Strike!" As though that were something to exult in. And they preach a gospel of hate of labor unions in criminal ignorance of the trend of the modern working world, when they should be explaining to Negroes the necessity of allying themselves with the workers' motive power and weapon—the Labor Union and the Strike.

Another evidence of the almost criminal incompetence and cringing compromise of the whole array of Negro leaders named in the beginning of this article is their recent endeavor to raise funds for the families of the colored men conscripted into the Army and Navy. A string of names of "so-called big Negroes" have given their endorsement and consent to the scheme.

Now a very elementary examination will reveal the farce of attempting to give any wholesome and fundamental relief to those families by the petty charitable scheme which they have adopted.

There are approximately one hundred thousand Negroes in the army. The smallest amount which might be considered as relief to a family in these days would be one dollar a day. One dollar a day to 100,000 families would be $100,000 per day or three million dollars per month. The impossibility of ever touching the surface of this problem by any hit and miss petty charity should have suggested itself to men like DuBois, Pickens, Kelly Miller and James W. Johnson, who must have had some study of elementary economics. And nothing more plausible and sound could be conceived of than that the government should take the matter in hand and handle it efficiently and scientifically. Yet not one of these "big Negro leaders" dares mention this either from ignorance or from lack of courage.

Again, we hear Prof. Wm. Pickens, DuBois and Kelly Miller talking in superlative sureness of how the Negroes' participation in this war will remove race prejudice. Since when has the subject race come out of a war with its rights and privileges accorded for such participation? Leaving out the question of color entirely where is the history to support this spurious promise? Did not the Negro fight in the Revolutionary War with Crispus Attucks dying first (which is not important nor material), and come out to be a miserable chattel slave in this country for nearly one hundred years after? Did not the Negro only *incidentally* secure freedom from physical slavery in the Civil War, only to have peonage fastened upon him almost immediately thereafter, become the victim of Ku Klux Klanism, oppression and unspeakable cruelty which were directly perpetrated by the South and condoned by the North. Did not the Negro take part in the Spanish-American War only to be discharged without honors and without a hearing by the president who rose into political prestige and power upon their valor in that war? And have not race prejudice and race hate grown in this country since 1898? The same story must be told of Ireland. She has always helped England in her wars, but she has remained under the feet of the English oppressor for the last eight hundred years. . . .

[d]
A REPORT FROM
THE TULSA RIOT SCENE
CALVIN CHASE
Washington Bee/June 11, 1921

The worst race riot in the history of the country occurred at Tulsa, Oklahoma, June 6. The toll of human life in the race riot here can only be guessed at, officials say. Many of the first to fall are still lying in the bullet and fire scarred district. The colored quarter, an area of a mile square, which was levelled by fire, has not yet been searched by the militia for bodies. It was there that most of the intense fighting took place, and many colored people are known to have been burned to death. Reports were received at military headquarters that white men carried Negro bodies from the ruins and had buried them outside Tulsa. Some were thrown into the river, it was reported. . . . Towns around here reported tonight that hundreds of colored people had passed, fleeing from Tulsa. Sperry, Oklahoma, reported that more than 1,000 of them passed there on their way to the Osage hills.

Trouble started when Richard Rawlings was arrested on the charge of "impudence and impertinence" to a white girl in an elevator. Police said he "assaulted" her, and there were threats of lynching.

A dozen colored men, hearing of the rumor, armed themselves, marched to the court house and asked to be sworn in as deputies to protect the prison. They were later reinforced by others, and a crowd of whites collected on the opposite side of the street. A white man started the riot by trying to take a gun away from a Negro. He was instantly killed.

The battle began. Colored men were outnumbered three to one and fell back into the colored section, which attacking whites immediately set on fire. The state militia was called out and the city put under martial law. Police disarmed colored men by the hundreds, leaving whites their arms. Militia also aided the whites. . .

Colored Rioters Poorly Armed,
But Casualty List Favorable Despite Handicap
   It is said that despite the preponderance of ammunition on the part
of the whites, who were abundantly supplied, the colored rioters put up
a good fight. The casualty list on the colored American side shows a
splendid spirit of defending themselves in the absence of protection
from the government. . .

Set Fire to Church
   One of the hottest engagements of the whole outbreak took place
around a colored church, where about fifty colored Americans barri-
caded themselves.
   Several massed attacks were launched against the church, but each
time the attackers had to fall back under the fire of the colored defenders. Finally a torch was applied to the building and the occupants
began to pour out, firing as they ran. Several of the colored people were
killed. . . .
   Race pride and confidence in the prowess of colored veterans of the
late war have been stirred to aid in the excitement. . . .

This article bore the headline "Bloody Race Riot Worst in the History of the
Country."

[e]
THE BURNING ALIVE
OF JOHN HENRY WILLIAMS
Washington Eagle/July 16, 1921

From Moultrie, Georgia, scene of the burning of the Negro Williams,
The Eagle has obtained the following facts by an eyewitness. It is
clearly shown that sworn officers of the law were leaders in mob violence and burning, acting with impunity.
   Says The Eagle's correspondent:
   "There are many things about the Williams burning more disgraceful
than have been published. A sick woman and her child, who had
nothing to do with the matter, were beaten into insensibility and left to
die because of hoodlumism of the mob. Colored churches were burned,

all colored farmers' fences were torn down and wealthy colored farmers chased from their homes.

"Williams was brought to Moultrie on Friday night by sheriffs from fifty counties. Saturday court was called. Not a single colored person was allowed nearer than a block of the courthouse. The trial took a half hour. Then Williams, surrounded by fifty sheriffs armed with machine guns, started out of the courthouse door toward the jail.

"Immediately a cracker by the name of Ken Murphy gave the Confederate yell: '*Whoo-whoo*—let's get the nigger.' Simultaneously five hundred poor pecks rushed on the armed sheriffs, who made no resistance whatever. They tore the Negro's clothing off before he was placed in a waiting automobile. This was done in broad daylight. The Negro was unsexed and made to eat a portion of his anatomy which had been cut away. Another portion was sent by parcel post to Governor Dorsey, whom the people of this section hate bitterly.

"The Negro was taken to a grove, where each one of more than five hundred people, in Ku Klux ceremonial, had placed a pine knot around a stump, making a pyramid to the height of ten feet. The Negro was chained to the stump and asked if he had anything to say. Castrated and in indescribable torture, the Negro asked for a cigarette, lit it and blew smoke in the face of his tormentors.

"The pyre was lit and a hundred men and women, old and young, grandmothers among them, joined hands and danced around while the Negro burned. A big dance was held in a barn nearby that evening in celebration of the burning, many people coming by automobile from nearby cities to the gala event."

[f]
FROM THE LYNCH MOB
TO THE LEGAL LYNCHER
OF THE COURTS
CARL MURPHY
Baltimore Afro-American/October 31, 1925

Foreign visitors to the Southern part of the United States must be struck immediately with the inefficiency of the police, sheriffs, and other rural constabulary.

In no other section of the country do the farmers quit work whenever a crime is committed, march to the court house by the tens and hundreds, have themselves sworn in as deputies, provided with a badge . . . and proceed, on foot, horse or by auto to hunt the criminal.

Bloodhounds used to be used to discover the scent and track the villain, so the hunt becomes something of a sport, but today the hounds have been discarded and as in Asheville, North Carolina, last week, 700 persons spent one night scouring the suburbs of West Asheville seeking a youngster who had attacked a white girl. All trains were stopped, searched, and colored passengers interrogated, colored homes entered, their occupants quizzed. Manifestly in a hunt of such proportions even the best bred bloodhound would be both confused and baffled, and so their use has been discontinued.

Perhaps most of the hounds now out of a job will be shipped to Jamaica . . . where the chasing of criminals is done chiefly by the cops and a perfectly good bloodhound will not be ruined by a hundred farmers yelling at him at once. Press dispatches last week said Jamaica had put in an order for bloodhounds. Even if they have not been purchased in this country, there are a lot of them down South, which have been discarded as criminal chasers and can be had for a bargain.

So it happens that the South has developed volunteer fire departments. Everybody down in Dixie is a policeman or a deputy sheriff . . . Once the poor culprit is caught, the volunteer police constitute themselves a volunteer judge and jury and volunteer executioners. Is the system effective? Well, records show that once a week on an average throughout the year, Dixie has her lynching parties.

Originally entitled "Southern Cops."

[g]
RESTRICTIVE COVENANTS
JULIUS A. TAYLOR
Chicago Broad Ax/June 11, 1921

Hon. Joseph E. Linquist, One of the Vice Presidents of the Central Trust Company of Illinois; at Which Bank the Colored People Have Thousands of Dollars on Deposit; J. W. Down of the New Down Dairy Co., 4326 Wabash Ave., Which Concern Supplies Thousands of Colored People With Their Milk and Cream; Martin Isaacs, Master-in-Chancery of the Superior Court, For Judge Joseph Sabath, and L. M. Smith, President of the Chicago Real Estate Board, Are the Guiding Spirits of the Grand Boulevard District Property Owners' Ass'n. The colored people residing on the South side should assemble together in a great convention and select two hundred men and women to form a delegation and let it march or call on L. M. Smith, President of the Chicago Real Estate Board, and the other high officials of the Grand Boulevard District Property Owners Association, and plainly inform them, that unless they refrain from attempting to boycott or black list them that they will endeavor to land them behind the prison bars at Joliet, Illinois, For Conspiracy.

This entire story was printed in headlines.

[h]
THE KU KLUX KLAN IN WATTS
California Eagle/April 10, 1925

This open letter which we are publishing clearly demonstrates the attitude of the Klan at Watts.

How long, Oh! how long, Lord, will the Negro suffer himself to be a political target? Watts, it seems, is almost solidly Ku Klux. Now Negroes who must play politics, should at least stay away from the Ku Klux political fold.

We are not so narrow as to believe that all white people are bad, but when we read this secret letter that was captured by the Watts Police Department, and digest its contents, we are forced to believe that this organization is made up of the worst brand of whites, and while it talks much of Americanism, in spirit, it is dangerously un-American, unprincipled and hellish.

"Our investigators are on the job twenty-four hours per day and we want to assure you that our office will leave nothing undone to bring to you and to your organization victory whenever 'Little Oscar' can be forced to call an election. He will be forced to do this within the next few days unless he files an appeal to the Supreme Court.

"We have taken steps to prevent the perfection of the appeal and we hope that we will be successful, though it must be remembered that Oscar has quite an extensive knowledge of the Recall Law. However, we have at our command several attorneys who are pledged to assist our organization in every possible way.

"I want to insist that you as my special organization follow instructions from this office. Remember that the committee that is working under your instructions must not know generally that you are representing this office, because you have on your campaign committee all races, creeds, etc., which is advisable on account of the fact that you have such a large Negro population in Watts, and also a large Catholic vote. Nevertheless you can use these aliens to forward the ideals of Americanism and can consequently relegate them to the rear.

"We have a special confidential investigator who is working among the Negroes. He makes the following suggestions, which I heartily approve:

"Place Cochrane, Bragg and Doram in charge of the Compton avenue district, and place McDaniels, Douglas, Thomas and the Groceryman Robnson in charge of the Wilmington avenue district. Neither of these Negroes have any racial pride and very little brains. We are about to line up a Negro woman by the name of Spurlock and she will be able to help out. Side in with the music of Dago Repeto. He claims that he can dictate to the Negroes in his neighborhood.

"The influence of Negro Knox is waning, and will be easily killed if we can bring proper pressure to bear. Negro Buford is wavering and might be bought over, though it will take much work to do so.

"Watch out for Oscar, Knox and Buford. They are much alive as yet. Knox uses the churches, but we are starting a fight against him in his own church and break his influence. We can trap Knox and Buford and break their influence. But great care must be used. This information must not be given out at any cost.

"We could plant a bottle of booze in an enemy's car and have on hand enough of the faithful to get a conviction before Judge Hunter or Wilson or some other of our fellow Klansmen who are pledged to give justice. And if these tactics fail, we can fall back on the old method of 'a woman.'

"The best way to get rid of our unprincipled antagonists is to make them leave Watts in disgrace. They will never come back.

"The Negro preacher Scott is a new man. He is a sleepy, pious man, and will hardly let politics be featured in his church. Cochrane is sure Scott can be kept quiet.

"The white people in Watts are tired of being run by people who are not 100% Americans. So it will be only necessary to corral the Negro vote. Manus must go. Oliver must be aided in every possible way. He may resign. He is disgusted. But faithful Klansmen will keep him in line and on the job.

"You will return these instructions to this office at once and not permit a copy to be made by anyone, under pain of expulsion.

"Faithfully yours in the Sacred Unfailing Bond,

G. W. PRICE, Imperial Representative, Realm of California,

604 Seventh and Hill Building,

Los Angeles, Calif., March 23rd, 1925."

[i]
LOOKING BACKWARD: THE NEGRO IN 1931
KELLY MILLER
New York Amsterdam News/December 30, 1931

Sizing up the stream of movements in which the American Negro has been caught, we are forced to reverse the ancient motto and say: "The past, at least, is insecure." Nineteen hundred and thirty-one has been a bad year for the world. Is it merely a readjustment from the convulsion of the World War? Or is it that man's smartness is again defeating itself by trying to reach the sky on a tower of science, as it did once long ago, by the vain attempt to build the tower of Babel on the plains of Shinar?

Machinery creates overproduction, for which mankind has not yet found a cure. Is more science to be the cure or the curse for too much science?

The Negro has been the incidental but inevitable victim of untoward world conditions. The bottom layer is always pressed thinnest by the weight superincumbent upon it. While it may do no good to lament after the manner of Jeremiah, yet courageous analysis and a frank facing of facts must precede any constructive scheme of relief.

Our greatest bank has failed. Our largest insurance enterprise is now in the hands of the receiver. Against these calamities we are heartened, to a degree, by the manful struggle which several of our notable enterprises are making to keep their head above water. There are over a million unemployed among us whom we have little or no power within ourselves to employ or to give substantial relief. The race should everywhere join in community movements to swell the Community Chest which engages to aid the needy on the basis of need, and not race. We must still beseech the white race each day for our daily bread.

Our public and private institutions have been keeping school and hearing lessons, without any constructive program for employment or self-help for the product of their tuition. Our highest institutions of learning have been put to their wits' end to justify the munificent grants which the foundations have been dumping into their laps. DuBois, the caustic critic, and Woodson, the iconoclast, have united in declaring our educational regime a failure, without any constructive suggestion.

Our religious life is at a lower ebb than it has been since the great awakening during the early years of the nineteenth century. Our oldest and most boasted and boastful denomination, in the language of the stock market, has reached "new lows." The churches have lost their militancy. Their efforts are too largely consumed in raising impossible financial budgets, to the comparative neglect of the missionary spirit and moral reform. The great temperance movement which is sweeping over the nation receives little or no enthusiastic support from the Negro church. Our youth no longer look to the church for moral guidance.

We stand appalled at the redivivus of lynching, like the man with the nightmare who cannot even move or scream at the imminence of danger. The church and state look on with paralyzed energies and impotency.

The N.A.A.C.P. has been carrying on its fight against instances of injustice and outrage, and has become practically the only voice warning the nation against the just requitement of iniquity and sin.

We have all but yielded up the ghost as to our Civil Service hope. Lately we have heard it triumphantly proclaimed that under Mr. Hoover we have 54,000 persons on the government payroll with an annual salary of $69,000,000. But it was carefully concealed that these low grade and low paid employees, for the most part, were handed down as a legacy from the Wilson administration, and during the year just elapsing there has been no augmentation in number nor elevation in dignity and rank.

For fully a year now Dr. Carter G. Woodson has been telling us in mournful numbers that the educational, economic, political, and religious life of the race is near the brink of collapse. We have the will to disbelieve him and branded him as a wild calamity howler, and yet we know that he tells much disagreeable truth. I have likened him to Cassandra, the blind prophetess of Troy, who spake the truth but the people were fated to disbelieve or ignore her, until it was too late. Dr. Woodson is undoubtedly serving a useful purpose at great sacrifice to his reputation as a research scholar and as a historian. His undaunted courage and intrepidity challenge our administration, even though we may not be able to follow out the unmitigated logic of his evil forebodings.

The Negro newspapers have on the whole proved to be our best sustained endeavor. . . .

Originally entitled "Looking Backward at the Negro's 1931 Movements."

[j]
AMERICA ON TRIAL
JOSEPH D. BIBB
Chicago Whip/August 22, 1931

The killing of three colored men in Chicago in so-called Communist "eviction riots" has provoked widespread comment, much like the "shot heard round the world" in the Revolutionary War. Most of the comment takes the form of bitter castigation of the Communists, and suggested remedies for prevention of recurrence of such a disturbance vary all the way from summary execution of all Reds to the quiet remedy of deportation of all who think and talk red or offer any adverse criticism against the present order of affairs. Obviously most of the critics are missing the mark. Regardless to what theory of government the Reds offer or advocate as a remedy for the present disorder the most casual observer sees and knows that there is something radically wrong with a system of government as rich in resources, brains and money as is America which permits millions who want to work to literally starve.

What the Reds have said about the failure of America to face its problems almost every person has said recently when the pinch of depression has hit him. What the critics have failed to do and what the brains of America has failed to do is to courageously correct the faults of which the Reds and millions of others are now complaining. The disturbances in Chicago may be in violation of the established laws . . . [but why did not] the Bailiff's Office and the charitable organizations of the city work out a plan whereby an unemployed man and his family are provided for before they are set upon the street, homeless and penniless. This plan could have been and should have been worked out BEFORE the riot and there would not have been the occasion for the riot.

If the critics are going to blame anyone for whatever happens in the next few years in America in which law and order is flouted, it should not be laid at the door of the Reds, but at the door of the governing heads and those who govern the governing heads of this country for their failure to assume a social responsibility and their lack of interest and courage to recognize any inadequacy of the system they uphold and their unwillingness to set in motion a plan to correct them. Why not place some at least of the blame where it belongs and why not devote the time used in fighting the so-called Red menace to a constructive correction of the evils about which we all know and feel? The Reds are not on trial, but America is, and so America, so the rest of the world, say our American boosters.

[k]
EVICTIONS AND RENT STRIKES
CYRIL V. BRIGGS
Harlem Liberator/May 20 and July 22, 1933

[May 20] The landlord of 16, 18, 24, West 134th street is threatening to evict 36 families from their homes. The tenants, most of them with large families, have been denied relief by the Home Relief Bureau due to discriminatory practices and are actually destitute. In one apartment the family of Mrs. C with four children, the oldest 14, has been without gas or electricity for six months. Due to exposure and undernourishment the children have contracted severe colds. . . . Harlem tenants must organize against evictions and high rents. The tenants of these houses should at once get together in a meeting in the apartment of one of their numbers. At this meeting they should then proceed to organize the whole block so that the tenants in the entire block can be rallied in a solid mass against this monstrous attempt to throw 36 families on the street. The Harlem Unemployed Council at 79 West 131st street has been doing excellent work in the organizing of tenants to fight against evictions. The workers in these houses should get in touch with the council.

[July 22] . . . Harlem is having one of its first organized rent strikes this week, the tenants of 129-30 East 111th street refusing to pay the landlord until he install kitchen doors and sanitary conditions in the building. The tenants also demand reduction of the present exorbitant rents which they are made to pay. They have organized a House Committee with twelve or fifteen tenants following the leadership of the Committee and the unemployed council, which is supporting the strike.

The landlord has informed the strikers he will go to the expense of thousands of dollars to evict them rather than install decent conditions in the house. The strikers are militantly picketing the house and call upon all workers to help them enforce their demands on the rent-hog landlord. Several tenants were brutally attacked by police thugs last night. Several tenants have been arrested while picketing the building. The workers have been refused bail.

2.
The Spirit of
the New Negro

The term "New Negro" was originated by political radicals as a means of distinguishing themselves from traditional black leadership. The "New Negro" title was coveted by nationalists, leftists, and angry young reformers. The title was proudly claimed for those who fought to defend black communities during the 1919 race riots—as shown in selection (a), from Cyril Briggs, one of the early black Marxists, in a 1919 issue of his *Crusader.* In selection (b), Roscoe Dunjee of the Oklahoma City *Black Dispatch* describes the depth of New Negro disillusionment with the traditional American system of justice. (This article was a reprint of a speech Dunjee delivered before a large interracial gathering at a meeting presided over by the governor of Oklahoma. Dunjee's paper, started in 1916, became the most widely read black weekly in the Southwest. Editor Dunjee was a prominent figure in the NAACP and an active force in Oklahoma politics.)

One of the most influential groups in the ranks of New Negroes were the black veterans of the World War. The attitude of the black soldier toward the war and the future of Black America is presented in excerpt (c), by Lt. Willian N. Colson, in the *Messenger.* (Colson was a staff writer for the *Messenger* until his untimely death in 1922. His wife was also on the staff of the magazine.)

By the mid-1920s the New Negro radicals had become divided among themselves over issues of program and ideology. The various approaches are discussed from the perspective of an integrationist by George S. Schuyler in one of his Pittsburgh *Courier* "Shafts and Darts" columns. (Schuyler's columns were carried in the *Messenger* and the *Courier.* A former army man, he came out of the World War to be secretary of the Syracuse, New York, Socialist party. In the 1930s he defined himself as an anarchist. Eventually he drifted into the political camp of the far right, his autobiography published in 1966 being titled *Black and Conservative.*) Schuyler's column is selection (d).

The optimism of New Negro radicals was in no small part attributable to their discovery of the power of psychological warfare. Among New Negro black nationalists, the war to liberate the mind from debilitating self-hate was seen as the first and most important step on the way to total liberation. "The Value of Propaganda" is discussed by Amy Jacques Garvey in selection (e) from the *Negro World.* (Mrs. Garvey contributed a woman's page to her husband's paper; edited his two-volume *Philosophy and Opinions;* was a noted orator for the movement; was involved in the building of the 1945 Pan-African Congress, and later in the Jamaican independence movement.)

The New Negro label was gradually co-opted by that very middle class which by radical definition was "Old Negro." Blacks who denounced radicals of all stripes commercialized the concept into a distinction between "new" aggressive individualists who capitalized on the social changes that came with the move to the city, and the lethargic Negro of the Old South. Selection (f) from the New York *Amsterdam News* should be compared with selection (a) from the *Crusader.* The hope and promise of communities like Harlem is extolled in selection (g), from John Lyon's New York *Dispatch.* (This paper was founded in 1920 with the stated purpose of attracting the young, involved black people. It was supported with funds from Fred R. Moore's New York *Age,* a major organ of traditional black business organizations and, in an earlier day, the main northern paper for the forces of Booker T. Washington.)

[a]
THE OLD NEGRO GOES: LET HIM GO IN PEACE
CYRIL V. BRIGGS
Crusader/October 1919

The Old Negro and his futile methods must go. After fifty years of him and his methods the Race still suffers from lynching, disfranchisement, Jim Crowism, segregation and a hundred other ills. His abject crawling and pleading have availed the Cause nothing. He has sold his life and his people for vapid promises tinged with traitor gold. His race is done. Let him go.

The New Negro now takes the helm. It is now OUR future at stake. Not his. His future is in the grave. And if the New Negro, imbibing the spirit of Liberty, is willing to suffer martyrdom for the Cause, then certainly the very least that the Old Negro can do is to stay in the background for his remaining years of life or to die a natural death without in his death struggles attempting to hamper those who take new means to effect ends which the Old Leaders throughout fifty years were not able to effect.

Can the Old Leaders deny that there is more wholesome respect for the Negro following the race riots in Washington, Chicago, Knoxville and other places than there was before those riots, and when there were only lynchings and burnings of scared Negroes and none of the fear in the white man's heart that comes from the New Negro fighting back? They cannot deny it, so let them go their way. The future is the New Negro's. It should have come to us safeguarded. But the Old Leaders have failed ignobly. Ours now is the task of safeguarding that future and of giving it to our children secured for all time. For us the future and all the great tasks that lie ahead. For the Old Leader *Requiescat in Pace!*

[b]
THE NEW NEGRO
ROSCOE DUNJEE
Oklahoma City Black Dispatch/October 10, 1919

The cornerstone upon which rests all of our difficulties is YOUR UN-WILLINGNESS TO RECOGNIZE THE NEGRO AS A MAN. Now the Negro is a man, and a free man. I might say to make clearer my point that you have now with you a NEW NEGRO. I do not mean the new Negro that you have had described to you. You have had what was termed a NEW NEGRO described to you as an insolent, arrogant in-dividual, a creature who would not assimilate himself properly into organized forms of government. I mean this, that out of the education that you have permitted us to get and which we have acquired out of our own efforts also, there has developed a different creature than the inert clod that you once knew as a slave. IN YOUR FAILURE TO RECOGNIZE JUST THIS ONE FACT RESTS ALL OF THE DIF-FICULTY.

This New Negro, who stands to-day released in spirit, finds himself, in America and in this state, physically bound and shackled by LAWS AND CUSTOMS THAT WERE MADE FOR SLAVES, and all of the unrest, all of the turbulence and all of the violence that now is charged to my people IS THE BATTLE OF FREE MEN, POUNDING UPON WALLS THAT SURROUND THEM AND THAT WERE MADE FOR SLAVES.

I am alarmed at the idea that some of the people of this country have as to the cause of the unrest among us. Some say, if I read correctly your newspapers, that there are I.W.W. agitators among us. Others say that it is Bolshevik or anarchistic influences that seek to draw us into their radical division. This is an improper conclusion. The Negro has arrived at the place where he now finds himself through his own processes of reasoning. For example, it does not take an I.W.W. to clinch the argument that the majority of the Negroes in the United States cannot vote. It does not take an anarchist to ride with us on the railroad for us to know that when we pay three cents per mile that we do not get what you get by paying the same and identical amount. It does not take a Bolshevist to inform us that freedom of movement is restricted to us and that, under the guise of law a separate status as citizens is designed for the black man.

I think you ought to know how the black man talks and feels at times when he knows that you are nowhere about, and I want to tell you, if you were to creep up to-night to a place where there are 10,000 Negroes gathered, you would find no division on this one point, I know that they all would say, 'WE HAVE NO CONFIDENCE IN WHITE POLICEMEN.'

Let there be one hundred or one hundred thousand, they would with one accord all say, WE HAVE NO CONFIDENCE IN THE WHITE MAN'S COURT. I think you ought to know this, for it is with what men think that we have to deal. They would say in such a meeting that they know before they get into the court what the verdict will be. If their cause is the cause of a black man against a white man they will say that they know that a verdict would be rendered in favor of the white man.

Now what is the psychology in this situation? How does the black man's mind operate under such conditions? If a Negro commits an offense he is apt to think like this, 'I cannot turn myself over to the police, FOR IT IS THE MOB; neither can I afford to turn myself over to the court, for it will lynch me of justice,' and he reaches this final conclusion, that there are two avenues open to him, EITHER SUC-CESSFULLY HIDE OR FIGHT AND DIE. How would you feel and how do you think that the Negro feels laboring under such conditions?

None of my race is dreaming of what you so often term SOCIAL 'EQUALITY.' . . .

What we want is 'SOCIAL JUSTICE.' We want to feel a larger secur-ity in our homes from the hand of the mob. We want the free, un-trammeled right at the ballot box. We want justice in the courts and the right, under the law, to do anything that other citizens of this govern-ment may do.

[c]
THE NEW NEGRO PATRIOTISM
WILLIAM N. COLSON
Messenger/August 1919

... Here we are principally concerned with the disillusioned, the new Negro and his new patriotism. The Negro soon found [during the World War] that the treachery of the white American was infinitely more damaging to him than that of the Hun. He was refused a square deal in the army and navy, and discriminations became more gruelling in the South. There was more exploitation of labor, more personal insult, more segregation, more degradation of women, more racial limitation and restriction than ever before. Now this state of affairs multiplies racial antagonism. . . . any lack of patriotism on the part of the Negro was and is the natural and logical consequence of unjust practices perpetrated against him.

It is noteworthy that his new patriotism was born during the time of the Negroes' active participation in all forms of war work, military and otherwise. Nor does it exist solely in the hearts of officers and true leaders for it is a sentiment which has gained its widest currency among the rank and file of the black soldiery and working class. Before the embarkation overseas of the 92d Division, it was frequently a matter of difficulty to instill the qualities of dash and vim into the enlisted personnel. The men asked without hesitation the reason for their fighting in the war. "Safe for democracy" became to them a mere mockery. They had no faith in their white officers and not much in the colored in that emergency. When discriminations were practiced at the cantonments like the customary equipping of white organizations before colored units and the assignments of the whites to the best camp locations, the most unlettered and provincial Negro soldiers often spent hours in discussing the justice of American military authority. In the 92d Division, the enlisted men as a whole were more outspoken and overt in their remarks and resentments than their colored officers. A few of them manifested their qualified loyalty by expressing sentiment of conscientious objection, nor was their conscientious objection always based on religious scruples. It was often a challenge to a mischievous patriotism. When black officers taught black men bayonet practice they usually substituted a picture of the rabid white

Southerner for that of the Hun. This method often times inspirited the soldier with the necessary dash and form.

What was the soul of the Negro in war-time? In the mood of seriousness it was the most usual thing for the Negroes to turn in their discussions to the fitness of their participation in the business of war. And in trench or camp, factory or school, the undeniable fact is that Negroes felt that they were fighting for false ideals.

While in France, the Negro soldiers got their bearings. They discovered that the only white men that treated them as men, were native Europeans, and especially the French with their wider social experience and finer social sense. The Frenchman was unable to comprehend American color prejudice. The Englishman was much more democratic than the American. Then the soldiers began to get letters from home. They brought the news that conditions in the States were no better than before; they were worse! For instance, a successful businessman from the South wrote that he felt relieved that his son was fighting on French soil for France, because France was at least democratic. A Negro clergyman whose church members subscribed $10,000 worth of Liberty Bonds wrote that he had no patriotism whatever. He had promoted the subscription in a spirit of hypocritical public service. A leading Negro banker, who had bought many thousands of dollars worth of bonds, stated in confidence that he joined in the public movement merely for the sake of retaining the good-will of his white business friends. But there was not one of these persons who would not have been glad to have given his all if he had felt that the war was fought for freedom and opportunity at home. Some Negro officers, just as many white officers did, largely volunteered and trained for commissions, not because of any real patriotism but because they wished to escape the draft and because they sought the distinction and remuneration which went with the officership. In all fairness, however, it may be said that many of the colored men trained for commissions out of a sense of race pride and prospect. Many of the black soldiers were divested of the little patriotism they possessed on their return from France. Their hearts sank as they hove in sight of these shores. The only reason for their joy in seeing America, was the fact that it meant a speedy discharge from a brutal military system and a meeting with home folks and friends. The way soldiers were discharged from the army and navy without prospective employment, is one of the national disgraces. The colored officer, maltreated and thrust aside, has cursed the flag and the country for which it stands a thousand times. Thousands of these soldiers now possess weapons to demonstrate if need be their legal right to self-defense against Southern encroachments and lynch-law.

Intelligent Negroes have all reached the point where their loyalty to the country is conditional. The patriotism of the mass of Negroes may now be called doubtful. The new Negro has put the question: "What will the shot of my bolt mean?"

It was on last November tenth, that a black platoon lay near the crest of a hill overlooking the placid Moselle. With their faces toward the battlements of mighty Metz, the soldiers awaited the order to attack. There was less singing and more thought. In one tense and bloody moment, the voice of a real doughboy, a new patriot, was heard amid the uncanny hiss of hot steel. It was the fervent wish that across the lines were the Huns of America, the convict leasers, the slave drivers, their domineering white American officers, the lynchers, their oppressors, instead of the Boches. The sentiment was that with the Huns of America over there the incitement necessary to the proper dash and courage would be forthcoming. They would then be fighting to make America safe for all classes. Shortly after the armistice members of this same platoon were anticipating the return home. Most of them were from the South. An ingenious fellow caused an endless round of merriment, when he cleverly placed each Southern state on an imaginary map of military operations. Georgia, Mississippi, Texas and Alabama were put in No Man's Land. The border states like Virginia and Kentucky, were the third line trenches, etc. The soldiers, all seated beneath an old apple tree, scarred by four years of German shrapnel, finally concluded that their next war for "democracy" would be in the land of "THE STAR-SPANGLED BANNER.". . .

Originally entitled "An Analysis of Negro Patriotism"; William N. Colson was "Formerly an Officer [Lieutenant] of the 367th U.S. Infantry."

[d]
THE INTEGRATIONIST VISION
GEORGE S. SCHUYLER
Pittsburgh Courier/June 11, 1927

In the consideration of our position as a minority group, there are items which we avoid discussing as a fish avoids dry land. Usually these are the very things that ought to be discussed very frankly. . . .

Firstly, we must courageously face the fact that there are only three possible solutions to the so-called Negro problem. One is wholesale emigration from these United States; another is segregation, either in ghettoes or a separate state; and third is amalgamation with the more numerous people in the midst of whom we live and have our being, such as it is. Our leaders and spokesmen hem and haw, pussyfoot and soft pedal, and generally avoid discussing our destiny on the basis of these three possible solutions. This is unfortunate because in the absence of a clearly defined goal our tactics, socially, politically and economically are necessarily bound to be confused, as they have been in the past and are at present. Aside from Marcus Garvey who advocated emigration and Hubert Harrison who advocates a separate state, hardly any Negro of prominence has had the courage to advocate any definite goal. Exceptions are the few radicals such as Randolph, Whiteman, Owen and others who frankly see a solution through labor organization and an ultimate democracy owned and controlled by workers, white and black.

Emigration, I think, can be dismissed because that remedy is worse than the disease. Likewise, the separate state idea, while not nearly so impracticable, is yet so difficult of attainment and fraught with so many dangers that the overwhelming majority of our people are at the present stage of thought, unalterably opposed to it. This, despite the fact that I cannot see how those who rant for Negro Nationalism, emphasize "racial differences" and whoop it up generally for the development of racial consciousness (like the Ku Klux Klan), can escape the logical conclusion of a separate state to which they must arrive if they reason correctly from such premises. For, surrounded as we are by this white civilization, indeed a part of it, how can we develop and maintain a separate Negro civilization and culture without breaking the physical and intellectual ties that bind us so closely to this white civilization?

Has it ever been done before, anywhere? I wish some of our brilliant thinkers would answer these questions.

Obviously there is a contradiction between whooping fervently for the development, maintenance and worship of everything Negro when at the same time, and with almost the same breath, we vociferously clamor for the breaking down of all social and economic barriers between the two peoples, which is bound logically to result in further cementing the two peoples into one people. Moreover, agitation for everything Negro—the propaganda of black nationalism—tends to further develop counter-propaganda of white nationalism which can only result ultimately in wholesale segregation or increased tension that may very possibly result in sanguinary conflict. Segregation, as I said before, is undesirable by most of us, and racial war would be suicidal for all of us. One is led to the inevitable conclusion then, and in spite of the gabble of the advocates of "Negro" culture, that such an ideal is visionary, undesirable, and even downright dangerous. I think we should soft-pedal it.

After all, my observation—which has been broad and deep—has led me to seriously doubt the sincerity of the so-called racial patriots and their numerous apostles and adherents. I am of the opinion that it is almost wholly an assumed attitude to counter the antagonistic attitude of the majority of whites. It is like the boy whistling while walking through a cemetery—it is done to keep up courage. Insofar it has psychological and social value, but as a goal I think it is extremely unsound. Most any intelligent and observing person will agree that the American so-called Negro is a Negro in color only, and not often then. In every other way he is the same as the white American. He has the psychology of a social caste; not of a race, for if there is such a thing as a Negro psychology inherent in us, then it ought to vary in accordance with the degree of racial mixture. I, for instance, should be more race conscious than A. Philip Randolph; Randolph should be more race conscious than Arthur Schomburg; and Schomburg should be more race conscious than Walter White. All of which is nonsense because I am probably less so than any of them, and I have no "white" or "Indian" blood in me at all.

Very well, then, so much for that. If there are any of our orators or writers who can break down the logic of that argument, by all means let them shoot in their letters addressed to me. As to the segregation in ghettoes, that is going on rapidly, in fact more rapidly than in the past. And I believe it is fraught with great danger. It ought to be strenuously fought at every turn. . . . All peoples throughout history have avoided it like the plague and accepted it only when they had to do so. Herein lies the great value of the work done by the N.A.A.C.P. and kindred organizations. For if we are to abolish the vicious caste system now extant and cement the two peoples more closely we must remove the social barriers that separate them. Ultimately we Americans must become one people socially and physically, as economically we are already. . . .

The labor movement is one of the most fertile fields for removing those antagonisms between the two peoples which are largely based on fear and ignorance. More young educated Negroes should get into it. There are more liberal white people (some almost devoid of prejudice) in the labor movement than in any other single group in America. Despite of the gabble of handkerchief-head Negro leaders, this has been true for the past hundred years or more, and is truer today than ever before. People who sit down together in union halls, struggle together for better wages and working conditions, celebrate their victories together with song and speeches, and arbitrate their differences across the conference table, are going a long way toward obtaining that mutual understanding that spells doom to the vicious color caste system.

Then Negro business men whenever possible should join all local business and trade organizations, and take an active part in their activities. Professional men such as physicians, dentists, pharmacists, lawyers and teachers should do the same. Our preachers should seek to get exchange pulpits. Efforts should be constantly made by Negro speakers to appear before white audiences, North and South, and white people of prominence should be constantly invited to address Negroes . . .

But above all—and this is probably the touchiest point of all—we should seek the association of white people. I mean social intercourse. After all, our opinion of any considerable people is largely based on our experience with one or two individuals of the group, I have heard people condemn all Englishmen because they once had difficulties with one. We need to chat, eat and dance with the other group, and should lose no opportunity to do so. In numerous places throughout the country, that can be done, yet Negroes have neglected to do it. Of course one often meets with rebuff and the business requires tact, but it is time that more of us started a little personal propaganda instead of depending on organizations to solve our problem for us. In this connection the Black and Tan cabarets and dance halls are exceedingly valuable. Think all this over before hurling your verbal brickbats.

[e]
THE VALUE OF PROPAGANDA
AMY JACQUES GARVEY
Negro World/March 6, 1927

The Associated press reports from Berlin that $5,000,000 will be spent for propaganda this year by the German government. This is a wise move, actuated perhaps by the bitter experiences of the war 1914-18 when Germany was defeated mainly by Allied propaganda. The horrible tales of atrocities in Belgium stirred the white world to united effort to "save civilization from Teutonic barbarians," as nothing else could have done. No one stopped to ascertain the truthfulness or source of the stories; every one was too high-strung to reason why "theirs was but to do or die," with the feeling of saving the world for democracy.

If we could tell how much England spends yearly for propaganda many of our readers would be surprised, as it is a very large figure, but it should be remembered that England controls her colonies, and bluffs the world by reason of her studied and systematic propaganda, disseminated in such a subtle manner that it is digested without the victim being aware of its poison. . . .

Marcus Garvey has been called one of the greatest propagandists of this age, because he is one of the few men that saw the great worth of propaganda in the year 1917, and started to use it in his efforts to educate black men to see the necessity for African Nationalism, and to get white men to appreciate the righteousness of his Cause.

One of his hardest tasks is to get "wise" Negroes to realize the value of propaganda. To them it is money wasted, because the benefits derived from it are not seen in dollars and cents, or brick and mortar. The Knights of Columbus, a Roman Catholic organization in America, voted $1,000,000 at its last convention for propaganda work for the year. If the U.N.I.A. had done this a howl of protest would have gone up from "big Negroes" "for wasting people's money." They would contend that the money could be invested in real estate in America; an investment that he has no means of protecting against white Christian mobs that covet it, and an investment that would not benefit Negroes outside America, who finance the organization. Nor could the tenants pay the rent when recession and depression comes.

To get Negroes of the world to know that there are 400,000,000 of them breathing God's air; to get this number to realize that they are men and women, not dogs or monkeys; to get them to know that the Creator made them lords of the earth, and not to be slaves or peons for other races; to remind those in alien lands that Africa is their ancestral home, and it is their duty, in common with those at home, to make of it an earthly paradise, this is the task Marcus Garvey, with God's help has set himself to do. Agents of white governments may persecute him, ignorant jealous Negroes may scoff at him, but the work goes on just the same. Handicapped by lack of funds, harassed and thrown in prison, yet his spirit soars high above the mean tactics of those who seek his destruction, and in a clear, determined voice he continues to cry, "Africa for the Africans," while the tom-toms relay the glad tidings to the remotest corners of the motherland, and languages and dialects re-echo the sounds to a startled world. Truly propaganda is a wise investment.

[f]
THE SPIRIT OF THE NEW NEGRO
New York Amsterdam News/circa 1929-30

To our way of thinking the New Negro, if there is such, is dependent upon himself for his food and thinking—a Negro who has the ideal of a spiritually and economically independent group working in harmony with and being a part of the larger American group. The New Negro is possessed of a new spirit. First, he believes in self-support. He supports his family; and helps to build a foundation for racial self-support. To do this, he believes it is not only necessary to talk 'race pride' but to act it. Hence he buys from a Negro grocer wherever he can; he goes to a Negro church; he has insurance in a Negro insurance company; he puts his money in a Negro bank; he acts race pride.

Second, the New Negro is a pioneer for his people. The New Negro launches out into business. (He may fail and the 'old' Negro may laugh at him.) The New Negro encourages the pioneer in other lines. He is willing to 'take a chance' to build for the future.

Third, the New Negro thinks straight. Because he is born of the new spirit of freedom, he is determined to have freedom in all its phases. He is willing to bear all its responsibilities. He wants all of its privileges. He refuses to believe he is different from or inferior to any other of God's children. But he is not raising too big a row about it.

The New Negro believes in God. He may be gradually changing his theology. It is perhaps wise that he should. But he believes in God. A hundred years ago a New Negro walked out of St. George's Church, Philadelphia, and preferred to worship in an old blacksmith shop which was bought by black people than in a fine house for which he did not pay. He believes that self-support is of God.

The New Negro has a new spirit, not necessarily a diploma, a white collar, a salary from charity organizations—he believes in God and himself and his future and is hard at work.

Reprinted in the *Negro Yearbook* 1931–32.

[g]
THE HOPE AND PROMISE OF HARLEM
New York Dispatch/January 7, 1921

It is a long way from the corn and cotton fields of the sunny South to the commercial enterprises of big, beautiful Harlem, but we are here, one hundred and fifty thousand of us, forming perhaps the largest Colored community in the entire United States. Here, where money will say more in *one moment* than the most *eloquent lover* can in years, a happy, thrifty people are working out a greater destiny for the Race, by solving their economic and political problems day by day. Fifteen years ago, Colored Harlem was confined to one or two city blocks. Today, Harlem's Colored People proudly claim almost the entire area north of 128th to 148th streets, from Park to Eighth avenues, a city "as it were," within the city. About two miles long by two miles wide, having more people than the entire combined population, whites and blacks, of Richmond and Lynchburg, Va., together. Here thrive many enterprises, such as light manufacture, commercial and professional life affords, with a large number of Colored people doing excellent business.

Large public schools, library, Y.M.C.A. and Y.W.C.A. buildings; casinos, theatres, political, social and music club houses; fraternal homes, and 80 percent of property in this area is owned by Colored people. There are two Colored representatives on the Board of Aldermen, and one in the State Legislature, all from *big beautiful Harlem,* to represent her interests. Our Churches are palatial. Our professional and business men are among the best in the country; here, too, the Colored artisans have commenced to grow strong. Our women, God bless them, are the prettiest and best dressed in the world.

Unity within the Race, *here as elsewhere,* is the Colored People's greatest concern; and when Harlem finds it, the so-called "Race Problem" will crumble before an intelligent, determined group, and Colored Harlem will not be *big* and *beautiful,* but will become *great* and *powerful.*

Originally entitled "The City."

II.

Questions
of
Ideology

3.
Black Identity
Old Style and New Style

During the Black Renaissance there was an unusual willingness to go beyond established institutions, social forms and political connections and build anew. For the radicals there was a fundamental state of psychic alienation from the United States of America and Western European culture. Those who rejected the established political alliances were the first of the New Negroes, those who accepted them were the Old Negroes. It was on this distinction that Dr. W. E. B. DuBois found himself glued to the old crowd.

The distinction between New and Old Negroes can be compared in the first two selections here. The DuBois declaration on the aims of the returning black soldiers of the World War, selection (a), has been widely republished as an example of the fighting spirit of that time; however, for DuBois it was quite clear that the troops were returning to change *their* country. On the other hand, there is the position taken by the avowed New Negro William Bridges in his *Challenge* selection (b), also discussing the returning black troops. For Bridges there seems little reason for loyalty to this government, or for confidence in the majority of its people. Selection (c), also from Bridges in the *Challenge*, reflects the same damning appraisal of American society. (Bridges' journal mixed support for socialism with favorable comment on the black nationalist Garvey movement. The *Challenge* had secret backing from Tammany Democrats, and the magazine did not last long after the disclosure of these connections in October of 1920. Bridges went into the real-estate business and contributed occasionally to the *Negro World*.)

The political distinction between the radicals and the "old crowd Negroes" reflected a power fight which found, on the one hand, nationalists, socialists and communists trying to build new bases of power in the community; and on the other hand, the combined forces of the NAACP and other civil rights groups, plus the old-line supporters of the late Booker T. Washington—the black business community. The DuBois and Washington fight of 1900 had been resolved. The Washington group had accepted the general tenets of the argument for full equality and political rights—within the system, of course. This is shown in selection (d), the statement of policy from the initial issue of Robert L. Vann's *Competitor,* one of a number of monthlies published for the black upper class. The *Competitor* specialized in society stories and testimonials of successful black businessmen. (Vann, who was also editor and publisher of the Pittsburgh *Courier,* had amassed $25,000 capital to start his magazine, which lasted but two years.)

With the coming of the Renaissance, DuBois found himself as titular head of the black establishment. His organization, the NAACP, once the most militant force in Black America, was now embraced by blacks who in previous years would have had nothing to do with it. As the New Negroes took to criticizing DuBois as a spokesman of tradition, DuBois in turn set himself apart from the new vanguard. In selection (e) DuBois explains in the *Crisis* why the NAACP had not joined the forces of "revolution"—by which he meant the advocates of class struggle among the New Negroes. In selection (f) Chandler Owen presents a *Messenger* reply.

[a]
RETURNING SOLDIERS
W. E. B. DU BOIS
Crisis/May 1919

We are returning from war! *The Crisis* and tens of thousands of black men were drafted into a great struggle. For bleeding France and what she means and has meant and will mean to us and humanity and against the threat of German race arrogance, we fought gladly and to the last drop of blood; for America and her highest ideals, we fought in far-off hope; for the dominant southern oligarchy entrenched in Washington, we fought in bitter resignation. For the America that represents and gloats in lynching, disfranchisement, caste, brutality and the devilish insult— for this, in the hateful upturning and mixing of things, we were forced by vindictive fate to fight, also.

But today we return! We return from the slavery of the uniform which the world's madness demanded us to don to the freedom of civil garb. We stand again to look America squarely in the face and call a spade a spade. We sing: This country of ours, despite all its better souls have done and dreamed, is yet a shameful land.

It *lynches.*

And lynching is barbarism of a degree of contemptible nastiness unparalleled in human history. Yet for fifty years we have lynched two Negroes a week, and we have kept this up right through the war.

It *disfranchises* its own citizens.

Disfranchisement is the deliberate theft and robbery of the only protection of poor against rich and black against white. The land that disfranchises its citizens and calls itself a democracy lies and knows it lies.

It encourages *ignorance.*

It has never really tried to educate the Negro. A dominant minority does not want Negroes educated. It wants servants, dogs, whores and monkeys. And when this land allows a reactionary group by its stolen political power to force as many black folk into these categories as it possibly can, it cries in contemptible hypocrisy: "They threaten us with degeneracy; they cannot be educated."

It *steals* from us.

It organizes industry to cheat us. It cheats us out of our land; it cheats us out of our labor. It confiscates our savings. It reduces our wages. It raises our rent. It steals our profit. It taxes us without representation. It keeps us consistently and universally poor, and then feeds us on charity and derides our poverty.

It *insults* us.

It has organized a nation-wide and latterly a world-wide propaganda of deliberate and continuous insult and defamation of black blood wherever found. It decrees that it shall not be possible in travel nor residence, work nor play, education nor instruction for a black man to exist without tacit or open acknowledgment of his inferiority to the dirtiest white dog. And it looks upon any attempt to question or even discuss this dogma as arrogance, unwarranted assumption and treason.

This is the country to which we Soldiers of Democracy return. This is the fatherland for which we fought! But it is *our* fatherland. It was right for us to fight. The faults of *our* country are *our* faults. Under similar circumstances, we would fight again. But by the God of Heaven, we are cowards and jackasses if now that that war is over, we do not marshal every ounce of our brain and brawn to fight a sterner, longer, more unbending battle against the forces of hell in our own land.

We return.

We return from fighting.

We return fighting.

Make way for Democracy! We saved it in France, and by the Great Jehovah, we will save it in the United States of America, or know the reason why.

[b]
SIX DEMANDS
WILLIAM BRIDGES
Challenge/August 1919

We demand, first, that instead of being re-Americanized into accepting sterner patriotic obligations we be thoroughly informed why we should be loyal to any Government that does not protect our lives and property the same as it protects those of other people with less claim to protection. Loyalty, fortunately for civilization, is no longer the outgrowth of traditional devotion to events written into histories with the blood of the people. It can only grow from and thrive on liberty and justice; out of and on the liberal equalization of every social, political, and industrial privilege necessary to the vigorous upbuilding of the human race. Loyalty in Negroes is not stimulated by proscription, lynching, and segregation. It is stunted and annihilated.

Second, that we be told why we should disclaim all previous respect for Germans and Germany, when, no matter how diminished the respect of white Americans for them may be, it still transcends that which white Americans have for us. Moreover, America has no social, political, and industrial opportunities, not within easy reach of the "detested" German, while being completely out of ours. Germany, on the other hand, does not lynch, Jim Crow, and disfranchise.

Third, that the full responsibility for lynching be placed where it properly belongs—on the American Government; not upon the feeble-minded groups that practice it, not upon the governors that permit it, not upon the States where it is carried on. Each and all of these are component parts simply of the organism of the United States subject to its laws and not above them.

Fourth, that we be told why we were shipped 3,000 miles oversea to wage war, brutal and insensate, on people against whom we had less real grievance than against that lawless element of America that robs us of life. We no more believe that it was to make the "world safe for those people who live upon it and have made it their own" than we do that satan rebelled in heaven to make it safe for angels.

Fifth, that the same Federal officers used now in hunting down illicit whisky makers all over the South, often using force to meet resistance from captives, be likewise employed to hunt out every white devil that lynches. Maybe white officers will refuse this. If so, there are millions of Negroes willing to enter the Government service, giving guarantees to stamp out mob violence in every section of the Republic.

Sixth, that to avoid threatening bloodshed both Congress and the President take immediate steps to make life better for the thousands of Negro soldiers who made as daring sacrifices "over there" and for the millions of civilians who gave as patriotic services over here as any other group amongst our citizenry. In a race conflict of any dimensions many of us will be slaughtered, but we have reached a point in the evolutionary stages of human development that we know it is more honorable to die defending our lives than to die pleading with some illiterate white dog to spare them. Until it is made as unsafe to lynch a Negro as it is to lynch a United States Senator there can be no peace.

[c]
"I AM PREJUDICE"
Challenge/September 1919

I am Prejudice—supreme monarch of the South, with vassal tributaries in the North and West.

Conceived in the "lily white" heart of the South, I was born, like sin, full-fledged and armed with terror.

My rage inspired the Rebellion—though resisted, baffled, beaten by a superior foe, I rose in brutal grandeur, the frightful genius of Vengeance.

The "Ku-Klux" and "Patrolers" were my ministering spirits. They executed my flaming decrees during the hideous nights and tragic days of the Reconstruction.

I have murdered Negroes without cause, hanged them without provocation—I have raped, robbed, maligned, segregated a defenseless people, and neither pulpit, press, nor President has disturbed my exalted peace of mind.

Enthroned in the heart of Dixie, I am more powerful than any church, I condemn all constituted authority, whether State or Federal.

The rope, torch, and shotgun are the sacred symbols of my majesty and power, and my will is enforced from Boston to Los Angeles, from Seattle to Miami—I am not a stranger at the Capitol!

I am protected by State rights—thanks be—and my bloody orgies have been dramatized and rehearsed in Atlanta, Springfield, East St. Louis, and Fort Sam Houston.

I am the acknowledged genius of church, division, race separation, city segregation, and I am supreme in the Navy and triumphant in the Army.

I am the cementing tie that binds the solid South—the patron goddess of white supremacy. I have the keys of the doors of culture, opportunity, and wealth.

I scorn the patriotism of him whose right to "life, liberty, and pursuit of happiness" I must forever deny.

I, alone, know how to keep him blind, poor, and degraded, for I recognize none of his distinctions, I acknowledge none of his merits, I ignore all of his "progress."

No law can shelter him from my hatred, no ethics can conceal him from my fury, for I am adored, worshipped—the young sing my praise, the old repeat the triumphs of my blessed brutality.

As the relentless "scourge of the race," I am coextensive with the breadth of this Republic.

My record of the past insures my supremacy for the future.

I am "Ruthlessness." I am "Frightfulness." I am "Brutality." I am "Inhumanity." I am, Mr. President, that "Intolerable Thing."

I am the disgrace of democracy, the shame of its justice, and the condemnation of its civilization!

In spite of the league of nations, in spite of the covenant of peace, in spite of Germany's defeat—I care nothing for the Negro's loyalty, his patriotism, his heroism, his supreme sacrifice—I thunder at him my eternal decree—thunder at him in Washington "down!"—I thunder at him in Chicago "back!" I thunder at his ambition, at his aspirations, at him in all his upward struggle—since the World's War.

    Negroes! "As you were."

    For I am Prejudice!

"A Confession of Prejudice, written by a Negro soldier."

[d]
AMERICANISM
ROBERT L. VANN
Competitor/January 1920

The Competitor has but one policy; a complete Americanization wrought by the proper blending of the co-operative efforts of all Americans for the mutual benefit of all Americans.

The Negro has been clothed with citizenship by Federal legislation, and any designation of him as a special American is highly improper. He is an American without any qualifying adjectives descriptive either of his color or of his condition. There is no such thing as half American.

If the Negro is an American then he can have but one demand upon his country: the right to compete fully with every other American, in everything American, for the identical fruits and blessings sought and achieved by any other American under our system of government. This must be the privilege of every American who meets the test of American citizenship.

The Competitor is not published in opposition to any organization or in opposition to any man or set of men. It has no selfish purposes to espouse. Rather, it is dedicated to the consummation of a profitable and dignified relation between all Americans. The Competitor will not bear aloft the burning torch of the Bolshevist, Anarchist or blind radicals, nor will it tolerate a cringing coward who declines to defend his honor or his home against any invading foe. The Competitor believes there is need of a new National Conscience; there must be a new system substituted for the old; there must be conference between the various races and groups with a sincere desire to instruct all Americans in progressive American ideals.

Originally entitled "Our Policy."

[e]

THE N.A.A.C.P.
AND THE CLASS STRUGGLE
W. E. B. DU BOIS
Crisis/August 1921

The NAACP has been accused of not being a "revolutionary" body. This is quite true. We do not believe in revolution. We expect revolutionary changes in many parts of this life and this world, but we expect these changes to come mainly through reason, human sympathy, and the education of children, and not by murder. We know that there have been times when organized murder seemed the only way out of wrong, but we believe those times have been very few, the cost of the remedy excessive, the results as terrible as beneficent, and we gravely doubt if, in the future, there will be any real recurrent necessity for such upheaval.

Whether this is true or not, the NAACP is organized to agitate, to investigate, to expose, to defend, to reason, to appeal. This is our program and this is the whole of our program. What human reform demands today is light—more light; clear thought, accurate knowledge, careful distinctions.

How far, for instance, does the dogma of the "class struggle" apply to black folk in the United States today? Theoretically we are a part of the world proletariat in the sense that we are mainly an exploited class of cheap laborers; but practically we are not a part of the white proletariat and are not recognized by that proletariat to any great extent. We are the victims of their physical oppression, social ostracism, economic exclusion and personal hatred; and when in self-defense we seek sheer subsistence we are howled down as "scabs."

Then consider another thing: The colored group is not yet divided into capitalists and laborers. There are only the beginnings of such a division. In one hundred years, if we develop along conventional lines, we would have such fully separated classes, but today to a very large extent our laborers are our capitalists and our capitalists are our laborers. Our small class of well-to-do men have come to affluence largely through manual toil and have never been physically or mentally separated from the toilers. Our professional classes are sons and daughters of porters, washerwomen, and laborers.

Under these circumstances, how silly it would be for us to try to apply the doctrine of the class struggle without modification or thought. Let us take a particular instance. Ten years ago the Negroes of New York City lived in hired tenement houses in Harlem, having gotten possession of them by paying higher rents than white tenants. If they had tried to escape these high rents and move into quarters where white laborers lived, the white laborers would have mobbed and murdered them. On the other hand, the white capitalists raised heaven and earth either to drive them out of Harlem or keep their rents high. Now between this devil and the deep sea, what ought the Negro socialist or the Negro radical or, for that matter, the Negro conservative do?

Manifestly, there was only one thing for him to do, and that was to buy Harlem; but the buying of real estate calls for capital and credit, and the institutions that deal in capital and credit are capitalistic institutions. If, now, the Negro had begun to fight capital in Harlem, what capital was he fighting? If he fought capital as represented by white big real estate interests, he was wise; but he was also just as wise when he fought labor, which insisted on segregating him in work and in residence.

If, on the other hand, he fought the accumulating capital in his own group, which was destined in the years 1915 to 1920 to pay down $5,000,000 for real estate in Harlem, then he was slapping himself in his own face. Because either he must furnish capital for the buying of his own home, or rest naked in the slums and swamps. It is for this reason that there is today a strong movement in Harlem for a Negro bank, and a movement which is going soon to be successful. This Negro bank eventually is going to bring into co-operation and concentration the resources of fifty or sixty other Negro banks in the United States, and this aggregation of capital is going to be used to break the power of white capital in enslaving and exploiting the darker world.

Whether this is a program of socialism or capitalism does not concern us. It is the only program that means salvation to the Negro race. The main danger and the central question of the capitalistic development through which the Negro-American group is forced to go is the question of the ultimate control of the capital which they must raise and use. If this capital is going to be controlled by a few men for their own benefit, then we are destined to suffer from our own capitalists exactly what we are suffering from white capitalists today. And while this is not a pleasant prospect, it is certainly no worse than the present actuality. If, on the other hand, because of our more democratic organization and our widespread interclass sympathy, we can introduce a more democratic control, taking advantage of what the white world is itself doing to introduce industrial democracy, then we may not only escape our present economic slavery but even guide and lead a distrait economic world.

Originally entitled "The Class Struggle." The article was unsigned; W. E. B. DuBois was editor of *Crisis*.

[f]
DU BOIS ON REVOLUTION: A REPLY
CHANDLER OWEN
Messenger/September 1921

In the August *Crisis,* Dr. W. E. B. DuBois, speaking editorially, writes an article entitled "The Class Struggle" which reads in part:

"The N.A.A.C.P. has been accused of not being a 'revolutionary' body. This is quite true. We do not believe in revolution. We expect revolutionary changes in many parts of this life and this world, but we expect these changes to come mainly through reason, human sympathy and the education of children, and not by murder. We know that there have been times when organized murder seemed the only way out of wrong, but we believe those times have been very few, the cost of the remedy excessive, the results as terrible as beneficent, and we gravely doubt if in the future there will be any real recurrent necessity for such upheaval."

For sheer cheap demagogy, for tawdry scholarship, for fragmentary thinking, for sham cerebration and shoddy mentality—this expression could hardly be surpassed. It is on par with the demagogy of the South in dealing with the Negro to pretend that revolution implies human murder. It is worthy of the discredited old Russian emigrés in referring to all phases of the Soviet government. . . .

For the benefit of the public we shall now give to our readers an explanation of revolution. By revolution recognized thinkers and scholars mean the change from one system to another and the substitution of the new system for the old. For instance, the change from the geocentric to the heliocentric theory was a revolution in astronomy. Nobody was murdered, but the sun was thereafter considered the center of the universe, instead of the earth. All astronomical thinkers know what an advance this new and correct conception was and is.

In biology the theory of evolution superseded the theory of divine creation. It constituted a revolution when by its thorough exposition Charles Darwin gave to the world the scientific view of unified rather than multiple origin of species.

In chemistry, the atomic theory revolutionized all chemical opinion. Molecules still remained; elements were not assassinated, and the early chemists were not murdered. Nevertheless a striking impetus was given to the development of chemical thought; the early chemical authorities were not murdered; nor did it prevent the still newer advances to the electronic theory of matter.

John Stuart Mill, Adam Smith and Herbert Spencer were staunch philosophers, economists and sociologists of the *laissez faire* school; they believed in the gospel of competition. A revolution in economics and sociology took place with the coming of Auguste Comte, Lester Ward, Richard Ely, Ross, and other economists and sociologists of the school of social control. As against the competition theory of the older group the newer group of economists and sociologists counterposed the higher concept of co-operation. The old group stood for competitive war; the new group for co-operative peace. It was a gigantic revolution in economic and social thought, still we did not learn of the murder of Herbert Spencer, John Stuart Mill and Adam Smith by Ward, Comte or Ely. . . .

Revolution has gone on steadily in social systems. Savagery, barbarism and cannibalism were followed by a revolution which brought on slavery. Slavery, while bad, was a great advance on the previous systems. It was the system by which man passed from savagery to civilization without being annihilated. Another revolution brought on feudalism—less inhuman and more desirable than slavery. A third revolution gave to the world capitalism. Here was a revolution produced by another revolution—the industrial revolution. From hand made products the world went to machine made products as the result of new inventions and discoveries—the invention of labor saving machinery.

This was the great revolution of the 19th century. Strictly speaking, it was the revolution from manufacture to machino-facture,—from the hand made article to the machine made article.

To-day we are upon the threshold of a new revolution—the revolution from capitalism to socialism. With it may come the shedding of blood just as the revolution from slavery to capitalism in the United States was accompanied by the mass murder of the Civil War of 1861. Whatever the condition of the transition, the labor and Socialist movement is making every effort for peace. It is engaged in constant education, agitation, organization. It endorses and brooks no violence. No responsible leader, no convention, no responsible group supports any cheap tawdry, petty force tactics. Not even the I.W.W., Dr. DuBois!

DuBois after making a veritably superficial scholar of himself on the revolution argument proceeds to make himself more ridiculous in trying to rule out the Negro from the proletariat class. His reason is that we are not a part of the white proletariat because we are not recognized by that proletariat to any great extent. This is about as asinine as saying we are not human beings or men because in the South we are largely not so recognized. Is manhood dependent upon recognition? Is proletariat a product of recognition or is it a state of economic position of human beings? Is a Negro not a Negro when not so recognized? Is he a capitalist if the white proletariat does not recognize him as a laborer? As a superficial sociologist and economist Dr. DuBois still holds his place. Besides, he shows a crass ignorance of the whole labor problem. Of 32 million white workers in the United States, only 4 million are organized. The 4 million constitute the organized proletariat to which DuBois refers. Are the other 28 million white workers not members of the working class because they are not organized?

Or let us take another illustration. There are 100 thousand Negroes members of the National Association for the Advancement of Colored People. There are ten and a half million Negroes in the United States. Are the 100,000 members to class the great bulk *as not Negroes,* or some such silly balderdash merely because they are not yet organized in the movement?

The next point is also badly reasoned. The Negro race is divided into laborers and capitalists, and their capitalists are of varied shades of opinion just as you find among the whites. Occasionally you discover a liberal and broad scholar among them, now and then public spirited, but on the whole narrow, visionless and reactionary. They charge the highest prices, give the lowest quality, gouge the poor tenants even more heartlessly than the white landlords, not because they are worse naturally, but because they can exploit a fallacious race pride which is little more than a bid for the many to fill the coffers of the few. . . .

As to Negroes moving into tenement houses in New York, there is nothing relevant in this whole argument. He says the Negroes moved into Harlem because the white capitalists could get sky high rents—that Negroes would have been mobbed had they gone into quarters where white laborers lived. The answer to this is most properly that the Negroes did live and live now surrounded by white laborers. Again, it is not true of all the laborers. Besides, the white laborers are living in white capitalists' houses also. Neither lives where he wants to but where he must. Nor does the history of this country support the effete and forceless argument of DuBois. In nearly every section of the country it has been the white capitalist who has fought most vigorously for segregation because of his property values. Witness the present bombing of Negro homes instigated by the Kenwood and Hyde Park Property Owners Association of Chicago. These gentlemen constitute the real estate capitalists who are mobbing and bombing Negroes who attempt to buy property. The Chicago Federation of Labor on the contrary, has frequently protested against it.

The third argument of DuBois which reveals his much over rated mentality is the confusing of capital and capitalism in his article. He says the Negro would have made a big mistake to fight the $5,000,000 capital paid on his real estate from 1915 to 1920. What has that to do with the control of the means of production and exchange by a few individuals? We do not fight capital such as the factory, the mill, the machine, money, the mine. We do not desire to burn up or sink the land beneath the sea. Nor would we injure (or murder, to use the Doctor's inappropriate language) the capitalist as a person. We do, however, propose to destroy capitalism—that is, the control of the machinery of production and exchange by the limited few for their private profit and benefit. Under Socialism we shall run factories, mills and mines. Food will have to be eaten, clothes worn, houses lived in, persons and property carried, messages transmitted, work done. But this will be done not merely for the benefit of a few Rockefellers, Morgans, Schwabs and Carnegies, but for the teeming and toiling millions who today produce food which they cannot eat, make clothes they cannot wear, build houses which they cannot live in.

In concluding, DuBois reflects on what might happen in a way to ventilate an ignorance which, if he understood political science, he would have stated not with such an air of novelty and original discovery. He continues:

"The main danger and the central question of the capitalistic development through which the Negro American group is forced to go is the question of the ultimate *control of the capital which they must raise and use. If this capital is going to be controlled by a few men for their own benefit, then we are destined to suffer from our own capitalists exactly what we are suffering from white capitalists today.* And while this is not a pleasant prospect, it is certainly no worse than the present actuality. If, on the other hand, because of our more democratic organization and our widespread inter-class sympathy we can introduce a more democratic control, taking advantage of what the white world is itself doing to introduce industrial democracy, then we may not only escape our present economic slavery but even guide and lead a distrait economic world."

Why, the control of the capital is the only issue! Nobody but a fool wants to destroy it. And this reveals that the distinguished doctor of philosophy is very short of the philosophy of the class struggle . . . It is not necessary for him [the Negro] to suffer all the evils of exploitation by Negro capitalists when he can now adopt the more democratic cooperative methods. And the Negro of New York, in particular, has had enough experience with Negro landlords to be perfectly sure that he is in every respect the equal if not the superior of the white landlord in the exploitation of Negro tenants.

Rest assured, Dr. DuBois, you are not getting by as easily these days with your scholarship laurels as in the old days when you were the literary philosophic lion. Persons in your own group like John Haynes Holmes, Mary W. Ovington, J. W. Johnson, R. W. Bagnall, Herbert J. Seligman, Osward G. Villard and others laugh at this discussion of revolution, the proletariat, capital and Negro capital. Unless you convalesce rather rapidly, we shall have to call out the first aid to doctor your philosophy, unless as a doctor of philosophy you can doctor your own.

4.
DuBois and Garvey

In black American history there are two personalized feuds which stand out beyond all others: W. E. B. DuBois vs. Booker T. Washington and W. E. B. DuBois vs. Marcus Garvey.

Garvey and DuBois had initially tried to establish friendly relations. When DuBois vacationed in Jamaica in 1915 he was hosted by the local UNIA as an honored visitor. However, in a report on his visit, DuBois declared the race problem in Jamaica had been virtually eliminated, and to this Garvey reacted angrily in a 1916 letter to R. R. Moton of Tuskegee Institute. When Garvey came to America in 1916, one of his first actions was to pay a visit to the NAACP office in New York. This visit would complete the split between the two men. Garvey was shocked to find that most of the workers in the NAACP headquarters were white. Fresh from his native land, Garvey equated the scene at the NAACP office with what it would have meant in Jamaica, where organizations for blacks which had whites in key roles were usually agencies for the perpetration of imperialism through black middle-class lackies. Garvey concluded that the NAACP was the "National Association for the Advancement of *Certain* People": the black middle class and their white friends, and not for the black masses.

In a 1919 issue of the *Crisis* DuBois criticized the UNIA separatist program without actually naming names. In 1920, Garvey made the first recorded open breach between the two men. It came in reaction to a report that DuBois had attended one of the meetings of the UNIA convention. Garvey declared, "If Dr. DuBois were a New Negro working for the freedom of his race we would have been glad to know that he was there. But association with an alien race, the size of the pocketbook, and the writing of a few books favorable to the Negroes is not enough for us. He must be 100 percent Negro. We do not care two pins for Dr. DuBois. When we think of big Negroes we do not think of him."

In the December 1920 and January 1921 *Crisis,* DuBois presented what he considered to be a favorable evaluation of Garvey and the UNIA economic program. Garvey thought otherwise of these articles. The feud was now out in the open and it would become a major issue in the black press. The Baltimore *Afro-American* printed excerpts of the January *Crisis* piece, and next to it a reply by Marcus Garvey. The *Afro* presentations—"What DuBois Thinks of Garvey" and "What Garvey Thinks of DuBois"—are included here as selections (a) and (b), and are significant not only for what they say about the feud but also as an example of how outsiders interpreted it.

By 1923 the battle had become, on both sides, a vicious attempt at character assassination. In selection (c), from a 1923 *Negro World* editorial reprinted in Garvey's *Philosophy and Opinions,* the UNIA leader replies to an attack DuBois made on him in *Century* magazine. Selection (d), a DuBois article in a 1924 issue of the *Crisis,* declares Garvey to be either a "lunatic or a traitor."

In his critiques of Garvey, DuBois avoided any serious criticism of Garvey's long-range goals. Garvey's objective was a separate black society. DuBois, on the other hand, was committed to integration and felt a special need to defend it during the nationalistic New Negro era, but he also believed deeply in the importance of having strong independent black institutions that would exist within an otherwise mixed American society; therefore, he preferred to dispute Garvey's methods and personality traits rather than his ends. In this regard it is worth noting that in 1934 DuBois resigned from the NAACP because of Association opposition to his advocacy of separate black institutions.

James Weldon Johnson, national secretary of the NAACP, was not nearly as touchy on the separatism-integration issue as was DuBois, and an editorial exchange between Johnson and Garvey brought out differences between the NAACP and UNIA that were apt to be clouded over in the diatribes between DuBois and Garvey. In selection (e) Johnson, in one of his New York *Age* columns, takes issue with a speech of Garvey's that was quoted in the *New York Tribune.* In selection (f) Garvey replies to Johnson in the *Negro World.* The *Negro World* ran Johnson's article next to Garvey's reply. (Johnson held his post in the NAACP between 1920 and 1930. He was a columnist for the *Age* for a decade, ending in 1923, when he had a falling out with the highly conservative editor-publisher of the *Age,* Fred Moore. Johnson was a prolific contributor to the writing of the Harlem Renaissance. Among his contributions are the Negro National Anthem, "Lift Every Voice and Sing," and the now classic book of black church poetry, *God's Trombones.*)

[a]
WHAT DU BOIS THINKS OF GARVEY
W. E. B. DU BOIS
Crisis/January 1921

... When it comes to Mr. Garvey's industrial and commercial enterprises there is more ground for doubt and misgiving than in the matter of his character. First of all his enterprises are incorporated in Delaware, where the incorporation laws are loose and where no financial statements are required. So far as I can find, and I have searched with care, Mr. Garvey has never published a complete statement of the income and expenditures of the Negro Improvement Association or of the Black Star Line or any of his enterprises, which really revealed his financial situation. A courteous letter of inquiry sent to him July 22, 1920, asking for such financial data as he was willing for the public to know, remains to this day unacknowledged and unanswered. . . .

This is a serious situation, and even this does not tell the whole story: the real estate, furniture, etc., listed above are probably valued correctly. But how about the boats? The Yarmouth is a wooden steamer of 1,452 tons, built in 1887. It is old and unseaworthy; it came near sinking a year ago and it has cost a great deal for repairs. It is said that it is now laid up for repairs with a large bill due. Without doubt the inexperienced purchasers of this vessel paid far more than it is worth, and it will soon be utterly worthless unless rebuilt at a very high cost.

The cases of the Kanawha (or Antonio Maceo) and the Shadyside are puzzling. Neither of these boats is registered as belonging to the Black Star Line at all. The former is recorded as belonging to C. L. Dimon, and the latter to the North and East River Steamboat Company. Does the Black Star Line really own these boats, or is it buying them by installments, or only leasing them? We do not know the facts and have been unable to find out. Under the circumstance they look like dubious "assets." . . .

Garvey himself tells of one woman who had saved about four hundred dollars in gold: "She brought out all the gold and bought shares in the Black Star Line." Another man writes this touching letter from the Canal Zone: "I was sent twice to buy shares amounting to $125 (numbers of certificates 3742 and 9617). Now I am sending $35 for seven more shares. You might think I have money but the truth, as I stated before, is that I have no money now. But if I'm to die of hunger it will be all right because I'm determined to do all that's in my power to better the conditions of my race." . . .

On the other hand, full credit must be given Garvey for a bold effort and some success. He has at least put vessels manned and owned by black men on the seas and they have carried passengers and cargoes. The difficulty is that he does not know the shipping business, he does not understand the investment of capital, and he has few trained and staunch assistants.

The present financial plight of an inexperienced and headstrong promoter may therefore decide the fate of the whole movement. This would be a calamity. Garvey is the beloved leader of tens of thousands of poor and bewildered people who have been cheated all their lives. His failure would mean a blow to their faith, and a loss of their little savings, which it would take generations to undo. . . .

Then too, Garvey increases his difficulties in other directions. He is a British subject. He wants to trade in British territory. Why then does he needlessly antagonize and even insult Britain? He wants to unite all Negroes. Why then does he sneer at the work of the powerful group of his race in the United States where he finds asylum and sympathy? Particularly, why does he decry the excellent and rising business enterprises of Harlem—intimating that his schemes alone are honest and sound when the facts flatly contradict him? . . .

And, finally, without arms, money, effective organization or base of operations, Mr. Garvey openly and wildly talks of "Conquest" and of telling white Europeans in Africa to "get out!" and of becoming himself a black Napoleon! . . .

To sum up: Garvey is a sincere, hard-working idealist; he is also a stubborn, domineering leader of the mass; he has worthy industrial and commercial schemes but he is an inexperienced business man. His dreams of Negro industry, commerce and the ultimate freedom of Africa are feasible; but his methods are bombastic, wasteful, illogical and ineffective and almost illegal. If he learns by experience, attracts strong and capable friends and helpers instead of making needless enemies; if he gives up secrecy and suspicion and substitutes open and frank reports as to his income and expenses, and above all if he is willing to be a co-worker and not a czar, he may yet ——* in his

* Word(s) missing in *Afro-American* reprint.

schemes toward accomplishment. But unless he does these things and
does them quickly he cannot escape failure.

As condensed and reprinted in the Baltimore *Afro-American* January 7, 1921.

[b]
WHAT GARVEY THINKS OF DU BOIS
MARCUS GARVEY
Negro World/January 1, 1921

The January number of the Crisis magazine contained a four page
article on Marcus Garvey. The first half of the article is devoted to a
survey of the Black Star Line, the second half is devoted to Mr.
Garvey's industrial enterprises and the feasibility of his general plans.
The article follows the general line of DuBois' articles when treating the
products of a Negro's brain, pen or hand. It is 75 percent criticism and
25 percent appreciation.

A brilliant student of sociology, a literary genius, a man of letters,
Dr. DuBois could grace a chair in any university in the world, but when
it comes to mingling with men and dealing with practical affairs, he
sometimes strikes the wrong note. When he taught in Wilberforce University and Atlanta University, and when he gathered facts in Philadelphia for sociological study he could rarely get close to the heart of
colored people. His literary ventures, the "Moon" and the "Horizon"
[magazines], did not pan out well. His Niagara movement died a natural
death. It was not until a few Boston and New York philanthropists
took Dr. DuBois under their aegis and threw around him the prestige of
their wealth and fame that he was able to make the Crisis and the
NAACP go. And if these men should withdraw their support and prestige the Crisis might go the way of the "Moon" and the "Horizon," and
the NAACP might go the way of the Niagara movement.

As we study the personality of Dr. DuBois, we find that he only
appreciates one type of men, and that is the cultured, refined type
which lingers around universities and attends pink tea affairs. The men
of dynamic force of the Negro race, the men with ability to sway and
move the masses, Dr. DuBois cannot appraise at their face value, and
that is why the author of the "Souls of Black Folk," while the idol of

the drawing room aristocrats, could not thus far become the popular leader of the masses of his own race.

To read Dr. DuBois' statement about the Black Star Line, one would imagine that no business concern ever made mistakes and that everything was always smooth sailing.

It took the Crisis, backed by millionaires, by big Negroes and edited by a distinguished scholar over five years to become self supporting. Suppose some over-inquisitive critic, before the NAACP was two years old, should demand an accounting and ask how much the philanthropists and Negro public were forced to contribute annually to keep the NAACP or the Crisis going, what would DuBois have said?

As a matter of fact, history is not made by the hypersensitive critics of the type of Walter Pater, Mark Pattison, Coventry Patmore, Prof. George Santayana and Dr. W.E.B. DuBois. But the men like Garvey, men of faith and vision, men of one idea, who have thrown their whole personality towards the realization of that idea, have been the makers of history and will be as long as men are men, created in the divine image and breathing the breath of a spiritual life. It was not the doubting Thomas but the crusading Peter and Paul who launched Christianity upon its world career.

Dr. DuBois is undoubtedly right when he says that there is no necessary antagonism between Garvey and other Negro leaders, between the UNIA and other movements for racial uplift. DuBois appeals to the "Talented Tenth," while Garvey appeals to the "Oi Polloi." The NAACP appeals to the Beau Brummell, Lord Chesterfield, kid gloved, silk stocking, creased trousers, patent leather shoe, Bird of Paradise hat and Hudson seal coat with beaver or skunk collar element, while the UNIA appeals to the sober, sane, serious, earnest, hard-working man, who earns his living by the sweat of his brow. The NAACP appeals to the cavalier element in the Negro race, while the UNIA appeals to the self reliant yeomanry. Hence, in no sense are Dr. DuBois and Mr. James Weldon Johnson rivals of Marcus Garvey. DuBois and Johnson as writers and speakers and Garvey as prophet, propagandist and organizer and inspirer of the masses are doing good work and all should be free and unimpeded in perfecting their plans.

The only objection that we have had to some of the Caucasian philanthropists behind Hampton, Tuskegee and NAACP selecting leaders for the Negro race was not because they elevated those Negro leaders who they thought were safe, sane and conservative and whom they could manipulate, but because they attempted to suppress those radical Negroes who manifested initiative, individuality and independence of character, regardless of their intellectual attainments and achievements and their worth as men.

As reprinted in the Baltimore *Afro-American* January 7, 1921.

[c]
W. E. B. DU BOIS
AS A HATER OF DARK PEOPLE
MARCUS GARVEY
Negro World/February 13, 1923

Calls His Own Race "Black and Ugly,"
Judging From the White Man's Standard of Beauty
Trick of National Association for the Advancement of
Colored People to Solve Problem by Assimilation and
Color Distinction

W. E. Burghardt DuBois, the Negro "misleader," who is editor of the "Crisis," the official organ of the National Association for the Advancement of "certain" Colored People, situated at 70 Fifth Avenue, New York City, has again appeared in print. This time he appears as author of an article in the February issue of the "Century" Magazine under the caption, "Back to Africa," in which he makes the effort to criticize Marcus Garvey, the Universal Negro Improvement Association and the Black Star Line. . . .

"Fat, Black, Ugly Man"

In describing Marcus Garvey in the article before mentioned, he referred to him as a "little, fat, black man; ugly, but with intelligent eyes and a big head." Now, what does DuBois mean by ugly? This so-called professor of Harvard and Berlin ought to know by now that the standard of beauty within a race is not arrived at by comparison with another race; as, for instance, if we were to desire to find out the standard of beauty among the Japanese people we would not judge them from the Anglo-Saxon viewpoint, but from the Japanese. How he arrives at his conclusion that Marcus Garvey is ugly, being a Negro, is impossible to determine, in that if there is any ugliness in the Negro race it would be reflected more through DuBois than Marcus Garvey, in that he himself tells us that he is a little Dutch, a little French, and a little Negro. Why, in fact, the man is a monstrosity. So, if there is any ugliness it is on the part of DuBois and not on the part of the "little fat, black man with a big head," because all this description is typical of the African. But this only goes to show how much hate DuBois has for the black blood in his veins. Anything that is black, to him, is ugly, is hideous, is monstrous, and this is why in 1917 he had but the lightest of colored people in his office, when one could hardly tell whether it was a white show or a colored vaudeville he was running at Fifth avenue. It was only after the Universal Negro Improvement Association started to pounce upon him and his National Association for the Advancement of Colored People that they admitted that colored element into the association that could be distinguished as Negro, and it was during that period of time that Weldon Johnson and Pickens got a look-in. . . .

DuBois and White Company

It is no wonder that DuBois seeks the company of white people, because he hates black as being ugly. That is why he likes to dance with white people, and dine with them, and sometimes sleep with them, because from his way of seeing things all that is black is ugly, and all that is white is beautiful. Yet this professor, who sees ugliness in being black, essays to be a leader of the Negro people and has been trying for over fourteen years to deceive them through his connection with the National Association for the Advancement of Colored People. Now what does he mean by advancing colored people if he hates black so much? In what direction must we expect his advancement? We can conclude in no other way than that it is in the direction of losing our black identity and becoming, as nearly as possible, the lowest whites by assimilation and miscegenation.

This probably is accountable for the bleaching processes and the hair straightening escapades of some of the people who are identified with the National Association for the Advancement of Colored People in their mad desire of approach to the white race, in which they see beauty as advocated by the professor from Harvard and Berlin. It is no wonder some of these individuals use the lip stick, and it is no wonder that the erudite Doctor keeps a French Beard. Surely that is not typical of Africa, it is typical of that blood which he loves so well and which he bewails in not having more in his veins—French.

Lazy and Dependent

In referring to the effort of Marcus Garvey and the Universal Negro Improvement Association to establish a building in Harlem, he says in the article: "There was a long, low, unfinished church basement roofed over. It was designed as the beginning of a church long ago, but abandoned. Marcus Garvey roofed it over, and out of this squat and dirty old Liberty Hall he screams his propaganda. As compared with the homes, the business and church, Garvey's basement represents nothing in accomplishment and only waste in attempt."

Here we have this "lazy dependent mulatto" condemning the honest effort of his race to create out of nothing something which could be attributed to their ownership, in that the "dirty old Liberty Hall" he speaks of is the property of Negroes, while in another section of his article he praises the "beautiful and luxurious buildings" he claims to be occupied by other black folk, making it appear that these buildings were really the property of these people referred to, such as, according to his own description, "a brick block on Seventh Avenue stretching low and beautiful from the Y.W.C.A. with a moving picture house of the better class and a colored 5 and 10 cent store, built and owned by black folks." DuBois knows he lies when he says that the premises herein referred to were built and are owned by black folks. They are the property of industrious Jews who have sought an outlet for their surplus cash in the colored district. . . .

Independent Negro Effort

Liberty Hall represents the only independent Negro structure referred to in the classification of DuBois about buildings up in Harlem, but he calls this independent effort "dirty and old," but that which has been contributed by white people he refers to in the highest terms. This shows the character of the man—he has absolutely no respect and regard for independent Negro effort but that which is supported by white charity and philanthropy, and why so? Because he himself was educated by charity and kept by philanthropy. He got his education by charity, and now he is occupying a position in the National Association for the Advancement of Colored People, and it is felt that his salary is also paid by the funds that are gathered in from the charity and philanthropy of white people. This "soft carpet" idea is going to be the undoing of W. E. B. DuBois. He likes too much the luxurious home and soft carpets, and that is why he is naturally attracted to white folks, because they have a lot of this; but if he were in Georgia or Alabama he would now be stepping on the carpets of Paradise; but that is not all of the man, as far as this is concerned. He ridicules the idea that the Universal Negro Improvement Association should hold a social function in Liberty Hall on the 10th of August, 1922, at which certain social honors were bestowed upon a number of colored gentlemen, such as Knighthood and the creation of the Peerage.

Social Honors for Negroes

In referring to the matter, he says in the article: "Many American Negroes and some others were scandalized by something which they could but regard as a simple child's play. It seemed to them sinister. This enthronement of a demagogue, a blatant boaster, who with monkey-shines was deluding the people, and taking their hard-earned dollars; and in high Harlem there arose an insistent cry, 'Garvey Must Go!' " Indeed DuBois was scandalized by the creation of a Peerage and Knighthood by Negroes, and in truth the person who is responsible for such a thing should go, because DuBois and those who think like him can see and regard honor conferred only by their white masters. If DuBois was created a Knight Commander of the Bath by the British King, or awarded a similar honor by some white Potentate, he would have advertised it from cover to cover of the "Crisis," and he would have written a book and told us how he was recognized above his fellows by such a Potentate, but it was not done that way. This was an enthronement of Negroes, in which DuBois could see nothing worth while. . . .

Comparison Between Two Men

Marcus Garvey was born in 1887; DuBois was born in 1868; that shows that DuBois is old enough to be Marcus Garvey's father. But what has happened? Within the fifty-five years of DuBois' life we find him still living on the patronage of good white people, and with the thirty-six years of Marcus Garvey (who was born poor and whose father, according to DuBois, died in a poor house) he was able to at least pass over the charity of white people and develop an independent program originally financed by himself to the extent of thousands of dollars, now taken up by the Negro peoples themselves. Now which of the two is poorer in character and in manhood? The older man, who had all these opportunities and still elects to be a parasite, living off the good will of another race, or the younger man, who had sufficient self-respect to make an effort to do for himself, even though in his effort he constructs a "dirty brick building" from which he can send out his propaganda on race self-reliance and self-respect.

Motive of DuBois

To go back to the motive of DuBois in the advocacy of the National Association for the Advancement of Colored People is to expose him for what he is. The National Association for the Advancement of Colored People executives have not been honest enough to explain to the people of the Negro race their real solution for the Negro problem, because they are afraid that they would be turned down in their intention. They would make it appear that they are interested in the advancement of the Negro people of America, when, in truth, they are but interested in the subjugation of certain types of the Negro race and the assimilation of as many . . . as possible into the white race. . . .

Garvey Challenges DuBois

DuBois says that "Garvey had no thorough education and a very hazy idea of the technique of civilization." DuBois forgets that Garvey has challenged him over a dozen times to intellectual combat, and he has for as many times failed to appear. Garvey will back his education against that of DuBois at any time in the day from early morning to midnight, and whether it be in the classroom or on the public platform, will make him look like a dead duck on a frozen lake.

Is DuBois Educated

DuBois seems to believe that the monopoly of education is acquired by being a graduate of Fisk, Harvard and Berlin. Education is not so much the school that one has passed through, but the use one makes of that which he has learned.

If DuBois' education fits him for no better service than being a lackey for good white people, then it were better that Negroes were not educated. DuBois forgets that the reason so much noise was made over him and his education was because he was among the first "experiments" made by white people on colored men along the lines of higher education. No one experimented with Marcus Garvey, so no one has to look upon him with surprise that he was able to master the classics and graduate from a university.

DuBois is a surprise and wonder to the good white people who experimented with him, but to us moderns he is just an ordinarily intelligent Negro, one of those who does not know what he wants.

The Man Who Lies

DuBois is such a liar when it comes to anything relating to the Universal Negro Improvement Association, the Black Star Line and Marcus Garvey that we will not consider his attacks on the Black Star Line seriously. He lied before in reference to this corporation and had to swallow his vomit. He has lied again, and we think a statement is quite enough to dispose of him in this matter.

This envious, narrow-minded man has tried in every way to surround the Universal Negro Improvement Association and Marcus Garvey with suspicion. He has been for a long time harping on the membership of the Universal Negro Improvement Association as to whether we have millions of members or thousands. He is interested because he wants to know whether these members are all paying dues or not, in that he will become very interested in the financial end of it, as there would be a lot of money available. DuBois does not know that whether the Universal Negro Improvement Association had money or not he wouldn't have the chance of laying his hands on it, in that there are very few "leaders" that we can trust with a dollar and get the proper change. This is the kind of leadership that the Universal Negro Improvement Association is about to destroy for the building up of that which is self-sacrificing; the kind of leadership that will not hate poor people because they are poor, as DuBois himself tells us he does, but a kind of leadership that will make itself poor and keep itself poor so as to be better able to interpret the poor in their desire for general uplift. He hates the poor. Now, what kind of leader is he? Negroes are all poor black folk. They are not rich. They are not white; hence they are despised by the great professor.

What do you think about this logic, this reasoning, professor? You have been to Berlin, Harvard and Fisk; you are educated and you have the "technique of civilization." . . .

[d]
MARCUS GARVEY: A LUNATIC OR A TRAITOR?
W. E. B. DU BOIS
Crisis/May 1924

In its endeavor to avoid any injustice toward Marcus Garvey and his followers, THE CRISIS has almost leaned backward. Notwithstanding his wanton squandering of hundreds of thousands of dollars we have refused to assume that he was a common thief. In spite of his monumental and persistent lying we have discussed only the larger and truer aspects of his propaganda. We have refrained from all comment on his trial and conviction for fraud. We have done this too in spite of his personal vituperation of the editor of THE CRISIS and persistent and unremitting repetition of falsehood after falsehood as to the editor's beliefs and acts and as to the program of the N.A.A.C.P.

In the face, however, of the unbelievable depths of debasement and humiliation to which this demagog has descended in order to keep himself out of jail, it is our duty to say openly and clearly:

Marcus Garvey is, without doubt, the most dangerous enemy of the Negro race in America and in the world. He is either a lunatic or a traitor. He is sending all over this country tons of letters and pamphlets appealing to Congressmen, business men, philanthropists and educators to join him on a platform whose half concealed planks may be interpreted as follows:

That no person of Negro descent can ever hope to become an American citizen.

That forcible separation of the races and the banishment of Negroes to Africa is the only solution of the Negro problem.

That race war is sure to follow any attempt to realize the program of the N.A.A.C.P.

We would have refused to believe that any man of Negro descent could have fathered such a propaganda if the evidence did not lie before us in black and white signed by this man. Here is a letter and part of a symposium sent to one of the most prominent business men of America and turned over to us; we select but a few phrases; the italics are ours:

"Do you believe the Negro to be a *human being*?

"Do you believe the Negro *entitled to all the rights of humanity*?

"Do you believe that the Negro should be taught *not to aspire to the highest political positions in Governments of the white race,* but to such positions among his own race in a Government of his own?

"Would you help morally *or otherwise* to bring about such a possibility? Do you believe that the Negro should be *encouraged to aspire* to the highest industrial and commercial positions in the countries of the white man in competition with him and to his exclusion?

"Do you believe that the Negro should be encouraged to regard and *respect the rights of all other races* in the same manner as the other races would respect the rights of the Negro?"

The pamphlets include one of the worst articles recently written *by a Southern white man* advocating the deportation of American Negroes to Liberia and several articles by Garvey and his friends. From one of Garvey's articles we abstract one phrase:

"THE WHITE RACE CAN BEST HELP THE NEGRO BY TELLING HIM THE TRUTH, AND NOT BY FLATTERING HIM INTO BELIEVING THAT HE IS AS GOOD AS ANY WHITE MAN."

Not even Tom Dixon or Ben Tillman or the hatefulest enemies of the Negro have ever stooped to a more vicious campaign than Marcus Garvey, sane or insane, is carrying on. He is not attacking white prejudice, he is grovelling before it and applauding it; his only attack is on men of his own race who are striving for freedom; his only contempt is for Negroes; his only threats are for black blood. And this leads us to a few plain words:

1. No Negro in America ever had a fairer and more patient trial than Marcus Garvey. He convicted himself by his own admissions, his swaggering monkey-shines in the court room with monocle and long tailed coat and his insults to the judge and prosecuting attorney.

2. Marcus Garvey was long refused bail, not because of his color, but because of the repeated threats and cold blooded assaults charged against his organizations. He himself openly threatened to "get" the

District Attorney. His followers had repeatedly to be warned from intimidating witnesses and one was sent to jail therefor. One of his former trusted officials after being put out of the Garvey organization brought the long concealed cash account of the organization to this office and we published it. Within two weeks the man was shot in the back in New Orleans and killed. We know nothing of Garvey's personal connection with these cases but we do know that today his former representative lies in jail in Liberia sentenced to death for murder. The District Attorney believed that Garvey's "army" had arms and ammunition and was prepared to "shoot up" colored Harlem if he was released. For these and no other reasons Garvey was held in the Tombs so long without bail and until he had made abject promises, apologizing to the judge and withdrawing his threats against the District Attorney. Since his release he has not dared to print a single word against white folk. All his vituperation has been heaped on his own race.

Everybody, including the writer, who has dared to make the slightest criticism of Garvey has been intimidated by threats and threatened with libel suits. Over fifty court cases have been brought by Garvey in ten years. After my first unfavorable article on Garvey, I was not only threatened with death by men declaring themselves his followers, but received letters of such unbelievable filth that they were absolutely unprintable. When I landed in this country from my trip to Africa I learned with disgust that my friends stirred by Garvey's threats had actually felt compelled to have secret police protection for me on the dock!

Friends have even begged me not to publish this editorial lest I be assassinated. To such depths have we dropped in free black America! I have been exposing white traitors for a quarter century. If the day has come when I cannot tell the truth about black traitors it is high time that I died.

The American Negroes have endured this wretch all too long with fine restraint and every effort at cooperation and understanding. But the end has come. Every man who apologizes for or defends Marcus Garvey from this day forth writes himself down as unworthy of the countenance of decent Americans. As for Garvey himself, this open ally of the Ku Klux Klan should be locked up or sent home.

[e]
AN ANALYSIS OF GARVEY
JAMES WELDON JOHNSON
New York Age/September 24, 1921

Recently Mr. Marcus Garvey, president-general of the Universal Negro Improvement Association, was quoted in one of the daily papers as making the following statement:

> The Universal Negro Improvement Association stands in opposition to the Pan-African Congress and to the leadership of Dr. DuBois because they seek to bring about a destruction of the black and white races by the social amalgamation of both. The Dr. DuBois group believe that Negroes should settle down in communities of whites and by social contact and miscegenation bring about a new type. The Universal Negro Improvement Association believes that both races have separate and distinct social destinies; that each and every race should develop on its own social lines; and that any attempt to bring about the amalgamation of any two opposite races is a crime against nature.

This is a statement in which Mr. Garvey consciously or unconsciously plays to the most deep-seated prejudices of the white man in America. It is the very sort of thing that Vardaman, Cole Blease and the rest of that ilk say and wish to have accepted. Does Mr. Garvey realize the full implication of his statement when he says that any attempt to bring about the amalgamation of any two opposite races is "a crime against nature"? Does he not see that a statement of this kind places the Negro in a position outside of the pale of the human race, somewhere between brute and man?

These are the exact words that have been used by men like Vardaman, who wish to infer that in any such relationship between the white and black races the white is guilty of something akin to bestiality. Furthermore, if such a relation between white and black were a crime against nature, the result of such relationship would be a monstrosity of sin. Is Mr. Garvey willing to say that Frederick Douglass and Booker T. Washington were such monstrosities?

If Mr. Garvey has the idea that the Negro, situated as he is in the United States, can fully duplicate the whole machinery of civilization, it is a sign of sheer simplicity.

When Mr. Garvey talks about social equality he should not do so in the loose manner in which Southern white people talk. He should say what he means by "social equality." If by "social equality" is meant the forcing of one's self into social intercourse with others, no self-respecting Negro wants it. But if by "social equality" is meant the right of the Negro to participate fully in all of the common rights of American citizenship and to arrange his own personal associations, wherever those associations are mutually agreeable, without being prohibited by any ban either of law or mob opinion, then no Negro can be self-respecting who does not stand for it.

It is on the cry of "social equality" in the loose sense that Negroes are refused in public places, driven out of Pullman cars, herded in "jim crow" pens, stuck up in the front end of street cars, given inferior schools and subjected to a hundred other humiliations and injustices. The only sensible definition of social equality is: The right of any person to associate with any other person when the wish to do so is mutual.

Social equality in its strict sense should be a matter left entirely to individuals; but it is not. It is regulated by law and mob opinion. The Negro must either protest against such caste regulation or accept the position of self-acknowledged inferiority. At the mere words "social equality" some white people froth at the mouth and some colored people grow panic stricken. There is no necessity for either action. To the rabid whites we would say that there is no one in these United States so weak that he can be forced against his will to accept anybody's society. To the dissembling Negroes we would say that absolutely nothing is gained by letting the white man feel that we consider ourselves unfit for human association with the other groups in this country.

We assume that Mr. Garvey is working for equality of opportunity for the Negro (we are discussing the Negro in the United States), and we assume also that he has too much sense to think it can be achieved by attempting to substitute black domination for white domination. By what feasible plan does Mr. Garvey propose to secure it?

The only possible end of the race problem in the United States to which we can now look without despair is one which embraces the fullest co-operation between white and black in all the phases of national activity. If that end can be reached save through the recognition of all kinds of equalities, we should be glad to have Mr. Garvey tell us.

Of course, there may some day arise one or two or three great empires in Africa that will compel the recognition of the full rights of men of African blood everywhere. Or there may come sooner than expected the ultimate downfall of the white race. But, as Kipling would say, that is another story—in fact, a couple.

Reprinted in the *Negro World,* October 1, 1921, in a column called "Views and Reviews" and headlined "A Crime Against Nature." This and the following selection (f) were featured on the same page under the banner headline "James Weldon Johnson and Marcus Garvey in a Tilt/The Immortal Question of Social Equality."

[f]
GARVEY REPLIES: "I DEMAND SOCIAL JUSTICE"
MARCUS GARVEY
Negro World/October 1, 1921

It is for me to inform James Weldon Johnson that I mean every word stated in the paragraph quoted . . . in the New York *Tribune,* and which paragraph he placed under review in the New York *Age* . . .

In making this statement Johnson will therefore realize that I am conscious of the import of the paragraph. Mr. Johnson states that in my statement I am supporting "every sort of thing that Vardaman and Cole Blease and the rest of that ilk say and wish to have accepted." It is for me to inform Mr. Johnson that I do not give two rows of pins for Vardaman and Cole Blease; I am concerned with the destiny of the Negro. If Vardaman and Cole Blease happen to say things that can be interpreted to mean the same things I say in the interest of my race, then Mr. Johnson is welcome to the comparison.

I will not question Mr. Johnson's intelligence to ask him if he realizes the full import of what he states, because I am forced to accept Mr. Johnson as a leader of the Negro race, and therefore, must give him credit for the intelligence of his own statement. Mr. Johnson and I differ in that Mr. Johnson and his associates and probably co-workers hanker after social equality with white people. I demand social justice.

There is quite a difference between fighting for social equality and fighting for social justice. I would like to see the man who would be able to compel me by law or otherwise to accept him as my companion if I did not care to do so. This is forcing the issue of social equality; but I demand from every man in the name of and by the law my constitutional right to go anywhere in the country of which I am a citizen. This is the difference between the Pan-African Congress, Dr. DuBois, Mr. Johnson and their followers, and the Universal Negro Improvement Association, the movement I represent.

If Negroes will stop making all this noise about social equality, giving the white people the idea that we are hankering after their company, and get down to business and build up a strong race, industrially, commercially, educationally and politically, everything social will come afterwards.

It is human to be prejudiced, it has been so since creation, and it will be so until Gabriel blows his horn; and where you have a race of slave masters admitting into citizenship a race of slaves, you are not going to expect the race of slave masters to yield up to the race of slaves, equality in everything, until the race of slaves has brought itself up to the standard of the race of slave masters.

It is all tomfoolery talking about a better time is coming when the white man's heart will be softened toward the Negro and will accept him as a social equal. You are crazy if you think that time will ever come on this side of Jordan until the Negro, either in America or elsewhere builds himself up as a great power to force the recognition of the world.

Mr. Johnson well knows that I have no imputation against great men like Frederick Douglass and Booker T. Washington, but these men were brought into the world under unfortunate circumstances; they were brought into the world through bastardy, the rape of the one race upon the other, and the abuse and advantage of the mothers of the one race by the men of the other. Does Mr. Johnson want us to perpetuate that order of society by which we must bring in a race of illegitimates to be called in the future a race of bastards rather than for us to get among ourselves now and regulate the social order under which we should live? The difference between Mr. Johnson's policy and the Universal Negro Improvement Association's is that he believes that the only society for the Negro is that of the white man's. We believe to the contrary. We think that the black man's society is as good as that of any other race, and we are determined to build up a Negro society even superior to that of the whites. Therefore, we are not going to make any noise about social equality among white folks; we are going to use our time in building up a social standard among ourselves, and if Mr. Johnson and his followers will get off the subsidized pinnacle of looking to the white people for everything social and financial and depend upon the brawn, sinew, sweat and ability of the Negro, it will be better for him and those who follow.

Mr. Johnson defeats his own argument when he says that "it is on the cry of social equality that Negroes are refused in public places, driven out of Pullman cars, herded in Jim Crow pens, stuck up in the front end of street cars, given inferior schools, and subjected to a hundred other humiliations and injustices." This is just what we want to prove, and that is why we are demonstrating to the white race that we do not give a row of pins about social equality with them, because we believe in our own good company; whilst on the contrary Mr. Johnson is aggravating this question of social equality by always wanting to be with the white folks. Now, who is doing more harm to the Negro race, Mr. Johnson or I? Johnson will agitate between now and eternity and he will never get social equality with white people, until he gets down and by a hard day's work builds up a race independently and then demand justice through the strength of the race.

I am not going to waste time with Mr. Johnson and his associates waiting for white people to recognize me. I am going to put in all my time with my race and help to bring them to a standard where they will demand things and get them, and not beg and be refused.

I am glad Mr. Johnson admits that one day two or three great empires in Africa will arise. The Universal Negro Improvement Association has traveled a long way to get Mr. Johnson and his followers to admit this. Thank God, the hour is drawing near. . . .

5.
Socialist Opposition to Black Nationalism

Black socialists had committed themselves to a coalition with the struggling white left. As the white radical movement declined during the early 1920s, black socialists were left out in the cold. A. Philip Randolph, Chandler Owen and others of the *Messenger* crowd now had to rely on the black community for support. There, among the masses, Marcus Garvey held sway with his black nationalist Universal Negro Improvement Association. Garvey argued that blacks could never gain ground through coalitions with whites of any type. For Randolph and others to argue that times were bad and that when conditions improved a coalition would bring results was extremely difficult so long as Garvey held a prominent position.

In 1922, Randolph and Owen, through their "Friends of Negro Freedom," an organization of trade unionists and some top NAACP officials, instigated a "Garvey Must Go" campaign, which, among other things, helped speed the U.S. Justice Department in taking action on its pending mail fraud indictment against Garvey and three of his lieutenants—the result of which was a five-year jail sentence for Garvey.

Randolph and his associates had long been disturbed by the black nationalism of Garvey and by what seemed to them Garvey's self-seeking demagoguery. To Randolph, Garvey's business ventures were unrealistic, his declarations on African Liberation were without a program that could carry through the struggle, and the UNIA "Back to Africa" idea was totally unrealistic. Like the dispute between DuBois and Garvey, this one also degenerated into petty haggling and personality slander. The evolution of socialist opposition to Garvey and his organization is traced here in three excerpts of Randolph articles in the *Messenger*. The first (1921) and the second (1923) reveal the progress of a

113

bitter hatred and frustration of Randolph over what appears to him as Garvey's meaningless position. The final excerpt, from a 1924 issue, suggests that in some quarters the battles within black society had reached the point of absurdity. In this excerpt Randolph conjures up an imaginary prize fight between "Battling DuBois" and "Kid Garvey," beginning with an analysis of the punching ability of the combatants in terms of their strong speeches and virulent writings, then going round by round through the verbal and literary assaults the two black leaders had hurled at one other.

[a]
GARVEYISM
A. PHILIP RANDOLPH
Messenger/September 1921

Garveyism is an upshot of the Great World War. It sprang forth amidst the wild currents of national, racial and class hatreds and prejudices stirred and unleashed by the furious flames of battle. Under the strains and stresses of conflict, the state power and institutions of the ruling peoples were mobilized. The intelligentsia of the Central Powers apotheosized "Mittel Europa," Kultur, the Bagdad Railroad, and hurled imprecations upon the heads of the ungodly Entente. So, in turn, the high priests of morals and propaganda of the holy Allies sang a hymn of hate to the tune of the "Hun."

"Britania, Britania rules the waves, Britons will ne'r be slaves," "self determination of smaller nationalities," "revanche, Italia irridenta," "100 per cent Americanism," "we are fighting to make the world safe for democracy," "Deutschland Uber Alles," "Pan-Slavism," etc., were the psychological armor and spear of Armageddon. Add to this psychic complex of blatant, arrogant and hypocritical chauvinism the revolutionary, proletarian internationalism of the Russian Revolution: "no annexations, no punitive indemnities and self-determination for smaller nationalities," and it is at once apparent how nationalisms, racialisms and classisms, strangled and repressed in the cruel and brutal grip of imperialism, under the magic and galvanic stimulant of such moving slogans, would struggle to become more articulate, more defiant, more revolutionary.

The Easter Rebellion of Sinn Feinism, in 1916; Mahatma Gandhi's non-co-operative philosophy of outraged India; Mustapha Kemal Pasha's adamant stand at Angora in the Levant, battling for a conquering, militant Pan Islamism; the erratic vagaries of d'Annunzio for a re-united Italy; together with the rumblings of unrest in Egypt and among other oppressed peoples, attest to the manner in which the war quickened the vision of hitherto adjudged backward peoples, and set free forces making for the overthrow of the institutions and the abolition of the conditions that gave it (the war) birth. Indeed, the war was fruitful of paradoxes. Movements grew both for and against the interest of society. Imperialism and revolution faced each other. The Kremlin and the Quai d'Orsay of the worker and capitalist, respectively, seemed to grow in power. Movements grotesque and sound, appear to flourish and decay for the nonce.

All of these varied and variegated associated efforts have their rooting in the sub-soil of oppression and fear. The oppressed struggle to be freed; the oppressors fear their struggles. Hence, movements for liberation, whether they function through a sound methodology or not, are reactions to age-long injustices; they are reflexes of the universal urge for human freedom.

In the light of these principles, it is clear to anyone that Garveyism is a natural and logical reaction of black men to the overweening and supercilious conduct of white imperialists. Garveyism proclaims the doctrine of "similarity."

To the fallacy of "white man first" Garveyism would counter with a similar fallacy of "Negro first." If there be a "White House" in the Capitol of the nation, why not a Black House also; if there be a Red Cross and an American Legion, why not a Black Cross and a Black or Negro Legion, says the movement. And at the summit of this doctrine of "similarity" stands the African Empire as a counter-irritant to the white empires, monarchies and republics of the world. Out of this doctrine it is, indeed, not strange that transportation should partake of the magic romanticism of color. Why do persons ask, then, why a Black Star Line? And this is not said in a vein of levity, for whatever might be said of the Garvey Movement, it, at least, strives for consistency.

A word, now, concerning the doctrine of "similarity." Upon its face, it would appear to commend itself as a sound and logical course of action. Upon closer examination, however, one is largely disillusioned.

It is hardly scientific, too, to make a sweeping condemnation of this doctrine on the grounds of its absolute inapplicability to the highly complex problems of the Negro. The stock argument raised by its proponents is that: "if a given thing is good for a white man, that very same thing is also good for the Negro." By this token of argument the conquest of Africa with a view to establishing an African empire, a Black Star Line, etc., is justified.

The fallacy of this logic consists in its total disregard of the relative value of the thing proposed to those for whom it is proposed. To illustrate: it does not follow that because there are subways in New York City owned and operated by white people that there should also be a subway in New York City owned and operated by Negroes. For in the first place it couldn't be done (the enthusiasts who proclaim the patent inanity that there is no such thing as "can't," to the contrary notwithstanding) and, in the second place, even if it could be done, it would be an economic injury instead of a benefit. The reasons for this are clear. The subways, elevated trains and surface lines are owned and controlled by the same financial interests. They are of the nature of a monopoly. These interests exercise great influence upon the City Administration which grants franchises to public utilities. Hence, a competing public carrier could not secure the necessary privilege; nor would the Money Trust extend the requisite capital, recognizing the inability of such a competitor to secure the same through the tedious and protracted method of small stock sales to an innocent public. Granting, however, that the necessary capital could be raised, a subway so established would immediately be thrown into bankruptcy through the rate cutting of fares by the older concern. . . .

What is true of transportation within cities, is also true of transportation between cities. No sane business promoter would think of advising anyone to invest in an enterprise to construct a railroad to compete with the great Pennsylvania, or Grand Central railway systems. Such a venture by people of color for people of color, in the circles of experienced and intelligent business men, would only be regarded as a joke. Obviously, from a business point of view, such aforenamed undertakings are unsound. If they are unsound business enterprises, by what stretch of the imagination and race patriotism could they be justified as a phase of the solution of the Negro problem? . . . Again while it is sometimes true that one profits from failures, it is also true that one may be destroyed by failures. Nor is it sufficient to counter with the argument that one must go through certain experiences in order to learn. *There is abundant evidence to show that experience is the most expensive and inconvenient method of acquiring knowledge....* The purpose of scientific research is to place, at the convenience of society, a body of knowledge which will make it unnecessary for every one to go through the same painful and protracted process of discovering and organizing the same....

[b]
THE ONLY WAY TO REDEEM AFRICA
A. PHILIP RANDOLPH
Messenger/January 1923

Of course, there is nothing more normal and logical than that the idea of building up a Negro empire should flow from the "Back to Africa" movement. A word about the difficulties to be overcome. First, with the opposition of the white powers, it would not be possible for the Garvey crowd to even land in Africa. Second, granting that they were allowed to land, they would have nothing to conquer Africa with, for it is not conceivable that Great Britain, France, Italy or America would supply their foe with the means for overthrowing their own dominion anywhere; and there is no spot in Africa where a landing can be effected which is not controlled by a great white power. In Africa, three obstacles would have to be overcome by the Garvey group, namely, the great white powers, the natives who are opposed to alien rule, and nature in Africa, such as the intensely hot tropical climate, the uncultivated soil, the wild beasts and deadly reptiles, together with a forbidding forest. *Neither one of these three obstacles could a group of uneducated, unarmed and unorganized Negroes—such as the Garvey crew—overcome.*

Establishing a Nation in Jamaica
In view of the foregoing difficulties, it ought to be clear to the most Africoid-Negro Garveyite that it would require unlimited technical, scientific skill and knowledge, together with billions of dollars of capital to subdue, harness up and develop the nature aspect of Africa alone, to say nothing of driving out the entrenched white powers and

subjecting the intractable natives. *Conquering Africa is not any less difficult than conquering Europe.*

Thus, I think that we are justified in asking the question, that if Mr. Garvey is seriously interested in establishing a Negro nation why doesn't he begin with Jamaica, West Indies (*not Jamaica, Long Island*). Jamaica is but a small island with a population of 850,000—the white population consisting of less than 20,000. Obviously, on a small island where the ratio of black and white inhabitants is 42 to 1 the Negroes ought to be able to overcome the whites and establish control. Then, too, Jamaica is Mr. Garvey's home. He ought to know the geography of the island, the language and customs of the people. In other words, he is far better qualified to establish a Negro nation in Jamaica than he is in Africa—a land which he has never visited, of the customs and languages of whose inhabitants he is entirely ignorant. Besides, I submit that it is much easier to over-throw one white power such as controls Jamaica, than it is to over-throw six white powers equipped with the greatest armies and navies the world has ever known, such as control Africa. And, too, it requires much less capital, less brains, less power. Don't you think that Jamaica is the logical place for Mr. Garvey to begin his plans for establishing a Negro nation?

There is also Liberia who tried to sell her independence to the invest-ment bankers of America for a loan of $5,000,000. If Mr. Garvey is so interested in a Negro nation, why didn't he come to the rescue of Liberia, by raising five millions, to save her from being gobbled up by the American Imperialist Eagle. *No, he didn't do that, but responsible persons say that he raised money presumably as a loan for a redemption fund for Liberia and that only an insignificant part of it was ever used in the interest of Liberia. As an evidence of the thought which Liberia gives the Garvey movement, when President King of Liberia was in the United States seeking a loan of five million dollars, he never had the slightest association in any way with the Garvey outfit.* Besides, Haiti is a struggling black nation which needs help. *Why doesn't Mr. Garvey expel the United States from Haiti?* Here is a black people who won their liberty over a hundred years ago. Now they are under the imperial heel of the United States. Why doesn't Brother Marcus help keep a Negro nation independent instead of trying to build up a new one? For if a Negro nation is all he wants, then he has two: Liberia and Haiti.

Passing of Empire Building

But granting that it were possible to establish a black empire in Africa, it would not be desirable. *Black despotism is as objectionable as white despotism.* A black landlord is no more sympathetic with black tenants than white landlords are. A Negro is no more interested in having his pocketbook stolen by a black thief than he is in having it stolen by a white thief. Death is no sweeter at the hands of a black murderer than it is at the hands of a white murderer.

Again, empires are passing. Witness Russia, Germany and Austria-Hungary. Garvey has begun Empire building too late. Even Germany started in the empire business too late. She wanted to build a "mittel europa" from Berlin to Bagdad, but she was thwarted. Great Britain, France, Italy, and Russia of the Czar were not interested in having any more competitors in the empire business. Hence they crushed her. Such would be the fate of an African empire, granting that one could be established. It is also of special moment to note that no people love empires save the ruling class who live by the exploitation of the subject or working class. Such was the reason for the revolt of the Russian people against the Russian empire. *The ruling and subject classes were both white, but that fact did not keep back the revolution.* Note also the revolutions in Germany and Austria-Hungary, and the revolt in Ireland, India and Korea against empire-rule. Then there is Mexico under Diaz. Oppression produced revolutions whether in white or black empires. *Thus, an African empire would last no longer than the African workers became conscious of oppression and their power to remove it, and then, they would overthrow and decapitate a black king as quickly as they would overthrow and decapitate a white king.*

The Black Star Line

In harmony with the "Back to Africa," "anti-white man" and "Negro First" doctrines, the Black Star Line is the maritime appositive of the White Star Line, the Red Star Line, etc. Mr. Garvey never took any thought of the existing monopoly in the shipping business, the need of hundreds of millions in capital, banking houses to manipulate international exchange, as well as the necessity of having experts in the shipping game to handle the business. The absence of either one of these indispensables would spell failure to any shipping project, and needless to say that Mr. Marcus neither had nor has either. Think of the

Black Star Line competing in maritime affairs when the United States Government is compelled to subsidize the United States Marine. It is difficult to make the shipping business pay when operated by the best brains with unlimited capital. *What will the Black Star Line do without brains or capital?* Negroes can no more expect to succeed in the shipping business than they can hope to succeed in the subway or telephone or gas business in New York City, or in the railroad business between New York and Chicago or New York and Washington, D.C. *These are monopolies that cannot thrive where duplication or competition exists. It is sheer folly to talk of building a ship line to transport Negroes only.* Not enough Negroes travel to Africa, the West Indies—*or to anywhere for that matter*—to support such an enterprise.

It would appear, then, that Mr. Garvey is not so much concerned about the soundness, feasibility or value of a project as he is about getting together something that will duplicate the efforts and works of the whites. As fortune or misfortune would have it, he always selects the most impossible things among the whites to imitate. His policy is to run the entire gamut of slavish imitation from empire building, ship lines, a Black House in Washington, D.C., a Black Cross Nurse, a Provisional President with a Royal Court. (Little different this, eh?) *Presidents don't have courts; it's the pastime of kings; but what's that ridiculous contradiction to the "Most Dishonorable," etc.*

Garvey's Imitation Doctrine

The Garveyites are so strong on imitation that they attempt to justify the Black Star Line disgrace by pointing to the millions of dollars that the United States Shipping Board lost. *In other words, if a white man takes arsenic, a Negro ought to take it too.* A sort of getting even policy, with the Negroes always the victim. *Think of Negroes competing in losing money with the United States Government, which has the power to tax both white and black to raise revenue.*

If Mr. Garvey was competing for the first prize for producing the largest number of failures among Negroes, he would win with hands down. All his efforts are of a piece with the Black Star Line in practicality. As fast as one little, dirty, mismanaged, junk grocery shop fails, he starts another one in his senseless efforts to compete with James Butler, Andrew Davey, The Atlantic & Pacific Tea Co. and Daniel Reeves, the largest chain store systems in the world, operating with hundreds of millions of capital, and the greatest business experts in their line.

In order to inveigle the enthusiastic but uncritical, the Brother proceeds from one pipe-dream to another, calling for each and every Negro of the 400 millions in the world, (*remember it's not one more and not one less*) to slip from one to one hundred beans into his various schemes, and new ones are always in the making. Note the Booker T. Washington University, if you please, the Negro Daily *Times,* The Phyllis Wheatley Hotel, the Universal Publishing House. These gestures are intended to impress the Garvey fanatics with the idea that they are owned by the U.N.I.A., that they represent great business strides of the organization, so that they will not be unwilling to dig down into their jeans again for more cash to drop into the Garvey bottomless money pits. *It is too evident that the running of the Negro Daily Times will rival the Black Star Line in not running.* It is well that the Negro is not fated to depend upon this *Times* to find out the *time* of the happening of anything. They will not be able to even buy the paper, to say nothing about printing it. And, of course, the Booker T. Washington University is mere moonshine. It will neither have students nor teachers. *Students will not trust it to give out knowledge; nor will teachers trust it to give out pay.*

Bogus Membership

But if there were any ground of reality to his rabid, sensational, theatrical, kaleidoscopic blandishments, then Brother Garvey ought to be able to operate some of the *smaller* things, at least.

For instance, if he actually had 4,500,000 members in his organization paying dues of 40 cents a month, he would have a revenue of $1,800,000 per month or $21,600,000 a year. But it is obvious that if he were getting that revenue, it would not be necessary for the "Yarmouth," a ship for which the U.N.I.A. paid the handsome sum of $145,000, and upon which, according to Mr. Garvey, testifying in the Seventh Municipal District Court, they had lost $300,000 on its first voyage, to be sold at auction, by the United States Marshal on December 2, 1921, for the pitiful sum of $1,625. Nor would it be necessary for the organization to be constantly sued for wages by its employees.

[c]
BATTLING DU BOIS VS. KID GARVEY
A. PHILIP RANDOLPH
Messenger/June 1924

. . . Battling DuBois and Kid Garvey face each other with sneers, refuse to shake hands. Gong sounds—fighters are off.

First round: Garvey leads, raining blows on DuBois' head: "DuBois goes to Peace Conference to betray Negro peoples of the world." DuBois parries, rushes Garvey to ropes.

Second round: Garvey lands staggering blow to jaw: "DuBois is the agent of the National Association for the Advancement of *Certain* People." DuBois looks dazed and with a lofty Mephistophelian sneer, grunts that "The answer is written in the stars," and flees to Europe; stages Pan-African Pow Wow. . . .

Fourth round: DuBois leads again with light tap: "Believes Garvey is honest and Black Star Line feasible, but—" Garvey, furious, rushes DuBois. They clinch. Garvey does vicious in-fighting: "DuBois is bought and paid for by the white people. The N.A.A.C.P. cannot lead Negroes because it is headed and controlled by white people." Scrappy Weldon Johnson rushes to ringside and threatens to join bout to defend N.A.A.C.P. DuBois, pale and groggy, gropes blindly to corner. . . .

Seventh round: DuBois returns from Africa and wades into Garvey with a smashing wicked haymaker to the mid-section: "Garvey is either a lunatic or a traitor"—editorial, May *Crisis*. Garvey crumples up and hits the mat with a deafening thud. Is almost counted out; rises and staggers to corner. DuBois, in a fierce rage, dancing like a wild Indian for Garvey's scalp, lands stiff right to solar plexus, but Garvey is too weak and badly beaten to return to fray. . . .

Decision reserved on account of charge by Kid Garvey that Battling DuBois struck foul blow below the belt, and that gloves were loaded.

The original headline reads, "Heavyweight Championship Bout for Afro-American–West Indian Belt, Between Battling DuBois and Kid Garvey . . . Referee–Everybody and Nobody."

6.
The African
Blood Brotherhood

The African Blood Brotherhood was in its day one of the most unusual Communist organizations in the world. It was nationalistic in an age in which Communists derided nationalism as a right-wing ideology. The Brotherhood developed independently from the worldwide Communist apparatus and remained independent for two years. Founded early in 1919 by Cyril V. Briggs, an immigrant from St. Kitts, the ABB was based in New York with branches spotted throughout the United States and in parts of the Caribbean. Initially Briggs aimed at a compact with Garvey and the UNIA, and a number of members of the Brotherhood "Supreme Executive Council" were active in the Garvey organization. The total ABB membership ran from three to five thousand, the exact number of this semi-secret society being unknown. The Brotherhood program called for the creation of a "worldwide federation" of black organizations, for which the ABB would provide the elite revolutionary cadre. In the colonies it would work to build up "a great Pan-African Army." In the U.S. the ABB proposed blacks organize in trade unions, build cooperatively owned businesses, and create paramilitary self-defense units to safeguard the community. The Brotherhood discussed, but never finalized, plans for a separate black state within the United States.

For an organ of black Communists, the ABB monthly *Crusader* carried surprisingly little economic analysis. Instead the magazine emphasized the arts, especially jazz music. A heavy black nationalist rhetoric pervaded the *Crusader*. The style of the magazine is shown in selection (a), a "Race Catechism," (b), a justification of the Brotherhood blood ceremony, and (c), a turning of the tables on white racism by J. Griffith, head of Art Publishing Co., which promoted race pride through the sales of reprints of the work of black artists. The *Crusader* urged blacks to employ self-defense against white violence and injected this idea into a number of articles on the Ku Klux Klan, an example of which is seen in selection (d).

Selection (e) is a *Negro World* reprint of a speech the white Communist-Anarchist Rose Pastor Stokes delivered to the Second Annual Convention of the UNIA. Briggs had Brotherhood members working in the UNIA who arranged for Mrs. Stokes to give this address, in which she asked for cooperation between the UNIA and the international Communist movement. In subsequent days of the convention, arguments over whether or not to accept Mrs. Stokes's offer resulted in the expulsion of the ABB members from the convention. The episode was a memorable one in the development of the now long-standing rift between black nationalism and communism. Explaining the Garveyite position on the expulsion, Robert L. Poston wrote in the March 4, 1922, *Negro World* that the essential difference between the ABB and the UNIA was that the latter "does not link up with white organizations, to quote the words of the *Crusader Bulletin,* 'whose interests are identical with our interests.' " According to Briggs's account, his group had been expelled from the UNIA convention not so much over the issue of the black-white alliance as over the differences in the overall programs of the ABB and the UNIA. Leaflets had been passed out to convention delegates explaining the Brotherhood program, and as Briggs stated in the November 1921 *Crusader,* his group had been expelled by Garvey "because he saw that program gaining favor in the eyes of most of the delegates who had given careful consideration to the printed forms distributed by the ABB."

In the late 1920s the Brotherhood was abandoned by Briggs and most of the ABB leadership, who felt they could work more effectively as a black cadre within the Communist party itself.

[a]
A RACE CATECHISM
CYRIL V. BRIGGS
Crusader/November 1918

Question: How do you consider yourself in relation to your race?

Answer: I consider myself bound to it by a sentiment which unites us all.

Question: What is it?

Answer: The sentiment that the Negro race is of all the races the most favored by the muses of music, poetry and art and is possessed of those qualities of courage, honor and intelligence necessary to the making of the best manhood and womanhood and the most brilliant development of the human species.

Question: What is one's duty to his race?

Answer: To love one's race above one's self and to further the common interests of all above the private interest of one. To cheerfully sacrifice wealth, ease, luxuries, necessities and, if need be, life itself to attain for the race that greatness in arms, in commerce, in art, the three combined without which there is neither respect, honor, nor security.

Question: How can you further the interest of the race?

Answer: By spreading race patriotism among my fellows; by unfolding the annals of our glorious deeds and the facts of the noble origin, splendid achievements and ancient cultures of the Negro Race to those whom alien education has kept in ignorance of these things; by combatting the insidious, mischievous and false teaching of school histories that exalt the white man and debase the Negro, that tell of the white man's achievements but not of his ignominy, while relating only that part of the Negro's story that refers to his temporary enslavement and partial decadence; by helping race industries in preference to all others; by encouraging race enterprise and business to the ends of an ultimate creation of wealth, employment and financial strength within the race; by so carrying myself as to demand honor and respect for my race.

Question: Why are you proud of your race?

Answer: Because in the veins of no human being does there flow more generous blood than in our own; in the annals of the world, the history of no race is more resplendent with honest, worthy glory than that of the Negro Race, members of which founded the first beginnings of civilization upon the banks of the Nile, developing it and extending it southward to Ethiopia and westward over the smiling Sudan to the distant Atlantic, so that the Greeks who came to learn from our fathers declared that they were "the most just of men, the favorites of the Gods."

Reprinted in 1918-1919 *Negro Yearbook.*

[b]
THE BLOOD OF AFRICA
CYRIL V. BRIGGS
Crusader/November 1921

The time has come when the sons of Africa should unite! The blood of Africa, richest, reddest and warmest of any that fuses in men's veins, challenges its sons to reappear for the ceremony of an exchange so that they may become blood brothers before the firesides.

There are some that misunderstand and think that we also have the idea of setting up ourselves above the chiefs and kings of Africa and impudently imposing our own dynasty upon the people of Africa. Such self-aggrandizement is not our idea, but ours the unselfish purpose of liberating Africa without thought or desire or reward other than to see our Motherland free and the Negro race independent and respected throughout the world; and the renewal of our own age-old custom, a custom as old as Time, is our recognition as "blood brothers." Yesteryear it was the custom of our early fathers to make recognition of all of Africa's sons through a ceremony by the exchange of blood. Such a custom exists in our midst spiritually and having touched the peculiar connecting link between us and the native African the message has traveled more than a thousand miles up the Congo, now discussed by Paramount chiefs under the very batter and terrors of Victoria Falls, within a stone's throw of the majestic Zambesi and on unkissed veldts and green and swardy meads of the awe-inspiring and mysterious Hinterland!

The proudest heritage of the millions of Negroes in the Occident should be the possession of that precious particle of African blood now fusing highest and healthiest in their veins. "Colonel" William Joseph Simmons, alien anglo-saxon of this continent, recently in an interview with a representative of the New York *World* said as much that under his mass of slick red hair there was not a drop of Negro blood, for which he thanked his God. The writer is gratified and thanks the Great Source that not a drop of Negro blood is mixed with the filth and shambles of his degenerate mind. Let us boast of Africa's blood which long ago comprehended the intricacies that still baffles red-haired Simmons and his ilk. Red hair apparently means cold mind, vacant cavits, cowards and hound packs that go in mobs to attack the defenseless! Let us boast of the "blood brotherhood" we possess with a past that understood the earth to such an extent as to have erected their largest and most accurate structure directly at the same degree of longitude . . . thereby proving their knowledge of the existence of a North Pole . . . which they believed the apex of their well imagined earth . . .

Originally entitled "Explaining the Historic Ceremony of Blood Brotherhood."

[c]
BLACK SUPREMACY
J. GRIFFITH
Crusader/September 1919

That the Negro mind instinctively believes in himself and his race is a fact beyond doubt or question. What the Negro needs to know is that in many qualities he is the superior of the white man. He needs to know these qualities and to believe in them and insist on them. Especially are the Negroes who live in America superior to the whites among whom they live. This may be accounted for by the fact that the Negro has not had the opportunity to be mean, brutal, cruel, and inhuman that the white have had for several centuries. Taken as a whole the Negro population are better looking than the whites. Take the colored women for instance; they are much more beautiful, judging them by every physical measure that might be applied. They are better formed, of better carriage and fuller of life and female vanity. As a rule they are never ungracious. Negroes have not realized this fact, merely because they have had instilled into them for centuries the false doctrine that that only is beautiful which is white, etc.

Originally entitled "The Negro and His Instinct."

[d]
DECLARATION OF WAR
ON THE KU KLUX KLAN
CYRIL V. BRIGGS
Crusader/January 1921

It is War!
War Whether the Negro Meets the Issue Courageously
or in Cowardly Surrender

The nation-wide mobilization under the Christian Cross and the Stars and Stripes of cracker America into the Klu Klux Klan [sic] is as plainly an act of war as was the mobilization in 1914. And the consequences of this latter mobilization will be quite as serious to the races living in North America as the German mobilization proved to be to the peoples of Europe.

It is war, and war of the cracker element of the white race against the entire Negro race. Whether the Negro race meets the issue courageously, demonstrating its essential humanity, or in cowardly surrender to the enemy, it will be war just the same—war against the Negro race. Whether other elements of the white race will be eventually drawn into the cracker onslaught against our rights and lives remains to be seen. History indicates its extreme likelihood. The only certainties are: (1) that it is war, (2) that the white government of the United States will take no effective steps to protect us in our rights, (3) that the white North and our so-called white friends will continue apathetic to our wrongs or at best maintain a benevolent neutrality and (4) that in the eventuality of further immigration from the South even this benevolent neutrality will not stand the strain of the resulting economic competition but will be metamorphosed into active hostility as at East St. Louis, Washington, Chicago, etc.

The Klu Klux Klan aims at our virtual re-enslavement, since it purposes to rob us of the few of the most elementary rights of human beings and American citizens which through half a century of battling we have been able to wrench from the unwilling hands of the white majority in the United States. . . . We confess we do not know how the Negro will meet this peril. However, we do know how it would be met by Real Negroes. And as we know that the Negro race is essentially human we can assume that it will react accordingly.

It is war to the hilt against our rights and liberties, and against our very existence! With us it will be a fight for life as well as for rights. And to the race fighting against mighty odds for its existence the use of any and every weapon at hand is not only permissible but compulsory. With the murderer clutching at our throats we can ill afford to choose our weapons, but must defend ourselves with what lies nearest whether that be poison, fire or what. As soon as it is demonstrated that the United States Government will not protect us in our rights, right then we must take steps to protect ourselves. The odds are mighty against us, but run or stand, the results are likely to be the same and if we must die let us with our brilliant poet, Claude McKay, resolve:

"If we must die, let it not be like hogs
    Hunted and penned in an inglorious spot
While 'round us bark the mad and hungry dogs,
    Making their mock at our accursed lot
If we must die, Oh, let us nobly die.
    So that our precious blood may not be shed
In vain; then even the monsters we defy
    Shall be constrained to honor us though dead!
O kinsmen! we must meet the common foe!
    Though far outnumbered let us show us brave,
And for their thousand blows deal one deathblow!
    What though before us lies the open grave?
Like men we'll face the murderous, cowardly pack,
    Pressed to the wall, dying, but fighting back!"

[e]
THE CAUSE OF FREEDOM:
BLACKS AND COMMUNISTS
ROSE PASTOR STOKES [introduced by Marcus Garvey]
Negro World/August 27, 1921

Marcus Garvey:

Ladies and Gentlemen: We have with us tonight a lady visitor who has been widely made known to the public by the press the world over as belonging to that class of agitators who are endeavoring to free struggling white humanity. This lady has been proscribed against, prosecuted, and persecuted, I believe, she and her husband, for the cause they represent. She desires to say a few words to us in convention, in her own way.

It is for me to explain that Liberty Hall welcomes all friends of liberty. (Applause.) We welcome the Irish, we welcome the Jews, the Egyptians, the Hindus, and all peoples struggling for liberty, because we are in sympathy with suffering humanity everywhere. But that does not mean to say that we support every program, every method that is being used. We are in sympathy with the cause of freedom everywhere, and this lady in her own way has linked up herself with the cause of bleeding Russia. It is her feeling, it is her belief, that certain things should be done to free the struggling ones of Russia. Her cause, I believe, is dear to her, even as our cause is dear to us. She has her own way of representing herself and of representing her cause, and we want to say that, representing as she does today the friends of Soviet Russia, it will be understood that the Universal Negro Improvement Association adopts no one form of government. We are not adopting any method or the methods of any government. Having been mingled and mixed with civilization during the last two thousand years at least, we have come to the conclusion that there is good in all and in every government. Therefore we are seeking to pick out the good in each government, let that government be monarchical, let that government be democratic, republican, or Soviet, we will pick out the good that is in each, and reject the bad. So that you will not mistake us to say that we are in support of the Soviet government while we invite this friend of Soviet Russia to speak to us. We are not Soviets; we are not monarchists; we are not entirely republican; we are, rather, a part of every good government in the world. (Applause.) Coming down in history from the time of the empires of Greece, Carthage, and Rome, and extending up to the present day, we pick out the good in each of them.

I trust, therefore, that the press will not misrepresent us as being Soviets, for I repeat, we are not Soviets. The press I wish to understand us as not being ultra-radicals, because we are not radicals, nor ultra-radicals. We are an organized body of people struggling towards freedom, and we are not going to stop at anything to get freedom. (Applause.)

So we welcome this friend of Soviet Russia to tell us a little of what her people are doing to get liberty, and if we can find any good in what she says we shall certainly be quick to seize upon it and adopt it for our own benefit. I take great pleasure, therefore, in presenting to you Mrs. Rose Pastor Stokes, a member of the Soviet Friends of Russia. (Applause.)

Mrs. Stokes Speaks

Rising, Mrs. Stokes Said:

Friends and Fellow-Workers: First I want to thank your president for his courtesy in permitting me to speak to you this evening. Wherever a Bolshevik like myself comes face to face with members of the working class, whether they be black, or yellow, or brown, or red, or white, whether they be Jew, or Christian, or Mohammedan, or heathen; whether they be believers or non-believers, whether they belong to one nation or another on the face of the earth—whatever their beliefs may be, whatever their color or nationality may be, the Bolsheviks are glad to face the workers, those who toil with their hands or with their brain for a living.

Friends and workers, Soviet Russia is today a government of the workers and the peasants of Russia. The working class of Russia have made their revolution; they have thrown off their backs those who oppressed them. The bourgeoisie, we call them, the capitalist class, those who regardless of whether they are people of our own color or people of your color; whether they be black or white, or any other shade or any other complexion, those people who themselves may be black, or white, or red, or brown, who have the whip with which to oppress their fellow men the world over. In every government, Mr.

President, I beg to say (and I am sure you wish me to express my opinion and my conviction from this platform) in every government on the face of the earth today, and wherever floats a flag, the working class, white or black, are being exploited to the limit of endurance; in the midst of industries, in the midst of factories, in the midst of technical developments, such as the world has never seen before.

We have millions of men and women unemployed in every line, hungry for work, seeking entry into those factories, seeking contact with the machinery of production, and not permitted to operate those machines. Why? Because at the present moment, fellow workers, it is unprofitable to the few who rule—those individuals, the few who are the power behind those governments—to employ every man and every woman who have the right to work, for the right to work is the right to live. Without work we cannot maintain existence. That, friends; that, fellow workers, is the condition existing in every government at the present time, and we who are Communists (and I am a Communist, I am a Bolshevik. I proclaim it from every platform. . . .) we Communists maintain that just so long as a nation, so long as a government permits the few to exploit the many for their own enrichment, just so long as capitalism, with its profit system, with its oppression of the broad masses of the people, is allowed to continue to exploit us, the working masses have but one mission, but one historic task before them, and that is to defeat, to take the power from the hands of the capitalist class and open the factories and give the land once more to the people. (Applause.)

Friends, Soviet Russia has done this thing, and Soviet Russia, to prove her faith, which is the faith of the Communists the world over, seeks not only to free herself from economic and social oppression and inequality, but it seeks to free also every people, every nation, every race upon the face of the earth.

Mr. President, you must know, and fellow workers, you all must know (because you read) that the Communists of Russia, that the international Communists, are setting up a Communist convention, a congress, sitting in Moscow. They give aid, they give unstinted help to the weaker peoples, to the darker races of the East. Wherever men are oppressed we say there is neither color, nor creed, nor nation. We stand together against all oppressors.

It is quite true, men and women—I admit it; we all must admit it who know anything of conditions today—that wherever we go there is prejudice; there is prejudice against a man or a woman because he does not happen to have a white skin, or she is a little darker than I am. We know that that prejudice exists; but it exists chiefly among the ignorant masses. It exists mainly among those who do not understand that if they, themselves, would be free, that they must free all workers together. (Applause.) We can have no liberty except in the liberty of all the people of all the world. (Applause.) In Soviet Russia they have decided that Persia shall be free; that India shall be free, (applause); that Africa shall be free. (Great applause.) And it is not merely words, it is not sentiment that they express; they have given of their gold; they have given of their wealth, which represents the labor power of the Russian workers and the peasants; and they have given not only of these things; they have given of their very all for the liberation of the darker races of the world. Go East and you will find the red armies of Russia are marching shoulder to shoulder with the black men; they march with the darker races. We say we will give you not only our wealth and our labor, but we will give you of our lives when necessary. (Applause.) And whenever necessary you will find us not wanting. (Renewed applause.)

And I want to say, fellow-workers, that until we can and do co-operate, and until you recognize, as we Communists recognize, that it is a matter of hard fact, a matter of clear experience, a matter of self-interest, if you please, that if we ourselves would be free, if you yourselves would be free, you must co-operate with the revolutionary working class of the world, the white working class of the world, revolutionary and determined, that every oppressed people, that the oppressed classes of the world, of all colors and all races must be free; you must co-operate with them, you must come with us, just as we are willing and eager to go with you in the struggle of liberty. (Applause.)

Imperialism

Friends, one other thought occurs to me. You want Africa. Africa should be yours. (Great cheering.) But Africa should be yours free, and not enslaved. Is it not true? You want a free Africa; you don't want an enslaved Africa, do you? (Cries of "No! no!") If your eyes are open to the conditions that prevail under capitalistic imperialism, you know, as well as we know, that there can be no freedom in the farthest parts of the world so long as capitalism maintains its power in the world. Do they not reach their tentacles out to the most remote places in the world? Is not imperialism placing its tentacles around Africa today? Is not Africa today the great prize, or one of the great prizes for which capitalistic imperialism is contending? It is true.

The Bolsheviki, friends and fellow workers, the Communists of Russia, and the communists of the world—and by Communists we mean the conscious revolutionary working class of the world—are seeking to destroy capitalistic imperialism, root and branch. They cannot, however, do it without the co-operation of the workers everywhere; and, fellow-workers, insofar as you are workers, insofar as you live by the labor of your hands, by tilling the soil, or by operating a machine, or in any other way serve your fellow-men; insofar as capitalism exploits you; insofar as you are one with us, the white workers of the world, there is a class conflict coming on in the world, and that conflict today overshadows every other element in the conflict of peoples and races and humanity. We must stand together as workers.

We must stand together as workers. We need not seek to place lines; or, I should say, on the contrary, if you prefer to draw lines, if you prefer to say: "Oh, we are black and you are white"; very well, fellow-workers. But co-operation, in the interest of your own freedom, is as necessary in relation to the great revolutionary working-class struggle of the world as it is necessary for you to build your own powerful organization. (Applause.) I am glad that you concur in this. I am glad that you see that it is essential for you, as workers, to struggle with the workers of the world against the powers that oppress us all.

We fought a great war. We fought it; that is, the workers of the world fought a great war. For whom did they fight? Did they fight for their own? Did they fight in the interest of their own class—black, white, yellow, brown, anything you like? No; they did not. They fought in the interest of that imperialism which happens to be in the white world; they fought in the interest of that imperialism in (I should not say it was in the white world only; so, I will qualify that statement); they fought in the interest of that imperialism which happens to be dominant in the white world. It is also in India, in Africa, in Persia, and everywhere else in the world. You will find the rich men, you will find princes in India, and you will find Shahs in Persia, you will find the strong and the mighty who live upon the blood and the tears of the common people. You will find them hand in glove with European imperialism; they work with them and enslave their own people. In Persia, recently, they had to defeat these Shahs and these princes; they had to overthrow them, and the land was brought back to the people, and all went back to the common masses for their use.

Well, then, we have capitalistic imperialism dominantly in the white world, and also in a measure wherever men can prey upon the labor of their fellows. Yes, we fought for them, but we have to strengthen the hands of those cut throats and their crew that are trying to destroy humanity. We fought for them. What was our reward? We did not know we were fighting for them; we thought we were fighting for ourselves. And when we returned here, you comrades, you fellow workers, you who went to the war with dark skins, you who came back with dark skins, the dominant press—which is the capitalist press—continued to foment and instill in the breasts of the white people all over the country the same old, dark, antediluvian prejudice that was before the war. But you fought back; some of you fought back. I glory in the fact that you fought back. (Applause.) We Bolsheviki were proud and glad that there were black workers in this country who had the courage and the manhood to stand up against their oppressors. (Applause.) You came back from an imperialist war to fight your own battles anew; and even at this moment, men and women, even at this moment, a new, a more deadly and more widespread, a more terrible imperialist conflict is preparing. And we shall have to send—no; we shall be driven by the millions, like so many ignorant, dumb-driven cattle—through whatever field it may be that we shall have to fight. That new war is preparing. And why? I want you to think of the causes.... There can be no peace—there can be no peace until the capitalist elements are eliminated from production and distribution. There can be no peace until capitalists are thoroughly defeated.... Soviet Russia appeals to Africa to cooperate with it in its efforts to defeat imperialism. In your own interest you must, and we in our own interest must work and cooperate with each other. I trust that you, Mr. President, and the other high officers of this organization, and the representatives who are attending this congress, I trust that before you have closed your congress you will have taken some stand in the battle.

I don't know whether I am overstepping your hospitality, or whether I am abusing your hospitality; but I believe, and I am sure, that your President must see that wherever there are workers, they must get together, to struggle onward together, to a new, a free world, until all shall have free access of the land, and wherever they want it; whether it be in Africa, in Asia or Europe; wherever the workers want the land, there they shall have it; wherever they wish to operate industrially, there they shall have free access to it; and those who will not work shall not eat. (Loud, enthusiastic applause.)

President General's Reply

The President General replied briefly to Mrs. Stokes' address as follows:

Mrs. Stokes: Liberty Hall being a great university, we call here to this forum of ours professors from the four corners of the world. (Applause.) Tonight we have had a Soviet professor. (Laughter.) Some few nights ago we had an Irish professor. Later on we will have a Republican professor, a Democratic professor, a professor from the monarchical system of government; and then we will decide, later on, what we will do. (Applause.)

I think, Mrs. Stokes, that you have made out a good cause for the Soviets. I hope that the capitalists will make out their cause; but when they come to Negroes they will find keen judges. (Applause.) We are going to give Mrs. Stokes a fair trial—after we have heard the other fellow. (Laughter.)

We give to you, Mrs. Stokes, the best wishes of the representatives of the Negro peoples of the world to the struggling workers in Russia and elsewhere. They are seeking, I understand from you, freedom from their capitalist oppressors. We are seeking freedom in Africa. Later on, if the Soviets can help us to free Africa, we will do all we can to help free them.

In behalf of the convention, I thank you for your splendid address, which I am sure was enjoyed and appreciated by every one here. (Applause.)

7.
Self-Defense Against White Violence

Support for the right of self-defense was an important feature distinguishing the outlook in the Harlem Renaissance from the period preceding it. The advocacy of self-defense against white violence has always been difficult for black Americans. Even in recent years, the Black Panther party was almost destroyed because of its self-defense stand, and Robert Williams was forced into exile.

In the post–World War I period, white mobs invading black communities were repeatedly met with armed self-defense by blacks. Militant journalists loudly applauded these actions, as shown in selection (b) from the *Veteran*. (This was the short-lived journal of William Y. Bell, James B. Adams and Thomas J. B. Harris published in New York during 1919.) Selection (a) is a news story from the Baltimore *Afro-American* on a call to arms issued by Hubert H. Harrison in New York after the bloody riot in Tulsa, Oklahoma. (Harrison was the most famous of Renaissance street-corner orators. Before the war he had been an organizer for the Industrial Workers of the World. In 1917 he produced one of the first New Negro magazines, the *Negro Voice,* and between 1919 and 1923 was on the staff of the *Negro World*. He was instrumental in the founding of the Schomburg Library in New York.)

Renaissance radicals occasionally employed allegory and metaphor to call for black retaliation against white violence. Marcus Garvey repeatedly conjured up images of a race-war Armageddon, as he did in the aftermath of the bloody 1919 race riot in Omaha, selection (c), from the *Negro World*. (This was one of hundreds of his public speeches reprinted in his newspaper. Actually, while the paper carried his name as chief editor, these duties were handled by a succession of assistants, including W. A. Domingo, Hubert Harrison, William Ferris, T. Thomas Fortune, and H. G. Mugdal.)

[a]
A CALL TO ARMS
HUBERT HARRISON
Baltimore Afro-American/June 10, 1921

New York, June 4—Negroes in New York were urged to arm by Hubert
H. Harrison, president of the Liberal League of Negro Americans, at a
meeting yesterday at 135th street and Lenox avenue to ask for contributions to a fund to relieve the suffering caused to the Negroes of
Tulsa. He denied that the Negroes of Tulsa were in any way responsible
for the rioting, and charged that the police and troops took sides with
the whites until restrained by the authorities.

"It is not only these Negroes, but those everywhere in the country,
of whom we are thinking," Mr. Harrison said in asking for funds. "I am
not making any predictions, but I should not be surprised if we saw
three splendid race riots by next September. There may not be any in
New York, but I advise you to be ready to defend yourselves. I notice
that the State Government has removed some of its restrictions upon
owning firearms, and one form of life insurance for your wives and
children might be the possession of some of these handy implements.
And it is absolutely necessary for your protection to join the Liberal
League, which is carrying on a wide campaign for the interests of our
race."

[b]
RACE RIOT IN KNOXVILLE:
UNCLE TOM IS DEAD
[EDITORIAL]
Veteran/September 6, 1919

[The white inhabitants were] anticipating great fun seeing the Negroes
scurrying before them like so many rats driven by the flames . . . They
went, they saw, they were defeated. They saw new things that day and
they met a new people. They saw fire—deadly well-directed fire, and
volley after volley of it, belched forth from the mouths of rifles and
revolvers held by the hands of black men who now have "stiff backs,

straight shoulders, and know how to shoot." They saw their vile comrades fall at their sides. They saw what others had seen at Chicago, at Washington, and at Longview, Tex.—that Uncle Tom is dead and that a new Negro rises in his tracks, a Negro who values liberty as he does not cherish life. One other thing they saw. They saw that the way behind them was more desirable than that before them. They turned on their heels, like the miserable cowards they have always been; they fled in confusion and fear.

Originally entitled "The Knoxville, Tennessee, Race Riot."

[c]
SOLDIERS OF ETHIOPIA
MARCUS GARVEY
Negro World/October 11, 1919

Fellow men of the Negro race:

Greeting. Once more the white man has outraged American civilization and dragged the fair name of the Republic before the court of civilized justice.

Another riot has visited the country and Omaha, Nebr., has placed her name upon the map of mob violence; so it can be seen that the mob spirit is spreading all over, going from South to East, to mid-West and then to the West.

Mobs of white men all over the world will continue to lynch and burn Negroes so long as we remain divided among ourselves. The very moment all the Negroes of this and other countries start to stand together, that very time will see the white man standing in fear of the Negro race even as he stands in fear of the yellow race of Japan to-day.

The Negro must now organize all over the world, 400,000,000 strong, to administer to our oppressors their Waterloo.

No mercy, nor respect, no justice will be shown the Negro until he forces all other men to respect him. There have been many riots in the United States and England recently, and immediately following the war of democracy, there will be many more as coming from the white man. Therefore, the best thing the Negro of all countries can do is to prepare to match fire with hell fire. No African is going to allow the Caucasian to trample eternally upon his rights. We have allowed it for 500 years and we have now struck.

Fellow men of the world, I here beg of you to prepare, for a great day is coming * * * the day of the war of the races, when Asia will lead out to defeat Europe, and Europe and the white man will again call upon the Negro to save them as we have often done. The New Negro has fought the last battle for the white man, and he is now getting ready to fight for the redemption of Africa. With mob laws and lynching bees fresh in our memories, we shall turn a deaf ear to the white man when Asia administers to him his final "licking" and place and keep him where he belongs.

If the white men were wise they would have treated Negroes differently, but to our astonishment they are playing the part of the dog biting the hand that feeds. If it were not for the Negro the white man would have been lost long ago. The black man has saved him, and the only thanks we get to-day is mob law.

Let every Negro all over the world prepare for the new emancipation. The Fatherland, Africa, has been kept by God Almighty for the Negro to redeem, and we, young men and women of the race, have pledged ourselves to plant the flag of freedom and of empire. Our forces of industry, commerce, science, art, literature, and war must be marshalled when Asia or Europe strikes the blow of a second world war. Black men shall die then and black women shall succor them, but in the end there shall be a crowning victory for the soldiers of Ethiopia on the African battlefield.

This article bore the headline "Negroes Should Prepare—Black Men All Over The World Should Prepare To Protect Themselves—Negroes Should Match Fire With Hell Fire."

8.
Opinions On
White Helpers

At the start of the Renaissance era, many blacks had high hopes for coalitions with white labor, and with reform or revolutionary political movements of whites. But the 1920s turned out to be a politically conservative decade for White America; and insecure white reformers and radicals reacted to the conservative mood by placating racist reaction. A commentary on this phenomenon is made by William Pickens in selection (a) from the *Crisis*. Pickens reviews the political convention of the Robert LaFollette Progressive party of 1924. Assembled at the convention were socialists, trade unionists, disillusioned Democrats and old "Bull Moose" reform Republicans. A revived Ku Klux Klan had been a major issue in politics that year, and the Progressive convention, like the Democratic and Republican ones, did not condemn the Klan, though Pickens had made a personal plea from the podium for a forthright statement on the KKK. One might have expected a rage of indignation by Pickens in his article; but his criticism was qualified with the notation that a minority caucus led by Socialists had pressed hard for a commitment from the Progressives. (Pickens was NAACP National Field Secretary. The son of a South Carolina sharecropper, he did not go to school until he was eleven. Ten years later he was a Yale graduate. Pickens was a heavy contributor to the *Crisis* and *Messenger*, and his columns appeared in dozens of weekly newspapers. He also contributed to a number of left-wing white magazines.)

Chandler Owen of the *Messenger* was one of many blacks who took their disappointment with white liberals and radicals with much bitterness. Learning that his brother had been refused a union card from a supposedly non-discriminatory trade union was the last straw. Owen wrote a scathing indictment of white trade-union racism, selection (b). By 1930 Owen had drifted out of politics entirely.

One hears often today the warning that white liberals involved in causes like ecology and women's liberation are becoming estranged from the basic struggle of blacks for economic security and civil rights. Back in the Renaissance period Dr. DuBois offered a similar warning on the estrangement of "white radicals," selection (c).

A black nationalist analysis of "white liberalism" is presented in selection (d), a *Negro World* editorial by columnist Ernest E. Mair. (A West Indian immigrant, Mair had been drawn into the Garvey movement by John E. Bruce and Duse Mohamed Ali. He was a contributor to the Garvey paper throughout the late 1920s.)

The nationalist appeal to Black America proved far more successful in attracting followers than did the socialist argument. Significantly, the nationalists addressed themselves to blacks, whereas the left seemed almost to talk more to a white audience than to a black one. The difference in style can be seen in selections (e) and (f), two articles on the shortsightedness of the white left in its relations with blacks. In the first, Amy J. Garvey comments in the *Negro World* on the English Labour government of Ramsey MacDonald in 1924; in the second, socialist Warner A. Domingo presents in his New York weekly *Emancipator* a critique on a statement by Leon Trotsky critical of the value of blacks to the proletarian revolution. (Prior to the start of his own paper in 1920, Domingo had edited Garvey's *Negro World,* but was fired for his "socialist and allied leanings." While Domingo did not like Trotsky's slap at blacks, he himself had voiced doubts about their militancy, in the *Messenger* and in a paper for the Socialist party—"Socialism Imperilled, or the Negro—A Potential Menace to American Radicalism." Always a Socialist, he joined the Communist-led African Blood Brotherhood because he felt the SP was prejudiced against West Indian immigrants. In later years he worked in his native Jamaica in the People's National party.)

[a]
THE LA FOLLETTE
PROGRESSIVE PARTY OF 1924
WILLIAM PICKENS
Crisis/September 1924

From a reading of the platform adopted by the Progressives in Cleveland it would not seem that much advance was made, except in the call for public ownership of necessary monopolies and large-power enterprises, such as railroads and mines. But in the immediate presence of the Progressive personnel one could get the impression that they are miles ahead of the average cog-wheel politicians of the "two old parties." There were perhaps some unnecessarily cautious tactics to avoid wrangles over divisive domestic issues, and some very unconcealable efforts on the part of those who managed the convention to carry out preconceived ideas and prearranged programs. And yet withal there was an atmosphere of honesty and sincerity in every procedure which is seldom or almost never found in a gathering of professional politicians.

For example, they had evidently decided before they came to Cleveland not to bring up the Klan issue, because, as they claimed, such a religious and racial issue might becloud the more essential economic issues,—and also because, as *we* claim, they had observed what a happy time the blessed Democrats were having over the Klan in Madison Square Garden [a bitterly split Convention]. But while a majority in the Democratic convention voted in favor of the Klan when the matter came to a roll call, the best information that could be gathered about the Progressive convention, where an actual "show-down" was prevented by the exclusion of the Ku Klux issue, was that not more than about ten per cent of the Progressive delegates were favorable to the Klan. This estimate was made by a prominent Socialist, and the Socialists were actively and decidedly anti-Klan. It was they who in a separate and subsequent meeting of their own wing of Progressives declared unequivocally against the Klan and in favor of the impartial recognition of Negroes in all labor unions. In this one exhibition of courage and consistency, the Socialists therefore hold the palm among all party groups.

And as to the Negro question, and more particularly as to his relationship to the labor unions,—one felt the same strange contradiction: that as to personnel here was a group of people who would be in the main fairer and juster and squarer with the Negro than any other group that had gathered in political convention since Reconstruction days, and yet that they (and especially their leadership) were unwilling or afraid to specify the Negro or to allow his case to become an issue in their effort to get together. Those who know the power and inclination, and the present distribution of the Negro vote, will count this omission a blunder in practical politics, that could only be offset by some very decided and straight pronouncements on the part of the Progressive presidential nominees, and some unmistakable recognition of colored people in the campaign of election. LaFollette must talk plain and straight and to the point, if he expects the unselfish and thoughtful part of the Negro vote, which is admittedly impatient with the "old parties," to have any feeling of conviction that his leadership and his party are more decently American than the others.

Nothing was said then, about the Negro in the office platform adopted in the Progressive Convention, for the reason that, as they say, the Negro is an American citizen and is included in all that the Progressives seek for American citizens; but it might have been well for the convention to specifically include the Negro, because, as we say, the four Railroad Brotherhoods which dominated the convention, do specifically *exclude* the Negro from their union rights.

The N.A.A.C.P. sent an observer to the Progressive Convention, simply to let the Progressives know that the Association and all intelligent colored people look upon the new political organization as upon all other parties, that they are inclined to give the new group the same chance to be heard, and that they are determined to act upon the merits of the case rather than upon any party name or party symbol— whether Elephants, Jackasses or other respectable creatures.

[b]
WHITE SUPREMACY
IN ORGANIZED LABOR
CHANDLER OWEN
Messenger/August 1923

Two decades ago it was Booker T. Washington who said: "In the South
the Negro can make a dollar but can't spend it, while in the North the
Negro can spend a dollar but can't make one." Here Mr. Washington
was referring to the comparative ease with which Negro bricklayers,
plasterers, painters, moulders, carpenters, and Negro mechanics in general, could get work in the South at their respective trades, but were so
proscribed in their privileges of entering such places of public accom-
modation and amusement as theatres, restaurants, pullman cars, and the
like as to amount almost to a denial of spending their money. At the
same time he noticed that whereas the Negro might freely (?) spend his
money in most of such places in the North, still there the labor unions
had so completely shut out of the trades all but "white-*black* men"
who could "pass"—to all intents and purposes the Negro could not
make a dollar.

In all parts of the United States the Negroes are generally opposed to
labor unions. They favor the open shop. It is not facetious to state that
many Negroes understand the term "closed shop" to mean "closed to
Negroes." Though such is not the etymological history, in substance the
closed shop has meant just about that. It still means that in a large area
of labor circles. This is true of the railroad brotherhoods and the machinists, who with brutal frankness have embodied in their constitu-
tions Negro exclusion clauses. Many other unions lacking the written
boldness to "write out" their black brother, nevertheless "read him
out" religiously in practice. The machinists put into their constitution:
"Each member agrees to introduce into this union no one but a sober,
industrious white man." Part of this rule is not lived up to judging from
the alcoholic breath which we have sometimes smelt at machinists'
meetings. Still it was white breath!

White Men's Jobs

Among the various methods employed for keeping out Negro

workers many unions have combined with their employers in proclaim-
ing certain lines of labor as "a white man's job." For instance, conductor is a white man's job. There is no question of efficiency involved
here since all it requires to be a conductor is the physical power to clip
and take up a ticket and a good memory. And every traveler will attest
these are exceptional possessions of the pullman porter. He can and
often does collect tickets from the passengers, while his memory is so
excellent he can quickly take in and bear in mind over several days each
passenger and the baggage which goes with him.

Motorman—street car, elevated and subway—is a white man's job.
(Detroit is probably the only city in America which employs Negroes.)
Yet Negroes make splendid chauffeurs. We submit, too, 'tis much more
difficult to run an automobile through a crowded city like New York,
Chicago or Los Angeles, where guiding and steering are demanded, than
it is to run a street car, subway or elevated train chiefly down a straight
track.

Next, railroad engineer is considered a white man's job. We cannot
resist the temptation to tell an incident which happened about two
years ago when the railroad brotherhoods were conferring at Chicago
relative to calling a strike. Southerners, of course, were present. At one
time when the strike call seemed imminent, Southern delegates from
Georgia and Texas, mind you, rose and opposed it. Said these gentlemen: *"We cannot afford to strike, because my fireman is a Negro who
can run the train as well as I can. In fact he does run the train most of
the time. So if we strike the bosses will put the Negroes in our places."*
It needs no comment that if the Negro can run the train, and does run
it most of the time, he ought to get both the pay and the name or
credit for being engineer. At the present time Negroes get everything
but the pay and the public credit.

Moreover, telephone operator is a "white woman's job." Telephone
companies nowhere employ Negro operators in the exchanges. We discover no justifiable reason—certainly no efficiency excuse. Colored girls
in New York frequently operate switchboards for apartment houses
which hold a population bigger than many American towns!

Again, even the telegraph companies attempt to make the messenger
boy service a "no-Negro" service, notwithstanding the fact that colored
boys can run across a city delivering messages as rapidly and as effi-
ciently as white boys.

At the outset I stated white employers and white unions combined in propagating the psychology of certain jobs as "white men's jobs." An illustration of this came to us a few years ago in the building trades. A Negro electrician went to an employer for a job. The employer informed him: *"We employ only union labor. If you get a union card we shall be glad to give you a job."* When the young colored electrician made application to the electricians' union for membership, the union officials informed him: *"We take in only persons who are working on the job. If you get on the job, we will grant you a union card."* Whereupon the Negro could get neither into the union nor on the job, because each party—employer and union—set up a condition which could only be met by the other.

Negroes Lost Confidence in White Unions

It is obvious the Negroes could not secure or retain confidence in white unions so long as everything—from pretext, ruse and evasion to brutal frankness—excluded them from the labor unions. Naturally and properly the *man of color* decided: *"What care I how fair she be, if she be not fair to me?"* It is better to have *low wages than no wages!* The Negro quite sanely prefers a *lower standard of living,* in the open shop, to starvation, or no standard of living, as a result of the closed shop!

Flirting With the Employers

Self-preservation is an instinct. All sentient organisms act upon this basic principle. The employers, understanding the psychology, have appealed to the Negro worker on the ground that white unions were the Negro's enemies. Proof was never lacking: on the contrary, the evidence was abundant. For the paucity of instances of trade union fairness to Negroes presented by union advocates the bosses could marshal a plethora of hostile instances. Most Negroes could fall back on their own experiences. Nor was it difficult to make a test case in any city any day. (It is not difficult even now!) Consequently Negro workers were and are ever ready to take the places of union strikers. They are coddled by the employers and repulsed by the unions. White employers are, and to a large extent have been, the Negro workers' patrons, while the white workers have been chiefly their competitors. Patrons aid while competitors fight. One is your friend, the other your enemy. Everybody likes to get in a blow at his enemy, revenge being sweet. Add to this sweet revenge the sweetness of economic income and the blow is sweeter! The labor unions of America have frequently felt this blow. Negroes have participated as strike breakers in most great American strikes. They have been a thorn in the strikers' side in such big strikes as the steel, the miners', packing, longshoremen's, waiters', railroad shopmen's and other strikes.

Employers Put Negroes in Unions

In business there is first competition, then combination. From 1873 to 1898 was the period of large scale business in the United States. The period was noted for railroad rate cutting, clashes between the Standard Oil and other independent oil companies, steel, automobile, tobacco and banking "cut-throat competition." Then came pooling, monopolies, trusts, syndicates—"combinations in restraint of trade." Competition was said to be the "life of business." It was really the death of more. Each business tried to destroy its competitor until the process grew so wasteful and destructive that those businesses which did survive decided that co-operation—combination, peace—was better than competition, opposition, warfare. Businesses then combined—businesses which had done all they could to kill each other.

The world of labor is little different from the world of business. White labor has constantly fought to keep Negroes out of the industries—not especially because of a dislike for Negroes but because to limit the supply of labor would increase the demand for white workers, raise their wages, shorten their hours, and extend their tenure of employment. The unions even try to limit white apprentices, also white women. But one day along would come a strike. White men walk out. They want more wages, shorter hours—some demand the employers are unwilling to grant. The white bosses send out an S.O.S. for Negro workers. The Negroes reply as it were: *"We are coming, Father Abraham, hundreds of thousands strong!"* White employers take on the Negroes, not because they (the white employers) particularly like the Negroes, but *because they like black labor cheap better than white labor dear!*

Then is it that white workers learn of the bosses' disregard for white supremacy. They (the white workers) see the Negroes in the industries. The white unionists cannot get them out. "How can the Negro workers be made to help us?" the white workers ask. "Lo and behold! the thing to do is to take them into our unions where we can at least get dues from them which will pay white officials' salaries in good jobs and help the union generally." And just as business in combining with its competitor does not do so because it likes the competitor any better (but because it could not kill its competitor), so the union white men in admitting Negroes do not do so because the white men like the Negro workers better, but because they could not keep the Negroes out of the industry—that is, they could not destroy their colored laboring competitors.

Herein we are called upon to state a truth which we have nowhere seen expressed in the radical and labor literature: *"The white employers and capitalists have placed the Negro workers both into the industries, and consequently into the unions, while the white trade unions have kept the Negroes out of both the unions and the industries, so long as they could!"* This question must be faced by labor leaders and organized white labor. The Negro worker may not be able to state the philosophy and the theories underlying the situation, but he is well aware of the facts. We have just returned from a long trip to the Pacific coast, during which time we passed through Topeka. Here the Santa Fe Railroad put in Negro shopmen, machinists, etc., during the shopmen's strike. The employers are keeping the Negroes in the shop despite labor union opposition. The unions are in a terrible dilemma. They cannot call upon the Negroes to join the unions because the unions exclude Negroes as members. The employers would no doubt discharge the Negroes if they did join the union. What inducement can the unions offer as presently constituted? And if the Negro workers are not right, wherein are they wrong?

Machinery and Labor Movement

There are two forces which capital is adopting today. Sometimes it moves the machinery or capital to the labor and raw materials. This is what generally happens as the result of imperialism in undeveloped countries like the West Indies, Mexico, parts of South America, Central America, Haiti and Nicaragua. Capital sends machinery right where the labor supply is overwhelming and the raw materials abundant.

The other method is to attract labor to the machinery, the raw materials and industry. That is what is going on in the case of the present large Negro migration. Negro labor, attracted from the South to the North by higher wages, is coming to the steel districts of Pittsburgh, Youngstown, Ohio, and Duluth, Minnesota; to the automobile center of Detroit; the packing districts of St. Louis, Chicago, Kansas City and Omaha; as longshoremen to the ports like New York, Philadelphia, Baltimore and Boston, and to the great industrial centers of the East and central West.

What Will the Unions Do?

The Negro workers at last are here. They are in many industries now; they will be in more shortly; eventually they will be in all. What will the unions do—take the Negroes in or permit them sullenly and inevitably to build up a veritable "scab union" ever ready, willing and anxious to take the places of the white workers? We are face to face with a serious problem . . .

[c]
RADICALS AND THE NEGRO
W. E. B. DU BOIS
Crisis/March 1925

Most Americans having secured the right to vote, the principle of free public schools, the right to trial by jury and the right to travel without insult are proceeding to use these foundation rights for the purpose of accomplishing economic freedom, more effective education, the abolition of crime and like reforms. Among such liberal and radical thinkers any reference to the right to vote, the abolition of lynching or admission to the public schools sounds archaic. It brings to them no recognition of the fact that these demands should be part of a radical program because their own program for white people has swept so far beyond these initial demands that these demands are no longer "radical"—they are almost reactionary.

If, therefore, you speak to the ordinary liberal minded white man of helping to secure to the Negro the right to vote, he immediately begins to discourse upon the inefficacy of voting among whites and the disappointment of the democratic movement which began with the right to vote. If you ask him to help stop lynching he inquires if lynching really does take place. He is then inclined to think that it must be very sporadic and at any rate he adds that there are many worse things in the modern industrial organization than lynching. If you are interested in securing elementary rights to common school education for black children you are reminded of the wretched school system in the city of New York; and if you wish to abolish the daily insult of "Jim Crow" cars you are talking about something that your auditor has never seen and cannot conceive of. And yet conceive the language of such a man if his vote were taken away, his children excluded from school and his wife compelled to travel in a smoking car!

Thus in a country where a tenth of the population has most of its voters illegally deprived of any voice in their government, where each week for forty years at least one of their fellows accused of crime has been lynched without semblance of a trial, where no schools at all are provided for a majority of the group's children, where no attempt is made to deal out even ordinary and primitive justice in the courts or in jail to large numbers of the group, and where discrimination in every walk of life is for them the ordinary rule,—in such a country you can have a program of public minded radicals which does not touch a single one of these wrongs except possibly by indirect inference.

The point which such radicals forget is that the oppression of the Negro in the United States is not simply the misfortune of the Negro. Even if that were not true surely the right of twelve million black people would call for at least as much space as 250,000 Indians. But the case is worse than this. Political cheating in the United States is directly traceable to cheating Negro voters in the South. The impossibility of securing a clear popular verdict in the United States on any question is directly chargeable to the rotten borough system of the Southern states. Education with us has been twisted out of its proper channels very largely because of the necessity of using it as a vehicle of propaganda against "inferior" races. There is no sense in a peace program which takes no account of the world wide economic war upon colored peoples. The insult to Japanese, Jews and southern Europeans in the pending immigration bill is a logical deduction from the American pastime of Negro-baiting. It is absolutely certain that the future of liberal and radical thought in the United States is going to be made easy or impossible by the way which American democracy treats American Negroes. Under these circumstances it seems to me impossible for any group of Radicals to write down any program which will in the slightest degree convince the world of its sincerity without touching the plight of American Negroes. . . .

[d]
THE HYPOCRISY OF WHITE LIBERALISM
ERNEST E. MAIR
Negro World/June 25, 1927

Most white people seem to think that Negroes are darned fools, or, rather, I should say, most white people of the ruling class. Much time is put into the current papers and periodicals . . . for the obvious purpose of hoodwinking the people most concerned.

To illustrate: Since the signing of the Treaty of Versailles the terms "colonies" and "spheres of influence" . . . have vanished completely from the vocabulary of the Society of Thieves when they meet at Geneva (of course, I mean the League of Nations). . . . It is about this time they begin to substitute the term "mandate" for "colony" and "protectorate" for "possession." Again: in the New York Times on occasion you will see an article setting forth the beneficent purpose of the English in Africa. On another occasion in the same paper you will see an article dealing with trade, which gives the lie direct to the claims of the previous issue. On one occasion, I remember that the magazine section of a certain large daily sang the praises of a white "African" administrator, while across the page from this was a review of a prominent women-writer's book which in its synopsis of the work discussed contradicted nearly everything said by the professional whitewasher on the other page. Now for whose benefit is all this much put out? Surely not for the whites who have not themselves any illusions as to why they are in Asia and Africa. And if not for themselves then—it must be for us (the oppressed) since we are the only other parties interested.

Many Negroes are blind enough to think that the studied hypocrisy of the white press is for the purpose of claiming the liberal elements of their own group. This I do not believe, for there are no liberal elements in whitedom with power enough and interested enough to make the pirates afraid.

To take them as they come:

Organized Christianity—What of them? And I answer, "They were the forerunners of the armies of conquest that consummated the rape of Africa and Asia. They are the liberals who teach us in the Southern

States of the United States that although God is the Father of all mankind, he is nevertheless opposed to Negroes and whites worshipping Him under the same roof . . ."

Organized Charity?—Have you ever heard of the man who stole a cow because (he said) he couldn't afford to buy meat for his dog? There you have organized charity in a nutshell. In ninety percent of all cases you will find that only an infinitesimal part of the funds collected for charity are actually spent upon the unfortunates . . . The rest goes to pay fat salaries to the professional helpers and uplifters of humanity. Which is not saying that they never do any good, but that the results are by no means commensurate to the outlay.

Socialists—These are the good folk who preach so much about the lot of the common man, who are perpetually getting excited about the policies of our government in China and Turkey; about what is happening to the Pogo-Pogo Indians, the Armenians, and indeed everybody that is remote and nobody that is right to hand. These same Socialists are eloquent in their preachments about the unfairness of the Capitalists and the injustice of being overfed while others starve, but if you think they are talking about the Negro, then you have another guess coming. . . . They tell you that they see no reason why they should single the Negro out for favor when there are so many of their own race in need, in which I concur, and by the same sign I will have none of them or their works.

Organized Labor—Here is the most conservative of all the supposed liberal movements. Ask any Negro who earns his bread in any of the lines of endeavor organized under the auspices of the American Federation of Labor, or, indeed, any other Labor organization in any other white ruled country (which is to say in nearly the whole world), and he will tell you that, although they expect us to protect them by refusing the employment they leave on strikes, they nevertheless practice the most rigid discrimination against us. I know myself of many capitalists who would like to open their shops to Negro labor, especially in the South . . . But does he dare to do it? He does not. Let him give ten out of a thousand available jobs to Negroes; and the white employees will walk out on him. And on the other hand, where is it that the Negro finds himself most considered in the awarding of employment? The non-union shops every time. Henry Ford is the largest single employer of Negro labor in the United States, and to him labor unions are anathema. The same applies to other large employers of labor, especially in the North and Middle West. If the plants are unionized the Negro is conspicuous by his absence or found only in the most menial jobs. If the plant is open shop you are likely to find Negroes in every kind of job from sweeper to foreman of a whole department . . .

I particularly want to impress upon the Negro who reads this that nothing here said is to be construed as opposition to the principle of unionizing. If one is to be honest he must admit that practically everything gained by the people that work with their hands has been due to the efforts of organized labor. Considered . . . as a movement for the general betterment of workingmen the labor movement is highly desirable. But we are not so considering it here. We are considering its usefulness as a liberal element of white society, able, if it will, to make life a whole lot more tolerable for the black man. And from that standpoint it is a miserable failure . . .

We come now to the Communists, those ultra-radicals . . . hated by all good capitalists. Well, I don't hate them, and I don't think the average Negro does either. Much of all this stuff bruited about the Negro's opposition to Communism is tosh, and the bruiters know it. The truth is that the average Negro does not know what Communism is, and cares less. But if he did know and then hated it, he would be a fool, for certainly no matter how wretched a system it may be, it cannot be worse than the system now in practice. Let us be truthful. We know that however well we thought of the system it would be economic suicide for us to embrace it, for the powers that be give us starvation wages now; if we developed Communistic leanings they would see to it that we had no jobs at all.

The same arguments adduced with regard to the movements mentioned above can be applied to the host of less well known ones that lay claim to liberalism. They do not constitute any check upon the greed and rapacity of the masses of their kind. . . . We may safely say . . . that it is no fear of his own liberal elements that leads the white man to indulge in his hypocrisy of speech when discussing the status of the darker people. Rather it is that he hopes so to confuse us as to his real aims that by the time we find out "what it is all about" we will then be already "past redemption point." But if this is his hope he is foredoomed to disappointment for the Negro is already aware of the concerted plot afoot to relegate him forever to the human scrap heap. And as determined as are his persecutors and detractors to accomplish his undoing, so is he determined, only doubly more, to climb to the very highest peak of human greatness and achievement . . .

[e]
LABOR AT THE BRITISH HELM
AMY JACQUES GARVEY
Negro World/February 2, 1924

Ramsay MacDonald, leader of the Labour Party, has assumed the Premiership of England and conjectures are rife as to what radical changes will be brought about during his regime.

The new Premier is a Socialist and Pacifist, but there is no occasion for alarm in England, as his speeches and actions indicate that he is fully aware of the delicate position in which he and his party are placed, and they are endeavoring to get the good-will of the nation.

The Labour Party is not yet strong enough to advance any radical measures, and the best it can do is to abstain from any controversial measures until its testing period is passed. Any incautious move at this time will ruin the future of the party now in power.

Premier MacDonald has shown inherent Scottish shrewdness in the selection of his cabinet, and has given appointments to men who, if overlooked, would have done incalculable harm by undermining the good intentions of his Cabinet.

A few days ago a Madras newspaper published a message from the new Premier to the Indian people, in which he pleaded for good-will and reason between India and England, and made it plain that "no party in England will be cowed by threats of force or by policies designed to bring the Government to a standstill, if any Indian sections are under the delusion that this is not so, events will sadly disappoint them."

This is a clear indication of a cautious policy, and unless the nation is in accord with certain measures Ramsay MacDonald will not jeopardise the success of his party to practise Socialism.

[f]
THE POSITION OF BLACKS IN THE REVOLUTIONARY STRUGGLE
W. A. DOMINGO
Emancipator/March 13, 1920

Everywhere bolshevism brings terror to the heart of Imperialism, secret diplomacy, hypocrisy and oppression, and yet, the chieftains of this liberating doctrine are afraid of some of the very races whom they would free.

This is a great paradox—the great tragedy, some of the very Indians and Negroes are the potential hangmen of their disinterested friend— Soviet Russia.

It is not idle fear that Trotzky voices. It is easy for propaganda to reach a literate people; but it is a tremendously more difficult task for it to reach an illiterate people. Poland and Roumania illustrate this.

However, there are signs of Negro awakening. All over the West Indies there are strikes and unrest; in South Africa, benighted and oppressed land, 40,000 natives are on strike, and two colored delegates to a labor conference in Johannesburg have been hailed as comrades and brothers. One of them even seconded a motion to support Soviet Russia to the limit. Social equality was also recognized as a prerequisite to industrial unity and racial harmony. The dawn is breaking in Negrodom.

Black soldiers from the West Indies, South Africa and a certain self-righteous republic, imbued with the spirit of the New Negro will not be willing tools of those who now rule Egypt, India, the West Indies and Arkansas with machine guns. . . .

We appreciate Trotzky's fear, but feel that it is a little overdrawn. The war has opened the eyes of the darker races a little. They will no longer be their own enslavers. On the Comrades of Trotzky in other lands devolves the duty of paying attention to the "needs" of the black masses whom the Russian war minister sees as the only possible material in the hands of the imperialists of the world.

9.
Garveyism and the Question of National Loyalty

This section contains three excerpts from the 1926 *Negro World* pertaining to the issue of national loyalty. In selection (a), first published in 1923 and reprinted in the June 26, 1926, issue, Marcus Garvey presents something of a Zionist interpretation. The following week, in the July 3, 1926, issue, T. Thomas Fortune offered an elaboration on a key paragraph (shown in italics) from this Garvey editorial. Fortune's piece is included as selection (b). (Fortune was at this time chief editor of the *Negro World*. He was the dean of black journalism, having founded the New York *Age* in the 1880s. In his youth, Fortune was an ardent supporter of Henry George and the single-tax reform concept. In the 1890s Fortune took a leading role in building the Afro-American Council and later supported Booker T. Washington in his battle with DuBois. Fortune became editor of Garvey's short-lived daily *Negro Times* in 1923, and during the mid-20s, in addition to editing the *Negro World* Fortune also served as chief editor for the New York *Interstate-Tattler*, a paper involved in Democratic party politics.)

In selection (c) Garvey defines the question of loyalty in psychological terms, declaring that the freedom from white ideology that would come from black American support for the struggle for nationhood in Africa would in and of itself be a revolution for black people in this country.

[a]
THE EMANCIPATION OF THE RACE
MARCUS GARVEY
Negro World/June 26, 1926

Gradually we are approaching the time when the Negro peoples of the world will have either to consciously, through their own organization, go forward to the point of destiny as laid out by themselves, or must sit quiescently and see themselves pushed back into the mire of economic serfdom, to be ultimately crushed by the grinding mill of exploitation and be exterminated ultimately by the strong hand of prejudice . . .

Without a desire to harm anyone, the Universal Negro Improvement Association feels that the Negro should without compromise or any apology appeal to the same spirit of racial pride and love as the great white race is doing for its own preservation, so that while others are raising the cry of a white America, a white Canada, a white Australia, we also without reservation raise the cry of a "Black Africa." The critic asks, "Is this possible?" and the four hundred million courageous Negroes of the world answer, "Yes." . . .

To fight for African redemption does not mean that we must give up our domestic fights for political justice and industrial rights. It does not mean that we must become disloyal to any government or to any country wherein we were born. Each and every race outside of its domestic national loyalty has a loyalty to itself; therefore, it is foolish for the Negro to talk about not being interested in his own racial, political, social and industrial destiny. We can be as loyal American citizens or British subjects as the Irishman or the Jew, and yet fight for the redemption of Africa, a complete emancipation of the race.

Fighting for the establishment of Palestine does not make the American Jew disloyal; fighting for the independence of Ireland does not make the Irish-American a bad citizen. Why should fighting for the freedom of Africa make the Afro-American disloyal or a bad citizen?

The Universal Negro Improvement Association teaches loyalty to all governments outside of Africa; but when it comes to Africa, we feel that the Negro has absolutely no obligation to any one but himself.

Out of the unsettled state and condition of the world will come such revolutions that will give each and every race that is oppressed the opportunity to march forward. The last world war brought the opportunity to many heretofore subject races to regain their freedom. The next world war will give Africa the opportunity for which we are preparing. We are going to have wars and rumors of wars. In another twenty or thirty years we will have a changed world, politically, and Africa will not be one of the most backward nations, but Africa shall be, I feel sure, one of the greatest commonwealths that will once more hold up the torchlight of civilization and bestow the blessings of freedom, liberty and democracy upon all mankind.

Written March 24, 1923, and entitled "The Negro's Place In World Reorganization."

[b]
A MAN WITHOUT A COUNTRY
T. THOMAS FORTUNE
Negro World/July 3, 1926

In all of the world there is no more miserable person than the one who can be said to be a man without a country. Edward Everett Hale has pictured for us the character of such a man, his sense of isolation, of despair, and we cannot but sympathize with such a man and rejoice when we are not as he. But, perhaps, there are more Negroes and Jews in the world who feel that they are persons without a country than any other race groups, as they find themselves scattered in the vine and leaf of every nation's life. It has been the despair and horror of such persons, who felt or were made to feel that they were persons without a country and were oppressed and persecuted in the countries where they were born. Millions of British Negro subjects feel this way, not only in the West Indies, but in Africa itself, and many Negro citizens of the United States as well. Whatever their status may be they still feel that they are residing in a far country, and among strangers, and long for a country of their own, peopled and governed by and for them. It is a natural feeling . . .

In his front page article in the last issue of The Negro World, President General Marcus Garvey succinctly explained and enlarged upon this question of a man without a country. . . .* The President General

* Here Fortune reprints the italicized passage in the preceding article.

covers the ground entirely and leaves no room for confusion. And it is important that there should be no confusion on this vital matter. Nationalization in Africa is the main objective, but in reaching it we cannot sacrifice our social, civil and economic values in the countries where we have been scattered as British subjects, French subjects, and the like, and as citizens of the United States, with our privileges and immunities specifically guaranteed by the Federal Constitution, and which no State may "deny or abridge." And the more we value our opportunities, the more we save and have, the better able will we be to assist the Universal Negro Improvement Association in its program of race upbuilding and national rehabilitation.

[c]
SACRIFICES FOR AFRICA
MARCUS GARVEY
Negro World/September 24, 1926

Fellow-Men of the Negro Race, Greeting:

Although my confinement prevents me from doing many things to aid our cause, I must send an occasional word of encouragement to my brothers all over the world who are struggling for manhood and freedom rights.

This is the age of helpful action, and it falls to the province of every Negro to help his brother to a fuller realization of the opportunities of life. Now is the time for all of us, fellow-men, to join in and help in the spreading of the doctrines of the Universal Negro Improvement Association. We have to utilize every energy we possess to redeem the scattered millions of our race. There is no time to waste about East, West, North or South. The question of the Negro should be the only question for us. We have remained divided long enough to realize that our weakness as a race is caused through disunity. We can no longer allow the enemy to penetrate our ranks. We must "close ranks" and make up our minds all over the world either to have full liberty and democracy or to die in the attempt to get it. The salvation of our race depends upon the action of the present generation of our young men. We fellows who could have died by the millions in battle fighting for the white men must now realize that we have but one life to give and since that life could have been given in France and Flanders for the salvation of an alien race, we ought to be sensible enough to see and realize that if there is to be another sacrifice of life, we shall first give that life to our own cause.

Africa, bleeding Africa, is calling for the service of every black man and woman to redeem her from the enslavement of the white man. All the sacrifice that must be made, therefore, shall be of the Negro, for the Negro and no one else. Whether we are of America, Canada, the West Indies, South or Central America or Africa, the call for action is ours. The scattered children of Africa know no country but their own dear Father and Motherland. We may make progress in America, the West Indies and other foreign countries, but there will never be any real lasting progress until the Negro makes of Africa a strong and powerful Republic to lend protection to the success we make in foreign lands.

The conflict of ideals between nations and races is causing a revolution among men. The royal and privileged classes of idlers who used to tyrannize and oppress the humble hordes of mankind are now experiencing difficulty in holding their control over the sentiment of the people. The people themselves have changed in their sentiments and outlook. This change is called a revolution, and one that will one day enthrone the rule of the masses and destroy the privilege of the classes. As far as this revolution extends its scope to the various races, it is for me to say that the Negro cannot afford to be silent nor stationary, he must also revolt from the slavish and subservient ideas of the past. The bloodless revolution of white society has taught the weak peoples of the world how to organize and how to act. There is no revolution as successful as that of the triumph of free thought over slavish ideas. The Negro has been a slave to the white man's ideas for three hundred years, and the hour has now struck for him to imitate the masses of white society and cut away from royalty and privilege.

Let every Negro think of the revolution that will one day sweep the continent of Africa. Let us dream of and plan for that day. Surely there is a time coming when all men shall greet others as brothers, but that time will mean the universal rise of man, when black, yellow and white men will all in their respective ways boast of their success and their civilization. No white men will respect and care for a black man who has nothing to show of his success in life, and so it is of the yellow man. All men must achieve, and then in the general success there will be an appreciation for all.

Every black man should, therefore, join the new revolution that seeks to place the mind of man in the realm of racial contentment and destroy the hideous monster of slave-thought. To be a successful revolutionist does not mean that you must use the sword and the gun, but to use the faculties of God's endowment and rise to the highest height possible for man. Let us therefore unite our forces and make one desperate rush for the goal of success. And now that we have started to make good by uniting ourselves, let us spare no effort to go forward.

This article bore the headline "The Sacrifices That Negroes Made For Alien Races Are Now Needed In Behalf Of Bleeding Africa."

10.
A Columnist Is Caught Between the NAACP and the UNIA

An example of how the fight between Garveyites and integrationists worked to polarize black society is found in the case of the firing of columnist Floyd Calvin from the staff of the socialist *Messenger*. Calvin was basically a writer of social satire and had worked on the *Messenger* throughout 1922, contributing a number of comical character sketches of leading Garveyites during the first months of the "Garvey Must Go" campaign. Then, in the February 21, 1923, issue of the weekly New York *Amsterdam News*, there appeared an article by Calvin in which he declared that the feud between the NAACP and the UNIA had gotten out of hand, that there was both good and bad in each organization and neither deserved to be ruined (selection [a]). He was promptly fired from his job with the *Messenger*. The *Negro World* of March 10, 1923, devoted substantial space on its editorial page to explaining this incident. Calvin himself contributed an article explaining why he had been fired (selection [b]). Elsewhere on the page was a reprint from Garvey's daily *Negro Times* congratulating Calvin for his "rational view" of the feud; and there was also a reprint from a 1920 *Negro World* article by Hubert H. Harrison on the creation of an alliance between the *Messenger* editors and their previous enemies, the leaders of the NAACP. These two articles are selection (c).

(Upon leaving the *Messenger* Calvin was hired by the Pittsburgh *Courier*. He was a regular columnist for that paper for over a decade, during which time he also worked as a field reporter, his feature stories on southern racism and unusual protest movements helping to build the *Courier* into one of the three top black weeklies in the country. A serious automobile accident in 1934 required years of recuperation and curtailed his active career as a journalist.)

[a]
THE N.A.A.C.P. VS. THE U.N.I.A.
FLOYD J. CALVIN
New York Amsterdam News/February 21, 1923

The fight between the National Association for the Advancement of Colored People and the Universal Negro Improvement Association has reached such a stage that it might not be unwise to impartially review both groups and see what should be preserved and what destroyed in each organization for the best interests of the public at large.

The names of both denote progress. One wishes to "advance," the other to "improve." One has for its objective building up the historic Motherland, Africa; the other, equality in America. If both carry out their programs, both will render a distinct service to the Negro race. But for either to forget its primary purpose for existing and devote its entire time to telling the other: "Your program is impossible," is like the pot calling the kettle black.

In the first place, neither program will be realized soon. The very foundations of each denote a continuous struggle in their respective fields. In the second place, if the public finds that the cardinal principles are suddenly forgotten and the controversy drops to the level of personalities, then both sides should be let severely alone. If members of two organizations cannot go about their business carrying out their respective programs—which are basically not programs of destruction—without being disgraced by personal fights between their respective leaders, then both leaders should be repudiated.

Now what about the charges flying to and fro? First, the followers haven't anything to do with those charges because they didn't make them. The followers joined with their respective leaders to carry out what they believed to be a good program. To be sure they have a right and ought to be loyal in a crisis. But they have no right to give their support until their cause denotes a public nuisance rather than a public service. They have no right to be worked into a frenzy until they hate every one who is not of their cult. They have no right to become suspicious of every one who is not as wild and excited as they. It is then that they become victims of personal grievances, rather than followers of constructive leaders. So that, rather than become demoralized and undermining, it is better to dismiss the leaders before the leaders destroy the unity of the people, for the people can always produce new leaders, but the same leaders cannot regain the confidence of their former supporters.

Who constitute the respective movements? What are the real differences between the two groups?

The N.A.A.C.P. has typical "American" ideas—"Advancement," "political equality." The U.N.I.A. has universal ideas—"improvement," "redeeming Africa." Now everybody wants to see the Negro "advance"—to political equality if he can. Likewise everybody wants to see the Negro "improve"—if he had a Motherland he would not be any the worse off.

The immediate program of the U.N.I.A. is businesses, self-respect, pride of race, race consciousness and general uplifting. Certainly this would be a blessing to all. The immediate program of the N.A.A.C.P. is civil rights. There is nothing wrong with this. What must be done? Simply "improve" and "advance"—the "leaders" to the contrary notwithstanding.

[b]
THE STRAW THAT BROKE THE CAMEL'S BACK
FLOYD J. CALVIN
Negro World/March 10, 1923

On February 1 I was assistant editor of The Messenger Magazine. On March 1 I am not. Why? I think it is because that between those two dates I gave utterance to the following words: "The fight between the National Association for the Advancement of Colored People and the Universal Negro Improvement Association has reached such a stage that it might not be unwise to impartially review both groups and see what should be preserved and what should be destroyed in each organization for the best interests of the public at large." This was spoken not in the columns of The Messenger, but independently in the general Negro press.

The editors of The Messenger have the unquestioned right to dictate just what should be expressed in the pages of their magazine. They are also justified in eliminating any factor which tends to create an outside impression that all is not well within their ranks. Therefore, to drop me from their editorial staff—for whatever reason—was both logical and correct.

But the settling of this point gives rise to another equally as important. Why should I, after some months of association, wilfully provoke such unavoidable action?

First, as assistant editor, I was in no way responsible to the public for what appeared in the magazine. Even though I believed every word that was written, or not a single word, it all remained my personal and private opinion. But if the time ever came when I felt disposed to object or disagree, that was also my personal right. So that the points involved are purely issues of public policy.

From editorial references to the position which I took it seems to be clear that I did not attack the rank and file of either the N.A.A.C.P. or the U.N.I.A. Also no one could deduce that I approved of Marcus Garvey or apologized for W. E. B. DuBois. Then where was my offense? Here: The very fact that I did not point an accusing finger at the entire membership of the U.N.I.A. was the straw that broke the camel's back.

As I understand it, Messrs. A. Philip Randolph and Chandler Owen advocate that not only must Marcus Garvey be destroyed, but the Universal Negro Improvement Association as well. To my mind this is unsound. Speaking particularly of racial uplift, I cannot countenance annihilating a whole group merely because the leader of that group comes into disrepute. Surely, the best of leaders may sometimes err—perhaps for a multiplicity of reasons—but it is not logical to presuppose that a majority of their followers have likewise gone astray.

But even so—granting that a certain group is on the wrong track—what would be the correct course for a would-be public servant?

First, what is a public servant? Concisely, he is either an elected or a self-imposed spokesman for the people. Second, in speaking or acting for the people, what rule must be his guide? In order to remain a servant—helpful, constructive, prophetic—he must seek to advance the people's interests. Third, how can these interests be best advanced? By lessening friction between groups, by calmly pointing out errors for the people to avoid, by presenting a practical program from which the majority may derive specific benefits. Thus, after much observation and serious reflection, I found I could not advocate that the U.N.I.A. be smashed simply because Marcus Garvey is suspected of being a bad actor. And I thought it at least no harm to express my honest convictions.

[c]
IN DEFENSE OF CALVIN
Negro World/March 10, 1923 [reprints]

[From *Negro Times*]
... Mr. Calvin has a very thoughtful article in the current issue of the New York Amsterdam News, in which he thinks the "fight between the National Association for the Advancement of Colored People and the Universal Negro Improvement Association has reached such a stage that it might not be unwise to impartially review both groups and see what should be preserved and what should be destroyed in each group for the best interests of the public at large."

That is the right way to go about getting at the truth of any organization or question in dispute. Mr. Calvin finds that the two organizations have well-defined purposes as an excuse for their existence, and that these purposes are good, and that the leaders of them should not compromise their membership by antagonizing each other, declaring the one to the other, "Your program is impossible." This is the rational view, but Mr. Calvin will not be able to convince the selfish and vindictive gentlemen of the Association for the Advancement of Colored People that it is. Nobody invited them to neglect their work in order to give most of their time and effort to the work of discrediting the Universal Negro Improvement Association, and nobody in the Universal Negro Improvement Association is going to invite them to discard the policy they have adopted with their eyes open and which they are killing themselves by pursuing ... What they need to do is to be about their own business, and they are learning the truth and force of this fact by the mistakes they have made and are making.

[From Hubert H. Harrison in the *Negro World,* March 4, 1920]

[Black socialists of the Messenger are now working] hand in glove with the N.A.A.C.P. Has the nature of that organization changed so much in the meantime, or has the Messenger changed [from its previous militant opposition to the NAACP]? We had heard that "the lion shall lie down with the lamb," but we had always understood that when that

blessed event came off the lamb would be in the same position as the
* * * young lady from Niger,
Who went out to ride on a tiger.
They came back from the ride
With the lady inside,
And a smile on the face of the tiger.
We hope that the six Socialists who are staging this grand transformation scene will not swallow the dear N.A.A.C.P. And, naturally, we hope that "the capitalist board of the N.A.A.C.P." which "will not permit the editor of the Crisis to lead Negroes in their own interests," will not swallow our Bolshevist Bonapartes. Either event would prove, we fear, a calamity of large dimensions. May we not say to both, "Beware of the dog!" Or, better still, "Beware of the Greeks, especially when they bring gifts."

We wonder what the N.A.A.C.P. will say to this offer of the olive branch thus adroitly tendered. We confess that it tickles us *demi à la morte,* as the schoolboys say, to see the lion and the lamb making friendly passes at each other. But, of course, we cannot help wondering (since we do not understand the Socialist philosophy) whether there isn't an economic advantage basis—past, present or expected—to this latest moral transformation.

11.
Communists in the 1930s

During the great Depression the Communist party made a concerted effort to win black American support. While there were roughly two dozen black Communists in 1927, there were ten thousand by the mid-1930s, and the impact of communism on Black America was much greater than their actual numbers.

The growth of Communist influence among blacks was helped by the adoption of a nationalistic program. In 1928 the Party proposed a plan for a Black Belt Republic in the southern United States. An area from Texas to Virginia, composing the counties of the "Black Belt" which had a majority black population, would be made a separate republic. The plan was promoted at meetings in the black community and through pamphlets distributed in the ghetto, but it was played down in the Communist press. One reason for this silence was a fear of antagonizing white comrades, many of whom grudgingly agreed to the principle of black and white working-class unity and were skeptical and suspicious of the special consideration given blacks in the republic plan. Selection (a) presents one of the rare discussions of the plan in the Communist Harlem weekly. This editorial by editor Cyril Briggs employs a nationalist rhetoric suggestive of the arguments put forth today by the Republic of New Africa in its plan for a separate black republic in the South.

The RNA apparently does not offer a place in the Republic for the white minority. The Communist plan did. Selection (b), a poem by Langston Hughes run in the international monthly *Negro Worker*, describes this goal of southern unity. (Hughes, the Renaissance poet and novelist, was in the early 1930s an avid supporter of communism and a voluminous writer of poems, plays and short stories for the Communist cause.) The footnotes for the poem presented here were added for the help of the international readership; even so, to explain Tuskegee and Booker T. Washington was suggestive of a patronizing attitude widely employed in this Communist monthly. (Doctored photographs were common. One of these was a picture supposedly showing a black addressing a large crowd in London. A third of the picture contains the silhouette of the speaker and in front of him are thousands of disproportionately small people who are looking attentively way to the right and far below the speaker.)

Communist efforts to save the defendants in the Scottsboro case were a major factor in the growth of black support for the Communist party. Between 1931 and 1935 the top news story in Black America was the attempted legal lynching of the nine "Scottsboro Boys." The case was fought through a series of trials and appeals, eventually resulting in the freedom of all but one defendant, who managed to escape from jail and write a highly successful book on his experiences. Arrested in Scottsboro, Alabama, for hitching a ride on a freight train, the nine teenagers were accused of raping two white women discovered in another part of the train. After the first trial, one of the young women admitted that she and her partner had framed the blacks to save face, and had done so on coaxing of the police. Communists had been there from the start with lawyers from the International Labor Defense—an organization which during the 1930s defended a number of blacks from lynch justice. Selection (c) presents some details of the case in an article from the *Negro Worker*. (The author, James W. Ford, was the initial editor of the magazine. He had been active in trade union struggles in Chicago after World War I, joined the Communists in 1925, and in 1932 and 1936 was their vice-presidential candidate.)

The NAACP also entered the Scottsboro case at the start, and had lined up an impressive battery of defense lawyers, including Clarence Darrow. But almost as quickly as the Association entered, it withdrew from the case, bitterly denouncing the Communists for mixing politics with an attempt to save lives. Selection (d) from editor William H. Davis of the *Amsterdam News* presents an evaluation of the Communist-NAACP feud.

In the Communist view, the only chance for saving the Scottsboro youths lay in a massive national and international outpouring of public indignation. Accordingly protest demonstrations and marches were conducted across America and in Europe and as far away as Buenos Aires. Moderate black editors like William H. Davis of the *Amsterdam News* had little choice but to give massive publicity to the Communist effort in order to try and save the nine young blacks. Davis, on his own, did organize a petition campaign. Selections (e) and (f), both from the May 10, 1933, *Amsterdam News,* report on two delegations to the White House which tried unsuccessfully to get President Roosevelt to inter-

vene in the Scottsboro case. One was led by Communists, the other by
the liberal Davis. The contrast between the aggressiveness of the former
and the hat-in-hand approach of the latter offers a clue as to how the
Communists won widespread sympathy in Black America. (The reporter on the Communist delegation, Ted Poston, was the younger
brother of former top Garveyite officials Robert and Ulysses Poston.
Ted Poston's involvement with the left would gain him a position on
the film crew that made an ill-fated mission to Moscow to make a
movie on U.S. racism. At the last minute Stalin changed his mind and
sent the crew home. Since World War II Poston has been a columnist
for the *New York Post*.)

[a]
THE BLACK BELT REPUBLIC PLAN
CYRIL V. BRIGGS
Harlem Liberator/August 1, 1932

In an immense territory of the South, a territory commonly known as
the Black Belt, live millions of Negro workers and farmers. These Negroes build and man the factories of this territory. The Negro farmers
and tenants till the land of this territory. They produce the wealth of
this territory.

But the rulers of this territory are not Negroes. The factories that
the Negroes man, belong to white owners. The land that the Negroes
till, and water with their sweat, belongs to white landlords. The officials
of the territory, from the governors of states down to the holders of the
lowest local offices, are white men. The courts of this territory are
presided over by white judges. The police and the sheriffs of this territory are white.

A handful of white bankers and landlords have imposed upon the
millions of Negroes a foreign bondage. And in order to maintain this
bondage, Negroes are held in slavery on the land, starved on the farms,
whipped on the chain-gangs, hanged from trees or legally lynched in the
courts.

The land of the Black Belt rightfully belongs to the millions of
Negroes who till it. These Negroes should own the land in this territory;
they should rule its territory and make its laws and sit in judgment in

its courts. They should have the right to determine what form of government they desire; and should they decide upon a government separate from the United States they must be free to act upon their decision.

This is, briefly, what is meant by the demand raised by the Communist Party; the right to self-determination in the Black Belt. The demand is part and parcel of the demand of the working class Party for equal rights. Without the right of self-determination in the Black Belt, all talk of equal rights is empty and futile.

But this slogan horrifies, not only the white bosses and landlords who grow fat by keeping the Negroes in subjection, but likewise the supporters, open and concealed, of these bosses and landlords. And one of those who cry out against the right of self-determination is Heywood Broun, mouthpiece of the Socialist Party.

To Broun, the idea of a handful of white bosses ruling millions of Negroes is entirely acceptable. But when the proposition is made that the Negroes of this territory shall govern this territory in which they are a majority, and govern the handful of white men who live there—then Broun and all his fellow-fakers are alarmed.

"It means a new form of Jim-Crowism," says Broun. Broun does not cry out against Norman Thomas, Socialist candidate for President, who regularly segregates Negroes in his meetings in the South. And although he has frankly stated that he is opposed to enforcement of the fourteenth and fifteenth amendments, Broun is much "concerned" over "Jim Crowism" in the Black Belt.

Does the right of self-determination mean Jim-Crowism? It means the opposite—freedom from bondage and inequality. The rule of Negroes in the Black Belt does not mean the setting aside of this territory for the Negroes alone, and forcing Negroes to live there. Equal rights for the Negroes in every part of the United States, with freedom to come and go as they wish—this is one of the main aims of the Communists. But the demand for equal rights is a hollow mockery unless the Negroes can throw off their backs this handful of white rulers who keep them in bondage. That is the meaning of the demand of the Communists: Equal rights for Negroes, self-determination for the Black Belt.

[b]
AN OPEN LETTER TO THE SOUTH
LANGSTON HUGHES [1]
Negro Worker/July 15, 1932

White workers of the South:
    Miners,
    Farmers,
    Mechanics,
    Mill hands,
    Shop girls,
    Railway men,
    Servants,
    Tobacco workers,
    Share croppers,
    GREETINGS!
I am the black worker,
    Listen:
That the land might be ours,
And the mines and the factories and the office towers
At Harlan, Richmond, Gastonia, Atlanta, New Orleans;
That the plants and the roads and the tools of power
Be ours:

Let us forget what Booker T. [2] said.
"Separate as the fingers."
He knew he lied.

Let us become instead, you and I,
One single hand
That can united rise
To smash the old dead dogmas of the past—
To kill the lies of color

1. Hughes is a young Negro revolutionary poet, the author of several volumes of poems, describing various phases of Negro working class life in America. He has recently written a play on the famous Alabama case, called the "Scottsboro Express."

2. Booker T. Washington, a Negro reformist leader who preached the policy of submission and segregation to the Negro masses, especially in the South.

[footnotes in original]

That keep the rich enthroned
And drive us to the time-clock and the plow
Helpless, stupid, scattered, and alone—as now—
Race against race,
Because one is black,
Another white of face.

Let us new lessons learn.
All workers.
New life-ways make,
One union form;
Until the future burns out
Every past mistake
Let us get together, say;
"You are my brother, black or white.
You my sister—now—today!"
For me, no more the great migration to the North
Instead: Migration into force and power—
Tuskegee[3] with a red flag on the tower!
On every lynching tree, a poster crying FREE
Because, O poor white workers,
You have linked your hands with me.

We did not know that we were brothers.
Now we know!
Out of that brotherhood
Let power grow!
We did not know
That we were strong.
Now we see
In union lies our strength.
Let union be
The force that breaks the time-clock,
Smashes misery,
Takes land,

---

3. Tuskegee,—a Negro college in Alabama, founded by Booker T. Washington
where the Negro youth is taught submission to white imperialist rule. The present
principal is R. R. Morton [sic], a disciple of Booker T. Washington and one of the
greatest misleaders of the Negro masses in America.

Takes factories,
Takes office towers,
Takes tools and banks and mines,
Railroad, ships, and dams,
Until the forces of the world
Are ours!

White worker,
Here is my hand.

Today,
We're Man to Man.

[c]
THE SCOTTSBORO CASE
JAMES W. FORD
Negro Worker/June 1931

Eight Negro boys framed-up on the charge of two notorious white prostitutes and sentenced to die by electrocution on July 10 by a farcical speedy trial of capitalist "justice" in the State of Alabama, U.S.A.

The "trial" was conducted in the midst of surroundings (a special carnival drawing hundreds of poor white farmers, thugs, police and other agents of the ruling class to the city) at which the Ku Klux Klan and other fascist agents of the ruling class made speeches, demonstrations, intimidations, letting loose the most vicious lynch law and mob violence spirit, with the object to make certain that lynch law would have its way and that the Negro workers would once again have an object lesson if they dare to rise against their oppression. . . .

Despite the stirring up of racial prejudices by the ruling class, confusing the minds of poor white farmers and workers and thus misdirecting their fight against unemployment and starvation from them (the ruling class) into lynching bees against the Negroes, interracial workers' solidarity is beginning to show itself by joint strikes against wage cuts and lengthening of hours of work, by joint mass demonstrations against unemployment and starvation and vicious jim-crow practices and against the whole capitalist system.

This is what is frightening the capitalist bosses not only in the United States but all the imperialist powers . . . That is why the capitalist bosses, frightened at the growing class consciousness of the Negro masses are intensifying white terror, lynch law, mob violence, police and soldiers massacre everywhere against the Negroes, trying to stop their rising revolts against oppression.

That is why the present wave of lynchings rage in the U.S.A. That is why over 40 Negro workers were lynched last year in the U.S.A. and over 15 already this Year. That is why only a few weeks ago in the State of Texas two white organizers of the Red Trade Unions, for organizing black and white workers, were kidnapped, beaten, thrown into a river and left to die by the fascist Ku Klux Klan of the ruling class.

Terror in Africa

Not only in the United States is the resistance of the Negro toilers against capitalist-imperialist oppression and exploitation being met with fascist white terror, in South Africa native workers are being murdered by the bourgeois state police for mass protest against taxation, pass laws and oppression. In Nigeria of West Africa native women and men are shot down by imperialist troops of the McDonald "Labour" Government for protesting against taxation. In Sierra Leone imperialist troops are suppressing the resistance of the natives by shooting down the population. In East Africa and the West Indies the imperialists are drowning the movements of the workers in blood.

The frame-up to burn these 8 young Negro workers in Alabama is but a link in the chain of imperialist terror against the Negro workers in order to try to stop their growing militancy. The frame-up to "legally" lynch these boys by the steel barons and landlords of Alabama is an attempt to destroy and outlaw the Communist party and the revolutionary Trade Unions and their growing influence among the Negro workers. This is a crime against the working class.

These 8 workers are sentenced to die on July 10th. **The International Trade Unions Committee of Negro Workers calls upon the International working class to rally to the support of our class brothers.** Only the firm hand of the International working class can stop this execution. Only mass protest and action of the international working class can stop the bloody fascist hands of the capitalist bosses of the state of Alabama.

The Negro masses in turning to the Communist Party and the Red Trade Unions in the U.S.A. are turning from the hired and paid petty bourgeois reformist Negro lackies who betray them into the hand of the capitalist bosses. The Negro workers in the U.S.A. are turning more and more to the International revolutionary movement in unity with their oppressed and exploited brothers in Africa, with their brothers in China and India and the other colonies, and with the revolutionary workers in the capitalist countries; and what is more the Negro workers are understanding more and more that the success of Socialist construction in the Soviet Union is the cause of the working class and oppressed peoples throughout the world.

We demand the release of these young workers!

We demand the release of our class brothers in South Africa and all class war prisoners!

We demand for the Negro Workers the right of revolutionary trade union organization!

We demand the right of Negro and white workers to fight jointly against unemployment, starvation and low wages!

Death to lynchers and imperialist slaughterers of Negro toilers!

Against forced labour, slavery, taxation and pass laws!

For full equality for Negroes! For the right of the Negro masses in the black belt of the south to self-determination!

For the complete independence and self-determination of the Negro colonies!

For a native republic in South Africa!

For the defense of the Soviet Union!

For international solidarity!

                    International Trade Unions Committee of Negro Workers

This article bore the headline "Smash Lynching 8 Young Negroes."

[d]
THE COMMUNISTS AND
THE SCOTTSBORO CASE
WILLIAM H. DAVIS
New York Amsterdam News/January 13, 1932

Last May, when the International Labor Defense and the National Association for the Advancement of Colored People were wrangling over the defense of the eight Scottsboro case defendants, The Amsterdam News, in an expression of editorial opinion, stated that "it would be better for the defense of the accused youths if the I.L.D. and the N.A.A.C.P. were co-operating, but since they are not, the main question to be decided" is their adequate defense. The editorial also expressed the opinion that "we cannot escape the suspicion that the Communists and the International Labor Defense are more interested in attracting converts to their cause than they are in preventing the eight lads from paying the extreme penalty," following a hasty and inadequate trial, for a crime they may not have committed.

THAT OUR SUSPICIONS were well-founded was proven a few days ago when Clarence Darrow and Arthur Garfield Hayes, two of the most distinguished and successful criminal lawyers in the United States, who had been retained by the N.A.A.C.P. to defend the youths, withdrew from the case after failing to reach an agreement with George W. Chamblee of Chattanooga, former Attorney-General of that state, who has been retained by the I.L.D. Darrow and Hayes before withdrawing proposed that all attorneys interested in the case should sign the following statement:

> We represent the defendants. We represent no organization. The lives of the eight boys are at stake. It is unimportant who enlisted our interests. We will engage in no controversy between groups. We have agreed to work together to try to save these boys and our responsibility is to them and to them only.

THIS STATEMENT the I.L.D. attorneys are reported to have refused to sign, insisting that Darrow and Hayes repudiate the N.A.A.C.P. and work with the I.L.D. Does not the failure to sign such a statement prove that the I.L.D. is interested, primarily, in spreading propaganda for the I.L.D.? Does it not prove that the interest that organization, and the Communists, has had so far in the boys themselves is a secondary one?

WITH THE WITHDRAWAL of the N.A.A.C.P., the I.L.D. is now left in sole charge of the defense of the Scottsboro case, which is probably just as well, since the two organizations and the attorneys could not get together, and the latter organization will have to accept full responsibility for whatever fate befalls the defendants. No longer will it be possible for the I.L.D. to insinuate that the N.A.A.C.P. is impeding the progress of the defense. And nothing could be more damaging to the propaganda efforts of the Communists among Negroes in this country than the execution of the eight defendants.

WHETHER OR NOT the Communist organization will now make the saving of the boys' lives its first consideration remains to be seen. There is certainly no excuse for not doing so, and their future status among Negroes will be decided by the outcome. Nor is there any reason why every possible co-operation, including that which the N.A.A.C.P. may be able to give, should not be extended to them. There is still but the one paramount issue in the Scottsboro case for those who believe that these defendants are innocent or that they have not had a fair trial—their freedom or a fair trial.

Originally entitled "The Scottsboro Muddle Clears," the editorial was unsigned.

[e]
MARCH ON WASHINGTON: 1
T. R. POSTON
New York Amsterdam News/May 10, 1933

WASHINGTON, D.C., May 8.—History was made in the nation's capital today.

Weary, drenched, and in many cases scantily clad and footsore, 3,000 of America's most oppressed peoples marched through the streets of this city and demanded the release of nine of their group in Alabama and the protection of 12,000,000 exploited citizens throughout the United States.

With the 3,000 Negro protesters there were approximately 1,000 white workers who added their voices to the demand for the release of the Scottsboro boys. Among these was Ruby Bates, defense witness in the celebrated case, and she with Mrs. Janie Patterson, mother of one of the condemned boys, led the parade through the rain-soaked streets of Washington.

Arm in arm, the woman who gave birth to Haywood Patterson and the girl who almost swore his life away led the shouting demonstration up Pennsylvania avenue and around the White House where a committee of twenty-five persons demanded the presence of the President of the United States so that they might seek his intervention into the course of Alabama "justice."

Refuse to Present Demands

The committee was received in the White House by Louis McHenry Howe, one of President Roosevelt's secretaries and special representative, but William L. Patterson, secretary of the International Labor Defense and spokesman of the group, refused to submit the group demands to the representative. Demanding the presence of the nation's chief executive, Patterson was informed that he was in conference with delegates from foreign nations.

Upon request of the spokesman, who refused to deal with Col. Howe, President Roosevelt was reached by telephone while the committee waited. As Col. Howe held the receiver from his ear, the voice of the chief executive could be heard plainly by the assembled listeners saying "I will not see the committee." He explained that he was busy in a conference.

Patterson termed Roosevelt's refusal "a gesture of contempt for the American Negro masses and the entire working class of the country," and refused to state his mission to the representative.

Ruby Bates at White House

Following this, Ruby Bates stepped forward and said: "Mr. Howe, I am Ruby Bates and I want to say to you that the Scottsboro boys are innocent." Mrs. Patterson, in a dramatic plea just before the committee retired, cried to Mr. Howe, "I do pray for you to ask the President to give me back my son, for my heart has been hanging heavy in my breast for two years now. The boys are innocent and I do pray that he will give me back my boy."

Others who spoke to Mr. Howe in demands for the presence of the

President included James W. Ford, Vice-Presidential candidate on the Communist party ticket last election; Louise Thompson, national secretary of the Scottsboro Action Committee which sponsored the march; Steve Kingston, "general" of the Scottsboro Army, and Richard B. Moore, young I.L.D. attorney. The group left petitions with 200,000 signatures for the President.

Mr. Howe was not familiar with the developments of the Scottsboro case. He insisted that the case was now before the United States Supreme Court and was only convinced of its present status after a short argument. Other members of the committee to the White House included A. J. Muste of the Conference for Progressive Labor Action; William N. Jones of the Baltimore Afro-American and George Murphy of the same periodical; Samuel C. Patterson of the Caribbean Union, Bruce Parker of the Unemployed Council and several representatives of various city march groups. . . .

Police Discourteous

The police escort [through the District of Columbia] was increased after the marchers started through the city carrying their "Free the Scottsboro Boys" and "We Demand Equal Rights for Negroes" placards. The motorcycle police, sneering openly, deliberately attempted to intimidate the marchers by riding close to the ranks and laying down a smoke and gas barrage. They laughed with each other at the sport and even cut through the parade to the other side when the wind would shift and the fumes would not be blown over the marchers. No one broke the strict discipline on the way to the White House, however. . . .

Datelined "Washington, D.C., May 8 [1933]," this article bore the headlines: "Roosevelt Refuses to See Leaders of Large Delegation/Led to Executive Mansion by Ruby Bates and Mrs. Janie Patterson, I.L.D. Secretary Declines to Present Demands."

[f]
MARCH ON WASHINGTON: 2
WILLIAM H. DAVIS
New York Amsterdam News/May 10, 1933

On behalf of the delegation which left New York Friday morning with 145,000 signatures to a petition requesting the Chief Executive of the nation to use his good office in securing for the nine Scottsboro boys a change of venue and to issue a new declaration of civil, political and economic justice and freedom aiming at the future strict enforcement of the Thirteenth, Fourteenth and Fifteenth amendments to the Federal Constitution, allow me to say that its members feel a deep sense of gratitude and appreciation for the generous manner in which you (the public) assisted to make their efforts a success.

The co-operation given the delegation by Congressman Joseph A. Gavagan and the manner and courtesies shown the delegation at the White House by the private secretary to the President, Louis McHenry Howe, who received the delegation, gave the assurance that petitions and appeal for justice will be laid before the President for his personal attention. The delegation feels that it has every reason to believe that the results will be favorable.

12.
Communists and Garveyites

The black Communist press conducted a withering attack on the entire non-Communist black leadership but in particular singled out Marcus Garvey, a man with widespread support among the working class. In selection (a), George Padmore, writing in the *Negro Worker,* awards Garvey all the sins of the black middle class. (Padmore took over editorship of the *Negro Worker* in 1931. His political awakening had come through work with the Garvey Club at Howard University. Rejecting Garvey as a reformist, Padmore became a top Communist critic of Garveyism. In 1933 Padmore learned that the Communist International was planning virtual abandonment of its work in the Third World in favor of conciliation with imperialist England and France, in the hope of cooperation in the fight to stop Hitler. Padmore rejected communism forthwith and became an anti-Communist zealot. In later years he would write rather favorably about Garvey.)

The Communists were in a bind concerning Garveyism. They knew they had to be nationalistic, as in their Black Belt plan, in order to win over a generation raised on the oratory of Garvey. But they were not in a position to cooperate with Garveyites, lest they help their main rival in the battle to win over the black working class revive his own movement. In selection (b) Arthur S. Gray, the top West Coast Garveyite, endorses communism in the *Negro World.* His support is rejected by Padmore in a reply to Gray run in the *Negro Worker,* selection (c). In selection (d), a Guyanan Garveyite writes a letter to the *Negro Worker* questioning Padmore's tirades against Garvey, and gets in reply another tirade. Another strategy involved the drawing of a division, putting

Marcus Garvey and his top lieutenants on one side and the Garveyite masses on the other. In selection (e) from the *Negro Worker* and selection (f) from the *Harlem Liberator,* Cyril Briggs writes favorably about the rank-and-file Garveyite.

[a]
THE BANKRUPTCY OF NEGRO LEADERSHIP
GEORGE PADMORE
Negro Worker/December 1931

Never since the days of chattel slavery, when millions of black men and women were brutally torn from Africa and enslaved on the plantations and in the mines of the New World, were the Negro workers faced with such misery as to-day.

Millions of these toilers and their families are starving in every town and village in Africa, America, and the West Indies, due to the greatest crisis which world capitalism has ever experienced. And it is just at this time, when the Negro toiling masses like those of other races and colors in every capitalist country, colony and semi-colony are looking to those who have paraded before them as leaders, to show them a revolutionary way out of their misery by organizing and leading them in struggle against the capitalist exploiters for food, clothing and shelter, we witness the most open acts of betrayal by the so-called "big" Negro leaders.

In every country where black men and women do the hardest and most dangerous work for the lowest wages under the most terrible conditions imposed upon them by the imperialists, we see the vast majority of the Negro middle-class leaders,—lawyers, preachers, doctors, and politicians, deserting the workers and unemployed toiling masses and going over in the most brazen fashion into the camp of the white capitalists and landlords.

For example: In America, **Mr. Oscar de Priest**, the Chicago politician and the only Negro representative in the United States Congress openly opposed a bill presented before that body demanding relief for the unemployed. Mr. de Priest's excuse was, that, although the Negroes are the greatest sufferers of the depression, he considered it Un-American (whatever that means) for the government to provide them with relief. In other words, Mr. de Priest has agreed with the policy of President Hoover and the other capitalist rulers of America, that the un-employed—black as well as white—must starve or depend upon the charity from the Salvation Army and other private institutions. The same can be said of **Major R. R. Moton** of Tuskegee Institute, who, in the face of the growing solidarity between the Negroes and the white workers in the South in joint struggles for their common class interest against the landlords and the capitalists, appeals to the Negro masses to disassociate themselves from their class conscious white allies and to peacefully submit to the system of lynching and mob-law of their op-pressors.

Not satisfied with such acts of treachery, de Priest and Moton, as well as the other black agents of international capitalism—like **DuBois, Walter White** and **Pickens** of the N.A.A.C.P. and **George Schuyler** in America; **Blaise Diagne** of Senegal, the Under-secretary for the French colonies,—the reformist trade union leaders, **Kadalie, Champion;** and **Professor T. D. D. Jabavu** in South Africa, and **Captain A. A. Cipriani,** in the West Indies, are all offering their services to their respective imperialist masters.

The chief role of the American wing of misleaders is to prevent the Negro workers from supporting the communist and revolutionary trade union movements, which alone are organizing and leading the fight in the interest of the working-class as a whole, and for full **economic, social, and political equality, as well as the right of self-determination for the Negro Masses in the Black Belt of the U.S.A.** In order to play their part as effectively as possible, DuBois, the ideological leader of the middle-class Negro Intellectuals, is trying to take away the lead from the revolutionary movement by playing with "left" phrases on the question of unemployment. However, his only advise [sic] to the Negro unemployed masses is, that they should "only spend their money where they get employment." What stupidity! What demagogy! Every jobless man knows that he must **first** have work before he is able to talk about "choosing" where to spend his money. This only shows the utter bank-ruptcy of the men at the head of the N.A.A.C.P. They have no program to lead the masses out of their misery. Only the militant labour move-ment can mobilize and show the masses **a revolutionary way out** of their hunger and starvation. Furthermore, these same black "hunting dogs" of the white capitalists are the very ones who are actively paving the way for the Negro toiling masses of America, Africa, and West India to be again used as cannon-fodder in the fast approaching imperialist war, and intervention against Soviet Russia, the most stalwarth [sic] friend and champion of the Negroes and all oppressed peoples, and the only country where there is no unemployment and where the working class is building up a Socialist society free from exploitation, race preju-dice, lynchings, jim-crowism, color bar, pass laws and the hundred and one other evils imposed upon the Negro masses under capitalism.

Chief among this array of international betrayers of the revolu-tionary struggles of the Negro masses, is **Marcus Garvey**. For years this demagogue has been exploiting the racial consciousness and national-istic tendencies of the Negro masses which began to express themselves during and after the war, in order to advance his own selfish interest and that of the class of "ghetto" capitalists and landlords whom he represents.

Before the outbreak of the world economic crisis and the sharpening of the conflicts between the workers and capitalists in America, Garvey by toying with the slogan **"Africa for the Africans,"** and coupled with a showmanship (semi-military corps and "royal" titles) which appealed to the psychology of the more backward sections of the Negro masses that had recently migrated North and were still possessed of a peasant ideol-ogy, was able to extort millions of dollars out of their sweat and blood, as they were misled in believing that Garvey's bombastic methods would liberate them from their misery. . . .

As the economic crisis gets worse, the Negro masses who are always the last to be hired and the first to be fired, are naturally not in position to continue to supply Garvey and his henchmen with money. So what is the reaction of this charlatan? Displeased that his exchequer is becoming more and more depleted, he has served notice to his few remaining followers, that if they don't make blood out of the stone and find money to maintain himself and his bootlickers in Jamaica, that he intends to sell out the newspaper, **"Black Man,"** and all the other prop-erty bought by the hard earned dollars of the masses, pocket the proceeds, and take up residence in London, the citadel of British Imperialism.

This announcement created a tremendous wave of protest and discontent among his followers and sympathizers, especially those in the United States, who have contributed the bulk of the money which Garvey is squandering in Jamaica. So in order to appease them, he dispatched his most "loyal" lieutenant, Madame de Mina to America and ordered his Hindu lackey, H. G. Mudgal, Editor of the **"Negro World,"** to launch a campaign for his return to the U.S. This having failed to win popular support, Marcus then decided to play another of his trump cards. And what is this?

In order to cover up his fakery and make it appear that he is still "on the war path," this trickster recently paid a flying visit to Geneva. Now, curious people will ask, what mission has Marcus Garvey in Geneva, Geneva being a place where ambassadors and the representatives of capitalist states are fond of assembling from time to time in order to mouth phrases about disarmament, while at the same time they are feverishly preparing for war.

Well, Mr. Garvey is neither an ambassador, nor representative of any state, his utopian African empire notwithstanding. But what this international clown is trying to do is to make the Negro toiling masses believe that, if they remain loyal to him and continue to supply him with money, he can compel the imperialists to free Africa by presenting a petition to the League of Nations. What nonsense! What absurdity! Garvey himself knows better, for he was the very one, who, twelve years ago, declared that the League of Nations was nothing but a **League of Thieves.** In so much so, that he even had enacted at the Universal Negro Improvement Association convention held in New York 1920, the following paragraph (45) in the Declaration of Rights of the Negro People.

"Be it further resolved, that we as a race of people declare the League of Nations **null and void** as far as the Negro is concerned, in that it seeks to deprive Negroes of their liberty."

But this fraud and unprincipled politician, realizing that his days are numbered, is trying to create the impression that the League of Nations represents the interest of the oppressed peoples and the colonial masses.

Now, what is really the League of Nations that this charlatan is trying to make the poor Negroes put faith in?

The League is composed of the biggest thieves, land grabbers, and exploiters that the world has ever known, namely, **Great Britain, France, Belgium, Portugal, Spain and Italy** (Germany having lost her share since the war) who, by the terms of the treaty of Berlin enacted in February 1885 solemnly declared "in the name of almighty God"—a name which the imperialists never forget to invoke when they are out to make war or enslave other peoples—that they were out to "civilize" Africa. We all know how their civilizing mission has been carried out. By machine guns, battleships, bombing planes, forced labor and confiscation of peasant lands.

Even at the present moment, we see Japan, one of the leading members of the League, with the open approval of the other big powers and the United States over running Manchuria in order to drown the Chinese Revolution in blood and prepare for the war against the Soviet Union on the eastern front.

This is the League of imperialist thieves, exploiters, and war mongers that Garvey, the self appointed black "ambassador" to Geneva would have the Negro masses put faith in.

Truly, those whom the gods want to destroy, they first make mad!

It should be clear to every honest Negro toiler in Africa, in America, in the West Indies,—wherever Garvey and his agents have carried on their reactionary propaganda, that despite the high sounding phrases behind which Garvey masqueraded while he was in America, his latest action exposes him as the greatest fraud and racketeer who has ever imposed himself upon an oppressed people.

The situation to-day is one in which opportunists such as **Garvey, DuBois, Pickens, Kadalie, Jabavu,** and others, are being more and more exposed before the masses. The Negro workers are quickly learning, who are their friends and who their enemies. Thousands of them are freeing themselves from their illusions about Garvey and Garveyism. They are beginning to understand that if Garvey was a real revolutionist and the slightest danger to British imperialism he would never be permitted to occupy a seat in the government of Jamaica (Kingston Municipal Council) much less to travel to Geneva on His Britannic Majesty's passport.

It is quite true that the British Empire is going to the dogs. That its ruling class is daily showing itself more and more incapable of holding down the growing tide of revolt among the English workers and the colonial masses in India and Africa. Nevertheless, they have not yet become so imbecilic as to permit a man whom they consider a real revolutionary leader of the most oppressed peoples under their yoke to run around the world demanding freedom for Africa.

Scotland Yard officials,—the watch dogs of the British Imperialists— know that behind all of Garvey's phrases of **"Africa for the Africans"** he is one of their most faithful lackeys and a traitor to the Negro workers.

[b]
ON CAPITALISM: 1
ARTHUR S. GRAY
Negro World/July 25, 1931

Capital which is used to sway the scales of justices, or to legislate against the poor, or to invade territories of backward peoples is an able description and cannot be defended by those seeking freedom from such oppression. It is this principle of capitalism that is opposed by Communist defenders.

The mere saving of one's honest earnings has never been opposed or resented by the most pronounced Communist thinker, but the accumulated **profits** of another's labour has [been] and will forever be attacked by the class-conscious workers. Capitalism was not created by individual saving and for anyone to make such a stupid comparison is positively childish and stupid.

In Russia we are told that the **workers** have first consideration in all matters of a political and economic nature, such a policy will protect the **weak** who most certainly need protection—if any is to be provided. In capitalist communities just the reverse is the condition: the wealthy dominate, dictate, and control all public matters to the despair of the poor, and uneducated masses. Charity is dispensed by these parasites— yes! But who wants a bone or a crust, when they are entitled to the wealth which their own labour produced. There are some workers that may wish to remain in this "beggar" state, but those who have been aroused to a consciousness of the class struggle want to end this vicious exploitation of the working class.

Any nation whose wealth does not belong to the people, is a state that is not controlled by the people; and to pretend that such communities are the people's governments is rank hypocrisy and deceit. In Russia, the workers are given an opportunity to **work**, because the state is dependent upon such income for its existence and progress; but in the United States you have little opportunity to secure employment— and they throw you in jail for vagrancy, if you fail to land a JOB.

As long as such intense misery and suffering prevails, as the records of this country reveal, wealth that has been amassed to the extent of the Rockefellers, Carnegie, Ford, Mellon, etc., should be confiscated by the state to relieve the nation wide depression of the masses. Can any of these millionaires dispose of such vast amount during their lifetime— normally? Then why not conscript such enormous savings to minimize the agonies of others, as man-power was conscripted during the war periods to "save civilisation?"

There should be no hesitation in the minds of Negro workers as to what course to pursue in this struggle, and particularly so by those who are advocating the overthrow of Imperialism in Africa, for all forms of Imperialism feed upon the support of capitalism. In America we find that capitalism condones lynching, jim-crowism, and all forms of race distinction. And in conclusion, I firmly believe that **communism** in its crudest state is more beneficial to the Negro worker than **capitalism** will ever be in its most modified form.

Originally entitled "Capitalism Is a Menace"; the following article (c) was printed as an "Editor's Note."

[c]
ON CAPITALISM: 2
GEORGE PADMORE
Negro Worker/July 1931

... We publish [the above article] in order to expose the "left" manoeuvres of the Negro petty-bourgeois national-reformists.

Mr. Gray is one of the chief supporters and ideological leaders of the "Back to Africa" Movement. Despite all of his "left" phrases that **Communism** in its crudest state is more beneficial to the Negro **worker** than **capitalism** will ever be in its most modified form. Mr. Gray still supports Marcus Garvey, who has been exposed over and over again as one of the greatest lackeys and defenders of capitalism, and a fakir who will stop short of nothing to utilize the oppression of the toiling masses of his race, to swindle them of their hard earnings in order to support all kinds of bogus schemes. Why does Mr. Gray come out in his attacks against capitalism? He realizes that the world economic crisis is undermining the very foundations of capitalism. He knows that the workers of the Soviet Union are achieving great victories in the building up of Socialism, and that the working class throughout the world and the toiling colonial masses in China, in India, in Africa, are carrying on a determined struggle against imperialist domination. Because of these facts, Mr. Gray realizes that the Negro bourgeois reformists are no longer able to befuddle and mislead the Negro masses, and that in order to maintain whatever little prestige he enjoys among the Negro workers in America it is necessary for him to adopt a more left-demagogic attitude about the evils of capitalism. We want to say to Mr. Gray and other "Left" Negro politicians inside and outside of the Garvey Movement that the only way that they can prove their sincerity and loyalty to the oppressed millions of their race is by breaking away from Garveyism and all other brands of Negro petty-bourgeois reformism, and actively supporting the revolutionary class struggle of the Negro workers and the national-liberation movements of their black brothers in the colonies for Freedom and Self-Determination. This can only be done by striving for the unity of workers of all colours and all oppressed peoples on the basis of the programme of militant class struggle, represented by the International Trade Union Committee of Negro Workers.

[d]
GARVEYISM IN THE WEST INDIES
GEORGE PADMORE
Negro Worker/August 15, 1932

Georgetown, Demerara
4 June, 1932

Dear Comrade Editor:—

After reading one of your leaflets entitled, "What is the International Trade Union Committee of Negro Workers?" I saw on the outside cover the words "Long live the freedom of Africa!" But in the inside I read these lines: "For years we have given our money to so-called big Negro leaders like the reformist Marcus Garvey."

Now I, as an African born in British Guiana cannot understand how you can talk that way of the Hon. gentleman Marcus Garvey. For I say with no apology that when he came forward and told us of a free Africa, and nationalism for the Africans at home and abroad,—that caused the other races to respect us as a people. Through the vision of Marcus Garvey also sprung up the U.N.I.A.,—yet still you, a man from the land of burnt men are talking bad about the man that is causing many a revolts the world over today. We want, and must have nationalism, before we as a race and people can get an international hearing in the line of politics, commerce, finance, employment, education, forced labour, etc. Without nationalism we are like a ship without a rudder.

Therefore, why you as a leader of the race too should count a man like Garvey among the crooks of the world? I say we of British Guiana do not like it and if you attack Garvey your work will not get as much hearing as it ought to get. I say stop criticizing Garvey and strike your blows at one side and leave Garvey on the other. For we are having a large tree to fell, and if you stop giving encouragement it would not fall at the time when we Africans are looking forward for it to fall.

I would like to be an agent for your "Negro Worker" and other good books which are showing the wrongs done to our people in Africa and all the world over. I like the Committee's work but for God Allmighty's sake leave the African's leader, the Hon. Marcus Garvey alone, the first man who put Africa before us.

I am a member of the African race.

Henry H. Kendal.

Dear Comrade Kendal:—

Thanks very much for your letter. Unfortunately space prevents us from publishing it in detail. However we are printing those parts which express your resentment of our criticism of Marcus Garvey. We are very sorry to offend you but ... we make no apologies for our uncompromising exposure of the reformist politician of Garvey, especially his capitalist utopian scheme of "Back to Africa."

We shall deal with this matter in greater detail in future issues of our magazine. In the meanwhile we would like to draw your attention to the article of comrade Briggs, published elsewhere in this issue.

We are against the reformist ideas of Garvey,—for, instead of giving some practical help to the Negro masses in their day-to-day economic struggles, especially at this time of mass unemployment and starvation—he has completely deserted the masses. Garvey has not done one single thing to help the workers in the fight for social insurance and other forms of immediate relief. Therefore it becomes more and more the duty of all class conscious revolutionary Negro workers to expose the demagogy behind which he has masqueraded for all of these years as the "great" leader.

We hope that you will write us again and continue to frankly discuss your problems with us. In the meanwhile, we would like you to give your assistance and support to the British Guiana Labour Union which is carrying on a splendid struggle in organizing the workers, especially the unemployed, for state relief, non-payment of rent and the other immediate demands of the working class. This is a practical way of helping in the struggles of the working class against British imperialism.

Don't wait until you go to Africa to begin the fight against your exploiters, for you might never get over there. You must start the fight right now. And you can only do this by joining up with the other workers in the union. You must not forget that the same British capitalists who are exploiting the masses in Africa are also exploiting you in British Guiana. And this is exactly what Marcus Garvey is not interested in, despite of all his big talk about, "Africa for the Africans, at home and abroad." He lives in ease and comfort, out of the millions of dollars which you and other misled workers have given to him. Garvey is so much at peace with the British imperialists that he does not even worry himself about trying to form a union in order to help the thousands of black men and women employed on the docks and banana plantations to get higher wages and shorter hours, much less to worry about the millions of Negroes in Africa,—thousands of miles away from Kingston. You must not permit yourself to be misled by Garvey's "radical" talk. That is exactly what he depends upon to fool the Negro masses. You must judge men not only by what they say but by their deeds and if we judge Marcus by this standard, every honest Negro can see that he is a fraud.

[e]
HOW GARVEY BETRAYED THE NEGROES
CYRIL V. BRIGGS
Negro Worker/August 15, 1932

Garveyism, or Negro Zionism, rose on the crest of the wave of discontent and revolutionary ferment which swept the capitalist world as a result of the post-war crisis.

Increased national oppression of the Negroes, arising out of the post-war crisis, together with the democratic slogans thrown out by the liberal-imperialist demagogues during the World War (right to self-determination for all nations, etc.) served to bring to the surface the latent national aspirations of the Negro masses. These aspirations were considerably strengthened with the return of the Negro workers and poor farmers who had been conscripted to "save the world for democracy." These returned with a wider horizon, new perspectives of human rights and a new confidence in themselves as a result of their experiences and disillusionment in the war. Their return strengthened the morale of the Negro masses and stiffened their resistance. So-called race riots took the place of lynching bees and massacres. The Negro masses were fighting back. In addition, many of the more politically advanced of the Negro workers were looking to the example of the victorious Russian proletariat as the way out of their oppression. The conviction was growing that the proletarian revolution in Russia was the beginning of a world-wide united movement of down-trodden classes and oppressed peoples. Even larger numbers of the Negro masses were becoming more favorable toward the revolutionary labor movement.

Distortion of National Revolutionary Movement by the Reformists

This growing national revolutionary sentiment was seized upon by the Negro petty bourgeoisie, under the leadership of the demagogue, Marcus Garvey, and diverted into utopian, reactionary, "Back to Africa" channels. There were various other reformist attempts to formulate the demands of the Negro masses and to create a program of action which would appeal to all elements of the dissatisfied Negro people. None of these met with even the partial and temporary success which greeted the Garvey movement.

The leadership of the Garvey Movement consisted of the poorest stratum of the Negro intellectuals—declassed elements, struggling business men and preachers, lawyers without a brief, etc.—who stood more or less close to the Negro masses and felt sharply the effects of the crisis. The movement represented a split-away from the official Negro bourgeois leadership of the National Association for the Advancement of Colored People which even then was already linked up with the imperialists.

The main social base of the movement was the Negro agricultural workers and the farming masses groaning under the terrific oppression of peonage and sharecropper slavery, and the backward sections of the Negro industrial workers, for the most part recent migrants from the plantations into the industrial centers of the North and South. These saw in the movement an escape from national oppression, a struggle for Negro rights throughout the world, including freedom from the oppression of the southern landlords and for ownership of the land. To the small advanced industrial Negro proletariat, who were experienced in the class struggle, the Garvey movement had little appeal.

While the movement never had the millions organizationally enrolled that its leaders claimed . . . the movement exercised a tremendous ideological influence over millions of Negroes outside its ranks.

Reflected Militancy of the Masses in Its Early Stages

The movement began as a radical petty bourgeois national movement, reflecting to a great extent in its early stages the militancy of the toiling masses, and in its demands expressing their readiness for struggle against oppression. From the very beginning there were two sides inherent to the movement: a democratic side and a reactionary side. In the early stages the democratic side dominated. To get the masses into the movement, the national reformist leaders were forced to resort to demagogy. The pressure of the militant masses in the movement further forced them to adopt progressive slogans. The program of the first congress was full of militant demands expressing the readiness for struggle.

A Negro mass movement with such perspectives was correctly construed by the imperialists as a direct threat to imperialism, and pressure began to be put on the leadership. A threat of the imperialists, inspired and backed by the leadership of the N.A.A.C.P., to exclude Garvey from the country on his return from a tour of the West Indies brought about the complete and abject capitulation of the national reformist leaders. Crawling on his knees before the imperialists, Garvey enunciated the infamous doctrine that "the Negro must be loyal to all flags under which he lives." This was a complete negation of the Negro liberation struggle. It was followed by an agreement with the Ku Klux Klan, in which the reformists catered for the support of the southern senators in an attempt to secure the "repatriation" of the Negro masses by deportation to Liberia.

Surrendered Right of Self-Determination
of Negro Majorities of U.S. and West Indies

While never actually waging a real struggle for national liberation the movement did make some militant demands in the beginning. However, these demands were soon thrown overboard as the reactionary side of the movement gained dominance. There followed a complete and shameful abandonment and betrayal of the struggles of the Negro masses of the United States and the West Indies. The right of the Negro majorities in the West Indies and in the Black Belt of the United States to determine and control their own government was as completely negated by the Garvey national reformists as by the imperialists. The Garvey movement became a tool of the imperialists. Even its struggle slogans for the liberation of the African peoples, which had always been given main stress, were abandoned and the movement began to peddle the illusion of a peaceful return to Africa.

At first giving expression to the disgust which the Negro masses felt for the religious illusions of liberation through "divine" intervention, etc., the Garvey movement became one of the main social carriers of these illusions among the masses, with Marcus Garvey taking on the role of High Priest after the resignation and defection of the Chaplain-General, Bishop McGuire. . . .

How completely the reactionary side came to dominate the movement is shown in (1) its acceptance of the Ku Klux Klan viewpoint that the United States is a white man's country and the Negro masses living here are rightfully denied all democratic rights; (2) the rejection by the leaders at the 1929 convention in Jamaica, B.W.I., of a resolution condemning imperialism. . . .

The recent decision of Garvey to sell the Jamaica properties of the organization (pocketing the proceeds) and take up his residence in Europe (far from the masses he·has plundered and betrayed), denotes a high stage in the collapse of this reactionary movement, whose dangerous ideology, bears not a single democratic trait.

Historically, however, the movement has certain progressive achievements. It undoubtedly helped to crystalize the national aspirations of the Negro masses. Moreover, the Negro masses achieved a certain political ripening as a result of their experience and disillusionment with this movement.

Before concluding, it is necessary to emphasize here that the Garvey movement, while in decline and on the verge of collapse, still represents a most dangerous reactionary force, exercising considerable ideological influence over large masses of Negroes. It will not do to ignore this movement which is most dangerous in its disintegration because of the desperate attempts being made by the national reformist leaders to maintain their influence over the Negro masses, either by saving the movement as it is or by luring the dissatisfied masses into other organizations under the control of the national reformists.

The situation affords considerable opportunity for the winning of the Negro masses away from the influence of the reformists which must be made one of the foremost tasks of the International Trade Union Committee of Negro Workers, specially in Africa and the West Indies.

[f]
OUR APPROACH
TO THE GARVEYITES
CYRIL V. BRIGGS
Harlem Liberator/September 23, 1933

In our approach to the Garveyites it is necessary to bear in mind the origin and source of the Garvey movement. Garveyism rose on the crest of the wave of discontent and revolutionary ferment which swept the capitalist world as a result of the post war crisis. The masses who joined the Garvey movement were sincerely seeking a way of struggle against imperialism, a way out of national oppression, subjugation and degradation.

Many of those who later became disillusioned with the leadership joined the revolutionary movement and have shown themselves among its best fighters. Many are today active leaders of the League of Struggle for Negro Rights.

Potentially the Garvey rank and file members are good fighters willing and ready to wage a relentless struggle to free Africa, the West Indies and the Black Belt of the Southern states from white imperialist domination and slavery . . . [But the Garveyite leaders] show political weaknesses, petty bourgeois wavering and helplessness before the sharpening attacks of the white imperialists against the Negro people.

13.
Black America
Looks at Communism

The impact of communism on Black America of the Depression period could be readily discerned in its press. Selection (a), from editor Joseph D. Bibb in his Chicago *Whip*, reflects on the social forces driving blacks to radicalism of Communist and other varieties. In selection (b), William N. Jones comments favorably on the Black Belt Republic plan in his column in the Baltimore *Afro-American*. (In 1932 Jones was an active campaigner for Communist candidates in that year's elections.) Selection (c) presents the views of six of ten leading black editors who contributed their analysis of communism to a symposium published in *Crisis*.

DuBois, editor of the *Crisis*, had a running battle with the Communists during this period. They labeled him one of the "arch race misleaders," and he in turn tabbed American Communists people of "pitiable mental equipment." In 1958 DuBois would take out membership in the Communist party of the United States. Actually, during the time he was at odds with the Communists, DuBois was far more objective and fair with them than they were with him. A 1933 DuBois analysis of "Marxism and the Negro Problem," from *Crisis,* is included here as selection (d).

[a]
RED AND BLACK
JOSEPH D. BIBB
Chicago Whip/August 1, 1931

Contrary to the conciliatory prophecies of Kelly Miller, Dean Pickens, Major Moton, Congressman DePriest, and other of our conservative leaders and erstwhile voicers of black public opinion, the overtures of the Communists and other radical political and economic groups to Negroes are not falling on deaf ears. In most of these cases, the prophecies are begotten of the wish, but the evidence to the contrary is too apparent everywhere about us to be contradicted on such slim rebuttal and words. When thousands of colored men and women gather every night of the week at the open air forums held by these radical groups in the parks and on the street corners of nearly all of our large cities to listen with rapt attention and enthusiasm to doctrines of a radical reorganization of our political and economic organization, the evidence to the contrary of the declaration that "Negroes will never take to Communist" is too strong to be ignored. When Negro miners in the coal and iron districts join in strikes and face starvation to cast their lot with the brother workers, no mere mouthing of platitudes will suffice to hoodwink the thinking masses of our people. When the enslaved and peon-ized share-croppers of the south dare bravely a certain threat of rope and faggot to follow radical leadership with organized demands for a newer and squarer deal, it fairly shouts from the house tops that the working Negro is part and parcel of the seething discontent which has swept across the entire world.

The rottenness, the injustice, the grim brutality and cold unconcern of our present system has become too irksome to the man farthest down to be longer endured in silence and pacificism. It is high time that those who would stem a revolution busied themselves in sweeping and lasting cures to the cancerous sores which fester upon our body politic and fiercely competitive society. The Communists have framed a program of social remedies which cannot fail to appeal to the hungry and jobless millions, who live in barren want, while everywhere about them is evidence of restricted plenty in the greedy hands of the few. Safety and security, peace and plenty are the things most dear to the hearts of the inarticulate lowly, and these are the things which the radicals hold out as bait to the masses, white as well as black. To argue that they cannot give them but begs the question, for the obvious answer is that our present systems HAVE not given them, and offer no promise of them.

If our two major parties would stem this rising tide of Communism, let them take steps to provide for such immediate needs as are virtually hurling the masses into the ranks of radicalism. Food, shelter and clothing, adequate employment are the only answer to the challenge of communism, not mere word of mouth denials. The demand among both black and white alike is insisting for improvement,—or change.

This editorial was unsigned.

[b]
SELF-DETERMINATION:
THE BLACK BELT REPUBLIC PLAN
WILLIAM N. JONES
Baltimore Afro-American/September 24, 1932

"Young white men and women here [White Plains, New York] working in shops and factories in New York City, discuss self determination for the Negro in what is known as the black belt of the South. By self determination these young Communists explain that wherever there is a majority of colored voters in any community city or state, that they should not only elect their own officers, but decide upon what kind government they should have.

"In their argument they point out that one of the things colored people in this country need is the administrative practice which will obliterate the inferiority complex and make them know they can construct governments as well as follow the white man's idea of government."

While this specific preachment won't be calculated to attract many voters for the Communist ticket, it is something young men and women might think about.

In this country we have been, in the main, just followers. Perhaps have not had time to be anything else. We started out following the Republican Party and to some extent we still trail the will-o-the-wisp . . .

Perhaps a wise and studied concentration of political strength would be a good thing. Perhaps the making of a unified political program, comprising the entire voting group in this country, would be a good thing. Set off to ourselves as a voting group, we could make alignments as dozens of minority groups do in European governments.

It might also be argued that such a concentrated voting population, dominating completely some state, could insure representation in both branches of the law-making bodies in Washington, become a powerful lever in close elections, and, most of all, become a practical training ground for future American citizenship.

For the working masses, however, there would be no reason to conclude that in a colored state they would fare any better than the white working class fares in white controlled states. But there would be no reason not to feel that a group of young colored radicals would not rise up to smash Negro capitalism just as white workers are trying throughout the world to smash white capitalism. Even this might be good training.

The idea of separatism, however, is not a popular one among colored people. Much that they suffer in this country has come through segregation. Marcus Garvey got kicked out of the country, not so much because he did the American act of misappropriating or squandering huge amounts of money, but because he threatened to build up a powerful Negro government somewhere in the world.

European powers have kept a choking grip on Liberia and Haiti, not merely because of the bad governments in those countries but because they feared there would really be at some time efficient and strong governments in these republics. There might come a crisis in international affairs when a few airplanes sent out from either Liberia or Haiti, might decide the outcome of a war. More than this, the white capitalistic world does not want the millions of dark-skinned people in Africa to wake up. One or two successful republics might give these exploited millions a hunch.

[c]
NEGRO EDITORS ON COMMUNISM: A SYMPOSIUM OF THE AMERICAN NEGRO PRESS
Crisis/April and May 1932

Carl Murphy, *The Afro-American,* Maryland
The Communist appear to be the only party going our way. They are as radical as the N.A.A.C.P. were twenty years ago.

Since the abolitionists passed off the scene, no white group of national prominence has openly advocated the economic, political and social equality of black folks.

Mr. Clarence Darrow speaking in Washington recently declared that we should not care what political candidates think of prohibition, the League of Nations, the tariff or any other general issue. What we should demand, Mr. Darrow said, is candidates who are right on all questions affecting the colored people. I agree with him.

Communism would appeal to Mr. Darrow if he were in my place.

Communists in Maryland saved orphan Jones from a legal lynching. They secured a change of venue from the mob-ridden Easton Shore.

They fought the exclusion of colored men from the jury, and on that ground financed an appeal of the case to Maryland's highest court. They compelled estimable Judge Duncan of Towson, Maryland, to testify that he had never considered colored people in picking jurors in his court for twenty-six years.

The Communists are going our way, for which Allah be praised.

P.B. Young, *Norfolk Journal and Guide,* Virginia
Because we recognize that throughout all ages new voices and new movements for the creation of a better social order have always been anathema to the "old guards" and the "stand-patters" of the period, it has been the policy of *The Journal and Guide* not to view Communism as a thoroughgoing, death-dealing evil but to regard it as just one of the factors in a growing world-wide ideal to improve the conditions of the under-privileged, to make government more the servant of all the people, to give the rank and file of those who labor a larger share in the

fruits of production, and to afford to all men equality before the law, and equal opportunity to work and live.

The Communists in America have commendably contended for and have practiced equality of all races, and in their many activities, have accepted Negroes into their ranks in both high and lowly positions; more, they have dramatized the disadvantages of the Negro by walking in a body out of a jim-crow Pittsburgh hospital, by aiding ejected tenement dwellers, and in industrial strikes directed by them fighting against the practice of excluding Negroes from labor unions. All these accomplishments go to the credit side for the Communists.

To the debit side must go, however, the fact that they in their efforts to "sell" Communism, have not taken into full consideration the economic dependence of the Negro race, its minority position, and the traditional aversion of the rank and file of Americans to the "blood and thunder" appeals of "revolution" and "mass action." Forgetful, they have aroused such charged feelings in many sections which make it difficult for the best of both races to get together and study and correct problems in an orderly way. Besides, because the Negro is marked racially, he becomes a ready target for anti-Communist venom whenever that develops as at Camp Hill [Alabama] and in Chicago.

The Negro is patriotic and loyal, if he is anything, and Communism has gained adherents, and will continue to do so, only because traditional American conditions with their race prejudice, economic semi-enslavement, lack of equal opportunity, and discrimination of all sorts have made the Negro susceptible to any doctrine which promises a brighter future, where race and color will not be a penalty.

These barriers to the more abundant growth of the Negro must be removed, but despite the theories behind Communism, we do not think it offers the way out for the Negro which shall be most beneficial and lasting in the long run. . . .

E. Washington Rhodes, *Philadelphia Tribune,* Pennsylvania

Whether for better or for worse, thousands of Negroes are playing with the Communists. They approach Communism, the glittering symbol of absolute equality, carefully and almost fearfully—as a child takes up a strange toy. But the evidence shows that Negroes *are* flirting with Communism. Many of them, perhaps, without understanding the deeper significance of its principles, are preaching the gospel of the "Reds."

. . . Is it not paradoxical that Negroes must seek protection under some flag other than the Stars and Stripes, the flag for which they have fought to keep flying in the cause of justice and human liberty?

The ideals of the Soviet Union of Russia have a fascinating appeal to American Negroes because they hold out a ray of hope for equality of opportunity which the present American system denies to them.

Thoughtful Negroes may reason that the philosophy and economic theories of Communism are unsound and will not obtain for them a more equitable distribution of the products of their labor, or a larger degree of justice—but a drowning man will grab at a straw.

When it is considered that equality is the theory of Communism, and that inequality is the result of the present system, it is amazing that millions of Negroes have not joined the followers of the Red flag, instead of a few thousands.

The Communists have been conducting a special drive for Negro adherents. They believe that racial prejudice makes the Negro a fertile field for the sowing of revolutionary propaganda. It will be difficult for the seeds to sprout and bring forth much fruit because of the peculiar love which Negroes have for America and American institutions—a love which transcends all human understanding.

I am told that there are more dark-skinned than white Communists in Philadelphia. If numbers mean success, then the drive for Negro members succeeded. In fact, the leaders of the movement are anxious now to prevent it from becoming a black party. This is undesirable because it is the purpose of the organizers to make the Communist party inter-racial. It is difficult to ascertain just how seriously Negroes are considering the Red movement. I doubt that many of those who are members of the "party" would participate in a revolution requiring physical violence. However, the Reds are masters of propaganda. They are painting vivid pictures of justice and equality for all men under a Communistic form of government. They went into Scottsboro and Salisbury with banners flying, condemning the persecution of Negroes. That these expressions of goodwill have had their effect in swaying Negroes is indisputable. Were not Negroes affected thereby, they would not be human.

Whether it is better for the Negro to endure his present ills or fly to others he knows not of, I am unable to say. But this one thing I know—Negroes are flirting with Communism; and if it develops into something more serious, the white American must blame himself.

Franklin M. Davis, *The Atlanta World,* Georgia

If, when the United States awoke some morning, it were suddenly discovered that everybody classed as a Negro had gone Red, it would cause an immediate change in race relations. There might be trouble for a day or so, but it would not last long. Whites, thoroughly aroused and afraid, would attempt to remove those injustices heaped upon Afro-America which cradled black Communists; for 12,000,000 souls, backed by the U.S.S.R. and possibly other jealous nations wishing secretly to wreck the United States, would be too big a group to deal with by force.

This is too remote and improbable, however, to merit serious consideration.

It is a fact that the Negro, getting the dirty end of the economic, social and political stick, finds in Communistic ideals those panaceas he seeks. Yet I believe that were our government adjusted according to Red standards, few members of this kaleidoscopic race would have sense enough to take advantage of it.

Actually, the Negro as a whole fears Communism—probably because white America has not accepted it. Some frankly believe Red promises would be forgotten were they in power, for aren't they white men too? Further: would the average, every-day white man be willing to forget his prejudices even if ruled by and imbued with Communistic ideals?

Small groups of Negroes in the South going Red have harmed themselves and others in the community. Violence and bloodshed have resulted. The defense that black Reds "started it" has been an A-1 excuse for police officials killing and wounding Negroes. Camp Hill bears this out and last year's sentiment in Alabama is proof of the damage done to race relations.

I have known personally some racial brethren going Red purely because of the chance to mingle freely with white women in the movement. Then they need no longer ogle secretly or with their personal safety threatened. Talks with a few Atlanta relatives of the Scottsboro boys showed me that Communistic friendliness, pronouncements of social equality, the use of "Mr." and "Mrs." and their treatment in Dixie as men and women instead of Negroes was what got 'em.

But I have no fear of the rainbow brotherhood going Red in wholesale numbers—at least not until white America takes long steps in that direction. This race is slow to change. It would prefer keeping its present status, no matter how low, than fly to a system, no matter what its worth, that is constantly lambasted by press and radio. Too, the Negro considers himself too dependent upon white America to take any chance at losing the crusts now thrown him. Nor is the Communistic policy of crude and noisy militancy liked by this race, for every Negro knows that what he has obtained from white men has been through diplomacy or basically intellectual campaigning.

The past two years has been a mating season for Reds with blacks, yet few of the 12,000,000 have wed. If the Communists cannot make headway amid the disgust of Negroes with our economic order by which they lose their jobs in times of industrial illness, there is hardly any chance of success when the nation rides high.

If enough of us would go Red, Okeh; when we get that way in little bunches it breathes nothing but new troubles for an already overburdened race.

Robert L. Vann, *Pittsburgh Courier*, Pennsylvania

... We have our serious doubts that the average American Negro understands communism. Communistic leaders are confused also. They think the radicalism of the present-day Negro fits him precisely for Communism. This is error. The radical Negro is nevertheless intelligent; he knows what he wants. He also knows he does not want Communism. It is significant to note that few intelligent Negroes are to be found in the Communistic movement. Almost all Negroes following Communism are being used chiefly to lend a semblance of democracy to the cause. The few intellectuals espousing the cause are no closer to the movement than the average ballyhoo man is to the circus he advertises. Communism will never make the Negro white, blue or green. In fact as long as the Negro retains his present identity his absorption is next to impossible. If the cause of Communism ever rises in power to the point of assuming government control, the Negro will be treated by his Communistic leaders then just as the Negro is treated by the Republicans and Democrats now. The Negro's hope of escape lies in a concentrated production to balance the ledger of his present consumption. To teach him to do this simple thing, the Negro perhaps needs a club more than he needs Communism.

We have no criticism of Negroes who desire to become Communists provided always they are thoroughly prepared to accept the ultimate consequences, whatever they may be.

Roscoe Dunjee, *Black Dispatch,* Oklahoma

By far, the most perplexing problem I have faced during my adult years, rests in the determination of the attitude I should assume towards Communism. For the past seven years, I am frank to say, my mind has been in virtual chaos on this important subject. Today my orientation is not complete.

I always have argued that sooner or later the poor white man here in America must come to the realization that his economic problems are wrapt up with the interests of the Negro; that the ruling class whites have subtly kept the masses of the two races apart. During the past twenty years, I have stood on many platforms and proclaimed this doctrine to mixed audiences. The mental picture I have carried of the day when the two races would sit down side by side on a basis of equality and brotherhood, has always been my rainbow.

My consternation today, however, develops out of the fact that I have at my door a poor white man who talks, acts and preaches the kind and sort of equality about which across the years I have given sanction. He wants to fight about it; he calls meetings and stages parades. Boldly he carries banners through the streets of Dixie, with inscriptions which fairly scream and say all my previous demoted citizenship must vanish. Jim Crow, segregation and anti-marriage laws, yes, everything which has hitherto separated the white and black here in America, is denounced by this poor white . . .

This same white man, who preaches brotherhood and equality, has, however, his faults as well as his virtues. With one mighty arm he draws me into his embrace, while with the other he casts bombs at our existing governmental system. His economic nostrums are anti-individualistic. Fear grips me and says: Alliance with him may cause the seldom used Negro labor unit to be boycotted; alliance with him may destroy the black man's traditional record of loyalty toward the Stars and Stripes.

What the black man's attitude should be towards this complex situation is the burning issue. Here, standing at our door is the poor white, who heretofore has constituted the major portion of the mob; who hitherto has joined with the ruling class in denying us equality and opportunity. Shall we turn our back upon the Communist entirely, because of his political notions and economic theories, or shall we join with him in wrecking the vicious social barriers, which he voluntarily expresses a desire to destroy?

Communism, as a political and economic theory, does not meet and join fully with my ideal notion of government . . .

Regardless of the foregoing viewpoint, I believe some definite course should be charted by Negro leadership with reference to Communism. I believe we are today standing on the brink of revolutionary changes in our social and racial attitudes. . . . Whatever the trend, Negro leadership should not overlook the chance to make the most of this moment.

The radical of today is the conservative of tomorrow. Ten years ago the N.A.A.C.P. was classified by many as dangerous to American institutions; so also were the Abolitionists, prior to the Civil War. In those days, motives and objectives were imputed to these two liberty loving organizations which were far from just and fair. The world has long since learned to accept and respect the brotherhood and justice in these two militant organizations. It is entirely possible that history may repeat itself. The Negro who fears the radicalism of Communism today may be classified by black leadership of another and future generation as traitors to the cause of liberty.

The important question for the Negro to decide is the method by which he may cement into lasting bonds of friendship this new relationship between the whites and blacks of America. We cannot afford to make a mistake.

Yonder stands the poor white with a bomb under his arm—yet love in his heart for me. What shall I do about it? Does that unsanitary looking human being hold within his grasp my rainbow of promise, and the power which I so sorely need? Is Communism the instrumentality through which I am to secure the racial opportunity which for years I have longed for and prayed?

Other contributors to the symposium not included here were: William M. Kelley, New York *Amsterdam News*; C. F. Richardson, Houston *Defender*; J. Alston Atkins, Houston *Informer* and *Texas Freeman*.

[d]
MARXISM AND THE NEGRO PROBLEM
W. E. B. DU BOIS
Crisis/May 1933

... There are certain books in the world which every searcher for truth must know: the Bible, the Critique of Pure Reason, the Origin of Species, and Karl Marx' "Capital."

Yet until the Russian Revolution, Karl Marx was little known in America. He was treated condescendingly in the universities, and regarded even by the intelligent public as a radical agitator whose curious and inconvenient theories it was easy to refute. Today, at last, we all know better, and we see in Karl Marx a colossal genius of infinite sacrifice and monumental industry, and with a mind of extraordinary logical keenness and grasp. We may disagree with many of the great books of truth that I have named, and with "Capital," but they can never be ignored....

The task which Karl Marx set himself was to study and interpret the organization of industry in the modern world. One of Marx's earlier works, "The Communist Manifesto," issued in 1848, on the eve of a series of democratic revolutions in Europe, laid down this fundamental proposition.

"That in every historical epoch the prevailing mode of economic production and exchange, and the social organization necessarily following from it, form the basis upon which is built up, and from which alone can be explained, the political and intellectual history of that epoch; that consequently the whole history of mankind ... has been a history of class struggles, contest between exploiting and exploited, ruling and oppressed classes; that the history of these class struggles forms a series of evolution in which, now-a-days, a stage has been reached where the exploited and oppressed class (the proletariat) cannot attain its emancipation from the sway of the exploiting and ruling class (the bourgeoisie) without, at the same time, and once and for all, emancipating society at large from all exploitation, oppression, class-distinction and class-struggles."

All will notice in this manifesto, phrases which have been used so much lately and so carelessly that they have almost lost their meaning. But behind them still is living and insistent truth. The *class struggle* of exploiter and exploited is a reality. The capitalist still today owns machines, materials, and wages with which to buy labor. The laborer even in America owns little more than his ability to work. A wage contract takes place between these two and the resultant manufactured commodity or service is the property of the capitalist.

Here Marx begins his scientific analysis based on a mastery of practically all economic theory before his time and on an extraordinary, thoroughgoing personal knowledge of industrial conditions over all Europe and many other parts of the world.

His final conclusions were never all properly published. He lived only to finish the first volume of his "Capital," and the other two volumes were completed from his papers and notes by his friend Engels. The result is an unfinished work, extraordinarily difficult to read and understand and one which the master himself would have been first to criticize as not properly representing his mature and finished thought.

Nevertheless, that first volume, together with the fairly evident meaning of the others, lay down a logical line of thought. The gist of that philosophy is that the value of products regularly exchanged in the open market depends upon the labor necessary to produce them; that capital consists of machines, materials and wages paid for labor; that out of the finished product, when materials have been paid for and the wear and tear and machinery replaced, and wages paid, there remains a surplus value. This surplus value arises from labor and is the difference between what is actually paid laborers for their wages and the market value of the commodities which the laborers produce. It represents, therefore, exploitation of the laborer, and this exploitation, inherent in the capitalistic system of production, is the cause of poverty, of industrial crises, and eventually of social revolution.

This social revolution, whether we regard it as voluntary revolt or the inevitable working of a vast cosmic law of social evolution, will be the last manifestation of the class struggle, and will come by inevitable change induced by the very nature of the conditions under which present production is carried on. It will come by the action of the great majority of men who compose the wage-earning proletariat, and it will result in common ownership of all capital, the disappearance of capitalistic exploitation, and the division of the products and services of industry according to human needs, and not according to the will of the owners of capital.

It goes without saying that every step of this reasoning and every presentation of supporting facts have been bitterly assailed. The labor theory of value has been denied; the theory of surplus value refuted; and inevitability of revolution scoffed at; while industrial crises—at least until this present one—have been defended as unusual exceptions proving the rule of modern industrial efficiency.

But with the Russian experiment and the World Depression most thoughtful men today are beginning to admit:

That the continued recurrence of industrial crises and wars based largely on economic rivalry, with persistent poverty, unemployment, disease and crime, are forcing the world to contemplate the possibilities of fundamental change in our economic methods; and that means thorough-going change, whether it be violent, as in France or Russia, or peaceful, as seems just as possible, and just as true to the Marxian formula, if it is fundamental change; in any case, Revolution seems bound to come.

Perhaps nothing illustrates this better than recent actions in the United States: our re-examination of the whole concept of Property; our banking moratorium; the extraordinary new agriculture bill; the plans to attack unemployment, and similar measures. Labor rather than gambling is the sure foundation of value and whatever we call it—exploitation, theft or business acumen—there is something radically wrong with an industrial system that turns out simultaneously paupers and millionaires and sets a world starving because it has too much food.

What now has all this to do with the Negro problem? First of all, it is manifest that the mass of Negroes in the United States belong distinctly to the working proletariat. Of every thousand working Negroes less than a hundred and fifty belong to any class that could possibly be considered bourgeois. And even this more educated and prosperous class has but small connection with the exploiters of wage and labor. Nevertheless, this black proletariat is not a part of the white proletariat. Black and white work together in many cases, and influence each other's rates of wages. They have similar complaints against capitalists, save that the grievances of the Negro worker are more fundamental and indefensible, ranging as they do, since the day of Karl Marx, from chattel slavery, to the worst paid, sweated, mobbed and cheated labor in any civilized land.

And while Negro labor in America suffers because of the fundamental inequities of the whole capitalistic system, the lowest and most fatal degree of its suffering comes not from the capitalists but from fellow white laborers. It is white labor that deprives the Negro of his right to vote, denies him education, denies him affiliation with trade unions, expels him from decent houses and neighborhoods, and heaps upon him the public insults of open color discrimination.

It is no sufficient answer to say that capital encourages this oppression and uses it for its own ends. This may have excused the ignorant and superstitious Russian peasants in the past and some of the poor whites of the South today. But the bulk of American white labor is neither ignorant nor fanatical. It knows exactly what it is doing and it means to do it. William Green and Mathew Wolf of the A.F. of L. have no excuse of illiteracy or religion to veil their deliberate intention to keep Negroes and Mexicans and other elements of common labor, in a lower proletariat as subservient to their interests as theirs are to the interests of capital.

This large development of a petty bourgeoisie within the American laboring class is a post-Marxian phenomenon and the result of the tremendous and world wide development of capitalism in the 20th Century. The market of capitalistic production has gained an effective world-wide organization. Industrial technique and mass production have brought possibilities in the production of goods and services which out-run even this wide market. A new class of technical engineers and managers has arisen forming a working class aristocracy between the older proletariat and the absentee owners of capital. The real owners of capital are small as well as large investors—workers who have deposits in savings banks and small holdings in stocks and bonds; families buying homes and purchasing commodities on installment; as well as the large and rich investors.

Of course, the individual laborer gets but an infinitesimal part of his income from such investments. On the other hand, such investments, in the aggregate, largely increase available capital for the exploiters, and they give investing laborers the capitalistic ideology. Between workers and owners of capital stand today the bankers and financiers who distribute capital and direct the engineers.

Thus the engineers and the saving better-paid workers, form a new petty bourgeois class, whose interests are bound up with those of the capitalists and antagonistic to those of common labor. On the other hand, common labor in America and white Europe far from being motivated by any vision of revolt against capitalism, has been blinded by the American vision of the possibility of layer after layer of the workers escaping into the wealthy class and becoming managers and employers of labor.

Thus in America we have seen a wild and ruthless scramble of labor groups over each other in order to climb to wealth on the backs of black labor and foreign immigrants. The Irish climbed on the Negroes. The Germans scrambled over the Negroes and emulated the Irish. The Scandinavians fought forward next to the Germans and the Italians and "Bohunks" are crowding up, leaving Negroes still at the bottom chained to helplessness, first by slavery, then by disfranchisement and always by the Color Bar.

The second influence on white labor both in America and Europe has been the fact that the extension of the world market by imperial expanding industry has established a world-wide new proletariat of colored workers, toiling under the worst conditions of 19th century capitalism, herded as slaves and serfs and furnishing by the lowest paid wage in modern history a mass of raw material for industry. With this largess the capitalists have consolidated their economic power, nullified universal suffrage and bribed the white workers by high wages, visions of wealth and the opportunity to drive "niggers." Soldiers and sailors from the white workers are used to keep "darkies" in their "places" and white foremen and engineers have been established as irresponsible satraps in China and India, Africa and the West Indies, backed by the organized and centralized ownership of machines, raw materials, finished commodities and land monopoly over the whole world.

How now does the philosophy of Karl Marx apply today to colored labor? First of all colored labor has no common ground with white labor. No soviet of technocrats would do more than exploit colored labor in order to raise the status of whites. No revolt of a white proletariat could be started if its object was to make black workers their economic, political and social equals. It is for this reason that American socialism for fifty years has been dumb on the Negro problem, and the communists cannot even get a respectful hearing in America unless they begin by expelling Negroes.

On the other hand, within the Negro groups, in the United States, in West Africa, in South America and in the West Indies, petty bourgeois groups are being evolved. In South America and the West Indies such groups drain off skill and intelligence into the white group, and leave the black labor poor, ignorant and leaderless save for an occasional demagog.

In West Africa, a Negro bourgeoisie is developing with invested capital and employment of natives and is only kept from the conventional capitalistic development by the opposition and enmity of white capital, and the white managers and engineers who represent it locally and who display bitter prejudice and tyranny; and by white European labor which furnishes armies and navies and Empire "preference." African black labor and black capital are therefore driven to seek alliance and common ground.

In the United States also a petty bourgeoisie is being developed, consisting of clergymen, teachers, farm owners, professional men and retail business men. The position of this class, however, is peculiar: they are not the chief or even large investors in Negro labor and therefore exploit it only here and there; and they bear the brunt of color prejudice because they express in word and work the aspirations of all black folk for emancipation. The revolt of any black proletariat could not, therefore, be logically directed against this class, nor could this class join either white capital, white engineers or white workers to strengthen the color bar.

Under these circumstances, what shall we say of the Marxian philosophy and of its relation to the American Negro? We can only say, as it seems to me, that the Marxian philosophy is a true diagnosis of the situation in Europe in the middle of the 19th Century despite some of its logical difficulties. But it must be modified in the United States of America and especially so far as the Negro group is concerned. The Negro is exploited to a degree that means poverty, crime, delinquency and indigence. And that exploitation comes not from a black capitalistic class but from the white capitalists and equally from the white proletariat. His only defense is such internal organization as will protect him from both parties, and such practical economic insight as will prevent inside the race group any large development of capitalistic exploitation.

Meantime, comes the Great Depression. It levels all in mighty catastrophe. The fantastic industrial structure of America is threatened with ruin. The trade unions of skilled labor are double-tongued and helpless.

Unskilled and common white labor is too frightened at Negro competition to attempt united action. It only begs a dole. The reformist program of Socialism meets no response from the white proletariat because it offers no escape to wealth and no effective bar to black labor, and a mud-sill of black labor is essential to white labor's standard of living. The shrill cry of a few communists is not even listened to, because and solely because it seeks to break down barriers between black and white. There is not at present the slightest indication that a Marxian revolution to attempt united action. It only begs a dole. The reformist pro-American far horizon. Rather race antagonism and labor group rivalry is still undisturbed by world catastrophe. In the hearts of black laborers alone, therefore, lie those ideals of democracy in politics and industry which may in time make the workers of the world effective dictators of civilization.

14.
Black Nationalism During the Depression

During the Depression years the Garvey movement, the singularly important promoter of Black Nationalism, went into headlong decline. The dispersal of the Garveyites is evaluated by *Negro World* columnist Samuel A. Haynes in selection (a).

Nationalism gained one very important convert. The principles of nationalism—black control of black communities; cultural, intellectual and economic independence from whites, etc.—were picked up by Dr. DuBois and enthusiastically described in the *Crisis*. He drew the distinction between forced segregation and voluntary separation and concluded that in a time when black institutions were everywhere suffering, there should be a special effort to support these institutions. A DuBois re-evaluation of "Segregation" in the *Crisis* is included as selection (b). A rebuttal by the NAACP's Walter White is selection (c). NAACP anger at DuBois's turning away from the integrationist goals led DuBois to resign his post in the NAACP as editor of the *Crisis*. In his letter of resignation he stated: "Today this organization, which has been great and effective for nearly a quarter of a century, finds itself in a time of crisis and change, without a program, without effective organization, without executive officers, who have either the ability or disposition to guide the National Association for the Advancement of Colored People in the right direction. . . . I have since the beginning of the Great Depression tried to work inside the organization for its realignment and readjustment to new duties. I have been almost absolutely unsuccessful. My program for economic readjustment has been totally ignored. . . ."

[a]
THE VISION AND VICTORY OF GARVEY
SAMUEL A. HAYNES
Negro World/May 6, 1933

Marcus Garvey, whose philosophy of racial solidarity and Negro auton-omy in Africa astounded the imperialists and scared the easy-going, patient, conservative Negro, can now drink deep of the cup of victory for which he paid dearly. Far, far away from the streets of Harlem and thoroughfares of American Negro life and culture, some of the very people foremost in fostering his persecution and sealing his exile from the country now find it safe to clothe Garveyism in a new name and dispense it fearlessly to a race dying because of the ineptitude of its leaders; stranded in the wilderness of American civilization because of the treachery and hypocrisy of its men of light and learning.

Garvey led the way in mass organization of Negroes; he blazed the trail in militancy; he sacrificed his freedom in one mighty effort to give to the Negro a higher emancipation. His absence from the American scene has not profited the Negro as was anticipated and heralded. The Bectons, the Father Divines, the Bishop Graces, the Moorish-Americans make no impress on the governments of the world; theirs is a program of consolation through emotional and spiritual complacency.

Garvey gave something to the Negro which neither time nor place can retrieve. Most of his enemies, particularly those of the Negro in-telligentsia, now agree that Garvey was essentially right in the funda-mentals of his program. They agree now that there can be no real freedom and independence for black men anywhere without mass ac-tion and uncompromising leadership.

Garvey erred, but his errors faded into insignificance before the concrete contributions he has made to Negro thought and culture. He gave to Negrodom a Black Philosophy, profound in depth, startling in its repercussions, inspiring in sentiment and in fact.

He brought the Negro people of the world into one family through the propagation of a program which gave birth to an international comity between them. The universality of this program bridged the chasm between Negroes everywhere.

Garvey demonstrated two things: (1) That Negroes can be organized. (2) That Negroes are eager to repose confidence in and support sincere Negro leadership.

By his uncompromising utterances, Garvey brought the Negro problem forcibly before the world.

Garvey deified black and gave Negroes a racial consciousness not before attained. When he invaded the United States he found "black" a symbol of regret, excuses, and pity; the trademark of inferiority. Garvey changed the order of things. He made "black" the symbol of honor and responsibility.

Garvey's clarion cry of "Africa for the Africans," those at home and those abroad, gave more publicity to Africa and the Negro than any similar effort since the Negro's emancipation.

Garvey sold the Negro to himself with the same zeal and enthusiasm that white Americans, Englishmen, Frenchmen, Italians and Japanese use preserving their racial identities.

His philosophy of a black culture has done much to bring the Negro into greater intimate fellowship and communion with the Motherland Africa, and with Negroes in distant lands.

Garvey, through his noble experiments, with the Black Star Line and the Black Cross Navigation and Trading Company, demonstrated the possibilities of the Race in the fields of commerce and industry. For years his organization provided honorable employment for Negro men and women. At one time there were more than 1,000 on the organization's payroll in the United States alone.

Garvey encouraged the Negro to scale the highest peak in human endeavor. He sent three delegations of black men to the League of Nations, two to the republic of Liberia. He appointed Commissioners and sent them to represent the Race in foreign lands. The gesture buoyed the Negro's self-respect and gave him a new hope, and a new vision.

Lest we forget, Garvey has not failed. Slowly but surely the mists of prejudice, jealousy, ignorance are being rolled away from the racial horizon. The American Negro's bitter experiences with the purposes of rugged Americanism, plus the sufferings he has absorbed during the depression, have served to convince him that Garvey was not, indeed, a charlatan, a devil, or a naive, but a FRIEND and COUNSELLOR, who came to serve him and his generation.

Lest we forget, Garveyism is now sweeping the lanes of Negro life everywhere; it is obscured by fictitious names and hedged in by renegades, but it is Garveyism just the same. Common gratitude, fair play, and a sense of justice demand that we give Garvey due credit for his vision and his courage to follow it through without counting the price.

[b]
ON SEGREGATION: 1
W. E. B. DU BOIS
Crisis/January 1934

The thinking colored people of the United States must stop being stampeded by the word segregation. The opposition to racial segregation is not or should not be any distaste or unwillingness of colored people to work with each other, to cooperate with each other, to live with each other. The opposition to segregation is an opposition to discrimination. The experience in the United States has been that usually when there is racial segregation, there is also racial discrimination.

But the two things do not necessarily go together, and there should never be an opposition to segregation pure and simple unless that segregation does involve discrimination. Not only is there no objection to colored people living beside colored people if the surroundings and treatment involve no discrimination, if streets are well lighted, if there is water, sewerage and police protection, and if anybody of any color who wishes, can live in that neighborhood. The same way in schools, there is no objection to schools attended by colored pupils and taught by colored teachers. On the contrary, colored pupils can by our own contention be as fine human beings as any other sort of children, and we certainly know that there are no teachers better than trained colored teachers. But if the existence of such a school is made reason and cause for giving it worse housing, poorer facilities, poorer equipment and poorer teachers, then we do object, and the objection is not against the color of the pupils' or teachers' skins but against the discrimination.

In the recent endeavor of the United States government to redistribute capital so that some of the disadvantaged groups may get a chance for development, the American Negro should voluntarily and insistently demand his share. Groups of communities and farms inhabited by colored folk should be voluntarily formed. In no case should there be any discrimination against white and blacks. But, at the same time, colored people should come forward, should organize and conduct enterprises, and their only insistence should be that the same provisions be made for the success of their enterprise that is being made for the success of any other enterprise. It must be remembered that in the last quarter of a century, the advance of the colored people has been mainly in the lines where they themselves, working by and for themselves, have accomplished the greatest advance.

There is no doubt that numbers of white people, perhaps the majority of Americans, stand ready to take the most distinct advantage of voluntary segregation and cooperation among colored people. Just as soon as they get a group of black folk segregated, they use it as a point of attack and discrimination. Our counter attack should be, therefore, against this discrimination; against the refusal of the South to spend the same amount of money on the black child as on the white child for its education; against the inability of black groups to use public capital; against the monopoly of credit by white groups. But never in the world should our fight be against association with ourselves because by that very token we give up the whole argument that we are worth associating with.

Doubtless, and in the long run, the greatest human development is going to take place under experiences of widest individual contact. Nevertheless, today such individual contact is made difficult and almost impossible by petty prejudice, deliberate and almost criminal propaganda and various survivals from prehistoric heathenism. It is impossible, therefore, to wait for the millennium of free and normal intercourse before we unite, to cooperate among themselves in groups of like-minded people and in groups of people suffering from the same disadvantages and the same hatreds.

It is the class-conscious working man uniting together who will eventually emancipate labor throughout the world. It is the race-conscious black man cooperating together in his own institutions and movements who will eventually emancipate the colored race, and the great step ahead today is for the American Negro to accomplish his economic emancipation through voluntary determined cooperative effort.

[c]
ON SEGREGATION: 2
WALTER WHITE
Crisis/April 1934

Numerous requests have been made of the National Association for the Advancement of Colored People for a statement of the position of the Association on editorials by Dr. DuBois on "Segregation" in the January and February issues of THE CRISIS. It is fitting and proper that the statement of the Secretary's position should first appear in THE CRISIS, the official organ of the Association.

Various interpretations have been placed upon Dr. DuBois's editorial, a number of them erroneous and especially the one which interprets the editorial as a statement of the position of the N.A.A.C.P. The historic position of the N.A.A.C.P. has from the date of its foundation been opposed to segregation. Dr. DuBois's editorial is merely a personal expression on his part that the whole question of segregation should be examined and discussed anew. There can be no objection to frank and free discussion on any subject and THE CRISIS is the last place where censorship or restriction of freedom of speech should be attempted. I wish to call attention to the fact that the N.A.A.C.P. has never officially budged in its general opposition to segregation. Since Dr. DuBois has expressed his personal opinion why this attitude might possibly have to be altered I should like to give my personal opinion why I believe we should continue to maintain the same attitude we have for nearly a quarter of a century, but I repeat that what I am about to say is merely my personal opinion just as Dr. DuBois's editorial expressed his personal opinion.

Let us put aside for the moment the ethical and moral principles involved. It is my firm conviction, based upon observation and experience that the truest statement in the January editorial is:

> "there is no doubt that numbers of white people, perhaps the majority of Americans, stand ready to take the most distinct advantage of voluntary segregation and cooperation among colored people. Just as soon as they get a group of black folk segregated, they use it as a point of attack and discrimination."

It is for this very reason that thoughtful colored people will be opposed to following the advice that "groups of communities and farms inhabited by colored folk should be voluntarily formed" where they involve government-financed and approved arrangements like the Homestead Subsistence projects.

It is unfortunate that Dr. DuBois's editorial has been used, we learn, by certain government officials in Washington to hold up admission of Negroes to one of the government-financed relief projects. Protests have been made to Mrs. Roosevelt and others by the N.A.A.C.P. against such exclusion. Plans to admit Negroes as a result of the protest are being delayed with the editorial in question used as an excuse for such delay.

To accept the status of separateness, which almost invariably in the case of the submerged, exploited and marginal groups means inferior accommodations and a distinctly inferior position in the national and communal life, means spiritual atrophy for the group segregated. When Negroes, Jews, Catholics or Nordic white Americans voluntarily choose to live or attend church or engage in social activity together, that is their affair and no one else's. But Negroes and all other groups must without compromise and without cessation oppose in every possible fashion any attempt to impose from without the establishment of pales and ghettoes. Arbitrary segregation of this sort means almost without exception that less money will be expended for adequate sewerage, water, police and fire protection and for the building of a healthful community. It is because of this that the N.A.A.C.P. has resolutely fought such segregation, as in the case of city ordinances and state laws in the Louisville, New Orleans and Richmond segregation cases; has opposed restrictive covenants written into deeds of property, and all other forms, legal and illegal, to restrict the areas in which Negroes may buy or rent and occupy property.

This principle is especially vital where attempts are made to establish separate areas which are financed by moneys from the federal or state governments for which black people are taxed at the same rate as white. No self-respecting Negro can afford to accept without vigorous protest any such attempt to put the stamp of federal approval upon discrimination of this character. Though separate schools do exist in the South and though for the time being little can be done towards ending the expensive and wasteful dual educational system based upon caste and color prejudice, yet no Negro who respects himself and his race can accept these segregated systems without at least inward protest.

I cannot agree with the statement made by Dr. DuBois in the February CRISIS that the N.A.A.C.P. opposed the establishment of the Veterans' Hospital of Tuskegee "although it is doubtful if it would have opposed such a hospital in the North." The N.A.A.C.P. did oppose, and successfully, the recent attempt to establish a segregated Veterans' Hospital at Chester, Pennsylvania. It was the feeling of many of us then and to now that the fight should be made for the acceptance of Negro physicians, specialists and nurses on the basis of equality to the staffs of *all* Veterans' Hospitals rather than to ask for jim-crow hospitals.

Nor can I agree that the failure of the citizens of Philadelphia to resist more persistently, intelligently and militantly the establishment of a partial system of elementary Negro schools is necessarily approval of the segregation which has been established. This opening wedge will undoubtedly result in more segregation in schools and other public institutions unless aggressively fought. Like cancer, segregation grows and must be, in my opinion, resisted wherever it shows its head.

It is admittedly a longer and more difficult road to full and unrestricted admission to schools, hospitals and other public institutions, but the mere difficulty of the road should not and will not serve as a deterrent to either Negro or white people who are mindful not only of present conditions but of those to which we aspire. In a world where time and space are being demolished by science it is no longer possible to create or imagine separate racial, national or other compartments of human thought and endeavor. The Negro must, without yielding, continue the grim struggle *for* integration and *against* segregation for his own physical, moral and spiritual well-being and for that of white America and of the world at large.

III.

Economic Issues

15.
Blacks and the
Trade Union Movement

With the coming of the New Negro era, blacks found themselves increasingly faced with the issue of how to relate to trade unions. The migrations had brought blacks to the city strongholds of organized labor. The American Federation of Labor was traditionally anti-black. Only a handful of its affiliated unions allowed blacks to be members on an equal basis with whites; others allowed blacks to join special segregated locals; and a large percentage of AFL unions excluded blacks entirely. A number of AFL unions had initially been part of the old Knights of Labor, but broke away from that integrated union movement expressly for the purpose of creating all-white unions. The racism of the AFL is the subject of selection (a), a 1918 article in the *Crisis* by DuBois.

An integrated arm of the labor movement was the Industrial Workers of the World, founded in 1905. Black and white were treated equally throughout the IWW, even in its attempts at organizing in the Deep South. The IWWs were Anarcho-Syndicalists, believing that the State would be abolished and all society would eventually be run by unions of laborers federated in "One Big Union," the IWW. New Negro militants enthusiastically endorsed the IWW in the *Messenger,* the *Crusader* and the *Challenge.* Selection (b) is a call to join the IWW run in the *Messenger.* The most successful IWW union in the United States was the Marine Transport Workers organization in Philadelphia. Nearly half of this longshoremen's union's members were black. The IWW suffered mob violence and government repression and the MTW was inundated by job requests from out-of-work IWW members on the West Coast, as well as demands for relief funds for other IWW unions. MTW leader Ben Fletcher comments, rather ungraciously, on this situation in selection (c). (Fletcher was a top official in the IWW, the one black on its executive board, and one of over a hundred IWW leaders imprisoned after World War I on Criminal Syndicalism charges.)

The reluctance of many unions to open their membership to blacks created situations where the employers used blacks as scab labor during strikes. This problem is discussed by Robert S. Abbott in selection (d) from his Chicago *Defender*. A solution to union discrimination, proposed periodically during the 1920s and 1930s, was the creation of a special black trade union organization to watchdog other unions and how they treated blacks. Such a proposal, from the *Messenger*, is selection (e).

The Brotherhood of Sleeping Car Porters, founded in 1925, was the most widely discussed of a number of black unions created during the New Negro era. For BSCP head A. Philip Randolph this union was to be an example for all black workers of the value of trade unions. As shown in selection (f) from the *Messenger*, Randolph depicted the union porter as a new man with a new-found dignity. Although the union was not set up exclusively for blacks, it was almost exclusively black because virtually all porters were black. The Pullman Company tried the divide-and-conquer tactic of hiring Filipinos as scab porters, hoping to play one group off against the other in the manner so often used to divide black and white labor. In selection (g), from the *Black Worker*, Randolph reflects on the problems of Filipino porters and his union.

Selection (h) from *Opportunity*, the National Urban League monthly, describes the situation for black workers in Los Angeles and looks at black and Mexican-American relationships in industry. (Charles S. Johnson obtained a doctorate from the University of Chicago in 1917, became the director of research and publicity for the Urban League, and edited *Opportunity*. He is the author of numerous sociological works.)

[a]
THE BLACK MAN AND THE UNIONS
W. E. B. DU BOIS
Crisis/March 1918

I am among the few colored men who have tried conscientiously to bring about understanding and co-operation between American Negroes and the Labor Unions. I have sought to look upon the Sons of Freedom as simply a part of the great mass of the earth's Disinherited, and to realize that world movements which have lifted the lowly in the past and are opening the gates of opportunity to them today are of equal value for all men, white and black, then and now.

I carry on the title page, for instance, of this magazine the Union label, and yet I know, and every one of my Negro readers knows, that the very fact that this label is there is an advertisement that no Negro's hand is engaged in the printing of this magazine, since the International Typographical Union systematically and deliberately excludes every Negro that it dares from membership, no matter what his qualifications.

Even here, however, and beyond the hurt of mine own, I have always striven to recognize the real cogency of the Union argument. Collective bargaining has, undoubtedly, raised modern labor from something like chattel slavery to the threshold of industrial freedom, and in this advance of labor white and black have shared.

I have tried, therefore, to see a vision of vast union between the laboring forces, particularly in the South, and hoped for no distant day when the black laborer and the white laborer, instead of being used against each other as helpless pawns, should unite to bring real democracy in the South.

On the other hand, the whole scheme of settling the Negro problem, inaugurated by philanthropists and carried out during the last twenty years, has been based upon the idea of playing off black workers against white. That it is essentially a mischievous and dangerous program no sane thinker can deny, but it is peculiarly disheartening to realize that it is the Labor Unions themselves that have given this movement its greatest impulse and that today, at least, in East St. Louis have brought the most unwilling of us to acknowledge that in the present Union movement as represented by the American Federation of Labor, there is absolutely no hope of justice for an American of Negro descent.

Personally, I have come to this decision reluctantly and in the past have written and spoken little of the closed door of opportunity, shut impudently in the faces of black men by organized white working-men. I realize that by heredity and century-long lack of opportunity one cannot expect in the laborer that larger sense of justice and duty which we ought to demand of the privileged classes. I have, therefore, inveighed against color discrimination by employers and by the rich and well-to-do, knowing at the same time in silence that it is practically impossible for any colored man or woman to become a boiler maker or book binder, an electrical worker or glass maker, a worker in jewelry or leather, a machinist or metal polisher, a paper maker or piano builder, a plumber or a potter, a printer or a pressman, a telegrapher or a railway trackman, an electrotyper or stove mounter, a textile worker or tile layer, a trunk maker, upholsterer, carpenter, locomotive engineer, switchman, stone cutter, baker, blacksmith, boot and shoemaker, tailor, or any of a dozen other important well-paid employments, without encountering the open determination and unscrupulous opposition of the whole united labor movement of America. That further than this, if he should want to become a painter, mason, carpenter, plasterer, brickmaker or fireman he would be subject to humiliating discrimination by his fellow Union workers, and be deprived of work at every possible opportunity, even in defiance of their own Union laws.

If, braving this outrageous attitude of the Unions, he succeeds in some small establishment or at some exceptional time at gaining employment, he must be labeled as a "scab" throughout the length and breadth of the land and written down as one who, for his selfish advantage, seeks to overthrow the labor uplift of a century.

[b]
BLACKS NEED THE I.W.W.
A. PHILIP RANDOLPH and CHANDLER OWEN
Messenger/July 1919

The I.W.W. is the only labor organization in the United States which draws no race or color line. It deals chiefly, too, with unskilled labor and most Negroes are unskilled laborers. They stand on the principle of industrial unionism, which would necessarily include, in its organization, any Negroes in an industry. For instance, the Brotherhood of Railway Trainmen has in its organization, the conductors, firemen, engineers, and switchmen. Negroes are not permitted to join, notwithstanding the fact that there are 149,000 Negroes engaged in the transportation work. The I.W.W. would include those 149,000 Negroes who have the power, by stopping their work, to tie up the railroads as completely as the Big Four Brotherhoods could. If the Negroes stopped loading the cars, repairing the track and producing the materials which are necessary for transportation, the engineers would have nothing to carry, but the Big Four Brotherhoods are so highly American that they are shot through with race prejudice which blinds them to their enlightened self-interest.

There is another reason why Negroes should join the I.W.W. The Negro must engage in direct action. He is forced to do this by the Government. When the whites speak of direct action, they are told to use their political power. But with the Negro it is different. He has no political power. Three-fourths of the Negroes in the United States are disfranchised. Over 2,000,000 Negro men pay taxes but can not vote. Therefore, the only recourse the Negro has is industrial action, and since he must combine with those forces which draw no line against him, it is simply logical for him to throw his lot with the Industrial Workers of the World. Nor do the Negroes need to bother about the abuse heaped on the I.W.W. Most of it is lies told by their opponents, just as the opponents of the Negroes lie about them. Again it needs to be noted that most of the forces opposed to the I.W.W. are also opposed to the Negroes; John Sharp Williams, Vardaman, Hoke Smith, Thomas Dixon, D. W. Griffith—who produced The Birth of a Nation— and practically all the anti-Negro group, are opposed to the I.W.W. Now, as a general proposition and principle, if we found John Sharp Williams, Vardaman, Hoke Smith, Thomas Dixon, and D. W. Griffith opposed to anything, we should be inclined to accept it on its face without an examination. And Negroes can not afford to allow those Southern bourbons and race-prejudiced crackers, together with their hand-picked Negro leaders, to choose for them the organizations in which we shall go. The editors of the Messenger have made a thorough study of the economic and social problems in the United States. We know the history of labor organizations. We know their record on race questions. We have compared them carefully. We know that the American Federation of Labor is a machine for the propagation of race prejudice. We, therefore, urge the Negroes to join their international brothers, the Industrial Workers of the World, the I.W.W.

Originally entitled "Negroes Should Join the I.W.W."

[c]
I.W.W. NEEDS ITS BLACK-LED UNION
BEN FLETCHER
Messenger/June 1923

During the month of May, 1913, the Longshoremen of Philadelphia went on strike and re-entered the Labor Movement after an absence of 15 years. A few days after their strike began against those intolerable conditions and low wages always imposed upon the unorganized workers, representatives of both the Marine Transport Workers' Union of the I.W.W. and the International Longshoremen's Union of the A.F.L. got before them and presented their various arguments favoring the Philadelphia Longshoremen's affiliation. At a mass meeting they made their choice, deciding to organize into the IWW and by May 20th had become an integral part of that organization.

After nine years' identification with the I.W.W. they have been forced to sever their connections with that organization in order to prevent the annihilation of their local autonomy by that unreasonable and inefficient Centralism that has grown upon the I.W.W. since 1916. Since that year innumerable assaults have been made by both the Central Administration of the Marine Transport Workers and the Central Administration of the I.W.W. upon their right to determine the local administration of the Union's affairs. Unacquainted in a practical way with the problems arising from a job-controlling organization, numbering 3,000 members; "Foot Loose Wobblies" from the I.W.W. Western jurisdiction, by abusing the I.W.W. Universal Transfer System, sought to (and sometimes succeeded) acquire a determining voice and vote on any question relating to Local Job or Financial matters.

Repeatedly the I.W.W. General Administration has attempted to force the Philadelphia Marine Transport Workers' Union to remit to the Marine Transport Workers' Central office, weekly, all net income balances above $100 and to confine all expenditures to those "permitted." Needless to state the organization consistently refused to do so. Last Fall the "Foot Loose Wobblies" succeeded in stampeding the Union into an insane attempt to wrest from the U.S. Shipping Board and Private Steamship and Stevedoring Interests the 44-hour week single handed. Immediately upon the collapse of the strike a representative of the I.W.W.'s General Administration appeared before a regular business meeting of the Philadelphia Longshoremen and delivered the following ultimatum: "You must strictly comply with the Constitution of the I.W.W. and remit all funds except a $100.00 or so from now on to the Central Office, or by the authority vested in the General Executive Board your charter will be annulled and your funds seized."

Pursuant to a motion under new business, steps were taken immediately to safeguard all property and funds of the Union. Last month (April) the organization of the Longshoremen in Philadelphia became a duly chartered Independent Union, known as the Philadelphia Longshoremen's Union. As heretofore it will embrace in One Union any and all workers engaged in the Marine Transport Industry.

The history of the Philadelphia Longshoremen's connection with the I.W.W. is one of unswerving loyalty to its fundamental principles. Some have died while hundreds of others have been jailed as its standard bearers in order to vindicate its cause. At no time during this connection was it necessary to appeal for outside aid to meet the expense incurred in defending its jailed militants. Into the coffers of the I.W.W. the Philadelphia Longshoremen dumped $50,000 in per capita tax alone during their affiliation, organization assessments, relief, defense and miscellaneous contributions in proportion.

Notwithstanding, the I.W.W. was not able in that period of time with that amount of finance at their disposal to organize one supporting job control port. The Philadelphia Longshoremen are of the opinion that they and they alone can rebuild their organization, just as it was they and they alone who did the trick in the past. They are confident that the organizing of the waterfront workers strictly upon the basis of and in conformity with their class interests will eventually overcome all the slander, baseless charges and race baiting now being propagated with avidity by those who were once loudest in their praise and boast of our power and righteousness.

Originally entitled "Philadelphia Waterfront's Unionism/The Philadelphia Longshoremen Become an Independent Union." Mr. Fletcher was identified by *The Messenger* as "the most prominent Negro Labor Leader in America."

[d]
BLACKS AND TRADE UNIONS
ROBERT S. ABBOTT
Chicago Defender/March 26, 1921

The air is rife with rumors of a strike in the packing industries. It is to be hoped that it is merely rumor. We cannot imagine a situation more fraught with ugly possibilities than a strike in this quarter, and yet if such a thing should come to pass public sentiment would be strongly on the side of the strikers. The packers, not content with reducing the wages of their employees, went a step farther by lengthening the hours of employment. While there may have been some shadow of excuse for wage reduction, due to the readjustment to be expected in all lines of industry at this time, we are at a loss to understand why further sacrifices should be demanded by exacting a ten-hour day. . .

There is another phase to the situation which cannot be overlooked, and that is the possibility of recurring race troubles. Many of our people are employed at the yards. They are not members of the union and will not be inclined to leave their employment. The fear of being supplanted by white workers will hold them at work. Naturally, they will become targets of pickets and strike sympathizers while going to and from their employment. Clashes under such circumstances are inevitable. . . .

We have not forgotten some past experiences with labor leaders. A few years ago the Colored waiters union inaugurated a strike against Chicago restaurants in which they were employed. They had received the most flattering promises of help from the white union leaders. Did they get it? Not by a jugful. The Colored waiters not only lost the strike and their position, but were forced to see their places taken by white union waiters. It is not difficult therefore to understand the reluctance of the Colored brothers to follow the union leaders in a walkout.

[e]
A UNITED NEGRO TRADES
A. PHILIP RANDOLPH and CHANDLER OWEN
Messenger/July 1923

The problems of the Negro worker are increasing, not diminishing. In and out of the labor movement, the element of race twists, contorts and distorts the Negro workers' relationships to white worker and employer alike. So distressingly menacing is the Negro-white-worker-equation to-day that it is becoming increasingly imperative that some comprehensive work of education and organization be instituted with a view to bringing about a greater measure of mutual understanding and co-operation where now exist bitterness, distrust, hatred and suspicion on the part of both races. While out of the unions, Negroes complain against the bars erected by certain unions against their joining. After they join the unions, they still complain about race prejudice within the unions. Still there is no machinery which can be set in motion either to get the Negroes in the unions that are out or to see that those who are in get justice both from the point of view of getting jobs in their trade and of being elected officials in their unions. If the Negro workers are to prepare themselves for the more serious business of workers' control of industry, which the signs of the times indicate is gradually approaching, they must receive the rigid discipline of self-government which only the union activities afford. Thus to the end of creating and stimulating in the Negro worker a larger, more active and substantial interest in the principles, policies, and tactics of the Labor Movement in general; and of generating a greater concern in the Negro union member in the practical work and struggles of his union, an organization known as the United Negro Trades should be formed.

Especially is such a piece of machinery in the Labor Movement necessary during the tremendous exodus of Negro workers, north, east and west. Only a very few unions are doing anything to organize the Negro workers in their trades. Still the Negro workers are pouring into the various industries daily, weekly and monthly by the hundreds and thousands. Without the work of such an organization, race riots are bound to flare up, especially when an industrial depression comes which creates a sullen army of white and black unemployed competing for the same jobs. Such an organization should conduct widespread propaganda among white and Negro workers, pointing out that the employers are robbing both without regard to race; that race prejudice is an injury to the worker and a benefit to the bosses. It should also issue pamphlets, booklets and manifestoes on the vital relations between the black and white workers on local, national and international problems. It should encourage, advocate and foster the formation of independent Negro unions only when the white unions deny Negro workers a union card. In short, the United Negro Trades should be to the Negro worker what the United Hebrew Trades and the Italian Chamber of Labor are to the Jewish and Italian workers, respectively. It should seek the affiliation of Negro workers in all unions, and supply the necessary intelligent leadership for their guidance and protection, education and organization.

This article was printed as an (unsigned) editorial.

[f]
THE NEW PULLMAN PORTER
A. PHILIP RANDOLPH
Messenger/April 1926

A new Pullman porter is born. He breathes a new spirit. He has caught a new vision. His creed is independence without insolence; courtesy without fawning; service without servility. His slogan is: "Opportunity not alms." For a fair day's work, he demands a fair day's wage. He reasons that if it is just and fair and advantageous for the Pullman Company to organize in order to sell service to the traveling public, that it is also just and fair and advantageous for the porters to organize in order to sell their service to the Pullman Company; that if it is to the best interests of the Pullman Conductors to form an organization of, by and for themselves, it is to the best interests of the Pullman porters to form an organization of, by and for themselves. . . .

The new Pullman porter is a rebel against all that the "Uncle Tom idea suggests. The former possesses the psychology of let well enough alone." The latter that of progressive improvement. The former relies upon charity and pity; the latter upon his intelligence, initiative and thrift. The old time porter is afflicted with an inferiority complex; the new porter logically takes the position that a man's worth in society is not the result of race, color, creed or nationality; but that a man's worth is based upon the quality of his service to society.

The old time porter assumed that a clownal grin or a "buck and wing" was a necessary part of the service in order to extract a dime tip from an amused and oft-times a disgusted passenger; whereas, the new porter believes that intelligence and dignity and industry are the chief factors in service of quality and value. As a service agent, the new porter seeks to anticipate the desires of his passengers with a view to making their travel ideal. He realizes that his service is a representative form of salesmanship for the Company to the public, and for himself to the Company and the public. His work is not alone regulated by the mechanical requirements of the service, but out of his rich and full experience, he is ever formulating new and higher forms of service. Many constructive and practical ideas lie in the heads of porters who are reluctant to reveal them because they feel that they neither get the proper appreciation or reward from the Company for them. A just wage stimulates the employees to give their best to their employer; it develops a larger interest in the job and a joy in performing a high type of workmanship.

The new porter is not amenable to the old slave-driving methods, his best service is secured through an appeal to his intelligence. Just as he demands fairer treatment than the old time porter, for the same reason, he gives a higher type of service. Just as he rejects charity and pity on the grounds that he is a man, and doesn't need such, so he refuses to make excuses, but performs his duties in accordance with the requirements of efficient service.

His object is not only to get more wages, better hours of work and improved working conditions, but to do his bit in order to raise and progressively improve the standard of Pullman service. The new Pullman porter takes the position that his ability to render the Company increased productive efficiency can only result from his increased physical, moral and mental efficiency, which rests directly upon a higher standard of living, which in turn, can only be secured by a higher, regular income. His insistence upon a regular, living wage is based upon the fact that not only is the tipping system morally unjustifiable, but because tips fluctuate violently in amounts, from month to month, and a porter is for ever uncertain as to how to regulate his household affairs, since he cannot definitely plan on how much money he can spend above his meager wage of $67.50 a month, on his wife's clothing, furniture for his home, or his children's education. No other group of workers are required to work under such distracting uncertainty. Of course, the reason is that they are organized.

The new Pullman porter believes in organization and is wont to convince the Company and the traveling public that the Brotherhood will be a distinct asset to the Pullman industry in the practical and efficient handling of service and personnel problems. He is cognizant of the fact that the security and well-fare of the porters are bound up with the steady, continued and sustained progress of the Pullman industry. He is confident that his experience in the service equips, adapts and furnishes him with a peculiar and unique type of training and knowledge which no other employee possesses, and, therefore, renders him highly capable of giving constructive cooperation to the Company which will reflect itself in better service, and, hence better business.

The new porter is not a Communist, but a simple trade unionist, seeking only to become a better and a more useful citizen by securing a higher standard of living and preserving his manhood.

The new porter is not a slacker either on the job or in his organization. He is not content to consume the fruits that the hands of others produce. He is willing and ready to shoulder his share of the responsibility in making conditions better for the porters in particular and the race in general. Nor does he assign his ills to the sinfullness of the officials of the Pullman Company, but to his own failure to sense his rights, duties and power to right them.

The new porter recognizes the necessity of cooperating with the Pullman conductor, since both are workers for the same employer whose policy is to pit one against the other in order to keep them at logger-heads. Each can get more through cooperation; both will be exploited the more should they permit themselves to be deceived by the Company into believing that their interests are opposed. Though they accidentally belong to different races, they belong to the same class.

The new porter is not flattered by the claim that he has a monopoly on a job which does not yield him a decent living. He maintains that a fuller consideration of the relation of wages to production costs will show wage rates accompanied efficient management, lower production costs, higher production efficiency and a higher type of workmanship.

Higher production efficiency is reflected in lower selling prices which makes possible service to a larger group of consumers, and a consequent larger volume of trade. The new Pullman porter contends that low wages encourages indolence, irresponsibility and dishonesty, and hence it is not an economical wage.

The new porter thinks hard but says little.

[g]
THE BROTHERHOOD: UNITED WE STAND
A. PHILIP RANDOLPH
Black Worker/February 1, 1930

When the Brotherhood began in 1925, Perry W. Howard then United States Assistant Attorney . . . said that if the porters persisted in organizing a union, the Company would place Filipinos on the cars. He cited this as a grave and ominous warning with the evident intention of frightening the porters away from the Brotherhood. Shortly afterward . . . a few Filipinos were placed on the Club Cars, and probably one or two had already been placed in the service. It is not because the Company loves Filipinos any more than it does Negroes, but because it found it convenient to use the Filipinos as a whip of intimidation over the porters to scare them away from a bonafide organization. We wish it understood that the Brotherhood has nothing against Filipinos. They have been used against the unionization of Pullman porters just as Negroes have been used against the unionization of white workers. The Brotherhood is interested in the organization of everybody on the Pullman cars who falls within the class of service which comes under the jurisdiction of the Union. We will take in Filipinos as members just as readily as we will anybody else who happens to be doing the work of Pullman porters. We want our Filipino brothers to understand that it is necessary for them to join the Brotherhood in order to help secure conditions and wages which they too will benefit from. While they have been put on the cars in violation of seniority rights, so long as they are there, they must be organized. Besides, just as the Company took the Pullman porters off some of the Club Cars and put Filipinos on, so when it feels disposed, will kick the Filipinos off and put the porters on again. The only security of the Filipinos as well as the Negro Pullman porters is organization in one common union, fighting for one common objective, namely, more wages, a 240 hour month and humane working conditions.

Originally entitled "The Brotherhood and the Filipinos," this was an (unsigned) editorial.

[h]

"INSTINCTS" IN INDUSTRY: BLACK AND CHICANO IN L.A.
CHARLES S. JOHNSON
Opportunity/June 1927

A recent survey of the industrial status of Negroes in Los Angeles, California, by the Department of Research and Investigation reached 456 plants of widely varying character and 23 unions. Equally as interesting as any of the figures on Negro inclusion in industry, skill, wages and comparative efficiency, are the various configurations of policy, in each case declared to be founded upon the same racial instincts.

The most frequently encountered policy was one based upon the belief that "Negro and white workers will not 'mix.' " They did "mix," however, in over 50 of the plants studied. In certain plants where Mexicans were regarded as white, Negroes were not allowed to "mix" with them; where Mexicans were classed as colored, Negroes not only worked with them but were given positions over them. In certain plants Mexicans and whites worked together; in some others white workers accepted Negroes and objected to Mexicans; still in others white workers accepted Mexicans and objected to Japanese. White women worked with Mexican and Italian women, but refused to work with Negroes. Mexicans and Negroes worked under a white foreman; Italians and Mexicans under a Negro foreman; Mexicans were in some places refused entirely because of plant policies against "mixing." In a hospital Negro nurses attended white patients, but were segregated from white nurses; in a manufacturing plant white workers refused to work with Negroes, but worked under a Negro foreman. Brick manufacturing was declared too hot and dusty for Negroes, yet the Negroes were reputed to be the best brick workers and were given a better scale of wages than Mexicans; peoples from southern climates were regarded as better adapted to work in the presence of heat, and the Consolidated Ice Companies, however, found the Mexicans best fitted to handling and storing ice. Because white elevator men and attendants in a department store disturbed the morale of the organization by constant chatting and flirtations with the salesgirls, Negro men were brought in to take their places and morale was restored, in spite of the fears that the races would not "mix."

II

Labor union practice merely traced the pattern of plant practice. Negroes were admitted freely when they were a menace to white workers, and when it was conceded that they held distinctly favorable positions with employers. The bricklayers were indifferent to Negro membership and refused to "mix" with them until they discovered that Negro bricklayers were "working independently for whatever wages they could get." The Asbestos workers bar Negroes, Mexicans and Italians. These are the three reasons they give: "Negroes cannot stand the heat of the work"; "There are no Negroes in the trade"; and "if we begin mixing the races they will get all of the good jobs." The Iron workers are certain that their work is "too dangerous for Negroes," besides, the work pays well. So they are kept out. On the other hand Negro musicians are readily sought by many unions. In these days when Negro musicians are liked as well by the public and frequently given preference over white musicians, the urge to preserve working standards for all musicians disregards many of the otherwise insistent "instincts." The white painters could not have Negroes or Mexicans in their locals, but they frequently worked for Negro contractors.

III

The fluctuations of racial feeling according to circumstance can be reduced to these generalizations. It increases when in instances of the union's assignment of work, white workers are given preference, and Negroes complain. It increases as white workers are exclusively favored by employers in work once shared by Negroes. It decreases when the question of job assignment is not present and the membership of Negroes is essential to the success of the white members. It appears on first contact where Negroes are taken into a trade, and disappears as members become accustomed to Negro members. It increases in unions of trades in which Negroes are given about the same chance for work as whites, on some notion of their special fitness, or on grounds of "fairness." It increases to the point that Negroes are sometimes given more than their numerical proportion of offices in locals of work in which Negro workers are given actual preference over white workers by employers.

This was an unsigned editorial.

16.
The Black
Business Community

Black capitalism never looked as promising as it did at the start of the New Negro period. Black bankers looked forward to turning profits on the savings of laborers in the war industries. As blacks flocked to northern cities, enterprising black realtors made small fortunes in renting and selling to the newcomers and by engaging in lucrative block-busting, which often included the tactic of moving a black family in and then extorting the neighboring racists for a payoff to move them out again. Black hotels did a boom business on the new arrivals; and there appeared to be good prospects for service industries catering to the black community.

The hope of the black capitalist is stated in selection (a), from Fred Moore in his New York *Age.*

In selection (b) from the *Messenger,* Randolph argues that black capitalism is doomed to failure. The *Messenger* ran numerous critiques on capitalism, all of which shared a heavy socialist polemical style. A third of the article excerpted here has been omitted because it carried only standard anti-capitalist theory rather than dealing with the black economy issue; still half of what remains is but broad theory.

Selection (c) is an excerpt from a two-part critique on black business in Chicago, in particular on the business dealings of Joseph D. Bibb and A. C. MacNeal of the Chicago *Whip.* The critique was written for the *Messenger* by Chandler Owen. The *Whip* was a notorious muckraking weekly, and its "Nosy Knows" column provides an excellent chronicle of the affairs of gangland Chicago. In discussing some of its exposés, Owen alleges the *Whip* was actually involved in crooked dealings of its own. Owen was out to discredit the *Whip* because of its anti-union stand and its acceptance of advertising from the Pullman Company at a time when that company was engaged in a trade union struggle with the Brotherhood of Sleeping Car Porters. Considering Owen's intriguing if debatable allegations, it is worth noting that on most issues the *Whip* took a militant stand. The *Whip* had been outspoken in its denunciation of the hypocrisy of the World War. Editor Bibb was a close associate of civil rights activist William Monroe Trotter of Boston and was a prominent figure in the early years of the Garvey movement in Chicago. The most spectacular of Bibb's muckraking endeavors was his campaign against discriminating businesses operating in the Chicago ghetto. He obtained, with the help of street agitators, figures on the number of blacks working in Southside stores, and also on the number employed by major industries and the telephone and electric company. Discrimination was spelled out and where possible blacks were urged to withhold patronage from these establishments. This "Don't Buy Where You Can't Work" movement proved highly successful.

Cooperative economics was a popular alternative to capitalist free enterprise. This form of economy was widely promoted in the black press, especially in the radical monthlies the *Messenger* and the *Crusader*, but also in some of the more moderate weeklies such as the New York *Age* and the Cleveland *Gazette*. In selection (d) from the Pittsburgh *Courier*, George Schuyler discusses one of the bigger cooperative movements of the 1930s, the Colored Merchants Association, which had branches in most American cities and also in the West Indies.

Selection (e) is an advertisement run regularly in the early 1920s in the *Negro World* calling upon blacks to support Garveyite businesses. Selection (f) is an advertisement in the *Messenger* for heavyweight champion Jack Johnson's Mexico Land Company. The *Messenger* and also the radical *Crusader* ran a number of ads dealing with the extension of black capitalism from the U.S. to the Third World. The emigration call in the Jack Johnson advertisement was common in these ads. As displayed in newspapers and magazine advertising there were half a dozen black shipping companies operating out of the U.S., the Caribbean, or England—a factor often overlooked in the controversy over the feasibility of Garvey's Black Star Line steamship company.

The "Don't Buy Where You Can't Work" jobs campaigns provided some of the major mass actions during the early years of the Depression. They involved the picketing and boycotting of white-owned businesses in the black community which refused to hire black workers. The movement started in Chicago in 1929, and by the mid-1930s campaigns had been conducted in almost every major city, the idea having spread without national coordination or any central organizing agency, growing spontaneously out of the dire need for employment.

The black press in general played a cautious role on the issue of the jobs campaigns. As the New York *Amsterdam News* noted with surprising candor, to have actively endorsed the campaigns could have cost "a fearful loss of advertising." Coincidentally, three weeklies that strongly endorsed local boycott movements did go out of business—the Chicago *Whip,* the New York *Interstate-Tattler,* and the *Negro World.* Selection (g) presents a call for a jobs campaign from the *Tattler.*

In addition to the jobs campaigns, the Depression spawned community mass action against evictions and for greater relief payments, and news of these actions was given broad coverage in the press. Among the many proposed actions for the hard-pressed black was the National Urban League's "Back to the Farm" movement, the idea being that during the economic crisis it might be easier for blacks to live off the land in the South than struggle on in the city. In selection (h), Robert L. Vann presents the *Courier*'s editorial views on this alternative.

[a]
BIG BUSINESS IN HARLEM
FRED R. MOORE
New York Age/March 30, 1920

The recent purchase by a Savannah banking corporation of a large plot of ground covered by eleven buildings on one of the most eligible corners in Harlem indicates the coming of big business to that humming centre of racial activities. While the transaction in real estate is important in itself, involving as it did the sum of two hundred thousand dollars, greater significance is to be attached to the fact that it signalizes the influx of outside capital from among the race to participate in the development located far from its source.

This investment of the funds of Southern investors in New York real estate is to be taken as promising good results, both for the individuals and institutions concerned in furnishing the funds, as well as for the community where the profits are to be realized. This new departure should mean the broadening and extension of business opportunities and housing facilities.

With the multiplication of real estate holdings in the hands of race owners, comes the opportunity for the use of such property in productive occupations, if only for the purpose of affording shelter to the many workers of the race gathered here from all parts of the country.

The colored people of the South are doing a wise thing in sending their capital here to work for them. Hitherto the South has sent mostly its surplus labor to the North, in search of industrial and civic opportunities. This is now being aptly supplemented by the diversion of accumulated capital to aid in furnishing the opportunities desired.

With this extension of big business, the need for a banking institution under race auspices in Harlem is accentuated. Such an institution is needed to take over the mortgages existing on the property of colored owners, as well as to encourage the habit of saving among colored workers.

Let the next move of big business in Harlem be made with an eye toward filling this need.

[b]
THE CRISIS IN NEGRO BUSINESS
A. PHILIP RANDOLPH
Messenger/March 1922

There is a crisis in business. It is national and international. It is an industrial, commercial and financial crisis. It began in the latter part of 1920. In the collapse of foreign exchange, in the closing down of factories and mines; in the restriction of credit; in wholesale lay-offs, slashing of wages and consequent widespread unemployment; in the deflation of prices, the crisis reflects itself.

No business or profession; no movement, spiritual or political has escaped the deadening blight of this worldwide economic scourge.

The present crisis followed the war, but the war was not its cause. Doubtlessly the war accelerated its rate, intensified and expanded its general effects.

As the Great War tore up ancient, historic, political kingdoms and empires by their very roots and hurled them into oblivion; so the Great World Crisis uprooted numberless financial, industrial and commercial empires and kingdoms and consigned them to the limbo of eternal obscurity. In the maelstrom of the war, the smaller nations suffered most. They were dismembered and appropriated by the larger powers, at will. With no less catastrophic ruthlessness, the small business units are torn limb from limb and, gobbled up by the great business Titans in industry, finance and trade. As out of the war a few big nations emerged with all of the world's power and control; so out of the panic a few trusts, syndicates and cartels, will emerge with the spoils of economic power and control, ready and prepared for a renewed, prolonged and more intense struggle with the forces of organized labor. In the arena of world powers, the smaller nations are building up little ententes such as Jugo-Slavia, Czecho-Slovakia and Roumania to re-enforce their position before the onward march of modern imperialism. By the same instinct of self-preservation, the petit businesses are organizing little economic ententes with a view to securing and safeguarding their trading spheres of influence. Such are the economic tendencies that stand out in bold relief in the present crisis.

So much for the nature and scope of the crisis.

What now is its cause? . . .

Its root cause is overproduction. Not overproduction in the sense that more commodities and services are produced than the people are capable of consuming; but over production as a result of the inability of those who produce to buy back what they have produced.

. . . Consequently production slackens up. For, according to good business economics, what is the use of producing more goods when the existing supply can not be sold at profitable prices. Such is the reason for the closing down of the factories, mines and shops, reducing all forms of services, etc.

. . . The small business man will fail if he does not sell his stock at a price below that which he paid for them, and certainly, he will fail if he does. The big businesses, on the other hand, find it eminently profitable to effect a more or less rapid liquidation. Their margin of operating capital is quite ample to safeguard them on a falling market. By cutting their prices below those at which the small businesses are able to sell, they drive them out of the field, thereby expanding their own economic domain. During these periods the small dealer is either destroyed entirely or he is so deeply involved in debt that he is virtually mortgaged for life and assumes the relation to the big capitalists of an economic vassal, a mere hired clerk.

Such is the process of the present panic, the full effects of whose far-reaching economic readjustments during the past year are exhibited in a new record of commercial failures throughout the country.

. . . The year's defaults were 928.8 per cent larger in number than those of 1920, in New England; 81.9 per cent greater, in the Middle Atlantic States; 186.3 per cent more numerous in the South Atlantic group; 195.5 per cent heavier, in the South Central division. . . .

In the southern district of New York 2,355 bankruptcy petitions were filed during the year. This is 852 more than in 1920, and is the largest number filed any year in a decade. . . .

Now a word about the application of these principles to Negro business.

At the outset let it be thoroughly understood that there are no peculiar economic laws that are specially adjusted for Negro business. The same causes that produce the success or failure of business run by white entrepreneurs are the causes also of the success or failure of business operated by Negroes. There are, however, certain businesses in which opportunities to succeed and the likelihood to fail are measurably increased as a result of the operation of certain crystallized customs founded upon race prejudice. Barbering and hair dressing among Negroes are instances in point. Such businesses are usually of the personal service kind.

In the main the behavior of the phenomena of Negro business is similar to that of the small business man. His turn-overs are small. His credit is small. His operating capital is always inadequate. Like most small business units of all races and nationalities, his system of accounting is bad and his management is not the best. Few far-reaching economies can be effected when a small volume of business is done. Still there are certain constant charges that are no different from those of the mammoth business enterprise. He must pay the same wages of the Trust. He is unable to contend with the organized power of labor through prolonged, expensive strikes. In short, the small business is a menace to itself and the public, because it must pay lower wages and sell at higher prices, and still its security is not assured.

Among Negro businesses the present depression has wrought havoc. Negro banks have failed all over the country. Several of his hotels and theatres have gone under. Only the more stable institutions can survive. The Negro business man finds himself hard put to the task of competing with gigantic combinations of capital—trusts who can excell him in service, price and quality.

For instance, in the retail grocery field, the small store, white or black, is driven to the wall by the great chain store corporations, such as James Butler, Atlantic and Pacific Tea Co., Daniel Reeves, etc. These stores have been selling sugar below the price at which the small grocer could buy it wholesale.

In the restaurant line, in New York, Chicago, Detroit and a few other larger cities, the Negro restauranteur finds that his field has been invaded by the chain restaurant and lunchroom corporations. These concerns buy their supplies by the tons, and sometimes by the carloads. One purchasing agent may be buying for 50 or more different stores or lunchrooms. They are serving millions of persons daily in one city. And these corporations ramify throughout a 100 or more cities. What economies can they not effect? One advertising agent is employed for a thousand or more stores. They can employ experts in every field affecting their line. Their fingers are on the pulse of the market. They know how to buy with a rising and falling market.

Not so with the small man. He is operating purely upon chance.

In Harlem, the St. Claire, the Manhattan and the Capital are all corporation chain lunches, and they are gradually capturing the field from the independent small Negro lunch and restaurant keepers. Only Tabb's Grill and Lunch has expanded since the advent of these chain lunch and restaurants into the neighborhood. But Tabb himself is adopting the chain system. He is competing with his competitors. The Pomona Bakery has also adopted the chain store system. So has the Hart 5, 10 & 25 cent store adopted the chain store plan. Most of the small Negro eating places are dying a slow death. What is true of New York is true of most of the big cities where Negroes are trying to do business on the old small unit-independent plan. The Negro groups can improve their status immensely by pooling their purchasing power.

In the insurance field Negroes are the beneficiaries of the operation of the law of race prejudice. This, of course, relates chiefly to the great life companies. The white sick and accident insurance companies are the keen competitors of the Negro companies. It can not be said that they are any superior to the Negro companies. In this field, however, the Negroes could strengthen their position immeasurably by combination. The white companies are already resorting to the merger principle. Unless the Negroes follow suit they will be forced out of the field, for the white companies will be able to give better premiums at lower prices, which is the chief inducement to a buyer. They will also be a safer investment for the Negro public, as a result of their greater power.

This is no advantage, however, which the Negro companies can not secure also.

In Banking, the Negro has lost ground as a result of the present crisis. In the future his only hope is the merger such as the white institutions are adopting everywhere. In Harlem, New York, the Chelsea Bank, one of the largest banking systems in America, has strangled every effort, on the part of Negroes, to establish a bank in this section. And it is a matter of common business knowledge that no group of people in any community can develop strong business institutions without favorable banking facilities. It is alleged by most Negro business men in Harlem that the Harlem branch of the Chelsea Bank will not accommodate Negroes with loans, despite the fact that they are depositors in the bank. Naturally, the only remedy for this is a Negro bank. A co-operative bank would be preferable.

Now a word about the remedy. As I have indicated above, the only remedies are combination and the co-operative business method. Pooling of buying power is the solvent key. Only a trust can face a trust in competition. The biggest efforts the Negroes have yet made in a business way are the Standard Life Insurance, Brown and Stevens, Bankers, the C. J. Walker and Poro, manufacturers of hair preparations, the Wage Earners Saving Bank, the North Carolina Provident and Mutual Insurance and the Nail and Parker real estate firm. All of these are doing well. They can do better if they adopt modern business methods in buying and selling and combining.

The second phase of the remedy is educational.

Besides actual economic combination in buying and selling, there must be moral and educational combination. This will take the form of business associations in the different cities such as the white chambers of commerce. They, in turn, must be linked up into a National Negro Chamber of Commerce, such as the United States Chamber of Commerce. At the same time Negro business men should join the white men's business associations when and where they can. These associations, however, must be more than social affairs for smoking and drinking. The laws, principles and facts of modern business must be discussed. Experts, in all lines, should be engaged to speak. A comprehensive educational program should be devised. Measures should be adopted for the protection and advancement of Negro business.

Combinations should be discussed. Loans devised for new ventures with the requisite safety. Methods of business ventilated. A consumers educational campaign should also be devised. No hostility should be advocated or engendered against white enterprise. This policy will fail. Only sound, modern, scientific economics will win. Race loyalty is an inconsequential and ineffective appeal. It is usually employed by the self-seeking, at the expense of the race. No Negro enterprise will succeed that is not compatible with the economic well-being of the masses of Negro consumers. And none should succeed. As between the interest of ten or more Negro business men in the community and a thousand Negro working class consumers, I stand by the worker-consumer everytime. I also stand for the unionization of the Negro workers in the Negro enterprise. For the wages of ten men working for a living are far more important than the profits of one. Furthermore, a Negro business man will pay as low wages to a Negro worker as a white business man will. As white workers organize against white employers so Negro workers must organize against Negro employers. And when white workers are working for Negro employers, they too must be unionized against the Negro employer for more wages, shorter hours and better working conditions.

My interest in this subject arises out of certain disadvantageous conditions to Negroes that are accentuated by the elements of race prejudice. We anticipate no great change in the conditions of the broad masses of working Negroes through a few successful Negro businesses. A greater development of the Negro business will afford, however, a wider opportunity to the Negro "brain worker" who is being turned out of the schools and colleges daily without hope of employment because of existing race prejudices.

Another essential form of education is the conference. The present crisis necessitates a national economic conference, in which all types of Negro business should participate. Even the great capitalist nations are adopting the conference methods for discussion of plans and policies for an economic rehabilitation. The Genoa Conference is a splendid example. Then the permanent annual convention has value. Something different from the National Negro Business League, however, is needed. It was useful at one time as a source of inspiration. That was the period of creating the desire in the Negro to do business; but today the chief need is a knowledge of method. Desire to do anything without a knowledge of the method by which one proposes to do that thing will simply lead to ruin.

In conclusion I want to add that the hope of the Negro business efforts today lies in the co-operative method which takes in the consumers.

The trust has advanced too far for the Negro to enter the fields where it controls on a purely capitalist-profit basis. Besides, the co-operative plan is more democratic. In it the consumers buy from themselves. Hence when properly run, it can not fail. In a future article, I shall discuss the co-operative and the future of Negro business.

[c]
PROBLEMS OF BLACK BUSINESS
CHANDLER OWEN
Messenger/January 1926

Chicago is a city of magnificent contrasts and extremes. It has the best and the worst. Here the richest and the poorest abound. It has the cream and the scum. It boasts an aristocracy and likewise a flotsam and jetsam of society. It has some of the best white newspapers, like the *Daily News, Tribune,* and *American,* and the worst, like *The Chicago Star.* It also has some of the best Negro newspapers, like *The Defender,* and *The Bee,* in contrast with the unspeakably poor *Chicago Whip.* . . .

For about six years colored Chicago has been bedeviled by a small, irresponsible publication edited by a man whose presumption is exceeded only by his ignorance. Publications must live off circulation and advertising—circulation usually comes from interesting news matter presented to one's readers. *The Chicago Whip* could command neither circulation nor advertising, so it thought out and presented a new policy in Negro newspaperdom; it inaugurated blackmail. . . .

The Brass Check
A few years ago Upton Sinclair wrote a little book called "The Brass Check." It dealt with the way journals were induced to publish, or to

refrain from publishing, news for pay. That pay might be direct or by the giving of advertising. *The Whip* editors have long been petty pastmasters in this putrid policy. We propose here to point out special instances of this damnable deviltry, giving names, places, and time.

Crusading Against Prostitution

Most decent people regret the conditions which have given rise to prostitution. They are also opposed to gambling, bootlegging, and general corruption. It is a popular chord one strikes when he attacks such evils. Therefore, apparently as a means of securing the support of decent, public-spirited colored people, in 1922 *The Whip* began a series of attacks on gambling houses and houses of prostitution. It will be noted that we say, "apparently." We use the word advisedly because it was only apparently. The object of the attack which began in the summer of 1922 was purely graft, blackmail and a "shake-down." In fact, Joseph D. Bibb and A. C. McNeal, in the offices of the McNeal Publishing Co. [of the *Whip*] thoroughly discussed the feasibility of attacking vice in the Second and Third Wards in the City of Chicago, and finally arrived at the decision that *The Whip* would attack every place of any note that was a vice den with the idea of a "shake-down." The few readers of *The Whip* will remember that not only was a series of articles carried in *The Whip,* but photos of the houses were published. This resulted in several hundreds of dollars passing from the hands of the Vice Lords into the coffers of *The Chicago Whip.*

First among the places attacked was "The Elite" . . . operated by Harvey Johnson, and doing business with craps and poker games and bootleg whiskey. The sum of five hundred dollars was paid into the offices of *The Chicago Whip,* then located at 3420 S. State street, said $500 being paid in the editorial room of Joseph D. Bibb to one Harold C. Thompson, who is a brother-in-law of Joseph D. Bibb. The said $500 was made in two payments.

Next to come under the hammer was the Douglass Buffet . . . alleged to be operated by Al Blum . . . This place housed more than twelve girls on the second floor, with bootleg whiskey on the first floor. Apparently, however, this dive went out of existence in a few weeks. It was still there, though, doing business in the same old way. The silence of *The Whip* was due to the changing of two hundred and fifty dollars from the hands of the Douglass Buffet management to one A. C. McNeal of the McNeal Publishing Co., which is now the Bibb-McNeal Publishing Co. This money was paid by Joe Bates, a white gangster, in the office of *The Whip*. He was directed to *The Whip* office by a Negro by the name of Klondike.

The Deer Inn, a house of ill repute, was said at that time to have been operated by Joseph G. Glasser. It paid tribute for immunity after having one write-up in *The Chicago Whip* to one A. C. McNeal in the sum of three hundred dollars. A fellow by the name of "Jew Kid," a white gangster, paid this over to McNeal around the corner, having first called up. McNeal went out and came back with the money.

An Exception

During that time there were three houses of ill repute located at the following addresses: 3617 and 3625 Indiana avenue, and 119 E. 36th place. They, too, were attacked by *The Chicago Whip*. Their owner was said to have been Al Capone, alias Al Brown, notorious Cicero, Illinois, gangster and bootlegger, who has now moved to New York. These places were attacked on several occasions, but Capone refused to give Bibb and *The Whip* any money. Instead, he threatened the lives of the publishers. And being a well-known gangster who was likely to carry out his threat, Bibb gave orders to "lie off that place," lest danger come to himself—a danger emphasized by a neat little package he received one morning containing several bullets, some of which were sticking out of a piece of cardboard cut in the shape of a heart. . . .

More Attempts at Blackmail

Even a *white* tooth was subject to *black*mail. A few years back certain dentists who advertised their crown work and bridge work on windows and billboards were listed by *The Whip* as "wild-cat dentists." These dentists had been solicited by *The Whip* and would not give "ads." *The Whip* attacked their methods and charged them with being fakes and "shake-downs." (Was that autobiography?) The little *Whip*, however, fought on until it got tired of giving the dentists free space. . . .

The Standard Life Affair

The first of 1925, when the Standard Life began to have difficulties, it was viciously attacked by *The Chicago Whip*. Do you, gentle reader, know the reason? Let us explain. Every business carries with it a certain element of risk. Herman Perry, a business genius, and a splendid business builder, had expanded the affiliated interests of the Standard Life too rapidly. To be perfectly clear, he had invested the Standard Life funds in laundries, drug stores, building and construction companies, and other enterprises. Now all these projects were perfectly feasible and practicable if times had kept normal. But like other men, white as well as colored, Perry did not foresee the World War which broke upon us suddenly. He could not have predicted the large migration of Negroes which took place with unprecedented speed, following the war's outbreak. Then, too, the war closed almost as rapidly as it began. Panic ensued. Negroes were thrown out of work. Many could not take out new insurance, while others had to drop their policies. The Standard borrowed money. It gave its stock as security. Times got harder still. The time came to pay its notes. The Standard could not meet its obligations. Unfortunately, it was in the hands of its Southern cracker enemies. When the time came to pay, true to Southern cracker principles, the Southern Life said, "Give us our money or give us the security." Southern Life took the Standard, which was the security.

Now what happened to the Standard was true of many great white companies. Sears, Roebuck Co., of Chicago, had such financial difficulties that Rosenwald had to loan them twenty million dollars. Wilson, the great packing concern, went into the hands of the receivers. The Chicago, Milwaukee and St. Paul, Ingersoll Watch Co. failed, owing different banks nearly three million dollars. . . . If the white papers had taken the same attitude toward these concerns that *The Whip* took toward the Standard, recovery would have been impossible. Instead, however, the great white publications preached sanity and optimism and poise, while New York banks loaned [funds to bail out many white companies].

Why did Bibb and *The Chicago Whip* so treacherously play the game of Southern cracker graft? This: Harry Pace had been with the Standard Life. He and Perry got into a fight, which resulted in Pace's leaving and Perry's staying. (We don't propose to pass upon the merits of the contest.) Now Pace had married Bibb's sister, a splendid woman against whom nothing should be held, even though she is Bibb's sister. Bibb took this personal sentiment as an excuse for injuring and destroying an institution which was a racial asset and which any high-minded man would have considered in the light of racial statesmanship and social vision.

A Similar Case

It is an old saying that *what is sauce for the goose is sauce for the gander*. Let us take two parallel cases. The inspiration and moving spirit of the Standard Life was Herman Perry. He was the organizer of the Standard Life and had sold a great deal of stock to colored people. The inspiration and organizer of the Black Swan Record Co. was Harry Pace, Bibb's brother-in-law. He had sold considerable stock in the Black Swan Record Co. to colored people. Among the Standard Life's difficulties must be listed the competition of big white companies like the Metropolitan, New York Life, and various local white insurance companies. They could sell a better policy at a cheaper rate. The Black Swan Record Co. met similar difficulties in trying to compete with the Victor, Columbia, and the Edison record companies. These companies could sell a better record at a cheaper price, too. Not only that, they were able to employ Pace's singers and artists by paying them higher wages and salaries.

Now both Pace and Perry were driven to the same conclusion. Pressed with obligations and debts Perry sold the Standard Life, a Negro insurance company, to the Southern Life, a white insurance company. Pressed with difficulties and debts Pace sold the Black Swan, a colored record company, to the Paramount, a white record company. Perry claimed that his deal with the Southern Life was a *merger*. Pace likewise, claimed that his deal with the Paramount was a *merger,* and those who remember will recall that the Paramount carried the name of the Black Swan in its advertising for several weeks after the deal. In each case the lion and the lamb had lain down together, but the lamb was in the lion's belly. Bibb's brother-in-law, Harry Pace, had done the very thing for which he and Bibb had severely criticised Herman Perry. If *The Whip* was so concerned about presenting all important deal transactions and enterprises to its handful of readers—why did it not analyze and present the Black Swan deal?

Originally entitled "The Neglected Truth."

[d]
ON ECONOMIC COOPERATIVES
GEORGE SCHUYLER
Pittsburgh Courier/November 8, 1930

... There is only one thing that can immediately get the Negro group
out of the barrel and that is consumer's cooperatives, the building up of
a Negro co-operative democracy within the shell of our present capitalist system ... Briefly, consumers cooperation means the organization
of ultimate consumers for the purposes of supplying themselves with
the necessities of life—the things they consume—by their own efforts
and management and without paying tribute to the retailer. Such societies are organized on the basis of one vote for each member regardless
of the number of shares owned. The surplus savings or profits, instead
of going to some one individual, are either put back into the business,
used for social service to the group, divided on the basis of purchases
made, or (and this rarely) divided on the basis of shares held. The
purpose of the cooperative is first and last to serve its members whereas
the capitalistic business is concerned with accumulating profits for its
owners ... In a cooperative system everybody owns private property.

Co-operative democracy means a social order in which the mills,
mines, railroads, farms, markets, houses, shops and all the other necessary means of production, distribution and exchange are owned cooperatively by those who produce, operate and use them.

Whereas the Socialists hope to usher in such a Utopia society by the
ballot and the Communists hope to turn the trick with the bullet, the
co-operator (who is really an Anarchist since the triumph of his society
will do away with the state in its present form—and I am an Anarchist)
is slowly and methodically doing so through legal, intelligent, economic
co-operation or mutual aid (of which Prince Kropotkin, the Anarchist,
spoke). Eventually, perhaps, the individualistic workingmen and women
of America will come to see that their much-vaunted individualism
amounts to nothing in the present economic system where they are at
the mercy of the DuPonts, Mellons, Rockefellers, Morgans, etc. . . . The
Negro being even poorer than the white must work that much faster at
cooperation . . .

[e]
UNEMPLOYMENT AMONG NEGROES: WHOM SHOULD WE BLAME?
[ADVERTISEMENT]
Negro World/February 19, 1921

The Universal Negro Improvement Association and its President-General Marcus Garvey preached for four years during the war period industrial preparedness among all Negroes.

The President-General told the people that they should save their money and invest a part of it in the Universal Negro Improvement Association and in the Black Star Line, so that these organizations could build factories, buy and build steamships, and open up industrial activities in Africa, to build up a country of our own and thereby take care of the millions of Negroes who would be thrown out of work after the war. Whilst Mr. Garvey preached this doctrine of preparedness and warned the people, some Negro newspapers in Chicago, New York, Philadelphia, Norfolk and Newport News, and men like Cyril Briggs of the Crusader, and DuBois of the Crisis, criticized Marcus Garvey and the Universal Negro Improvement Association and the Black Star Line. They wrote terrible things to discourage the people and make them suspicious, as if someone was trying to rob or exploit them. The Negro being over-suspicious, having been exploited so often, turned a deaf ear to the plea of Marcus Garvey. Everybody said Garvey and his followers were crazy and that they were a "bunch of illiterates." Very few of the race had the sense and confidence to appreciate the doctrine that Marcus Garvey taught for four years. The few who understood, bought shares in the Black Star Line, through which the corporation was able to purchase two ocean going ships fitted only for coastwide trade between America and Central America and West Indian ports, but the corporation was not supported to the extent of purchasing bigger ships for the trans-Atlantic route for trading with Africa. Our critics of the Negro newspapers tried their best to defeat our plan by harassing us in public print under the guise of friendly criticism as some of them tried to camouflage. What's the result? Some of the newspapers not mentioned are now out of business. Some of them were paid by white men to write down the Universal Negro Improvement Association, the Black

Star Line and Marcus Garvey, so that they could perpetually keep down the Negro, as this man Garvey and his movement were doing too much to open the people's eyes. The critics succeeded and now thousands, and later on millions of Negroes will be out of employment and no one to help them, because they harkened to the ways of the critics and did not support the Black Star Line nor the Universal Negro Improvement Association.

You men who earned $100, $80, $70, $60, $50, $40, $30 and $25 per week during the last five years, who are you going to blame for unemployment among you? Who earned your money for you? Did you not earn it for yourself? What did you do with it? Buy silk shirts at $10, $15 and $20? Silk socks at $2, $3, $4 and $5 each? ... Buy expensive furniture for thousands of dollars, which is not yet paid for, and which will be lost to you and forfeited to the furniture company if you don't pay up every month regularly even though you are now out of work? You drove in automobiles. You went to every dance and party held in town. You flirted with half a dozen girls and bought expensive presents for each and every one. . . . You lived as though you were millionaires. . . . You spent one hundred per cent. of what you earned during the war. *You shouted, "Oh, Garvey is crazy." "That Crazy Garvey Bunch."* WHO IS CRAZY NOW? WHO IS OUT OF A JOB NOW? WHO HAS NOWHERE TO GO? WHAT CAN THE NEWS-PAPER CRITICS DO FO YOU? Go to their offices and ask them for bread and see what they will do. . . .

If Negroes during the time of prosperity had subscribed the $10,000,000 capital of the Black Star Line we would today have at least twenty large ocean going ships, and we would be able to ship at least 5,000 unemployed Negroes from America and other parts every week during these hard times.

Africa is calling with her untold opportunities, but we haven't the ships on which to send away the people.

Negro critics are a curse to the race. They criticize and condemn everything, and of themselves can do nothing to help when the crisis comes.

Whom must we blame for unemployment? ANSWER YOURSELF.

[f]
SOUTH OF THE RIO GRANDE
[ADVERTISEMENT]
Messenger/1919, various issues

[g]
DON'T BUY WHERE YOU CAN'T WORK: A CALL FOR A BOYCOTT
[EDITORIAL]
New York Interstate-Tattler/January 28, 1932

Harlem has 165,000 persons over twenty-one years of age, nearly all of whom are working. Recent statistics place the figures for Harlem unemployed at around 45,000 . . . The earning power of those employed means spending power and we might use the spending power selectively for pressure for jobs to give more power to the community . . . Not only do Negroes have spending power in local stores of Harlem but there is a vast amount of money paid by Harlemites to instalment houses both in and out of the community and millions more go to the public utilities like the electric and gas companies and telephone company . . . It is therefore quite obvious that with this great spending power, intelligently directed mass pressure could be brought to bear upon any store or utility company, even upon the transportation companies, by either the boycott or passive resistance method that would literally compel them to employ a full Negro quota, and in some cases an entire staff, or go out of business.

If just five thousand Negro telephone subscribers organized themselves and cancelled their phone service dramatically on the same day, and at the same time told the company that they were doing so because they had failed to employ Negro girls at their Harlem stations, there is absolutely no question about the attention the company would give such a demand.

Also, if there were a concentrated action carried out against such stores as the 5 & 10 in this community coupled with systematic picketing by paid pickets, the store managers would be forced to terms on Negro employment by sheer economic pressure, the same as they were forced in Chicago. The 5 & 10 cent stores in the Spanish section of Harlem employ Spanish clerks because the difference in language compels them to do so, but the Negro can resort only to an economic weapon.

Pending the application of such a program as stated above, it is highly desirable that the Harlem merchants themselves, through their business organizations, start "Buy in Harlem" campaigns. Negro business men, and white merchants who employ Negroes, should come together at some place like the Association of Trade and Commerce, and map out a plan whereby more money can be put in circulation in this community and more colored people given employment. Although we are still asleep, we must not starve.

[h]
BACK TO THE FARM?
ROBERT L. VANN
Pittsburgh Courier/September 24, 1932

During these dark days of depression there is much talk among thoughtful persons in Aframerica over the feasibility of the Negro returning to the farm, from whence he trekked hopefully to the Southern and Northern urban centers during and after the World War.

There should be more discussion of this proposition, especially in those cities where there is a considerable unemployed Negro population subsisting precariously on the dole. Certainly the chances of a Negro obtaining food, clothing, shelter and wholesome recreation are not growing any better in our cities with the passage of time. Even more than the impoverished white worker he is becoming an authentic proletarian, without economic security or hope for anything better.

If by these conferences we can formulate some plan by which scores of thousands of these black paupers and dependents may become self-supporting and useful citizens on their own farms, we shall have gone a long way on the road to solving our economic problems as a group. Any plan, however, must reckon with the fact that thousands of farms are being abandoned in all parts of the country because of high taxes and low prices for crops. How can the Negro returning to the farm defeat these inexorable economic forces that are driving millions away from rural areas and into the gilded vortex of the city?

We might with great profit study the history and development of agriculture in Denmark, Holland, Scandinavia and Ireland, where through producer's co-operative associations under intelligent, informed leadership, so much has been done to elevate the farmer to a position of security and independence realized by very few followers of agriculture and stock raising in the United States.

But in urging Negroes—or whites for that matter—to return to the soil we must take care that only farmers are included. . . . Useless people on a farm are as bad as useless people in the city.

IV.

The
Black American
and the
Third World

17.
Pan-Africanism vs.
Africa for the Africans

In the introduction to his anthology *The New Negro,* published in 1925, Alain Locke speaks in glowing phrases of the black American's new "consciousness of acting as the advance-guard of the African peoples in their contact with Twentieth Century civilization." Afro-American interest in Africa had two distinct focal points; one was the Garvey movement, the other the DuBois Pan-African Congress movement. The former was led by a generally younger crowd than the latter. The Garvey movement had a large number of immigrants to the U.S. in leadership positions, whereas the Pan-Africanists in the U.S. were overwhelmingly native-born. The rank-and-file Garveyites were primarily from the working class, whereas the Pan-Africanists, from leaders to the nominal followers, were from the professions, the academic community and other middle-class backgrounds. The Garveyites had a mass movement—the Pan-Africanists represented an enlightened elite.

The rudimentary distinction between the Garveyites and the Pan-Africanists in the United States is revealed in a February 1919 *Crisis* article by DuBois, selection (a). At this point in time, DuBois could chime the slogan of Garvey that "Africa is for the Africans," and even accept Garvey's idea for emigration of a small representative group of black Americans. But at this early point in the New Negro movement, DuBois was already leery of the "separatism" in Garvey's program in the United States, i.e., Garvey's alienation from America.

The concern of the Pan-Africanists over Garvey's alleged distraction of black American interest in the struggle here was voiced by James

Weldon Johnson in a New York *Age* editorial column of August 21, 1920, that stated in part, "Africa should be redeemed and Africa will be redeemed, but the main work of its redemption must be accomplished by the Africans themselves. Their blood brothers in this country can aid them more effectively by fighting out their own destiny in America than they can by embarking upon a crusade." This statement should be compared with what Johnson wrote a year earlier in another of his *Age* columns (selection [b]), in which he displayed the strongest support for African liberation and saw no cause for disclaimers on the connection of Afro-American and African struggles.

Again, it is interesting to compare Johnson in selection (b) with the militant black nationalist expression of Marcus Garvey in selection (c), from a 1921 issue of *Negro World.*

The specific plans of the Garveyites revolved around establishing a beachhead in the African nation of Liberia. Their critics claimed that Garvey's emigration plan was a sham, a misleading of the black masses with hopes of massive escape that could never be accomplished. Garveyites repeatedly denied they were planning a wholesale exodus from the United States; a *Negro World* explanation of their plan for sending a few thousand pioneers to Africa is included here as selection (d).

In selection (e), from a 1921 *Crisis,* DuBois describes the first Pan-African Congress and mentions some of the movements growing in Africa and other parts of the Third World that he would like to see represented in the Second Pan-African Congress, called for September of 1921. Selection (f) from the *Crisis* presents the Manifesto of the Second Pan-African Congress.

[a]
AFRICA FOR THE AFRICANS
W. E. B. DU BOIS
Crisis/February 1919

. . . The suggestion has been made that these territories which Germany has lost should not be handed over to any other nation of Europe but should, under the guidance of *organized civilization,* be brought to a point of development which shall finally result in an autonomous state. This plan has met with much criticism and ridicule. Let the natives develop along their own lines and they will "go back," has been the cry. Back to what, in Heaven's name?

Is a civilization naturally backward because it is different? Outside of cannibalism, which can be matched in this country, at least, by lynching, there is no vice and no degradation in native African customs which can begin to touch the horrors thrust upon them by white masters. Drunkenness, terrible diseases, immorality, all these things have been the gifts of European civilization. There is no need to dwell on German and Belgian atrocities, the world knows them too well. Nor have France and England been blameless. But even supposing that these masters had been models of kindness and rectitude, who shall say that any civilization is in itself so superior that it must be superimposed upon another nation without the expressed and intelligent consent of the people most concerned. The culture indigenous to a country, its folk-customs, its art, all this must have free scope or there is no such thing as freedom for the world.

The truth is, white men are merely juggling with words—or worse— when they declare that the withdrawal of Europeans from Africa will plunge that continent into chaos. What Europe, and indeed only a small group in Europe, wants in Africa is not a field for the spread of European civilization, but a field for exploitation. They covet the raw materials,—ivory, diamonds, copper and rubber in which the land abounds, and even more do they covet cheap native labor to mine and produce these things. Greed,—naked, pitiless lust for wealth and power, lie back of all of Europe's interest in Africa and the white world knows it and is not ashamed.

Any readjustment of Africa is not fair and cannot be lasting which does not consider the interests of native Africans and peoples of African descent. Prejudice, in European colonies in Africa, against the ambitious Negro is greater than in America, and that is saying much. But with the establishment of a form of government which shall be based on the concept that Africa is for Africans, there would be a chance for the colored American to emigrate and to go as a pioneer to a country which must, sentimentally at least, possess for him the same fascination as England does for Indian-born Englishmen.

Not "Separatism"

This is not a "separatist" movement. There is no need to think that those who advocate the opening up of Africa for Africans and those of African descent desire to deport any large number of colored Americans to a foreign and, in some respects, inhospitable land. Once for all, let us realize that we are Americans, that we were brought here with the earliest settlers, and that the very sort of civilization from which we came made the complete adoption of western modes and customs imperative if we were to survive at all. In brief, there is nothing so indigenous, so completely "made in America" as we. It is as absurd to talk of a return to Africa, merely because that was our home 300 years ago, as it would be to expect the members of the Caucasian race to return to the fastnesses of the Caucasus Mountains from which, it is reputed, they sprang.

But it is true that we as a people are not given to colonization, and that thereby a number of essential occupations and interests have been closed to us which the redemption of Africa would open up. The African movement means to us what the Zionist movement must mean to the Jews, the centralization of race effort and the recognition of a racial fount. To help bear the burden of Africa does not mean any lessening of effort in our own problem at home. Rather it means increased interest. For any ebullition of action and feeling that results in an amelioration of the lot of Africa tends to ameliorate the condition of colored peoples throughout the world. And no man liveth to himself.

From an editorial, this part entitled "Reconstruction and Africa."

[b]
THE AFRICAN QUESTION AND THE RIGHTS OF THE NEGRO
JAMES WELDON JOHNSON
New York Age/February 8, 1919

People of African descent everywhere should be interested in the fact that one of the first great questions to come up before the Peace Conference was internationalization. And for the reason that, before the Peace Conference, "internationalization" is simply another way of saying "the African question."

Internationalization and the African question mean one and the same thing, because the consideration of internationalization is concerned almost entirely with the status of the former German colonies in Africa.

We said in this column some weeks ago that the question of Africa was sure to loom up large in the Peace Conference because of the international position held by it. We also expressed grave doubts that the question of the conditions of the American Negro would be allowed to rise at the peace table because the Powers would be only too glad to regard it as a domestic question, a question between American citizens and their own government. *We therefore reached the conclusion that the wisest step that could be taken by the colored people of the world would be to put the African question up to the Peace Conference so strongly that it would compel a consideration of the rights of Negro people everywhere.*

We arrived at this conclusion by simply looking facts in the face; and by doing so through ordinary, plain glass rather than through rose-colored glasses.

In our opinion, the best claim that the colored people of the world could put before the Peace Conference in behalf of Africa would be a claim for the internationalization of the former German Colonies. We held this opinion for the very evident reason that no questions regarding any new disposition of French and British possessions in Africa would arise; that these questions would be confined to the former German colonies; and that the question regarding the German colonies would come up in only three forms: the return of these colonies to Germany, their division among the Allies, or their internationalization.

Of course, a great deal has been said about self-determination; but no group of people, in spite of all that has been said, is going to get self-determination as a result of petition or even plain justice; the only ones who will get it are those who are in a position to force it. *The natives all over Africa can get self-determination as soon as they are in a position to force it from their overlords.* It seems to us that the quickest step by which they may reach such a position is through internationalization; through an internationalization which will give them a large and increasing share in their own government.

Such an internationalization of the former German colonies should eventually lead to the whole of Central Africa being ruled by native

Africans, and that in turn should lead to an Africa for Africans. And an Africa for Africans would make a great change for the better in the status of people of Negro blood all over the world. In the meantime, the American colored people should realize that the greatest advantage they have gained from the war is the opportunity and the right to fight more effectively at close quarters, here at home, for the things in the name of which the war was waged.

[c]
THE AFRICAN REPUBLIC AND WHITE POLITICS
MARCUS GARVEY
Negro World/February 12, 1921

We are going to build up in Africa a government of our own, big enough and strong enough to protect Africa and Negroes anywhere.

Here you have three men, one white, one black, one yellow, all come into the world at one and the same time. The white man has guns and swords, daggers and other implements and keeps them with him; the yellow man does the same, and this foolish black man stands up in the middle—between these two men—with two bare hands. You must realize that you are flirting with your own future, your destiny, and your race . . . What is the idea of Japan having a big navy? The idea is to protect the rights of the yellow man in Asia. The nations of Europe have navies to protect the rights of the white man in Europe. Negroes, the time has come for you to make and create a nation of Africa and have the greatest army and navy in the world.

Africa must be redeemed. There is no doubt about it, it is no camouflage. The Universal Negro Improvement Association is organizing now, and there is going to be some dying later on. We are not organizing to fight against or disrespect the government of America, I say this plainly and for everybody to hear—we are organizing to drive every pale-face out of Africa. [Applause] Do you know why? Because Africa is mine; Africa is the land of my fathers; and what my fathers never gave to anybody else, since they did not will it to anybody, must have been for me. . . . Some of you turn up your noses against the Africa of Africans. Africa was the land from whence our fore-parents were brought three hundred years ago into this Western Hemisphere. They did not probably know what the consequences would be. But that God who rules, that God who sees and knows, he had his plan when he inspired the Psalmist to write: "Princes shall come out of Egypt, and Ethiopia shall stretch forth her hand unto God."

If anybody should be a radical it should be the Negro. We are not radicals, even though some men think we are. The I.W.W. are radicals, and so are some Socialists; but they are white people, so let them "raise Cain" and do what they please. We have no time with them; we have all the time with four hundred million Negroes . . . So, please understand that Marcus Garvey is no I.W.W.; he doesn't even know what it means; he is no anarchist, as far as Western civilization is concerned; but if anarchism means that you have to drive out somebody and sometimes kill somebody, to get that which belongs to you, then when I get to Africa I am going to be an anarchist.

If it is right for the white man and the yellow man to rule in their respective domains, it is right for the black man to rule in his own domain. Remaining here you will never have a black man as president of the United States; you will never have a black Premier of Great Britain; you need not waste time over it. I am going to use all my time to establish a great republic in Africa for four hundred million Negroes, so that one day if I desire to be president, I can throw my hat in the ring and run as a candidate for the presidency.

From a speech by Marcus Garvey.

[d]
LIBERIA, LAND OF OPPORTUNITY
WILLIAM SHERRILL
Negro World/April 5, 1924

The Universal Negro Improvement Association has set a record for tackling big jobs and, here in the last few months, it has tackled one of the biggest jobs in the history of this organization, and that is the job of building up industrially and commercially the great Republic of Liberia. This job that the Universal Negro Improvement Association has tackled now is one which will not only benefit the race as a whole, but it is one in which there is much for each of us individually, especially if we have the courage and ability necessary to play our part.

What Liberia Offers

Liberia offers to the Negro one of the greatest opportunities the race has had the privilege of taking advantage of for several centuries. Liberia offers those of us individually who plan to take part in it individually the opportunity for building that big business necessary to make the race respected everywhere. Liberia, with her 40,000 square miles of rich, alluvial land—Liberia with her vast timber forests—Liberia, with her zinc, her coal, her copper and diamond mines—with her oil fields and her 350 miles of coast line—Liberia, with her vast, untouched resources, offers to the ambitious, energetic, capable Negro today an opportunity for becoming a man. Her 350 miles of coast line beckon and call for harbors, warehouses and docks; her mines are simply waiting for the touch of scientific apparatus to exploit her untold treasures. Her forests await the touch of the axe and the buzz of the sawmill. These untouched resources in Liberia are simply awaiting the genius, the ability, and the finance of Negroes who are able to take advantage of them. Liberia calls for Negroes with ambition—Negroes who are able to work and see shafts sunk deep into the bowels bringing to the surface precious minerals for export to the various countries of the world: men who are able to stand in the forests and see in their mind's eye those giant trees turned into beautiful homes and cottages; those giant trees made into every conceivable thing that you can make out of wood; men who are able to see with their mind's eyes its harbors dredged, docks built; men who can go to that vast, untouched territory of Liberia and see there a mighty nation of flourishing cities and see there great corporations and centers of industries.

Become Producers

Liberia offers to the race that opportunity of becoming not only consumers in the world, but becoming the producers of those things we must consume. You know, we as a race today are simply a race of consumers. As Mr. Garvey said to me a couple of days ago, practically everything that we of the race have built up in America which we boast of is consumed, in our banks, our insurance companies, our grocery stores. Boast of our progress as much as you want, but all is on the end of consumption. The producers hold the other end, which is the important end; and in 30 days, it matters not how big our banks are, it matters not how big our insurance companies are, it matters not how large our retail stores are, they can be put out of commission because they must depend upon your ability to get a job and earn wages to support them. But Liberia offers to the Negro an opportunity to build up that financial strength which will enable the retail stores, whether they be in America or the West Indies, or on the continent of Europe, the banks and insurance companies to have thousands of men and women who control the tools of production, feeding them in order that they will not be dependent on or at the mercy of alien peoples or alien races.

Real wealth after all has its origin in the natural resources of a country. About 400 years ago, the Pilgrim Fathers came to this country—they brought nothing practically but themselves. They landed in a vast wilderness and, after a lapse of 400 years they have built up a country the total wealth of which is estimated now at more than $300,000,000,000. They did not bring it here, but simply because they were wise men, scientifically exploited the natural resources of the land and built up a country of gigantic wealth which now controls practically the commerce of the world.

It is such an opportunity that the opening up of Liberia offers to each and every one of us who takes part in that opening. It gives you that opportunity for which we are now hoping. It is the hope and ambition of each and every one sitting here before me tonight that at some time or other in your life you will reach that independence where next month's house rent will not worry you; where your grocer's bill will not worry you; where you will not be disturbed about your children's welfare; to reach that point in your life when you will become financially independent and have an opportunity to enjoy some of this world's goods. But you will never be able to do that if you have to gain that independence simply by what you earn; you have got to be in a position where you can take your earnings and savings and place them in a position to earn you more money. . . . It is such an opportunity that Liberia offers you. Liberia is to be built. Who knows but some of you tonight have the plans in your minds for organizing certain industries in the Republic of Liberia. . . .

Who knows but what I am talking tonight to young men who will write again the history of Rockefeller; young men who will write again the history of Edison; young men who will write again the history of Gary; young men who will write again the history of those who have built up other countries; young men who will see the opportunity—who will catch the vision and who will go into that little country of Liberia and build up there a financial and industrial force that will make the Republic respected by the nations of the world. . . .

[e]
PAN-AFRICA
W. E. B. DU BOIS
Crisis/March 1921

The growth of a body of public opinion among peoples of Negro descent broad enough to be called Pan-African is a movement belonging almost entirely to the twentieth century.

Seven hundred and fifty years before Christ the Negroes as rulers of Ethiopia and conquerors of Egypt were practically supreme in the civilized world; but the character of the African continent was such that this supremacy brought no continental unity; rather the inhabitants of the narrow Nile Valley set their faces toward the Mediterranean and Asia more than toward the western Sudan, the valley of the Congo and the Atlantic.

From that time even in the rise of the Sudanese kingdoms of the 13th, 14th and 15th centuries there was still no Pan-Africa; and after that the slave trade brought continental confusion.

In 1900 at the time of the Paris Exposition there was called on January 23, 24, and 25 a Pan-African Conference in Westminster Hall, London. A second conference was held at Tuskegee Institute about 1912.

Finally, at the time of the Peace Conference in Paris, February, 1919, the first Pan-African Congress was called. The interest in this congress was worldwide among the darker peoples. Delegates were elected in the United States, the West Indies, South and West Africa and elsewhere. Most of them, of course, were prevented from attending as a result of war measures and physical difficulties.

However, there did assemble in Paris 57 delegates from 15 countries where over 85,000,000 Negroes and persons of African descent dwell. Resolutions were adopted taking up the question of the relation of Africa to the League of Nations, and the general question of land, capital, labor, education, hygiene and the treatment of civilized Negroes. Blaise Diagne, Deputy from Senegal and Commissioner in charge of the French Colonial Troops, was elected president of a permanent organization, and W. E. B. DuBois of the United States, Editor of THE CRISIS, was made secretary. A second congress was called to meet in Paris in September, 1921.

Meantime, the feeling of the necessity for understanding among the Africans and their descendants has been growing throughout the world. There was held from March 11–19, 1920, the National Congress of British West Africa. This body after careful conference adopted resolutions concerning legislative reforms, the franchise, administrative changes, a West African University, commercial enterprise, judicial and sanitary programs. They also stated their opinion concerning the land question and self-determination and sent a deputation to the King. The deputation, consisting of three lawyers, two merchants, an ex–Deputy Mayor, a physician and a native ruler, went to England and presented to the King their demands, which included right to vote, local self-government and other matters.

Other movements have gone on. In the agitation for Egyptian independence there is a large number of men of Negro descent. In South Africa, the African Political Organization and the Native Congress have had a number of conferences and have sent delegates to London, protesting against the land legislation of the Union of South Africa.

In the Canal Zone and in the West Indies have come movements looking toward union of effort among peoples of African descent and emphasizing the economic bond. In the United States there is the National Association for the Advancement of Colored People, with its 90,000 members and its very wide influence and activities.

Many of these movements will be represented in the second Pan-African Congress next fall, and out of this meeting will undoubtedly grow a larger and larger unity of thought among Negroes and through this, concerted action. At first this action will probably include a demand for political rights, for economic freedom—especially in relation to the land—for the abolition of slavery, peonage and caste, and for freer access to education . . .

[f]
MANIFESTO OF THE
SECOND PAN-AFRICAN CONGRESS
W. E. B. DU BOIS
Crisis/November 1921

The absolute equality of races,—physical, political and social—is the founding stone of world peace and human advancement. No one denies great differences of gift, capacity and attainment among individuals of all races, but the voice of science, religion and practical politics is one in denying the God-appointed existence of super-races, or of races naturally and inevitably and eternally inferior.

That in the vast range of time, one group should in its industrial technique, or social organization, or spiritual vision, lag a few hundred years behind another, or forge fitfully ahead, or come to differ decidedly in thought, deed and ideal, is proof of the essential richness and variety of human nature, rather than proof of the co-existence of demigods and apes in human form. The doctrine of racial equality does not interfere with individual liberty, rather, it fulfills it. And of all the various criteria by which masses of men have in the past been prejudged and classified, that of the color of the skin and texture of the hair, is surely the most adventitious and idiotic.

It is the duty of the world to assist in every way the advance of the backward and suppressed groups of mankind. The rise of all men is a menace to no one and is the highest human ideal; it is not an altruistic benevolence, but the one road to world salvation.

For the purpose of raising such peoples to intelligence, self-knowledge and self-control, their intelligentsia of right ought to be recognized as the natural leaders of their groups.

The insidious and dishonorable propaganda, which, for selfish ends, so distorts and denies facts as to represent the advancement and development of certain races of men as impossible and undesirable, should be met with widespread dissemination of the truth. The experiment of making the Negro slave a free citizen in the United States is not a failure; the attempts at autonomous government in Haiti and Liberia are not proofs of the impossibility of self-government among black men; the experience of Spanish America does not prove that mulatto democracy will not eventually succeed there; the aspirations of Egypt and India are not successfully to be met by sneers at the capacity of darker races.

We who resent the attempt to treat civilized men as uncivilized, and who bring in our hearts grievance upon grievance against those who lynch the untried, disfranchise the intelligent, deny self-government to educated men, and insult the helpless, we complain; but not simply or primarily for ourselves—more especially for the millions of our fellows, blood of our blood, and flesh of our flesh, who have not even what we have—the power to complain against monstrous wrong, the power to see and to know the source of our oppression.

How far the future advance of mankind will depend upon the social contract and physical intermixture of the various strains of human blood is unknown, but the demand for the interpenetration of countries and intermingling of blood has come, in modern days, from the white race alone, and has been imposed upon brown and black folks mainly by brute force and fraud. On top of this, the resulting people of mixed race have had to endure innuendo, persecution, and insult, and the penetrated countries have been forced into semi-slavery.

If it be proven that absolute world segregation by group, color or historic affinity is best for the future, let the white race leave the dark world and the darker races will gladly leave the white. But the proposition is absurd. This is a world of men, of men whose likenesses far outweigh their differences; who mutually need each other in labor and thought and dream, but who can successfully have each other on terms of equality, justice and mutual respect. They are the real and only peacemakers who work sincerely and peacefully to this end.

The beginning of wisdom in interracial contact is the establishment of political institutions among suppressed peoples. The habit of democracy must be made to encircle the earth. Despite the attempt to prove that its practice is the secret and divine gift of the few, no habit is more natural or more widely spread among primitive people, or more easily capable of development among masses. Local self-government with a minimum of help and oversight can be established tomorrow in Asia, in Africa, in America and in the Isles of the Sea. It will in many instances need general control and guidance, but it will fail only when that guidance seeks ignorantly and consciously its own selfish ends and not the people's liberty and good.

Surely in the 20th century of the Prince of Peace, in the millennium of Buddha and Mahmoud, and in the mightiest Age of Human Reason, there can be found in the civilized world enough of altruism, learning and benevolence to develop native institutions for the natives' good, rather than continue to allow the majority of mankind to be brutalized and enslaved by ignorant and selfish agents of commercial institutions, whose one aim is profit and power for the few.

And this brings us to the crux of the matter: It is the shame of the world that today the relation between the main groups of mankind and their mutual estimate and respect is determined chiefly by the degree in which one can subject the other to its service, enslaving labor, making ignorance compulsory, uprooting ruthlessly religion and customs, and destroying government, so that the favored Few may luxuriate in the toil of the tortured Many. Science, Religion and Philanthropy have thus been made the slaves of world commerce and industry, and bodies, minds, souls of Fiji and Congo, are judged almost solely by the quotations on the Bourse.

The day of such world organization is past and whatever excuse be made for it in other ages, the 20th century must come to judge men as men and not as material and labor.

The great industrial problem which has hitherto been regarded as the domestic problem of culture lands, must be viewed far more broadly, if it is ever to reach just settlement. Labor and capital in England, France and America can never solve their problem as long as a similar and vastly greater problem of poverty and injustice marks the relations of the whiter and darker peoples. It is shameful, unreligious, unscientific and undemocratic that the estimate, which half the people of earth put on the other half, depends mainly on their ability to squeeze profit out of them.

If we are coming to recognize that the great modern problem is to correct maladjustment in the distribution of wealth, it must be remembered that the basic maladjustment is in the outrageously unjust distribution of world income between the dominant and suppressed peoples; in the rape of land and raw material, and monopoly of technique and culture. And in this crime white labor is *particeps criminis* with white capital. Unconsciously and consciously, carelessly and deliberately, the vast power of the white labor vote in modern democracies has been cajoled and flattered into imperialistic schemes to enslave and debauch black, brown and yellow labor, until with fatal retribution, they are themselves today bound and gagged and rendered impotent by the resulting monopoly of the world's raw material in the hands of a dominant, cruel and irresponsible few.

And, too, just as curiously, the educated and cultured of the world, the well-born and well-bred, and even the deeply pious and philanthropic, receive their training and comfort and luxury, the ministrations of delicate beauty and sensibility, on condition that they neither inquire into the real source of their income and the methods of distribution or interfere with the legal props which rest on a pitiful human foundation of writhing white and yellow and brown and black bodies.

We claim no perfectness of our own nor do we seek to escape the blame which of right falls on the backward for failure to advance, but *noblesse oblige,* and we arraign civilization and more especially the colonial powers for deliberate transgressions of our just demands and their own better conscience.

England, with her Pax Brittanica, her courts of justice, established commerce and a certain apparent recognition of native law and customs, has nevertheless systematically fostered ignorance among the natives, has enslaved them and is still enslaving some of them, has usually declined even to try to train black and brown men in real self-government, to recognize civilized black folks as civilized, or to grant to colored colonies those rights of self-government which it freely gives to white men.

Belgium is a nation which has but recently assumed responsibility for her colonies, and has taken some steps to lift them from the worst abuses of the autocratic regime; but she has not confirmed to the people the possession of their land and labor, and she shows no disposition to allow the natives any voice in their own government, or to provide for their political future. Her colonial policy is still mainly dominated by the banks and great corporations. But we are glad to learn that the present government is considering a liberal program of reform for the future.

Portugal and Spain have never drawn a legal caste line against persons of culture who happen to be of Negro descent. Portugal has a humane code for the natives and has begun their education in some regions. But unfortunately, the industrial concessions of Portuguese Africa are almost wholly in the hands of foreigners whom Portugal cannot or will not control, and who are exploiting land and re-establishing the African slave trade.

The United States of America after brutally enslaving millions of black folks suddenly emancipated them and began their education; but it acted without system or forethought, throwing the freed men upon the world penniless and landless, educating them without thoroughness and system, and subjecting them the while to lynching, lawlessness, discrimination, insult and slander, such as human beings have seldom endured and survived. To save their own government, they enfranchised the Negro and then when danger passed, allowed hundreds of thousands of educated and civilized black folk to be lawlessly disfranchised and subjected to a caste system; and, at the same time, in 1776, 1812, 1861, 1897, and 1917, they asked and allowed thousands of black men to offer up their lives as a sacrifice to the country which despised and despises them.

France alone of the great colonial powers has sought to place her cultured black citizens on a plane of absolute legal and social equality with her whites and given them representation in her highest legislature. In her colonies she has a widespread but still imperfect system of state education. This splendid beginning must be completed by widening the political basis of her native government, by restoring to the indigenes the ownership of the soil, by protecting native labor against the aggression of established capital, and by asking no man, black or white, to be a soldier unless the country gives him a voice in his own government.

The independence of Abyssinia, Liberia, Haiti and San Domingo, is absolutely necessary to any sustained belief of the black folk in the sincerity and honesty of the white. These nations have earned the right to be free, they deserve the recognition of the world; notwithstanding all their faults and mistakes, and the fact that they are behind the most advanced civilization of the day, nevertheless they compare favorably with the past, and even more recent, history of most European nations, and it shames civilization that the treaty of London practically invited Italy to aggression in Abyssinia, and that free America has unjustly and cruelly seized Haiti, murdered and for a time enslaved her workmen, overthrown her free institutions by force, and has so far failed in return to give her a single bit of help, aid or sympathy.

What do those wish who see these evils of the color line and racial discrimination and who believe in the divine right of suppressed and backward peoples to learn and aspire to be free?

The Negro race through its thinking intelligentsia is demanding:

I. The recognition of civilized men as civilized despite their race or color

II. Local self-government for backward groups, deliberately rising as experience and knowledge grow to complete self-government under the limitations of a self-governed world

III. Education in self knowledge, in scientific truth and in industrial technique, undivorced from the art of beauty

IV. Freedom in their own religion and social customs, and with the right to be different and non-conformist

V. Co-operation with the rest of the world in government, industry and art on the basis of Justice, Freedom and Peace

VI. The ancient common ownership of the land and its natural fruits and defence against the unrestrained greed of . . . capital

VII. The establishment under the League of Nations of an international institution for the study of Negro problems

VIII. The establishment of an international section in the Labor Bureau of the League of Nations, charged with the protection of native labor.

The world must face two eventualities: either the complete assimilation of Africa with two or three of the great world states, with political, civil and social power and privileges absolutely equal for its black and white citizens, or the rise of a great black African state founded in Peace and Good Will, based on popular education, natural art and industry and freedom of trade; autonomous and sovereign in its internal policy, but from its beginning a part of a great society of peoples in which it takes its place with others as co-rulers of the world.

In some such words and thoughts as these we seek to express our will and ideal, and the end of our untiring effort. To our aid we call all men of the Earth who love Justice and Mercy. Out of the depths we have cried unto the deaf and dumb masters of the world. Out of the depths we cry to our own sleeping souls.

The answer is written in the stars.

18.
The
Afro-American Press
On the Third World

One mark of the New Negro period was the heightened interest in news reports of events in the Third World, not only from Black Africa but from red, brown and yellow people as well. The passive resistance efforts of Mahatma Gandhi were widely reported in the black weeklies. Selection (a) is an analysis of the worldwide significance of Gandhi written by Robert L. Vann of the Pittsburgh *Courier.* Cyril Briggs, in selection (b) from a 1919 *Crusader,* asks how the U.S. could justify an armed intervention in Mexico to preserve law and order in that country when mob rule and lynching had replaced law and order in the U.S. Selection (c) presents one of a series of articles in the *Messenger* on labor conditions in the Union of South Africa by Clements Kadalie, president of the largest black trade union in that country. The rise of China and Japan were of major interest to Garveyites. Amy J. Garvey, in a 1927 editorial on her Women's Page of the *Negro World,* declared that the rise of Asia was striking fear in the white world; and in her imagery Mrs. Garvey seems to prophesy Pearl Harbor. The editorial is included as selection (d). In a 1931 *Negro Worker* article, selection (e), George Padmore warns blacks not to be fooled into supporting an Asian fascist show of strength, such as the one the militaristic Japanese displayed in their invasion of Manchuria.

One of the most important organs in the creation of New Negro Third World consciousness was Duse Mohamed Ali's *African Times and Orient Review* published in London from 1912 to 1917 and distributed internationally on five continents. After World War I, Mohamed produced a similar magazine, the *Africa and Orient Review*, which was published until 1921. Among the contributors to Mohamed's magazine were Marcus Garvey and fellow Garveyites William Ferris, John E. Bruce and T. Thomas Fortune; Liberian Garveyites Gabriel Johnson and Justice James J. Dossen; Rudolph B. Smith of Guyana; George O. Marke of Sierra Leone; the Ghanaian barrister, Pan-African Congress delegate and Garveyite Casely Hayford; George F. Downing and James Weldon Johnson of the Pan-African movement; Richard B. Moore of the African Blood Brotherhood; and the black intellectuals Arthur Schomburg and Hubert H. Harrison. Dr. DuBois was one of the few important people involved in the development of an international black consciousness who was not involved with "the Duse Mohamed crowd."

A discussion of the background of the Egyptian-born Mohamed and of the importance of his journal is presented in selection (f), an article by William Ferris from his Chicago *Champion* magazine reprinted in the *African Times and Orient Review*.

Selection (g), a *Review* reprint of an article from the Lagos, Nigeria, *Standard*, presents an argument that the fight of England in the World War, in the cause of the rights of independence for smaller nations, is certainly applicable in the case of Liberia, which during the War was threatened with annexation.

[a]
ON GANDHI: AN EMPIRE AT STAKE
ROBERT L. VANN
Pittsburgh Courier/May 17, 1930

The eyes of the entire world are on India. There the great Hindu leader, Mahatma Gandhi, once an obscure lawyer in South Africa but now the spiritual leader of 300 million dark people, defies the power of the British Empire with his program of civil disobedience.

Passive non-resistance has given way here and there to violence as the situation has grown more acute. The Mayor of Calcutta, the Indian metropolis, has been imprisoned, as have many other prominent Indian leaders including Gandhi's son; officials all over the vast country have resigned their positions in answer to the call of the great man and even certain units of the Indian Army have shown signs of disaffection. The wild tribesmen of Afghanistan are beginning to raid the northern border and the British have been compelled to close the Khyber Pass. Meantime, Soviet Russia, fomenter of mass revolts, has completed a 1,000-mile strategic railroad nearby that will constitute another thorn in the side of British imperialism.

It is quite possible that the whole of India may spring into violent revolt within a few weeks and even the Indian soldiers will join with the impoverished masses. In that event, Soviet Russia is very likely to assist the revolutionists through the Third Internationale, and Afghanistan, which is suspiciously friendly with the Soviets, will also find a way to help the struggling Indian masses. In that event Great Britain stands a chance of losing her rich empire which has contributed so much to her position as the dominant world power.

If the Indians do succeed, in spite of their myriad conflicting castes and prejudices in launching a great revolution, it will sound the death knell of the British Empire, the foremost exploiter of black labor in the world. Australia, South Africa, Canada and the Irish Free State are practically independent nations already. An Indian revolt will very likely start a Mohammedan revolt in Africa and Asia. At the same time, the British working people, still disgruntled by the losses in the great war and the subsequent hard times, and on the verge of Socialism, are not disposed to fight another war to guarantee the security of those who deny them the right to work.

Altogether, the work of Gandhi tends to make the future look rather bright for the dark peoples of the world. To be sure, the British imperialists will not give up an empire without a fierce struggle, but against a united India they cannot prevail. They only got a foothold there in the first place because of the wars between Indian princes.

An unsigned editorial.

[b]
ON INTERVENTION IN MEXICO
CYRIL V. BRIGGS
Crusader/October 1919

Intervention is in the air, and strange as it may seem to those uninitiated in the mysteries of that ancient fetish, "law and order," it is not to be intervention by some civilized powers in the interests of "law and order" and the suppression of the race wars and mob rule in the United States, but intervention—please don't laugh, it's serious—by these same barbarous and benighted United States in the affairs of the Mexicans—a people who, by all indications, seem quite able to live together without engaging in race wars, mob violence, and the fiendish torture of human beings, which are so freely and heartily indulged in on this side of the Rio Grande, and which, more than any other thing in contemporary American history, are the salient and identifying features of the much-vaunted American civilization.

But Mexico is rich in oil minerals. And it is inhabited by a colored race. And what's more human life—especially when it's colored human life—when there's such wealth to be reaped by the American capitalists and junkers and nothing on the Mexican side strong enough to oppose the might that is admiringly held up as the right?

[c]
KEEPING THE NIGGER IN HIS PLACE: WHITE LABOR IN AFRICA
CLEMENTS KADALIE
Messenger/July 1924

I am conscious of the fact that if I continue to run a series of articles in this indispensable New-Negro-Thought magazine, without making some explanation of the relations existing between white and black workers on this continent, it is clear that I shall be committing a serious blunder, and will soon find myself in conflict with the fundamental policy of this journal. I take it to be a journalistic creed that all correspondents of a newspaper at home and abroad should at all cost preserve inviolate the policy of a paper. Since my association with THE MESSENGER, not long ago, I have learnt that it is the desire of the well-read editors of this magazine to advocate the "Mixed Unions" as between white and black labor in the United States of America, with a view to ensuring a permanent victory for all toilers irrespective of their creed, color or nationality. This is admittedly the philosophical theory of the labor movement the world over. I have decided in this article to enlighten American labor, both white and black, of the actual situation in Africa; not only for the benefit of American labor, but primarily for the good of the African native on whose behalf I have . . . acceded to act as the South African correspondent of THE MESSENGER.

In my last article I mentioned amongst many other things that the African native was suffering under the iron heel of capitalism; that he was continually at the mercy of the various Colonial British Governments for the purpose of exploitation, and that year after year he is subjected to rifle and bayonet. I did not mention, however, the part played by the white workers of this continent in assisting the authorities to "keep the nigger (?) in his place." The great mineral wealth and abundance of raw material in this sunny land of our forefathers are subjects for advertisements in England, Europe and the western hemisphere by the South African capitalists, but they deliberately and grossly neglect to advertise the plight of the African native, who is here surrounded by two enemies—capitalism and his fellow white workers. . . .

Recruiting System

The African native has been a victim of this recruiting system since its inception. The recruiting system in Africa is carried on on the principles of slavery and barbarism, and as such, there is no difference between it and the "Slave Fleet" that carried thousands upon thousands of black souls from the coast of Africa to toil in the plantations of the new colonies in the Western Hemisphere. The white trade unionists advocated the necessity of this practice to avoid competition with African labor, and the Government (a white Christian government!), without giving the matter serious consideration, welcomed the suggestion, and took the initiative by making it lawful for African native workers to come under this system. It must have been predestined that I once worked as a clerk and timekeeper in some of the largest mines in this sub-continent, and witnessed my people groaning, early in the morning and late at night, in all kinds of weather, forced by their white shift bosses, who had no regard for the health of these poor souls, recruited from distant territories, and not daring to quit. If they made any attempt to quit, they were immediately lodged in jails. An African native worker can be dismissed from work without notice, in spite of the existence of a contract between him and the employer, whilst such worker, should he absent himself from work, is there and then made a criminal.

Under this system the African native workers are debarred from forming themselves into industrial unions. They are forced to accept any wage offered, which does not include his expenditure to his family, nor is it the full value of his labor, but simply what one would call hand-to-mouth wages. Notwithstanding such disabilities, the African natives still survive.

Then we have another scandal which manifests the brutality of the authors of this recruiting system. The African workers are engaged to do piecework. Some of them take 45 days to complete a task of 30 days' shift. This is effected in a most devilish way. At the end of each book, where the number of days worked are marked, is appended 15 or 20 "loafers' tickets," or paper forms. These forms serve the purpose of docking their fragmentary earnings at the pleasure of the white trade union boss. The result is that the native worker labors for twelve months for six months' wages. The African native workers are paid in the mining industry a maximum of 50 cents per day, while his fellow white worker earns his $5 per day.

White Labor Versus Black Labor

The mining operations in South Africa are carried on in the Northern Provinces, and the white trade union movement is much stronger in the Transvaal Province than it is in the Southern Provinces, where the political and industrial "Color Bar" is very acute, and from whence "A White South Africa" slogan was born, and is at present echoed by every white man and woman through the mediums of the public press, platform and pulpit. I have endeavored to point out here that the white workers of this country subscribed to this unchristianlike recruiting system and have ever since been responsible for widening the gulf between themselves and their fellow black workers.

In the Transvaal gold mines there are 29,276 white workers as against 264,051 black workers. With this recruiting system in operation plus various mine regulations (which the white workers have not only accepted, as hitherto shown, but have actually agitated for), we find that the trade union door is barred to the bulk of the black workers. It is indeed humiliating to the labor movement to know that no definite attempts have ever been made by the white workers to organize their fellow brethren without whose labor the existence of these white trade unionists would unquestionably be impossible. No human law based on selfishness can be permanently respected. With such odds against them, these oppressed sons of Ham were not in the least despondent since several attempts were made to dash for liberty. When strikes were organized by the black workers in defiance of these inhuman restrictions, the white trade unions scabbed on these unfortunate men, and when it came to pass that the authorities adopted repressive measures, the white workers were either employed or took the law into their own hands and shot down their fellow black workers.

During the great Cape Town Dock strike of 1919; a strike in which both the Cape Federation of Labor Unions and the Railway Union (both white organizations), were equally responsible and interested in its successful issue, they left us in the lurch, instead of rendering us moral and financial support—support which we so richly deserved in view of the fact that the great issue of the strike was to check the exportation of foodstuffs, which was responsible for the higher prices on what remained in South Africa.

The white workers did much more evil than this. Three days after the strike was declared, when the Government announced through the press not to export foodstuffs, the white labor unions, the railway union in particular who kept their members driving cranes, assisted the authorities in putting on poor whites . . . to scab on the native African workers. Instead of keeping to their pledges, the fresh African labor recruited from other centres where the issue of the strike was unknown, were brought to Cape Town on railways, the drivers of which were all white members of the railway union.

To survey in detail the part played by the white workers in Africa in assisting capitalism to exploit a section, a formidable section, too, of the labor movement, I am afraid would discredit the cause of labor by humanity as a whole. In every instance when the African workers have made up their minds to no longer tolerate the making of bricks without straw; building great pyramids and castles for others, and have demanded a new order in their economic life, no direct or indirect support was ever accorded them by the white workers. . . .

A White South Africa

An African native is a sensible human being created in the likeness of God. He would ask himself what was the matter with this intruder (the white man), who was supposed to come to Africa principally to proselytise my forefathers into Christianity and Civilization. . . . He soon discovered that Christianity and western civilization were simply used as a disguise to realize a "white South Africa." This new slogan aroused great enthusiasm amongst the white people. It has ever since been openly propagated in Parliament by all parties and on the public platform, in the pulpit, in school and press. . . . Thus in the early part of the year 1922, this "white South Africa" slogan was put to a test. A handful of white miners irritated by the Transvaal Chamber of Mines, took the opportunity to bring about a "white South Africa" by employing the industrial weapon. The Status Quo agreement which made it possible to reserve exclusively all skilled jobs at the mines for white miners was publicly illustrated as the only security for a "White South Africa." During those dark days in the history of this country, white men and women emphatically and militantly stated that it would be fatal to a "white South Africa" to permit African natives to work on a trade. The white miner had previously taken no steps to organize the black workers, and yet [during the strike] the former were crying for help. This desired help was not forthcoming, so, instead of taking defeat like men, the white workers declared war on the black workers. It was no longer an ordinary industrial upheaval. The forces of the state and those of the white workers were in battle, wounding and killing each other, while the latter insisted on a brutal slaughter of the innocent black men and women who had shown no hostile attitude to the white miners.

The I.C.U. [Industrial and Commercial Workers Union], which is always alert in safeguarding the interests of the African race in general, made it possible on Sunday, March 12th, 1922, at a mass meeting held on the Grand Parade, Cape Town, which was very largely attended, to voice the feeling of the African people in the following resolutions:

> In view of the fact that the disturbances on the Rand and events leading thereto are influenced mainly by the color bar, this meeting is of the opinion that the success of the strikers means the retarding of our people in their praiseworthy ambition to secure a livelihood for themselves and their families, and, if possible, to receive a higher wage that would enable them to make provision for the education of their children and lift themselves to a higher place in the civilization of South Africa; that as long as artificial restrictions are placed on citizens simply on account of their color, great trouble will be in store for this South Africa of ours. Therefore, we call upon the Government to take such measures as will immediately effect the abolition of this obnoxious and unjust discrimination, and so insure for South Africa a full and free development of its industries and wealth, and permanent and lasting contentment for its population regardless of color, creed or race.

In these resolutions the attitude of the native African worker is clearly shown. It is our desire to establish a mutual understanding between the two wings of labor. . . .

Black Trade Unionism

. . . With the rapid growth of industrial unionism amongst the native African workers, backed by race consciousness, it must, indeed, sooner or later create uneasiness in the white trade union camp. Although oppressive statutory laws debar us from every privilege, yet the African race is making great advances. . . . Thus quite recently it was rumored that the South African Mine Workers' Union, the largest trade union amongst the white workers of this country, had decided to admit native African workers into their union. This declaration is indeed a moral surrender for the white trade unions, and a great moral victory for the native African workers who had all these years kept on fighting organized capital on one hand, while fighting the selfishness of white labor on the other. All honor to the pioneers of the I.C.U., who once having discovered the insincerity of the white workers, decided to carry on the struggle alone. We have been successful in building up a great labor organization without the assistance of white labor. It is a deliberate challenge, this, to the white trade unions of this country.

. . . Time will tell when the forces of native African labor will make it possible to bring about the disastrous defeat of selfish, organized white labor. Trade unionism can only succeed when it realizes that if one member of the family suffers, be it white, black or yellow, the whole family will eventually suffer.

I have tried to show that the defeat of white labor in Africa is inevitable unless the white workers change their attitude toward the aboriginals, and they must also show deeds of true repentance instead of vain phraseology. The tendency of unifying the various tribes into one solid bond is growing stronger day by day. The rapid growth of the membership of the I.C.U. illustrates this tendency. From all parts of South Africa and far beyond its borders, the growing desire of the masses of native African workers to form themselves into branches of this great labor movement of the aboriginals, threatens the very existence of the white trade unions. It is not intended to drive the white workers out of any industries. The desire of the masses of the African workers is that the doors should be thrown open to them: that they have a just right and certainly more claim to the great industries of this country. South Africa has great potentialities, a vast country indeed, and to deny the aboriginals the right to share in the management of its industries or to obtain a decent livelihood, is considered by the new black man to be a gross injustice, which, if added to the many criminal evils already inflicted upon the sons of the soil, may eventually bring a greater catastrophe to all concerned. Thus we find that the white man here in Africa theoretically constitutes himself as an "aristocrat" and forgets all his responsibilities as a workingman.

Our forthcoming "African National Congress," to be held at East London, another important seaport, beginning January 17th next, is where the minds of the masses of our race are focussed, while "white South Africa" is restless at the coming events. . . .

Whatever the path may be, the forthcoming Congress must determine to establish a formidable labor organization by which the native African worker will more and more win a real emancipation for himself, and take his rightful place in the ranks of those who do the world's useful work.

Note—This article was written in the Fall of 1923.

Originally entitled "Aristocracy of White Labor in Africa." Mr. Kadalie was identified by *The Messenger* as "General Secretary, Industrial and Commercial Workers' Union of South Africa, and Editor of the Workers' Herald, Cape Town, South Africa."

[d]
AWAKENED ASIA
AMY JACQUES GARVEY
Negro World/March 19, 1927

A guilty conscience has begun to torture the white race. They foresee in awakened Asia the stern hand of retribution preparing to return measure for measure all that it has received. They are in the throes of a horrid nightmare, superinduced by their own sharp practices that cause them to see everything red.

England draws closer to America as she thinks of Canada and Australia in the Pacific. The cycle of civilization is shifting, and with it the battleground of the future. The age of the Atlantic has passed, the age of the Pacific is here.

Soon a United Asia, with a population of over 900,000,000, will look across the Pacific at Canada of 3,730,000 square miles, sparsely populated with 8,800,000, and a U.S.A. of 3,027,000 square miles, with a population of 100,000,000 prejudiced whites and 15,000,000 disgruntled Negroes. The question that agitates one's mind is how long will the white people continue to treat Asiatics as inferiors? America and Canada are in the danger zone. They must either acknowledge the rising progressive powers of Asia as equals, or be made to do it within the next ten years by a superior force of Asiatic arms.

The people of the East are not aggressive, but they are a proud people and resent the badge of inferiority placed on them by their pale-faced brothers. While they may not make wars of aggression, they will certainly prove to their neighbors across the Pacific that yellow planes can fly as high as white ones, and yellow poison gas is as deadly as white gas. The 15,000,000 oppressed Negroes are asking themselves now the question: "What are we going to do when yellow rain comes down?" Will they say that the Asiatics are wrong to demand racial equality, or will they sing, "My country 'tis of thee, sweet land of liberty"?

White America can prevent further Pacific conflict by an intensive program of enlightenment among her arrogant population, which has been taught to regard dark-skinned people like dogs. Her statesmen should stretch out the hand of fellowship to China, and sympathize with her struggle for national independence, remembering the depths from which she came to be what she is today. This friendly gesture would counteract the bitterness and revengeful feeling of the Chinese, and all Asia would then respect America's sense of justice.

But it seems as if the inevitable must happen; Nordic arrogance refuses to treat with young Asia, and so war clouds thicken, as the blacks of Africa and America and the yellow and brown peoples of Asia nurse a common resentment for being called inferior by white nations that spend their time exploiting and keeping them underfoot.

A dreadful fear is clutching at the white man's heart; he knows he is wrong, he sees the futility of his continued struggle, yet for mere "cussedness" he will not be fair. He is in the throes of a nightmare. He hears the rattle of the slave chains, he sees an army of the black victims of his lust and greed rise from their graves and with pointed fingers at him say, ominously, "Remember!" He sees the sons of brutalized yellow peons dressed in his own armor, and on their caps are the words "I will repay." He arms the coolies of India and Afganistan to "suppress the revolutionaries," and behold! They advance, but they halt suddenly and about face with drawn swords they turn on him. He [awakes] exhausted from his dream but determined to kill and destroy before the phantom gets him.

Know ye, white men, that the East [has] a soul; ye cannot judge darker peoples by your own materialistic selfish nature. Africa and Asia are not out to destroy Europe by bloody reprisals; all they ask is that you respect their rights as human beings, entitled to enjoy God's green earth.

Originally entitled "A Conscience-Stricken White Race."

[e]
THE JAPANESE INVASION OF MANCHURIA
GEORGE PADMORE
Negro Worker/October-November 1931

Negro Workers, Defend the Soviet Union and the Chinese Revolution!

A new act of war has been committed by the Japanese imperialists in Manchuria, North China, where troops are being sent under all kinds of flimsy excuses to bomb defenseless cities and to annex Manchuria and turn it into a Japanese colony like Korea. The highhanded policy of Japan has once more shown the utter futility of the League of Nations and the Kellog "Peace" Pact as instruments for preventing war.

China, which, like Japan, was a signatory to the Kellog Pact against war, has now appealed to all the nations (including Britain and the U.S.A.) which signed this pact, to intervene, but is certainly unlikely to get any satisfaction. . . .

Japan and China are both members of the League, nevertheless, the attitude of the League has been such that Japan has been permitted the full right to send troops to implant herself firmly in the Chinese territory of Manchuria.

Hunt for Iron and Coal

Among the reasons why Japan wants to steal Manchuria away from China is because coal and iron, two indispensable minerals in the economic life of any imperialist nation, are both lacking in Japan, while Manchuria is rich in these minerals. Besides this, the Japanese capitalists already experiencing the effects of the world crisis are desperately attempting to find new colonial markets for their commodities and an outlet for the investment of their finance-capital. Furthermore, they hope that by starting a war they will be able to distract the attention of millions of peasants and workers who are actually starving from their class interests and turn them into national patriots—thereby mobilizing them as cannonfodder in carrying out the robber policy of Japanese imperialism.

Preparing Attack Upon Soviet Russia

This imperialist expansion of Japan into Manchuria brings her into conflict with the Soviet Union, for she realizes that it will be dangerous to have Soviet territory bounding to her newly annexed colony, as the freedom which the toilers of the Soviet Union enjoy will be an incentive to the oppressed Chinese masses in Manchuria to follow the path of revolutionary struggle against their Japanese oppressors.

This is another reason why Japan, like the other imperialist powers America, England and France, are not only interested in dividing up China among themselves in the same way as the European powers did with Africa during the last century, but are hoping to be able to compromise their imperialistic differences and unite together in launching an armed attack upon the revolutionary government in the Soviet districts of China and Soviet Russia, which they all hate and would like to destroy.

The capitalist powers of the West are all hoping that the Japanese militarists will succeed in provoking Soviet Russia into war, which will provide them with the opportunity of joining in the fight under some pretext or another.

The provocative attitude of the Japanese imperialists is shown by the lying reports which they are spreading with the aid of the capitalist press of Europe and America that the Soviet Union is supplying Chinese generals with ammunition to defend Manchuria against the Japanese militarists. The Soviet Government has categorically refuted these lies.

The Japanese imperialists require lies and slanders as an excuse in order to stretch out their robber hands against the stronghold of the revolutionary workers of the world, which has just celebrated its 14th anniversary; and which, with the greatest sacrifice and with utmost exertion of all its forces, is completing the third year of the **Five-Year-Plan.**

The new turn in the Manchurian war is an alarm signal to the workers throughout the world. Whilst hitherto the protests against Japanese imperialism have been isolated, it is now necessary to strengthen them and to carry out a mass mobilization of the revolutionary proletariat in all countries. . . .

Class–Not Race War

This new war of enslaving the Chinese people and stealing their country points an important lesson to the Negro workers and the toilers of the other darker races. It exposes the whole misleading reformist programme of the Negro capitalists, landlords and intellectuals in America who try to hide up the class policy of the Japanese imperialists behind idle talk of "unity of the darker races." Never will all the people of any race be united under capitalism, where there is rich and poor, exploiters and exploited. These fakers know this, but in order to make the poor working class blacks forget their misery, the so-called Negro leaders are trying to create the impression among the Negro masses that all people with a dark skin, whether they belong to the capitalist or working class, have the same interests.

In the present Manchurian war we see through this lie. For here we find the Japanese imperialists, members of the same yellow race (Mongolian) as the Chinese workers and peasants, using machine guns, bombing planes, battleships, and other devices of modern warfare to conquer and then enslave people of their own colour in just the same way as British imperialism oppresses the white toiling masses in Ireland, and the black Americo-Liberian ruling class their kinsmen in Liberia.

This is not the first time that the Japanese imperialists have shown themselves the same type of robbers and enslavers like their white imperialist brothers in Europe and America, by using arms to massacre people of their own race. They did the same to the Koreans, and since then, the Japanese imperialist policy in Korea can only be compared with that of the French, Portuguese, British and Belgian in Africa, where terror, forced labour and the most brutal forms of oppression exist. The Negro workers must not forget that in all capitalist countries whether the population happens to be white as in Europe, yellow as in Japan and China, brown as in India, or black as in Liberia and Haiti, it is not colour that counts, but **class.**

Rich Chinese, Japanese, Indians and Negroes exploit the poor of their own race in just the same way as white capitalists oppress white workers. **Exploitation knows no color-line.** A capitalist and landlord is the same bloodsucker, no matter what colour he might be. This is what every Negro worker must recognize in the present conflict in Manchuria; for only in this way will the Negro masses be able to expose the deceptive plans of their own capitalists, landlords and other schemers

who like Marcus Garvey, in order to build up their capitalist business enterprises in America and Africa are trying to get the masses of his race to believe that all black people have the same interests—whether they be capitalists, landlords or workers.
Originally entitled "The War Danger/War in the East."

[f]
DUSE MOHAMED
WILLIAM H. FERRIS
African Times and Orient Review/October 1917

We received as a pleasant surprise a few days ago the mid-January number of "The African Times and Orient Review," edited by Duse Mohamed, 158, Fleetstreet, London, E. C., England, which, after a two years' silence, makes its bow again to the reading public. When the news spread over the world that the European War had caused a temporary suspension of the publication of "The African Times and Orient Review," the judicious grieved. But who is Duse Mohamed and what is the "African Times and Orient Review?" the surprised reader may ask. We will briefly tell of the career of one of the men of might who has come out of Africa.

Duse Mohamed (Mohamed Ali) was born in Egypt about fifty-one years ago. His father was a distinguished Egyptian and his mother a Soudanese. He was sent to England while a lad to complete his education. But he was called home on account of the Egyptian War. His father was killed and the property was confiscated. Then young Mohamed travelled over Europe, England, and America as an actor. Finally he settled in England, and became a playwright, poet, and novelist. He wrote the Hull Coronation Ode, a novel and a history of Egypt. Five years ago a vast idea took form and shape in his mind. It was to publish a magazine that should circulate throughout Africa and the Orient, the West Indies of America, and be the voice of the darker races. John E. Bruce, the veteran writer of Yonkers, but now of New York City, encouraged the idea. Wealthy West Africans furnished the needed means five years ago.

"The African Times and Orient Review" issued first as a monthly magazine. It circulated in Egypt, West Africa, England, the Federated Malay States, Japan, British Guiana, the United States, Australia, Canada, Republic of Panama, India, Ceylon, South Africa, Jamaica, and Nigeria. The demand for the magazine was so great that it was published as a weekly. Prior to the European War it had grown into an organ through which the black, brown, and yellow races could voice their longings. It interpreted the darker races to the white race. As it resumes publication it has the same perspective as before. It has an interesting article on the Darker Races in the Press of the World. But its reprinting a famous essay overshadows the other interesting features of the magazine. The essay is entitled, "Ancient Egyptians, Abyssinians, and Ashantees: Their Common Superstitions, Customs and Arts," by T. Edward Bowdich. We extend our congratulations to our Duse Mohamed, and wish him and his journal a long and happy life.

Reprinted from *Champion* Magazine.

[g]
LIBERIA AND THE WORLD WAR
African Times and Orient Review/December 1917

America, casting her lot with our Imperial Allies, has presented Liberia to both belligerents and neutrals in a very new light. Before this most welcome alliance, Liberia was looked upon with very grave suspicion. So grave was this suspicion that Liberia was considered "Pro-German," which in consequence created a trade retaliation, which, if continued, might have ended in . . . economic crisis, as merchant vessels of England called at very long intervals at the trade ports of this black republic. . . .

To Western Africans enjoying the protection of the British flag Liberia is, and should be, a country in and around whose interests their energies should be directed and their hopes centered. Liberia's future, we feel, must and should be the great problem of Europe and America after the war. Her independence we certainly plead for . . . Bent on securing the freedom and independence of weaker states and nations, such as are our Imperial claims on entering this war . . . Liberia should have its share of consideration.

. . . If even the war brought about what would seem almost a super-human change of colonial administrative policy, if even the Crown Colony system of government falls before an almost Divine substituted institution and form of government, the present war policy founded on the preservation of weaker states demand that Liberian independence remains intact and inviolated. Reverting to Liberia's position: "Destiny seems to have forbidden the extension of Sierra Leone to the north-ward, and to have favoured her growth to the south-east, so that now that her territory adjoins that of Liberia, we have a continuous English-speaking Negro state from the Sierra Leone River to the San Pedro River—a distance of 800 miles."

Can we see from so favourable a position the possibilities of Britain and her Allies holding spheres of influence from Dakar to the Came-roons, using Liberia as the "Middle Way" to the gateway of half-slumbering West Africa's progress? It may seem Utopic! It may appear in the reading the wild dream of a faddist when we say that Liberia may in the years to come prove the highway by sea and land to West Africa's "El Dorado." . . . Although Sierra Leone continues a Colony under a powerful Imperial Government, and Liberia is a nation still struggling with the problems of independent nationality, yet our political institu-tions have the same origin. The same jurisprudence which contributes to the prosperity and elevation of Sierra Leone, which protects property, maintains order, and punishes crime here, has been adopted by Liberia, upholds the majesty of the law there, and guards us in the exercise and enjoyment of the rights of freemen. The form of government is a mere incident, and does not interfere with the original idea and special work of the Colony. . . . So, if the paths of the two countries seem to be divergent, they diverge only that they may the more effectually perform their work, by taking within the circle of their influence wider interests and bringing together larger contributions for the upbuilding and honour of the race. The American Alliance [entry into the World War], we hope, will create greater possibilities for Liberia, her foster-child. The provisions of international trade that the alliance will create and make after the war we hope will mean much to America. With the proposed and possible monopoly of trade that the successful end of the war will mean, we hope America will extend early facility for the trade prosperity and economic prosperity of this struggling Republic. May no stone be left unturned to obtain the huge capital of financiers that Liberia may have free course and development, thereby enabling its peoples to sing with one heart and mind

"Hail! Liberia, Hail!"

_____

Reprinted from the Lagos *Standard* and entitled "The American Alliance: Its Importance to Liberia."

19.
Africa and
the Afro-American:
An Editorial Debate

In the internecine wars between factions of New Negroes, there were
regrettably no face-to-face public debates between the leading proponents of integration and nationalist separatism. There were many exchanges of opinion between editorialists in the press, but few of them
extended beyond a one-shot commentary on an opponent's article. One
that did become an extended confrontation involved on one side the
avid integrationist George S. Schuyler, writing in the Pittsburgh *Courier,* and on the other Samuel Alfred Haynes, columnist for the *Negro
World.* The first exchanges occurred in 1927 and were renewed in 1929.
At issue was the question of the black American's relations to the
struggle in Africa. It was Schuyler, the satiric wit, ridiculing the entire
idea that Afro-Americans were concerned with Africa, versus Haynes,
the Garveyite idealist, willing to ignore some of Schuyler's fine points
of logic in order to win ground with a projection of a future international black unity. The four excerpts here start with Schuyler's opening, Haynes's retort, Schuyler's rebuttal and Haynes's final shot in the
1927 debate. (Haynes was for many years the head of the Pittsburgh
UNIA and later of its Philadelphia division. During World War II he
wrote for the *African* magazine, the organ of the Pan-African Congress
movement. His comment in selection (d) on his saving of white lives
occurred during the Belize uprising in British Honduras in 1919. At the
time, Haynes was head of the Belize UNIA, and bitterness that developed over a prohibition on the import of copies of the *Negro World*

into the colony had helped spark the uprising which destroyed some
$20,000 worth of white property in the colony and was eventually put
down by a shore party from a British naval warship.)

[a]
PAN-AFRICANISM:
A WASTE OF TIME
GEORGE S. SCHUYLER
Pittsburgh Courier/July 9, 1927

... The Pan-African Congress is a sheer waste of money, time and
energy ... insofar as the Negro peoples of the world are concerned it
might as well not be held. In that respect it is as useless as the U.N.I.A. In
the first place no other Negroes except a handful in the United States
are interested in the idea of Pan-Africa. . . .

It might just as well be understood that this talk of organizing the
Negroes of the world and getting them to understand one another and
work in unison is about as nonsensical as talk of hewing down Mt.
Everest with a toothpick. To the majority of Negroes of the world the
words "Negro" and "African" mean nothing whatever. They call themselves French, British, Yorubas, Vais, Fantis, Basutos, Zulus and so
forth. Only the blacks in the United States and the West Indies refer to
themselves by that uncertain term. . . .

The fact is that the dark peoples everywhere, like the light peoples
everywhere, are nationalists. There is no unanimity of opinion on anything among the light or "white" peoples of the world, not even on the
race question. It is just as [difficult] to get American, British, French,
Belgian, Spanish and Italian Negroes to agree on any one thing as it is to
get the white peoples of various countries to agree on any one
thing. . . .

[b]
PAN-AFRICANISM: A MIGHTY FORCE
SAMUEL A. HAYNES
Negro World/July 16, 1927

... This is one of the most crushing indictments against the Race and its intelligence that has ever emanated from the pen of a prominent writer. It is sensational because of the apparent incompetency of the writer to deal scholarly with the subject matter under review. It does not in any way enhance Mr. Schuyler's reputation as a journalist and would-be advisor on racial matters. The criticism is foolish. It comes at a time when Africa and Asia are about to join hands in combat against western imperialism, at a time when the peoples of both countries are reaching out for sympathy and understanding from these shores of light and learning. It will be received with much surprise in England, home of the West African Students' Union, in Africa, home of the African National Congress, and in the West Indies and Central America, where the idea of "Africa for the Africans" is a mighty spiritual force. . . .

If Mr. Schuyler's statement that no other Negroes except a handful in the United States are interested in the idea of Pan-Africa is true, then why is it that hundreds of others in Europe, Africa, Asia, Canada, the West Indies, South and Central America ... are supporting the U.N.I.A., the West African Students' Union of Great Britain, and the African National Congress? Why is it that the Negro World is barred in South Africa, more especially in the ... diamond fields of Kimberley and the Rand? ... Why do the British and French governments take such pains to admit only a certain class of Africans from abroad to their territories in Africa, and ignore the right of the African at home to communicate freely with his brethren abroad? What have these powerful governments to fear from a handful of Negroes in the United States?

That internationalism is foreign matter to Mr. Schuyler is evident when he states there is no unanimity of opinion on anything among the light peoples of the world, not even on the race question. What is more unanimous than the agreement between white peoples of the world to so shape the destiny of society that they will always remain strong and other races weak? They the masters, we the slaves? . . .

From a column entitled "Through Black Spectacles."

[c]
PAN-AFRICANISM:
A WILD SCHEME
GEORGE S. SCHUYLER
Pittsburgh Courier/July 23, 1927

... A couple of weeks ago in commenting on the coming Pan-African Congress, I stated that no other Negroes except a handful in the United States were interested in the idea of Pan-Africa. Mr. S. A. Haynes, a columnist on the staff of the Negro World, hastens to take me to task. After claiming that what I wrote is "one of the most crushing indictments against the race," "sensational because of the apparent incompetency of the writer," and much more to the same effect. As would be expected by me from an adherent of Garvey and his moonshine schemes, the writer claims that "Africa and Asia are about to join hands in combat against western imperialism," and waxes wroth because I am unable to see it. My friend, Mr. Haynes, with the characteristic insight of a Garveyite, assumes that because a few psychopaths here and there in Europe, Africa and America are screaming about "the race" and "Africa the Homeland" that means that the Negroes of the world are awakening and about to join hands. One might as well say that the world is going Bolshevik because there is a Communist Party in every country in the world. Agitation doesn't mean organization.

... Fellows like Mr. Haynes upbraid me because I do not "see the world through black spectacles." Well, I am content to see the world as it is, and not through black, red or yellow spectacles. No more wild and insane scheme than that of NEGRO NATIONALISM has even been promulgated. The idea of anyone talking of founding a nation on the basis merely of skin coloration! As well talk about getting all the long-eared people like Mr. Haynes together in one nation. These fellows are nothing more than lampblacked Ku Klux Klansmen, leading their followers astray with absurd doctrines of fanatical racialism destined to cause infinitely more pain than pleasure.

Mr. Haynes' logic is amusing. He takes me to task for telling the American Negro to attend to his own business and put his own house in order, saying heatedly, "What house? Any Negro who calls these United States or Europe or Asia, his house is impertinent and unreasonable.

Ownership denotes rights of possession, and rights of possession denote authority. The Negro has but one house that is divinely and legally his own. This is the house of Africa. It needs to be put in order very badly. That's why we need the U.N.I.A." Passing over the obvious comment that the U.N.I.A. just had to get rid of its own house on 135th street at the earnest solicitation of creditors and sheriffs because it wasn't in order, let us examine this fellow's logic. If ownership denotes rights of possession, and rights of possession denote authority, then Africa properly belongs to Great Britain, France, Italy, Spain, Belgium and Portugal. Aside from Abyssinia and Liberia, the Negroes are only inhabiting the land of sufferance, toiling to make the owners rich. I may not, as this gentleman says, know anything about internationalism, but I know that Negroes in Africa have no rights of possession and almost no authority, except in a couple of native states, such as Basutoland and Zululand.

Mr. Haynes is also wrong when he states that there is unanimity of opinion among whites as to their treatment of Negroes. That is to argue that the attitude of Elihu Root is the same as that of "Pat" Harrison; that the Governor of Arkansas thinks the same about Negroes as Branting, the Swedish Socialist; that the views of the late E. D. Morel and Roger Casement were identical to those held by Imperial Wizard Evans and Bibb Graves of Alabama; that Mary White Ovington thinks the same of the Negro as Premier Hertzog of South Africa; that Frank Harris looks upon his darker brother with the prejudiced eye of Thomas Dixon; that J. E. Spingarn and the Governor of Mississippi are equally bitten by the bug of colorphobia. . . .

If there had been no difference of opinion among white people, the Belgian atrocities would never have been investigated, slavery in this country would never have been abolished, most of our Negro schools and colleges would never have been founded and would not now be supported, there would be much more persecution of the black man than there is; there would be no black men voting at the polls and Mr. Haynes wouldn't be able to preach unreasoning hatred against white folks. . . .

From Schuyler's column, "Views and Reviews."

[d]
PAN-AFRICANISM: THE ONE AND ONLY WAY
SAMUEL A. HAYNES
Negro World/August 13, 1927

In one of his reviews some weeks ago Mr. George S. Schuyler referred to me as a black klansman and a preacher of hatred against white people. Writing in the Pittsburgh Courier he informed the public that Negro Nationalism is a wild and insane scheme. He called the writer a "lampblacked klansman," leading his followers astray with absurd doctrines of fanatical racialism destined to cause infinitely more pain than pleasure. This brilliant young man, ignorant of what is going on behind the scenes in Africa, says: "But I know that Negroes in Africa have no rights of possession and almost no authority, except in a couple of native states, such as Basutoland and Zululand." He does not agree that "there is a unanimity of opinion among whites as to their treatment of Negroes," and calls me a "shallow-pated propagandist" for broadcasting the contention that Elihu Root and "Pat" Harrison, the Governor of Arkansas, and Branting of Sweden, E. D. Morel and Roger Casement, Imperial Wizard Evans and Bibb Graves of Alabama, Mary White Ovington and Premier Hertzog of South Africa, Frank Harris and Thomas Dixon, J. E. Spingarn and the Governor of Mississippi are equally bitten by the bug of colorphobia. That there is a difference of opinion among white people in the treatment of Negroes, Mr. Schuyler cites the investigation of the Belgian atrocities, the abolition of slavery in this country, the birth and support of our Negro schools and colleges, the right of Negroes to vote at the polls, and closes his argument by saying that "Mr. Haynes wouldn't be able to preach unreasoning hatred against white folks."

When Black Sees White

Such contentions as these are the logical conclusions of a white mind encased in a black body. Like millions of others, alien education and environment have not made Mr. Schuyler "see the world as it is," but as it should be seen from the white man's point of view. No white journalist speaks of a "United States of Europe" as a wild and insane scheme, nor does a Scotchman refer likewise to the program for "Scottish independence," "Chinese Nationalism," "Egyptian independence," "India for the Indians." These are slogans accepted by those who shape the destiny of mankind as within the bounds of justice and reason. And an awkward public conscience looks upon "Negro Nationalism" as a valid demand, though belated. It is only wild and insane in the opinion of white men who fear its success, and Negroes like Mr. Schuyler who are like "dumb driven cattle." Years of travel and experience coupled with a persistent study of those problems which make for jealousy, hatred and war, have convinced me that peace on earth may be realized only when the families of the human race recognize the rights and privileges of each other, remain within the bounds of their habitation, and dwell together in brotherly love. Two families with the same ambitions cannot live peacefully under the same roof . . . Let the white man rule in America and Europe, let the yellow man rule in Asia, and let the black man live at peace with the world in Africa, the land of his fathers. If this is Ku Klux Klanism, then make the best of it.

Courage, Man, Courage!

Mr. Schuyler says that such absurd doctrines of fanatical racialism are destined to cause infinitely more pain than pleasure. . . . Who ever heard of pleasure in the quest for freedom? The thought of pain and suffering frightens Mr. Schuyler. There is no pleasure in the struggle for freedom and independence, save the knowledge that truth and justice always triumph. . . .

The One and Only Way

Because the thoughts and actions of certain white men and women in the higher walks of life, as they affect the treatment of Negroes, appear more civilized than that of their brethren, this cannot be used as a criterion of the whole. Ethical standards demand that responsible leaders of the white race eloquently deny and upbraid the actions of their fellowmen in mistreating Negroes; this is but a means to an end and no definite proof that they are really in earnest. . . .

How Hatred Is Engendered

The Belgian atrocities were investigated not because of a difference in heart on the part of Belgian citizens, but because of the pricking of a guilty conscience and fear of open rebellion in the Belgian Congo, and probably all Africa. It is well established by now by responsible historians that Lincoln did not free the slaves because of humanitarian impulses. The safety of the Union and the force of peculiar circumstances which then existed made the Emancipation Proclamation expedient. Negro schools and colleges are not given us because of any special desire to make us equals, but the white man knows from his experience that it is far easier to subdue a group educated through his tutelage than one dependent only on its primitive faculties. To boast of Negroes voting at the polls is like a doctor without patients boasting of his skill. If telling the Negroes the truth about certain phases of life as I see and understand it, if inviting Negroes to redeem Africa from the hands of those who exploit and ravish her is preaching hatred against white folks, then I have no apology to offer. In July 1919, I saved a number of white men—British, Scot, Irish, German and American—from probably wholesale massacre at the hands of an infuriated contingent of returned soldiers in a British colony, receiving the commendation of the Secretary of State for the Colonies in a special dispatch to the Governor of the Colony for my restraining influence. I volunteered for service in 1915 and served four years in Egypt and Mesopotamia, earning two medals and an honorable discharge. Hatred finds no haven in my youthful life. I am for peace and good will between men and races. I don't believe in hypocrisy, in deceit between races. Herein lies the incentive to race hatred which the U.N.I.A., to which I am proud to belong, is endeavoring to wipe out. No one need waste his time preaching to Negroes to hate white folks. Only white folks can make Negroes hate them ... I understand well Mr. Schuyler's position and sympathize with him, but when men of his type go so far as to incite hatred against Negroes who are earnestly seeking the truth about black and white relationship, they court the disrespect of their fellowmen.

From the column, "Through Black Spectacles."

20.
The Liberian-American Plan

Relations between New Negroes and Liberia were extensive. Through-out the period there were periodic visits by leading black Americans to Liberia, and excursions of prominent Liberians to this country.

One of the more historically significant New Negro involvements in the African republic involved William N. Jones and his Liberian-American Plan. Jones, a columnist for the Baltimore *Afro-American*, travelled to Liberia in the fall of 1933 to investigate a troubled situation there. Liberia had been continually threatened by colonial powers since its founding in 1817. There were periodic annexations of its territory by England and France, and consistent threats of intervention for payment of international debts. In the early 1930s the U.S. State Department, working through the League of Nations, devised a scheme whereby the League would send in white administrators to run the finances and civil service of the black nation, a move predicated on the view that there was a complete breakdown of Liberian governmental and financial stability. As analyzed by historian Charles Henry Huber-ich in his *Political and Legislative History of Liberia*, the League design was "ingeniously framed to deprive Liberia of its territorial sovereignty and place it in the position of a mandated territory or a virtual protec-torate." In selection (a), Jones describes the plotting of the U.S. State Department and outlines his idea for a plan of assistance from black Americans for Liberia, the objective being one of offering Liberia the opportunity to politely reject the League scheme on the grounds of being able to obtain help elsewhere. Selection (b) is one of the promo-tional articles for Jones's plan, run in the Baltimore weekly. At the

October 1934 meeting of the League of Nations, the Liberian delegate did refuse the League administrators on the grounds that Liberia felt it could obtain specialists "otherwise than under the Plan of Assistance" of the League.

A sidelight of the Liberian-American Plan was the propagation by Jones of some of the earliest statements about value of indigenous African Socialism in the process of modernization (selection [c]). In recent years the idea that communal native African social institutions could help Africa to bypass capitalism and leap from colonialism to a modern socialist system has been promulgated by a wide assortment of African leaders. That a South Carolina-born black journalist on a one-month visit to Africa should on his own uncover African socialism must say something about the concept. (Jones had worked with *Afro-American* editor Carl Murphy in the Maryland Socialist party during World War I. In the 1930s Jones was one of the more highly touted Communist fellow-travellers, until he hit upon the African socialism idea and the Liberian-American Plan, which the Communists interpreted as "petty-bourgeois nationalism." If it was black nationalist it may have been influenced by Jones's experience as an *Afro-American* reporter at UNIA conventions of the 1920s. In addition to his regular column, Jones was the first editor of the Philadelphia *Afro-American,* and during World War II was a European war correspondent for the *Afro-American* chain.)

[a]
AFRO-AMERICA
MUST HELP LIBERIA
WILLIAM N. JONES
Baltimore Afro-American/December 23, 1933

... I do not think I can impress upon you too seriously that the republic [of Liberia] is facing a serious crisis. The Firestone Company, backed by the U.S. State Department, seems bent upon instituting a white man control. Their ultimate aim, I believe, is to so change the land laws so that they can own, instead of hold under lease, their plantation.

Shortly after arriving here I had a dinner invitation from the American charge-de-affaires and spent most of a night talking to him. He was blunt in his insistence that for Liberia it was either the league plan or the end [a League of Nations proposal to have a team of white directors administer the finances of Liberia]. At first he suggested that I urge the people to accept the league plan. I told him that my mission here was simply one of good will and that I did not come to give any voluntary advice.

I made it plain, however, that if my advice was asked I was bound by the opinion of those who sent me, as I understood it, to advise that Liberia should not sign away her autonomy. When later I was called into a joint session of the senate and house of representatives and asked to take part in a discussion on this matter, I did express to them that it was my understanding that colored people in America would be sorry if Liberia had to make such a sacrifice for help under the league plan.

State Department Cable

Shortly following this session, the sentiment of which got to the American legation shortly after its close, there was released here a cable from the U.S. State Department in which it was bluntly said that the United States' State Department expected Liberia to accept the plan. This cablegram was mimeographed by the Firestone Company and distributed here and was intended to halt any sentiment I might make along this line. . . .

Standing Pat

. . . I might say that the present situation is this:

The government is standing pat. The League of Nations meets again in January. Liberia is expected to give her answer in January. As you know the league plan imposes an additional burden on Liberia of $150,000 and that $72,000 of this is to pay salaries of white advisers. The objectionable part, however, is that feature which makes the chief advisor the absolute dictator in all governmental affairs.

In private conferences Liberian officials advised that Liberia would gladly prefer to accept colored experts from America and cooperate fully in a plan which could be worked out to interest America in the future development of the country. Everybody here, even the opposition party, would welcome American help. It seems the only way out. Personally I believe it is a great chance for the colored people in America. It ought to meet a patriotic response in every little nook and corner of the country. Africa is now the most vital issue on this side of the Atlantic.

While I was in Sierra Leone I was impressed with the profound interest leaders there had in the matter. Every colored man or woman to whom I talked expressed the hope that the "great" American colored group would come to the aid of the Liberian republic so that it would remain a republic.

The same sentiment exists along the entire West Coast and every native chief to whom I talked made an appeal that Liberia be kept under colored control.

Even Japan

If the colored people institute a crusade to save Liberia and formulate a practical plan, it would open up a wide field of opportunity for our youth. There is opportunity for all of the higher fields of constructive endeavor, including road building, engineering, business, educational and cultural expansion.

All countries in Europe and Asia are pouring their young men into Liberian territory. Even Japan is bidding for trade there and in fact making headway. Only we in America are off the job.

Although Liberia needs money, her most serious need is intelligent manpower. She needs new blood. . . .

A Clean Start

In the present crisis the hard pressed Liberians are in the disposition to make a clean start. This, it seems to me, affords one of the greatest opportunities ever presented for the American people to lay a firm foundation for a real republic which will increase the prestige of colored people throughout the world. Our people are now linked up in a historical way with any development in Liberia. Americo-Liberians, as well as natives, feel that the good will mission came in the nick of time. They spoke of this expression of American interest as sent from God. I therefore suggest that our people further stimulate its development by:

1. A country-wide crusade to induce the U.S. government to at least sanction the effort on the part of Americans of African descent to help develop a strong republic in Liberia. Widely expressed sentiment on our part to this effect would no doubt make it possible for the Liberian government to reject the League of Nations plan with good grace on the

ground that their brothers and sisters in America had volunteered to come to their aid with a more feasible plan.

2. The promotion of a program whereby there would be provided a trained group of Afro-Americans to go to Liberia and help in governmental administration and internal development.

Save Liberia

3. That a country-wide "Save Liberia" campaign be immediately instituted to show the world that we mean to stand by the republic.

4. That in addition, some group, headed by men like Spaulding, Moton, or others, sponsor the organization of an American Liberian Trading Company to promote trade relations between Liberia and America.

Of course these are merely outline suggestions and are given more to suggest the trend of needs than an attempt at detail.

Reforms

The venerable Arthur Barclay who represented Liberia on the commission to investigate slavery told me that the present situation in Liberia left no room at all for any nation to say that the republic is not meeting squarely the problem of reforms. Even the well known "pawn" system formerly used extensively by the Vai people has been practically eradicated, he said.

Excerpted from Jones's report; the *Afro-American* introduced the article with a series of headlines: "Jones Returns from Liberia on the Bremen/Afro's Editor Home Friday After 3-Mo. Good-Will Tour/Finds Liberia Looking to U.S./Crisis Serious; White Dictator Opposed/All Elements in the Nation Are United/Less Real Hunger in Liberia than in Many Countries More Advanced . . . [Special to the AFRO.] "

[b]
LAUNCHING
THE LIBERIAN-AMERICAN PLAN
Baltimore Afro-American/January 6, 1934

MOVEMENT IS STARTED TO AID LIBERIA
AFRO-AMERICAN WILL CALL GROUP TO STUDY IMMEDIATE ACTION
WILL SEEK TO SEE THE PRESIDENT
NATION-WIDE DRIVE ALSO SUGGESTED

Plans for immediate action looking towards cooperation between the Liberian republic and American citizens were made this week when Carl Murphy, president of the AFRO-AMERICAN company, suggested an early meeting in Washington of interested persons to study the situation.

The first step in the plan will be to put the Liberian situation directly up to President Roosevelt and the State Department. Preceding this, however, a carefully worked out plan of cooperation and help is expected to be worked out.

To Call Leaders
This plan will be made public after it has been formulated by a group of white and colored leaders interested in the Liberian situation.

When William N. Jones, good will ambassador, was in Liberia the legislature passed a resolution which set forth in principle the fact that the government would gladly cooperate with American people in future development of the republic. This action of the legislature was approved not only by President Barclay but in a mass meeting of the Liberian people, and represents what is believed to be an earnest conclusion of the Liberian people that it is to the American people that the country must look.

Wide Possibilities
That a cooperative program between the people of Liberia and the American citizens offers wide possibilities for help, groups [of] citizens both here and there are agreed. It has been pointed out that in addition

to the historical and sentimental relations of the two groups, there are many mutual helpful reasons why there should be cooperation.

From the Liberian standpoint, of course, unless interested persons in America take an active step in her behalf she has hard sledding ahead. Not only are her troubles growing out of the Firestone Loan threatening, but neither England nor France wants her to live as a republic. Only the marshaling of tremendous moral sentiment in her behalf can save her and this alone American citizens can do. . . .

It is believed that should our 14,000,000 citizens show an earnest intention of joining hands in building a strong and self-supporting republic in Africa our government should give them every assistance from every consideration of American welfare. . . .

The page of the *Afro-American* on which this and the following article appeared was devoted entirely to news of Liberia.

[c]
LIBERIA TODAY AND TOMORROW
WILLIAM N. JONES
Baltimore Afro-American/January 6, 1934

Editor's note:—This is the second of a series of twelve articles on the Liberian situation as observed by Mr. Jones, who spent several weeks recently on a good-will tour to and in Liberia as a representative of the AFRO-AMERICAN.

The present Liberian governmental system is unique among all governments in the world. Theoretically it is a republic and in so far as Monrovia, Montserrado County, Grand Bassa County, Sineo County, Grand Cape Mount and Maryland County, are concerned, it is a genuine republic with well functioning governmental machinery based wholly on a constitution similar to that of the United States.

When you regard Liberia as a whole, however, you have a mixture of governmental set-ups which are all tending towards the republican representative forms. While every male person 21 years or over in the whole of Liberia as a citizen of the republic, could qualify as a voter and take part in the election of its officers under its constitution, fully 90 per cent of them are governed under a system similar to the colonial set-up used throughout Africa.

There is, however, even here a vast difference between white colonial governmental policies and that used by the Liberian government in native towns; for while the white colonial government is based on the ultimate objective of a white controlled Africa, the Liberian government is based upon the ultimate attainment of self-government.

Native Units

Since the further development of the Liberian system means that the big native population will ultimately come into practical citizenship and exercise more and more the ballot, their present status is important. The smallest native unit is the town which comprises a group of homes with their own selected chief, corresponding to our mayor. He is responsible to a council of elders which in most cases he obeys when it comes to important town matters. Two or more, some times many more, of these towns, make up a paramount chieftancy which corresponds with that of our governor and these paramount chiefs are responsible to the Liberian government at Monrovia through a district commissioner.

Socialized Unit

What may become very significant is the fact that as now constructed each of these towns is a purely socialized unit. The main items of wealth, including the land, is owned jointly by the whole group. The children are owned by the whole group and the whole group is responsible for the care of the aged. In other words there are no orphans or homeless old folk in a native village. The hard cold law of the bush has brought some evils, but it has also prevented some more subtly brutal benefits of civilization. Most of all it has left the native unit town a model in community control. As they become modernized they can take their places in the republican government as have the other more modern settlements of Liberia. . . .

District Commissioner

The district commissioner, an official appointed by the government to supervise native towns, is that part of the Liberian system which follows the colonial idea. He is the most important factor in native development. Representing the president he is in direct touch with the everyday life of the people. It is obvious that he can be a great factor for either good or evil and some of the most troublesome criticisms aimed at the government have come because of the acts of district commissioners.

When a town or paramount chief cannot settle a local matter it is taken to him. If his decision is not satisfactory to the natives involved, it can be taken to the courts at Monrovia or directly to the president.

President Barclay

... As matters now exist any native may bring a grievance to Monrovia with much more freedom and less relative expense than any of our citizens now living in the far South can bring to our government when they have been treated unjustly. My own observations as to how these appeals are treated leads me to conclude that the government is striving to cultivate and cement friendship between the natives and the government, and that it is only a matter of time when the district commissioner will become a locally selected representative ... The Liberian government is working towards that end.

Carrying On

On the whole, therefore, despite mistakes and successes, Liberia's official family is carrying on. The important thing is that it is the only government in all Africa except Abyssinia which is headed towards self-government. Other parts of Africa will of course attain self-government, but it will be through the bloody way of war or revolution. They will have to fight for their independence as America once fought, and as India, Ireland and other colonial dependencies are now fighting. To my mind this is one great reason why colored folk throughout the world should strive to preserve this one beacon light of hope on the continent, that this 50,000 square miles of African territory should be preserved forever as a laboratory of self-government. . . .

Presidential Grind

... The one outstanding thing about him, it seems to me, he understands the trust imposed upon him in maintaining the autonomy of the republic. He understands every move that is made to make Liberia a country in which its native people would have no rights any white man is bound to respect. He understands what is going on in other parts of Africa.

The Tshedeki case [in South Africa] dramatized white policy in Africa in that it set forth clearly that as white men enter this black continent they automatically become, because of their race, superior to native laws.

The fact is, it was a similar incident, involving a trial of a white official of a big corporation in Monrovia which brought into action the events out of which the present League of Nations controversy arises. When we, therefore, think of the government of Liberia as that of a republic we must also think of it as a Negro republic in which white men may be brought to account.

Against such black republic are arrayed colonial England, colonial France, and the joint combination of the Firestone corporation and the State Department of the United States.

V.

The
Harlem
Renaissance

21.
The Blooming
of the Renaissance

The initial call for the cultural renaissance was directly related to the social and political militancy of the postwar period. New Negro militants saw the creation of a vibrant black culture as a necessary parallel to social and political struggle. In selection (a), William Ferris presents in the *Negro World* a call for historical study and literary endeavor as an adjunct to the world awakening of the black masses. In its first years, the creative writing of the Renaissance was largely in poetry. Much of this poetry was highly political, as in Claude McKay's "If We Must Die" (quoted in an earlier section of this anthology). The theme of the inhumanity of white racists ran through much of the early New Negro poetry, as shown in selection (b) from A. V. Bernier's *New Negro*. The militant mood was captured in the work of artists who generally lacked a radical political perspective. Archibald H. Grimke, a man of academic circles, a political moderate, and an official in the NAACP, wrote in 1919 a poem that was rejected as too radical by the *Crisis* and the *Atlantic* monthly. It was picked up by the *Messenger,* from which it is produced here as selection (c). Grimke's "Her 13 Black Soldiers" is a eulogy to black troops executed by the U.S. Army for their involvement in a Houston race riot. While on leave in Houston, black soldiers had been insulted and threatened by a group of whites; enraged, the black troops struck against the racists. Reaction followed in the form of a white mob assault on Houston blacks, troops and citizens. Selection (d) presents another poem on black troops, one of several poems by A. Razafkeriefo printed in the *Crusader.* (A member of an immigrant family from Madagascar, Razafkeriefo is better known as Andy Razaf, the librettist for most of Fats Waller's pop music.)

In the early 1920s a number of anthologies of black poetry were published but few received much attention from the critics. Two collections that received wide acclaim were James Weldon Johnson's *The Book of American Negro Poetry* and Claude McKay's *Harlem Shadows.* A review of these books by Jessie Fauset in the *Crisis* is selection (e). (Fauset assisted DuBois in the editing of the NAACP monthly and wrote a regular book review column. She was a highly regarded novelist of the Renaissance period and was active in the Pan-African Congress movement.) In selection (f) Theophilus Lewis presents a *Messenger* review of another anthology of black poetry, and discusses the reasons for the preponderance of poetry over novels and short stories during the early Renaissance years. (Lewis competed on the *Messenger* with George Schuyler in the art of biting social commentary. In the 1930s Lewis was part of the black contingent that went to the Soviet Union to produce a motion picture exposing American racism; production was stopped by Stalin, and the film crew and writers were sent home.) In selection (g) Bennie Butler talks about the Negro's knowledge of "whitey." (Butler, a columnist for the *Interstate-Tattler,* had formerly been a sports writer for Garvey's daily *Negro Times.*)

[a]
THE ARTS
AND BLACK DEVELOPMENT
WILLIAM FERRIS
Negro World/April 30, 1921

The history and literature of any race are the credentials on which that race is admitted to the family of civilized men and are the indications of its future possibilities. Through all ages and in all nations civilized man has justified his existence by pointing to his history and literature not only as his proofs of development, but as evidence of his contribution to the total sum of human betterment and of the torch he has lent to light the path of man's onward march. The Jew, the Greek, the Roman, the Hindu, the peoples of China and the people of Western Europe are known and esteemed for what history and literature reveal of them and for the contribution they have made to man's knowledge and welfare. The descendants of these races may well study with pride and profit the history of their fathers and justly look with confidence towards the future.

The ancient history and literature of Negroes in Africa have not been emphasized by other races which have dominated the world with their language and civilization of other nations and races, know little of the ancient civilization and customs which still find expression in native tribes of the mother land. It is entirely possible that the destruction of the great Alexandrian library deprived the world of much of the history and literature of ancient Africa.

The campaign for the study of Negro history and literature conducted by the Omega Psi Phi Fraternity during the week of April 24 should meet the approval and secure the co-operation of all Negro men and women who are interested in the intellectual growth of the race and its future achievements.

[b]

THE VILLAGE LYNCHSMITH
New Negro/September 1919

Under a spreading chestnut tree
A red-eyed cracker stands
(A champion of democracy)
A rope is in his hands
And a veteran warrior is he
Of Southern Ku Klux Klans.

His head is hammer-shaped and long
And brainless as a pan,
His brow is wet with moonshine sweat;
He loves to "rush the can"
And boast that common decency
He owes no colored man.

Week in, week out, from morn till night
You can hear him madly blow
Against social equality;
Yet he will slyly go
And hound some helpless colored girl
When the evening sun is low. . . .

Raping, hanging, and burning
Onward through life he goes;
Each morning sees some crime begun,
Each evening sees its close;
Hatred attempted, hatred done
Has earned a night's repose. . . .

[c]
HER 13 BLACK SOLDIERS
ARCHIBALD H. GRIMKE
Messenger/October 1919

. . . And what did she do, she who put that uniform on them,
And bade them to do and die if needs be for her?
Did she raise an arm to protect them?
Did she raise her voice to frighten away the reptilian thing?
Did she lift a finger or shy a word of rebuke at it?
Did she do anything in defense of her black soldiers?
She did nothing. She sat complacent, indifferent in her seat of power.
She had eyes but she refused to see what Houston was doing to her
    black soldiers;
She had ears but she stuffed them with cotton,
That she might not hear the murmured rage of her black soldiers.
They suffered alone, they were defenseless against insult and violence,
For she would not see them nor hear them nor protect them.
Then in desperation they smote the reptilian thing,
They smote it as they had smitten before her enemies,
For was it not her enemy, the reptilian thing, as well as their own?
They in an hour of madness smote it in battle furiously,
And it shrank back from their blows hysterical,
Terror and fear of death seized it, and it cried unto her for help.
And she, who would not hear her black soldiers in their dire need,
She, who put her uniform on them, heard their enemy.
She flew at its call and hanged her brave black soldiers.
She hanged them for doing for themselves what she ought to have done
    for them.
She hanged them for resenting insult to her uniform,
She hanged them for defending from violence her brave black soldiers.
Loyal to the last were they and obedient.

[d]
DON'T TREAD ON ME
A. RAZAFKERIEFO [ANDY RAZAF]
Crusader/September 1919

There is a wondrous symbol
Which has come from 'cross the sea;
It's worn by every member
Of the Fifteenth Infantry.
A snake curled up, prepared to strike,
And one can plainly see
That by its threat'ning attitude
It says: Don't tread on me!
O race, make this your battle cry,
Engrave it on your heart.
It's time for us "to do or die,"
To play a bolder part.
For by the blood you've spilled in France
You must and will be free.
So from now on let us advance
With this: Don't tread on me!

[e]
BLACK POETRY: 1
JESSIE FAUSET
Crisis/June 1922

One of the poets whom James Weldon Johnson quotes in his "Book of American Negro Poetry," himself defines unconsciously the significance of this collection. This poet, Charles Bertram Johnson, after noting in the development of Negro Poets "the greater growing reach of larger latent power," declares:

We wait our Lyric Seer,
By whom our wills are caught.
Who makes our cause and wrong
The motif of his song;
Who sings our racial good,
Bestows us honor's place,
The cosmic brotherhood
Of genius—not of race.

Not all of the 32 poets quoted here give evidence of this cosmic quality, but there is a fair showing, notably Mrs. Georgia Douglas Johnson whose power however is checked by the narrowness of her medium of expression, Claude McKay and Anne Spencer. Of Claude McKay I shall speak later, but I wonder why we have not heard more of Anne Spencer. Her art and its expression are true and fine; she blends a delicate mysticism with a diamond clearness of exposition, and her subject matter is original.

This anthology itself has the value of an arrow pointing the direction of Negro genius, but the author's preface has a more immediate worth. It is not only a graceful bit of expository writing befitting a collection of poetry, but it affords a splendid compendium of the Negro's artistic contributions to America. Mr. Johnson feels that the Negro is the author of the only distinctively American artistic products. He lists his gifts as follows: Folk-tales such as we find in the Joel Chandler Harris collection; the Spirituals; the Cakewalk and Ragtime. What is still more important is the possession on the part of the Negro of what Mr. Johnson calls a "transfusive quality," that is the ability to adopt the original spirit of his milieu into something "artistic and original, which yet possesses the note of universal appeal."

The first thought that will flash into the mind of the reader of "Harlem Shadows" will be: *"This is poetry!"* No other later discovery, a slight unevenness of power, a strange rhythm, the fact of the author's ancestry, will be able to affect that first evaluation. Mr. McKay possesses a deep emotionalism, a perception of what is fundamentally important to mankind everywhere—love of kind, love of home, and love of race. He is extraordinarily vivid in depicting these last two. "Flame-heart" and "My Mother" fill even the casual reader with a sense of longing for home and the first, fine love for parents. The warmth and sweetness of those days described in the former poem are especially alluring; the mind is caught by the concept of the poinsettia's redness as the eye is fixed by a flash of color. But Mr. McKay's noble effort has been spent in the poems of which "America" (quoted in this issue's *Looking Glass*) is the finest example. He has dwelt in fiery, impassioned language on the sufferings of his race. Yet there is no touch of propaganda. This is the truest mark of genius.

From a column entitled "As To Books," the article reviewed, among others, James Weldon Johnson, ed., *The Book of American Negro Poetry* (New York: Harcourt, Brace and Co.); and Claude McKay, *Harlem Shadows* (Harcourt, Brace and Co.).

[f]
BLACK POETRY: 2
THEOPHILUS LEWIS
Messenger/October 1926

... I announce that I take no pleasure in the current jubilee in celebration of the "Renaissance" of Negro culture—that is, in so far as the "Renaissance" applies to the Aframerican.

I lead off with the cardinal heresy of denying that the spirituals are triumphs of art. I further depose and declare that I am aware of no Aframerican musician of the first order, barring a concert singer or two; that I do not concede the Aframerican any pronounced racial talent for dramatic or histrionic art; that not one of the expensive churches Negroes are building or buying indicates that the preacher has taste enough to prevent an architect or a passel of Jews from selling him a granite barn; that in the whole roster of colored prose writers under forty years old there are only two producing work which can be called literature without insulting the term: George S. Schuyler is a genuine humorist and Jean Toomer is the only story teller able to create a striking and original character; "promising" is the best you can say about the rest of the lot, and most of them are not promising very much. In fact, to make it snappy, the celebrazione of chocolate culture is 99 44-100 per cent pale pink whootle dust.

The only thing that saves the hullabaloo from being entirely bogus is the solid and stable work of a platoon of poets. With Langston Hughes at their head, or, if you prefer, Countee Cullen or Georgia Douglas

Johnson, such full throated singers as Claude McKaye [sic], Arna
Bontemps, Wallace Thurman, Gwendolyn Bennett, Helene Johnson
and at least half a dozen more are producing poetry every whit as
lyrical and mature and as critical of life as the work of their white
contemporaries from Edgar Lee Masters on down.

You certainly can't match this band of competent poets with any
group of prose writers of anything like equal ability. The reason is
obvious. It is because Negro life furnishes the poets with an adequate
cultural and technical background while denying the prose writers a
similar advantage. Maturity of spiritual expression is a social as well as
an individual development. A people lays the foundation of its literature by breeding illiterate rhymsters and story tellers who recite their
sagas for the entertainment of the customers of taverns, country stores
and barber shops or for the diversion of their fellow workers in the
cotton fields. . . . Next writers appear and begin to evolve a rudimentary technique. It is only after this pioneer work has been done that a
people can begin to produce effective artists; for even if a prodigy
appears before that time he will merely dissipate his energies creating
his material and devising means to present it to the best advantage, with
no time nor strength left to refine it toward perfection.

The development of poetry and the progress of prose do not proceed
along together with an even pace. Poetry is essentially the expression of
emotion while prose is essentially a medium for the expression of ideas.
Since in the common relations of life, love, anger, sadness, pity and the
desire for revenge are feelings everybody experiences daily while only a
few people either possess the ability or meet the necessity for sustained
thinking it is inevitable that words and phrases packed with emotional
meaning should multiply faster than terms invented to convey ideas.
Thus the poet finds both the language and the habits of thought of a
people prepared for him much earlier than the writer who wants to
express himself in prose. In the case of American Negroes universal
oppression has kept the entire race in a constant fever of emotion, but
only two men, Booker Washington and Dr. DuBois, have contributed
any original or effective thought to the problems of the race; and
perhaps you can add Fred Douglas [sic]. As for cultural ideas which
grow out of a refined way of living the race has produced none at all,
simply because there has been no refined way of living. With a background so saturated with feeling and so barren of ideas and refinement

it is not at all suprising that we have swarms of respectable poets while we have not yet produced six fiction writers capable of consistently writing up to the standard of Snappy Stories.

A refreshing and instructive book on the subject of Aframerican poetry is Poetry by American Negroes, an anthology compiled by Professor Newman Ivey White and Professor Walter Clinton Jackson, of Trinity College and the North Carolina College for Women, respectively. I take it for granted that both professors are southerners and up to the time of the appearance of their book eligible for membership in the Ku Klux Klan. Still, both the compassionate patronizing of the old line Southerner and the sickening cant and kudos of the current Stallingses and Van Vechtens are agreeably absent from their book. The authors neither profess a profound love for Negro poetry because they had black wet nurses nor intimate that because Claude McKay is capable of weaving an intricate rhyme scheme he is peer to Dante Alighieri and John the Baptist to a renaissance of Negro art.

Instead they discuss their subject in the sober manner of men with a sound understanding of the mechanics of English verse, a catholic knowledge of its variety and development and an abiding appreciation of its beauty. From this point of view they con the entire output of Aframerican bards from Phyllis Wheatly to Georgia Douglas Johnson. Their method is to submit samples of a poet's representative work together with a brief biographical sketch and a critical remark or two. Their book represents not only a prodigious amount of research, but also a faculty for detective work rarely possessed by literary men; for much of their material was to be found only in out of print periodicals and pamphlets nobody but the publisher himself ever saw.

The anthology includes samples of the work of six poets before Dunbar, with Phyllis Wheatly heading the list. Excepting the work of Phyllis Wheatly, none of the verses submitted can be called poetry except by courtesy. This, of course, is to be expected, for it is the work of writers who began to function before the illiterate bards of the cotton field and cane brake had adequately fertilized racial thought. All of these poets were simply verse writers ʟoying with primitive ideas. As these jejune ideas were culled from books, mainly European history, they were quite innocent of any distinctive Negro flavor. Dunbar was first to plow under the thin layer of tinsel ideas into the feelings of the people; hence he was the first Aframerican to produce mature poetry.

Since his time the poets of the race have gone deeper and deeper into the realm of feeling with the result that we now have a body of poetry as distinctively Aframerican as the spirituals. . . .
A review of Newman Ivey White and Walter Clinton Jackson, *Poetry by American Negroes* (Durham, N.C.: Duke University Press).

[g]
CONNING THE OFAY: WHITE REVELERS IN HARLEM
BENNIE BUTLER
New York Interstate-Tattler/March 17, 1932

Harlem is so popular with Nordic night life revellers. They come to Harlem night after night, year after year and never seem to tire of it, never get enough of it. Why? In my limited way I have undertaken the gigantic task of analyzing the Nordic mania for carousing in semi-Ethiopian centers. . . . The tentative answer is the fact that white America, in a very limited sense knows the Negro. But the Negro, in a very large sense knows white America. Negro knowledge of the white man is the reason the Negro is not extinct like the Indian. The Indian never figured out how to fight the superiority in numbers of whitey. . . . How does the Negro use his knowledge of whitey . . . The Negro takes full advantage of the white man's vanity, arrogance, ambition and fears. The Negro cons the Nordic superman. The ofay eats it up. He does not give the Negro credit for any intelligence whatsoever. A pullman porter will make the most insipid, insignificant white man feel like the president of the United States. And the funny thing about it is that the white man for years after will tell his friends how old Sam the pullman porter put him in the same berth where President Roosevelt or some other illustrious man had once slept. He actually believes, swallows hook, line and sinker, the porter's yarn about presidents having slept in that berth.

Dispensing sympathy is a specialty with the Negro. He can feel sorrier and express more regret over the illness of a white man's dog than that same white man could feel over the death of his own mother. The way the average Negro coddles and cons a white man and the way the average white man eats it up is a Ripley.

22.
Black Nationalist Intellectuals

Two distinct coteries of black intellectuals had been formed in the years just prior to the World War. But it took the coming of the New Negro to bring the differences between the two groups into the open. The New Negro brought a student rebellion to the campuses of the leading black colleges and universities. When the students of Howard University protested restrictions on academic freedom and the ties to whites coveted by the conservative deans of the university, Garvey's *Negro World* picked up the student cause and ran a series of articles criticizing the Howard academic situation. This solidified the split in the black intelligentsia. Two factions now congregated around distinct historical study groups (the uncovering of the Afro-American and African past was a vital part of the Renaissance): on the one hand was the Carter G. Woodson–Benjamin Brawley-led Association for the Study of Negro Life and History; and on the other, the John E. Bruce–Arthur A. Schomburg-led Negro Society for Historical Research. The former was based in the black colleges and had the support of white philanthropists; the latter was based in the Garvey movement. With Woodson's financial connections, his group was able to publish the *Journal of Negro History* and run the successful Associated Publishers to produce monographs. The Bruce forces had only the Garvey weekly and daily newspapers. The one outstanding achievement of the Bruce-Schomburg group was the amassing of the Schomburg Library, now a part of the New York Public Library, and the world's most comprehensive research collection for Afro-American, Black Caribbean and ancient African history. During the 1920s the Schomburg Library held regular public forums and conferences and earned the title of the "Mecca of the New Negro."

The Black Nationalist intellectuals—Bruce, Schomburg, William Ferris, Hubert H. Harrison, Joel A. Rogers, Richard B. Moore, Duse Mohamed Ali and others—found themselves ostracized from the American academic mainstream; and as William Pickens explains in a biographical essay on Harrison, there was a heavy hand of blatant racism in this situation—selection (a) from the *Amsterdam News.* In 1922 there was a direct clash between Schomburg and Woodson. The latter published *The Negro in Our History* with a number of photographs and other pictorial matter from the Schomburg collection but failed to acknowledge the source in his book. This slight was deeply felt by the nationalists, who needed any publicity they could get. Schomburg wrote a scathing review of the Woodson book in the *Negro World,* selection (b).

William Ferris had long been at odds with the black academic establishment. From sad experience Ferris had concluded that the black academicians were tragically alienated from the black masses. The Connecticut-born Yale graduate had been at the turn of the century a most perfect example of the white-educated alienated black, bouncing from one patronizing group of whites to another showing off his superficial talents. To escape from this way of life he first tried the ministry in the South, then discovered the Garvey movement. Selection (c), a Ferris review of DuBois's *Darkwater,* published in the *Africa and Orient Review,* presents a standard Garveyite argument on the isolation of DuBois from the black masses.

Selection (d) is a *Negro World* review by Duse Mohamed of the Dunbar Players' black theatrical group. Selection (e) is a John E. Bruce column from the Garveyite daily *Negro Times* on the significance of the discovery of King Tut's tomb. Bruce's pride in King Tut's blackness and the sarcasm Bruce hurls at white archaeologists exemplify the unabashed pro-black attitude which was common to the writing of nationalist intellectuals but which was toned down or purged from the "objective" scholarship of Woodson and his associates. (Bruce was one of the patriarchs of black journalism. He had edited a number of newspapers of his own; and "Bruce Grit's Column," of which the above selection is an example, was originated almost half a century prior to World War I. Bruce was known as a columnist with a "down-home" wit. He was founder of the Negro Society for Historical Research and was one of the few early aides of Marcus Garvey in the organizing of the UNIA.)

[a]
HUBERT HARRISON, SIDEWALK PHILOSOPHER
WILLIAM PICKENS
New York Amsterdam News/February 7, 1923

It is not possible that Socrates could have outdone Hubert Harrison in making the most commonplace subject interesting. Here is a plain black man who can speak more easily, effectively and interestingly on a greater variety of subjects than any other man we have ever met, even in any of the great universities. We do not like a platitude or a hackneyed phrase, but we know nothing better than to say that he is a "walking cyclopedia" of current human facts, and more especially of history and literature. And it makes no difference whether he is talking about "Alice in Wonderland" or the most extensive work of H. G. Wells; about the lightest shadows of Edgar Allen Poe or the heaviest depths of Kant; about music, or art, or science, or political history—he is equally interesting.

We know how hard it is to believe this, and we confess that we would never have believed it ourself, by report. But continual visits to the lectures which Harrison has been giving this winter in the New York Public Library, and elsewhere under the auspices of the public school system, have convinced us. That is all. We had heard Harrison talk on the street corners before—and one is apt to be disgusted or disappointed with street-corner talks, because of the hearer's psychological state and discomforts, and because he seldom hears the tale out. But go and sit down comfortably, anywhere under the dome of heaven, and hear Hubert Harrison TALK; evenly, easily, readily, wittily, but not too wittily, about ANYTHING under the sun, and if you have brains you will concede him the palm as an educational lecturer. . . .

The unfortunate thing is, that a man like Hubert Harrison cannot yet find his proper place among us. He ought to be a lecturer in some great American university. Not one out of a hundred of those lecturing in the universities have half his real information, and not one out of a thousand can convey it so interestingly. And we poor American people, white and black, have been so used to the white ideal, that it is next to impossible for us to believe that of any black man—until we become convinced. And most of us will never become convinced, for we will not even allow ourselves enough preliminary faith in the proposition to "Come and see!"

There is hardly a place for such a black man in America. If Mr. Harrison were white (and we say it boldly), he might be one of the most prominent lecturers and professors of Columbia University, under the shadow of which he is passing his days. Many white university people can be found sitting among the colored people at the Public Library on West 135th Street, or in some public school auditorium in Harlem, patiently listening to Harrison and writing rapidly in their note books—gathering material for their classes at the institution. And the strange human thing is, THAT THESE SAME WHITE DEVOTEES WOULD OBJECT AND PERHAPS WOULD EVEN REFUSE TO ATTEND COLUMBIA UNIVERSITY, IF HARRISON WAS TO BE THEIR LECTURER AND LEADER THERE. Of such poor stuff is human nature made. And yet these same students, if they bravely confessed, would acknowledge that they can listen interestedly to Harrison lecturing at ten o'clock at night on a subject in which their university professors could hardly interest them at ten o'clock in the morning.

Well, people used to go and sit on the hard rocks by the river to hear the Nazarene, or trudge thru the woods to the wilderness to listen to the Baptist, who would not have accepted either Jesus or John as heads or leaders of their synagogues. Fellows were charmed by Socrates on the corners of the small streets and in the market places, who would have felt too "proud" to enroll in a school or university course headed up by that bare-foot, pot-gutted old gentleman.

Such is human nature—and when you add race prejudice and color mania to that!

Just as Charles Gilpin might have gone on in cheap vaudeville and back street shows for the rest of his life—but for an accident—so Hubert Harrison may go on for the rest of his life, with his full mind and most instructive deliverance in the less prominent corners of public education—for accidents do not work so readily in his class of performance.

[b]
"THE NEGRO IN OUR HISTORY"
ARTHUR A. SCHOMBURG
Negro World/November 4, 1922

We expected, upon opening Dr. Carter Woodson's "The Negro in Our History," to find the treatment of the Negro in Africa from "a cursory examination" based on the people who were in touch with them—Iban Batuta, Leo Africanus, and Ildriel, and Dr. Barth's excellent works, not to mention others. His premises are not based on careful examination and research of these sources, but rather on speculative opinion and finding of latter-day writers.

The people of Africa at one time were, according to certain records, such as to compel Dr. Woodson to reach a conclusion that they were largely of the mulatto type. Whereas, any one who has travelled extensively in Africa must reason against the author, for it appears that the masses of Africans have been decidedly of pure black stock, becoming lighter by degree and time.... The word culture is used with much freedom and looseness in the treatment of the movement of people in their relation to early civilizations. It is too big a subject to be condensed in a paragraph. Dr. Woodson would have us believe "Drawing no color line these Arabs blended readily with the Negroes and gave rise to the prominence of certain Arabises blacks represented by Antar" (p. 9). Gibbons in his "Decline and Fall of the Roman Empire" relates that the believer in Mohammetanism has no scruple between his wives and the females attached to his harem. It is not a question of drawing lines but of religious belief and peculiar toleration of cult....

The book takes for granted opinion, whereas the historian should of necessity deal with naked facts.

"... cannibalism is practiced as the taste of human flesh does not differ materially from that of other animals" (p. 4).

It is unfortunate for a history in the form of a text book for school children to be marred by such improper statements....

Dr. Woodson would have us believe that Negroes were "so common" in the city of Seville, Spain, in 1474, that Ferdinand and Isabella nominated a celebrated Negro, Juan de Valladolid, as the "Mayoral of the Negroes" in that city. The writer has quoted this from W. E. B. DuBois's "The Negro" (p. 146). As this is somewhat misleading let us examine the source. Diego Ortiz de Zuniga, author of the "Ecclesiastical and Secular Annals of Sevilla, 1246-1671" (v. xii, 1475; p. 374), Madrid, 1677, gives us the transcripts of the patent creating Valladolid a Negro Count. Arthur Helps in his excellent work "Spanish Conquest in America, etc." (v. 1; p. 32), London, 1855, commenting on the case, says, "But the above merely shows that in the year 1474 there were many Negroes in Sevilla, and that laws and ordinances had been made about them." Dr. DuBois in "The Negro" ... says, "We find, for instance, in 1474, that Negroes were 'common' in Seville." Dr. Woodson goes one better on Dr. DuBois when he says "they were so common." Neither Dr. DuBois nor Dr. Woodson can show any right for adorning language at the expense of fact. Diego Ortiz de Zuniga in his able work only stated from the records that outside the small Negro village with its Roman Catholic Church and its brotherhood there was nothing to show that [Negroes] were as common as we find them in Harlem. Sometimes paraphrasing is a dangerous thing.

Here we have another instance. It would have been more appropriate for the Doctor to have called the discoverer of the city of Cibola, Esteban, as his foot-note from Channing's history (p. 75, v. 1) proves, rather than for him to have dubbed him diminutively Estevanecito; even George Parker Winship in his elaborate work on the "Coronado Expedition, 1540-1542," printed in the fourteenth annual report of the Bureau of Ethnology (p. 348), holds to the dignity of the proper name of "Esteban" (or Stephen).

Delving into the slavery of the West Indies, while he states that it "was most unfortunate" (p. 25), he says it can not be compared with the slavery of our own borders. . . . A peep into Coke's West Indies, Bryan Edwards' "West Indies" (5th edition), Southey's "Chronological History of the West Indies" (3 vls.) would have aided Dr. Woodson to a more stimulated and definite understanding of the slavery of the West Indies.

We do not feel like going into 340 pages to show omissions and palpable errors and enter into conflicting conclusions for a book seeking to enter the school room as a text-book with subject unsuited for the immature scholar in quest of positive information not after controversial arguments leading to endless discussion. . . . [But we do] question the propriety of the extensive treatment of miscegenation as dealt by the author to place before school boys. We need not parade before their eyes the palpable sins of omission and commission for which they are, as a race, irresponsible. Perhaps Dr. Woodson forgot that Dr. James W. C. Pennington, a runaway slave of Maryland, printed at Hartford in 1841 a "Text Book of the Origin of the Colored People." But why claim that William C. Nell and William Wells Brown are the "first actual historians produced by the race?" What proof is there that Denmark Vesey was born in St. Domingo, whereas it is known he was born in St. Thomas, Virgin Islands? . . .

A charitable appreciation for those who helped Dr. Woodson with rare prints, engravings, etc., would not have in any way harmed him in the preface. It is one of the few books lacking this feature of long-established custom.

The book is splendidly and profusely illustrated, but unfortunately out of tune with the rules of chronology. There is much information promiscuously scattered through the 342 pages for those who may want to read and enjoy the "dry bones of history."

This review bore the headline "Schomburg Tears Carter Woodson To Pieces for Historical Narrowness."

[c]
"DARKWATER"
WILLIAM H. FERRIS
Africa and Orient Review/June 1920

The much-heralded "Darkwater," By Dr. W. E. Burghardt DuBois, author of "The Souls of Black Folk," has issued from the Press, published by Harcourt, Brace and Howe of New York. The publishers say of the book: "A companion volume to 'The Souls of Black Folk,' dealing with the place of the darker races in the modern world, not a dry contribution to the sociology of the Negro problem, but a human document of extraordinary intensity and insight, describing the awakened conscience and aspirations of the darker races everywhere; how it feels to be a black man in a white world. Even more than the late Booker Washington, Mr. DuBois is now the chief spokesman of the two hundred million men and women of African blood." "Darkwater" is unquestionably a wonderful book, but we think that the last sentence could be somewhat modified and toned down. When we consider how one of DuBois' "Close Ranks" editorials and his aspiring to be a captain in the U.S. Army and editor of the *Crisis* at the same time was raked fore and aft by the Negro Press of the country in the summer of 1918 and how the Washington division of the N.A.A.C.P. rose in open rebellion, it tempts one to put an interrogation point after the statement that "Mr. DuBois is now the chief spokesman of the two hundred million men and women of African blood."

But it is not our purpose in this review to go into the extravagant and exaggerated claim of Dr. DuBois' friends and followers. We will not consider whether Oswald Garrison Villard was spiritually blind when he regarded DuBois as the only intellectual luminary in the African plane. We will not consider whether DuBois is too aristocratic and hypercritical, too touchy and sensitive, too dainty and fastidious, too high and holy to lead the masses of his race. We will not consider whether DuBois did or did not make fatal blunders when he attempted to referee the work and worth of other coloured men and to determine "who was who" in the Negro race. We believe that, if our Anglo-Saxon friends and well-wishers will cease trying to select leaders for the Negro race, thereby putting men into positions which their natural tastes and aptitudes and inclinations and previous training and preparation unfit them for, there would be more peace and harmony within the black ranks. Neither do we think that every educated Negro is to be relegated to the ash pile if he does not successfully lead a Negro group.

A book ought to be judged wholly and solely on its merits. The question as to whether the author is rich or poor, as to whether he does or does not possess social and political prestige and pull, as to whether he is a successful teacher, preacher, social worker or business man, should not enter into the discussion at all. A book, like any other work of art—like a poem, a musical composition, a painting, a sculpture, or creation in architecture—ought to be judged solely and only on its merits. And it is from this standpoint that we will consider DuBois' "Darkwater." "Darkwater" is a revelation of the soul of the author, as much so as Cardinal Newman's "Apologia Pro Vitâ Suâ." The strength and the weakness of DuBois, and his genius and limitations, are clearly revealed in that book. It was finished on his fiftieth birthday, after he had reached the years that bring the philosophic mind, and after he had twenty-five years' experience as a writer and a leader of various groups. It represents the matured thought of a man who has been somewhat

hardened and chastened by experience. All that DuBois has to contribute to the discussion of the race problem—the message that he brings
to his race—is contained in "Darkwater." His place in Negro history and
in American literature will be determined by that volume. . . .

Anglo-Saxon Civilisation

What shall we say of the book? "Darkwater" is neither a philosophical, psychological, scientific, historical, or sociological masterpiece, for
philosophical analysis is not DuBois' *forte*. The book is, however, a
powerful arraignment of Anglo-Saxon civilisation. It, with a master's
skill, exposes the arrogance and presumption of the Anglo-Saxon, who
was indebted to the Jews for his religion, to the Ethiopians, Egyptians,
and Greeks for his philosophy and theology, to the Romans for his law
and colonial administration, and who learned much from France in
literature and art, much from Germany in philosophy and music, much
from Italy in music and art, and much from India in philosophy, and
then oppressed the various races and nations who laid the foundations
of the civilisation upon which he serenely reposes. Nearly all of the
ideas underlying his civilisation the Anglo-Saxon derived from other
lands and ages. His ascendancy lies in representative government, in
applied science, in perfecting machinery, and in his aggressive and
adventurous spirit. He has shown genius in putting into execution the
ideas and thoughts of other races and nations.

When DuBois says, "Run the gamut, if you will, and let us have the
Europeans, who in sober truth overmatch Nefertari, Mohammed,
Rameses and Askia, Confucius, Buddha and Jesus Christ. If we could
scan the calendar of thousands of lesser men, in like comparison, the
result would be the same, but we cannot do this because of the deliberately educated ignorance of white schools, by which they remember
Napoleon and forget Sonni Ali. Why, then, is Europe great? Because of
the foundations which the mighty past have furnished her to build
upon: the iron trade of ancient, black Africa, the religion and empire-
building of Yellow Asia, the art and science of the 'Dago' Mediterranean shore, east, south and west, as well as north," he utters generali-
sations which are worthy of serious consideration.

Then, "Darkwater" is an amazing revelation of the soul of a cultured,
refined Negro of mixed blood. We see in it the agony of soul of a Negro
of mixed blood, writhing and twisting and turning in the cage in which

the Anglo-Saxon has confined it. It is the white blood of DuBois crying
for its own. It is the disinherited coloured offspring and offshoot of the
Caucasian, weeping and wailing and cursing and damning because he has
been disinherited by his Caucasian brother. If one desires to learn how
it feels to be cultured and intelligent and coloured at the same time, he
can find it in pages 32 to 35, pages 221 and 224, and pages 228 to 230
of "Darkwater." But, while the black and brown masses resent the
exploitation of Africa by Europeans, and lynching, restricted economic
and industrial opportunity, jimcrowism, segregation and disfranchisement in America as keenly as DuBois does, they are not as sensitive
about social ostracism as DuBois and the mulattoes, quadroons, and
octoroons are.

    ... the Anglo-Saxon who is mainly interested in a coloured man
because of his influence with his own people, and as to whether that
influence will be wielded in the interest of Anglo-Saxon domination,
will mainly be interested in the reflex psychological reaction of the
book upon the black masses. Coloured men will be grateful to DuBois
for his artistic pruning of Anglo-Saxon arrogance and Anglo-Saxon
hypocrisy. They will regard "Darkwater" as a literary masterpiece, and
doff their hats to DuBois as a supreme literary artist. But there are
three reasons why they will not go into ecstasies and hail him as a
Messiah and Deliverer, as they did when "The Souls of Black Folk"
issued from the Press and when they spontaneously hurled him to the
saddle of Negro leadership, although he did not seek the honour. In the
first place, DuBois is a Jeremiah who lyrically sings the woes and lamen-
tations of his people, but not a prophet who brings a message of hope,
not a Moses or Joshua who is bent on reaching the Promised Land.
DuBois eloquently expresses what is in the soul of the Negro, eloquently voices his protest and indignation against a blind, irrational, and
artificial caste prejudice, based upon colour alone. The other members
of the race know that they are in the bottom of the ditch in Africa, in
Purgatory in the northern and western States in America, and in an
earthly hell south of the Mason and Dixon's land. And their problem is
how to get out. Dr. DuBois has no constructive plan and programme.

    Dr. Booker T. Washington had the advantage in this respect, for he
had a constructive plan and programme. But that was defective becase
it vainly imagined that a suppressed and ostracised racial group in a
nation could rise by acquiring industrial efficiency and attaining eco-

nomic independence without the training of the mind and the ballot. Men who are in trouble, whether that trouble is moral, religious, social, physical, financial, or political, desire a way of escape or a plan of salvation. They want, whether they know it or not, some Messianic hope. I intimated in the *African Abroad* that Dr. DuBois lacked a philosophy of history, lacked what theologians call the vision of God. No oppressed or suppressed or ostracised race or nation can rise in a day or generation. The Negro race must progress and struggle upwards through a long, slow, and painful progress. It must cry out for justice and acquire what the races on top have in their possession—the weapons of destiny. These weapons are intellectual strength, political strategy, industrial efficiency, mechanical skill, commercial knowledge and economic independence.

How Negroes will Look at "Darkwater"

Now for the second reason. The chapter "Of Work and Wealth" is both a sociological study of East St. Louis and a dramatic portrayal of the economic, political and social facts that precipitated the East St. Louis riot in the summer of 1917. It is a chapter that one cannot easily forget. But as one reads the absorbing story, as one sees that vivid picture, one reflects why did Dr. DuBois and the N.A.A.C.P. make no move to prevent Dr. LeRoy Bundy, the black hero in that tragic episode, from being sentenced to prison for life? Dr. Bundy was a successful dentist . . . He was a manly man. He was, perhaps, not perfect in every respect; but his only offence was that he protested against the oppression of his race and advised his men to fight like men, when attacked, rather than die like dogs. One would have thought that this was a type of manly Negro that the N.A.A.C.P. would endorse. The fact that he used his own judgment about lecturing throughout the country should not have prevailed upon the N.A.A.C.P. to permit him to be sent to gaol without one protesting voice. As it is, others have rescued him.

Now, it is the failure of Dr. DuBois to translate his idealistic dreams into reality, his falling down when a practical case for need or aid appears, that causes many of his erstwhile admirers to ask the reason why.

Now we come to the third reason why the black masses . . . will not throw up their hats when they read "Darkwater," and that reason is the critical and hypercritical attitude that Dr. DuBois has seemed to assume toward other aspiring or unfortunate members of his own race. He has impressed them as looking down upon their infirmities from the heights of his own greatness.

Some of his critics claim that Dr. DuBois, like Lord Bacon, possesses a great intellect, but a petty soul. But they err. No man could have written "The Souls of Black Folk" and "Darkwater" who lacked soul. It is my custom to go to a man's own writings for an interpretation of the dominant motives of his life. In the first chapter, the autobiographical chapter entitled "The Shadow of Years," we find this interpretation. On page 10, DuBois says of his boyhood days: "I cordially despised the poor Irish and South Germans who slaved in the mills, and annexed the rich and well-to-do as my natural companions. Of such is the kingdom of snobs." On page 20 he said, "The coloured people of Philadelphia received me with no open arms. They had a natural dislike to being studied as a strange species." On page 21 he says, "At Wilberforce I was their *captious critic.*" These passages, and especially that phrase, "captious critic," explains DuBois' attitude towards the members of his own race. He was interested in them, but seemingly felt himself immeasurably superior to them, and looked down upon them from the august heights of his superiority in a patronising manner. And that is what the coloured people in Philadelphia and Wilberforce unconsciously resented twenty years ago, and what they have resented ever since—that attitude of a captious critic.

DuBois' Personality and Place in Literature

But DuBois' limitation is an intellectual, rather than a moral limitation. He is a man of thought rather than a man of action. He enjoys more the library and the desk than rubbing elbows with the man of the street. . . . He is of a studious, brooding, meditative and reflective turn of mind, and is impressed by the sad and sombre rather than by the bright and joyous aspects of nature and life. He possesses a keen and aesthetic sensibility, which is easily affected by the jars and discords of life. And he possesses the power of clothing his observations and reflections in prose that is imaginative and luminous, and that has the beauty, suggestiveness and aerial quality of poetry.

Let a man of this temperament be placed in a congenial and joyous environment, let the course of his life run smooth and clear, and you might have a Donald G. Mitchell, who gave to the world "Reveries of a

Bachelor" and "Dream Life," and those delightful studies in English literature called "American Land and Letters" and "English Land, Letters, and Kings." Now, let this man's fur be rubbed by a reactionary president of a coloured college, let him be greeted with indifference by the coloured people of Philadelphia, and let him then go to teach in Atlanta, Ga., where, as he says, "I saw the race-hatred of the whites as I had never dreamt of it before—naked and unashamed," and we may expect the sad, pensive note, the hot indignation of a "Souls of Black Folk."

And then followed sixteen years of mingled happiness and unhappiness. He received cordial appreciation as a scholar and writer, but the white people as a whole impressed him that he was not one of them. His own people did not understand him, and he felt that he was not one of them. With a man not temperamentally religious or optimistic, and facing the hard experience that all educated and refined coloured men must face more or less, it would be unreasonable to expect his works to ring with the buoyant note of a Browning or the serenity of a Ralph Waldo Emerson.

Not a great sociologist or philosopher, Dr. DuBois is a remarkably well-read and widely-informed man, and he possesses that magic of style and witchery of phrase which will not only give him a permanent place in Negro literature, but a high place in American literature. Let us not deify him as his friends have attempted to do, and let us not find fault with him because he cannot do everything equally well as his critics have done. But let us accord him a full meed of praise for his scholarly attainments, his psychological insight, his manliness and inimitable charm of style which ranks him with the masters of English prose.

[d]
THE DUNBAR PLAYERS, WHERE BLACK IS WHITE
DUSE MOHAMED ALI
Negro World/April 22, 1922

Did I see the Dunbar Players?

Yes, I saw them at Washington.

My opinion? Well, I don't think my opinion will be appreciated by them.

Naturally I believe in drama as an adjunct to higher education and culture, and of course, it obviously follows that in proportion to the class of drama enacted so we estimate the intelligence not only of the actors but of the audience.

I cannot say that the Dunbar Players have quickened Negro intellect; that is, if the samples of third-rate white melodrama which they are producing at present is any criterion of their ability. As a matter of fact, I think that they are misusing the name of Dunbar. If Dunbar stood for anything he stood for all that was best in the Negro, and it must not be forgotten that Dunbar was black, whereas the Dunbar Players are colored men and women who try to look as white as they possibly can on the stage. As a matter of fact it was difficult to tell that they were colored people when I saw them in December last at Washington. I repeat, this is not art; at any rate, not Negro art.

Of course, I agree that the black actor, when impersonating a white character, should whiten his face, even as the white actor performing a black part will be forced to blacken his face in the interests of artistic proportion. And here the comparison ends.

White men performing a Negro drama where the characters are all black is ludicrous. In like manner where the black—I beg your pardon, I mean colored—man attempts a drama of a third-rate quality that is white and whitens his face in order to appear white is also incongruous.

Oh, no. Do not think for a moment that I underrate the ability of the Dunbar Players. Quite the contrary. My main contention is that they are prostituting their artistry. The white man claims that the Negro and Negroids are apes—aping the white men—and the Dunbar Players are simply aping the third-rate white actor by performing a third-rate white drama.

What about Shakespeare? That is just it. Were these actors performing Shakespeare or any other brand of classic drama it would be necessary for them to whiten their faces. But then Shakespeare has some educational value and there would be legitimate reason for their doing so, which does not apply to the very mediocre plays they are performing at present. . . .

[e]

KING TUTANKHAMEN, BLACK EGYPTIAN

JOHN EDWARD BRUCE
Negro Times/February 21, 1923

The discovery of the tomb of King Tutankhamen's at Luxor, Egypt, and the finding of so many valuable evidences of the high state of civilization which existed among the blacks in Egypt 3,000 years ago has aroused the Savants, the scientific and daily press of the world to the point of making a more intensive study of this particular Pharaoh.

. . . That he was a black man, there can be but little doubt, reigning as he did in the south . . . we may therefore expect when his tomb is opened as is contemplated a year hence, and his mummy exposed to view to see a typical African-Egyptian whose features and fleecy locks will at once identify him with the race which has worn them for unnumbered years.

"This shadowed livery of the burnished sun" . . . This is what is worrying the scientists, the savants and the press. Mennon, who was also an Egyptian, invented the first letters, which Codum introduced into Greece. . . . Egyptians-Africans understood navigation, the principles of Commerce, the art of forging and working metals, of embalming the dead. . . . thousands of years before Europe or America were known the mighty blacks of Egypt were practicing the art of reading, writing letters and figures, building, making moulding, carving, spinning, weaving, dying, sowing, ploughing, planting, reaping, threshing, winnowing, grinding, preserving, embalming, navigating, fighting.

The flute owes its origin to the great Egyptian ruler and legislator Osin's. The celebrated Egyptians or Africans of Egypt, were at an early age a people who took an elevated stand in the civilized world and were familiar with all the varieties of knowledge which flourished in those days. The influence of their civilization extended to the people inhabiting adjoining countries.

The character and quality of the workmanship upon the jewellry, articles of furniture, and other objects removed from the tomb at Luxor, show that these early artisans were at least the equal, if not in some things the superiors of our twentieth century skilled mechanics and artisans. The opening of this tomb is a significant happening and its effect may be to revise the white man's estimate of the Negro and induce him to treat him more considerately and justly since the discovery in the tomb of King Tutankhamen [provides] tangible proof of the Supremacy of the black race in civilization, the arts, science, religion, etc. Inferior races cannot do the things which the "Superior" race now admits were done by the Egyptians three thousand years ago.

From the column, "The Passing Show."

23.
"Home to Harlem" and Other Works

The novelists and short-story writers of the Harlem Renaissance were short-changed by white publishers and literary critics. Neither the publishers nor the critics knew black society and consequently they established false standards and encouraged superficial rather than perceptive writing. In addition, publishers were out to sell to the white public, and if black books for whites offered little for blacks, so what—blacks were only 10 percent of the potential market, and a poverty-stricken 10 percent at that.

The manner in which the black literary critic reacted to this predicament varied according to the importance he placed on having black literature acknowledged by white judges. The distinction is traced in this section through four reviews which deal in part or entirely with Claude McKay's controversial novel *Home to Harlem.* Selection (a) is a review of the Renaissance output for the year 1928 by Alain Locke in *Opportunity.* Significantly Locke offers here a more critical appraisal than that found in his anthology *The New Negro,* the book which did more than any other to bring the Renaissance to the white public. In selection (b) James W. Ivy, writing in the *Messenger,* reviews McKay's book and finds in it a story of the working class that is "beautiful but frank." *Messenger* reviewers generally liked anything with a labor theme, and McKay's novel included a trade-union struggle. (Ivy would later become the editor of the *Crisis.*) In selection (c) Marcus Garvey roasts McKay's book and others like it in a page-one *Negro World* review. In Garvey's opinion, the sex and sensationalism of Renaissance writers fed the negative stereotypes of black people, offering neither guidance nor insight into the black experience. DuBois, in selection (d) from the *Crisis,* agrees with Garvey's judgment of McKay's novel.

[a]
1928:
A RETROSPECTIVE REVIEW
ALAIN LOCKE
Opportunity/January 1929

The year 1928 represents probably the floodtide of the present Negro-phile movement. More books have been published about Negro life by both white and Negro authors than was the normal output of more than a decade in the past. More aspects of Negro life have been treated than were ever even dreamed of. The proportions show the typical curve of a major American fad, and to a certain extent, this indeed it is. We shall not fully realize it until the inevitable reaction comes; when as the popular interest flags, the movement will lose thousands of supporters who are now under its spell, but who tomorrow would be equally hypnotized by the next craze.

A retrospective view ought to give us some clue as to what to expect and how to interpret it. Criticism should at least forewarn us of what is likely to happen. In this, as with many another boom, the water will need to be squeezed out of much inflated stock and many bubbles must burst. However, those who are interested in the real Negro movement which can be discerned behind the fad, will be glad to see the fad subside. Only then will the truest critical appraisal be possible, as the opportunity comes to discriminate between shoddy and wool, fair-weather friends and true supporters, the stock-brokers and the real productive talents. The real significance and potential power of the Negro renaissance may not reveal itself until after this reaction, and the entire top-soil of contemporary Negro expression may need to be ploughed completely under for a second hardier and richer crop.

To my mind the movement for the vital expression of Negro life can only truly begin as the fad breaks off. There is inevitable distortion under the hectic interest and forcing of the present vogue for Negro idioms. An introspective calm, a spiritually posed approach, a deeply matured understanding are finally necessary. These may not, need not come entirely from the Negro artist; but no true and lasting expression of Negro life can come except from these more firmly established points of view. To get above ground, much forcing has had to be endured; to win a hearing, much exploitation has had to be tolerated. There is as much spiritual bondage in these things as there ever was material bondage in slavery. Certainly the Negro artist must point the way when this significant movement comes, and establish the values by which Negro literature and art are to be permanently gauged after the fluctuating experimentalism of the last few years. Much more could be said on this subject,—but I was requested to write a retrospective review of the outstanding literary and artistic events of 1928 in the field of Negro life.

The year has been notable particularly in the field of fiction,—a shift from the prevailing emphasis in Negro expression upon poetry. In this field there were three really important events,—Claude McKay's *Home to Harlem,* Rudolph Fisher's *Walls of Jericho* and Julia Peterkin's *Scarlet Sister Mary.* An appraisal of the outstanding creative achievement in fiction a year ago would not have given us a majority on the Negro side. That in itself reflects a solid gain, gauged by the standard I have set,—for no movement can be a fad from the inside. Negro fiction may even temporarily lose ground in general interest, but under cover of the present vogue there has been nurtured an important new articulateness in Negro life more significant than mere creativeness in poetry. For creative fiction involves one additional factor of cultural maturity, —the art of social analysis and criticism. If *Home to Harlem* is significant, as it notably is, for descriptive art and its reflection of the vital rhythms of Negro life, *Walls of Jericho* is notable in this other important direction,—the art of social analysis. The ironic detachment of the one is almost as welcome as the emotional saturation of the other; they are in their several ways high-water marks in fiction for the Negro artist. Those who read *Home to Harlem* superficially will see only a more authentic *"Nigger Heaven"*; posterity will see the peculiar and persistent quality of Negro peasant life transposed to the city and the modern mode, but still vibrant with a clean folkiness of the soil instead of the decadent muck of the city-gutter. Moreover *Home to Harlem* will stand as a challenging answer to a still too prevalent idea that the Negro can only be creatively spontaneous in music and poetry, just as Mr. Fisher's book must stand as the answer to the charge that the Negro artist is not yet ripe for social criticism or balanced in social perspective.

The scene of Harlem is of course more typical of modern Negro life than a South Carolina plantation, but the fact that the year has produced another novel from the South almost equal to *Porgy* is one of outstanding importance. *Scarlet Sister Mary,* by a veteran protagonist of the new school of Southern fiction, represents not only an acme of Mrs. Peterkin's art, but evidence that the new attitude of the literary South toward Negro life is firmly established. To be rooted deep enough for tragedy, layers beneath the usual shallowness and sentimentalism of the older Southern fiction, is of course an achievement for the literature of the South, apart from the fact that this artistic growth has been achieved in the field of Negro fiction.

Indeed this new attitude of the white writer and artist toward Negro life has now become an accepted attitude, it registers more than the lip service of realism, for it is equally a tribute to the deeper human qualities of black humanity. . . .

I have reserved for brief final treatment what is in my judgment the most significant of all recent developments; the new interest in Negro origins. If there is anything that points to a permanent revaluation of the Negro, it is the thoroughgoing change of attitude which is getting established about Africa and things African. Africa has always been a subject of acute interest; but too largely of the circus variety. A sudden shift from the level of gross curiosity to that of intelligent human comprehension and sympathy is apparent in the current literature about Africa. In their several fields, recent publications like the translation of Blaise Cendrar's anthology of African folk-lore, *The African Saga,* Captain Canot's *Adventures of an African Slaver,* Mrs. Gollock's two informative books—*Lives of Eminent Africans* and *Sons of Africa,* Donald Fraser's *The New Africa* and Milton Staffer's symposium entitled *Thinking with Africa,* the publication of the new quarterly journal of the International Institute of African Languages and Culture called "Africa," and very notably, I think, J. W. Vandercook's *Black Majesty* represent in about the space of a year's time a revolutionary change not only in interest but in point of view and approach. Really this is not to be underestimated, because a revaluation of the Negro without an equivalent restatement of the Negro background could easily sag back to the old points of view. But with so thoroughgoing a transformation of opinion and an approach which implies cultural recognition to the Negro in his own intrinsic rights, no such reaction can reasonably occur; it will encounter the resistance of facts instead of the mere fluid tide of sentiment. Even when the reaction comes that was predicted at the outset of this article, there will be a vast net gain that can be counted upon as a new artistic and cultural foundation for a superstructure which it really is the privilege and task of another generation than ours to rear.

[b]
"HOME TO HARLEM": A SLICE OF LIFE
JAMES W. IVY
Messenger/May-June 1928

A series of episodes linked together through the presence in each of Jake Brown, longshoreman, ex-soldier, and lover of Harlem's teasing browns, who give themselves so neatly to sluttery. Two tales in the book stand out: that of Gin-Head Susy of Brooklyn, fat, black and ugly, but tolerated for her good gin; and that of "Rhinocerous," a much hated Pennsylvania chef, "a great black bundle of consciously suppressed desires." Of Susy, McKay writes: "Susy was wonderfully credited. She was of the Complexion known among Negroes as spade or chocolate-to-the-bone. Her eyes shone like big white stars. Her chest was majestic and the general effect like a mountain."

"The burning passion of Susy's life was the yellow youth of the race," "Susy's life of yellow Complexity was surcharged with gin. There were whisky and beer also at her sociable evenings, but gin was the drink of drinks—all-male were her parties and as yellow as she could make them.

"Yet for all of her wages drowned in gin, Susy carried a hive of discontents in her majestic breast. She desired a lover, something like her undutiful husband, but she desired in vain. Her guests consumed her gin and listened to the phonograph, exchanged rakish stories, and when they felt fruit-ripe to dropping, left her place in pursuit of pleasures elsewhere."

Susy, of course, is well aware "that the men's was most buyable themselves," and after keeping Zeddy for a time loses even him. Of the Pennsylvania Chef cook: "The short, stout, hard-and-horny chef was terrible as a rhinoceros. Against the second, third, and fourth cooks he bellied his way up to the little serving door and glared at the waiters. His tough, aproned front was a challenge to them. In his oily, shining face his big white eyes danced with meanness." His philosophy is "Keep 'em (the waiters) up a tree all the time, but don't let 'em get you up there." Those who objected to Nigger Heaven will, if they are honest, howl with rage when they read *Home to Harlem*. It is not a book for old maids, neither he nor she: it is frankly a story of the so-called common nigger; and pimps, bulldykers, faggots, "snoweaters," wild parties, razor fights, and sluttish women, are all written of in a free and open manner. McKay is not ashamed of this throbbing life of "Nigger Heaven." The book is beautiful but frank to the verge of cruelty. Many of the paragraphs are in reality poems in prose. Take the one about the "blues" on page 54, or the one on page 8 about "brown girls." McKay is surely a writer of talent, and we are hoping that he will try his hand at another novel.

This book is not a picture of *Harlem Life,* it is a slice of Harlem Life. The social milieu treated is actually and faithfully portrayed. McKay, however, does not include the variety of types pictured by Van Bechten.

[c]
"HOME TO HARLEM":
AN INSULT TO THE RACE
MARCUS GARVEY
Negro World/September 29, 1928

Fellowmen of the Negro Race, Greeting:
    It is my duty to bring to your attention this week a grave evil that afflicts us as a people at this time. Our race, within recent years, has developed a new group of writers who have been prostituting their intelligence, under the direction of the white man, to bring out and

show up the worse traits of our people. Several of these writers are American and West Indian Negroes. They have been writing books, novels and poems, under the advice of white publishers, to portray to the world the looseness, laxity and immorality that are peculiar to our group, for the purpose of these publishers circulating the libel against us among the white peoples of the world, to further hold us up to ridicule and contempt and universal prejudice.

McKay's "Home to Harlem"

Several of these books have been published in America recently, the last of which is Claude McKay's "Home to Harlem," published by Harper Bros. of New York. This book . . . is a damnable libel against the Negro. . . . Claude McKay, the Jamaican Negro, is not singular in the authorship of such books. W. E. B. DuBois, of America; Walter White, Weldon Johnson, Eric Walrond, of British Guiana, and others, have written similar books, while we have had recently a large number of sappy poems from the rising poets.

White Publishers Use Negroes

The white people have these Negroes to write [this] kind of stuff . . . so that the Negro can still be regarded as a monkey or some imbecilic creature. Whenever authors of the Negro race write good literature for publication the white publishers refuse to publish it, but wherever the Negro is sufficiently known to attract attention he is advised to write in the way that the white man wants. That is just what has happened to Claude McKay. The time has come for us to boycott such Negro authors whom we may fairly designate as "literary prostitutes." We must make them understand that we are not going to stand for their insults indulged in to suit prejudiced white people who desire to hold the Negro up to contempt and ridicule. We must encourage our own black authors who have character, who are loyal to their race, who feel proud to be black, and in every way let them feel that we appreciate their efforts to advance our race through healthy and decent literature.

Writers to Fight Negro Cause

We want writers who will fight [for] the Negro's cause, as H. G. Wells of the white race fights for the cause of the Anglo-Saxon group. Let us imagine Wells prostituting his intelligence and ability as an author to suit Negro publishers, as against the morals or interest of the Anglo-Saxon race. It is impossible. Yet there are many Negro writers who prostituted their intelligence to do the most damaging harm to the morals and reputations of the black race. . . .

The preceding bore the following headlines: " 'Home to Harlem' . . . Should Earn Wholesale Condemnation/Marcus Garvey, Foremost Negro Leader, Condemns Harmful Trend of Books of a New Group of Race Writers/Says Jamaican Negro's Latest Offering Is an Insult to Black Race/Sappy Poems and Pernicious Novels Written by 'Literary Prostitutes' to Suit White Publishers/Halt Must Be Called on Libelous Writers So That Negro Race May Develop Helpful Authors."

[d]
"HOME TO HARLEM" AND "QUICKSAND"
W. E. B. DU BOIS
Crisis/June 1928

I have just read the last two novels of Negro America. The one I liked; the other I distinctly did not. I think that Mrs. Imes, writing under the pen name of Nella Larsen, has done a fine, thoughtful and courageous piece of work in her novel. It is, on the whole, the best piece of fiction that Negro America has produced since the heyday of Chesnutt, and stands easily with Jessie Fauset's "There is Confusion," in its subtle comprehension of the curious cross currents that swirl about the black American.

Claude McKay's "Home to Harlem," on the other hand, for the most part nauseates me, and after the dirtier parts of its filth I feel distinctly like taking a bath. This does not mean that the book is wholly bad. McKay is too great a poet to make any complete failure in writing. There are bits of "Home to Harlem," beautiful and fascinating: the continued changes upon the theme of the beauty of colored skins; the portrayal of the fascination of their new yearnings for each other which Negroes are developing. The chief character, Jake, has something appealing, and the glimpses of the Haitian, Ray, have all the material of a great piece of fiction.

But it looks as though, despite this, McKay has set out to cater for that prurient demand on the part of white folk for a portrayal in

Negroes of that utter licentiousness which conventional civilization holds white folk back from enjoying—if enjoyment it can be called. That which a certain decadent section of the white American world, centered particularly in New York, longs for with fierce and unrestrained passions, it wants to see written out in black and white, and saddled on black Harlem. This demand, as voiced by a number of New York publishers, McKay has certainly satisfied, and added much for good measure. He has used every art and emphasis to paint drunkenness, fighting, lascivious sexual promiscuity and utter absence of restraint in as bold and as bright colors as he can.

If this had been done in the course of a well-conceived plot or with any artistic unity, it might have been understood if not excused. But "Home to Harlem" is padded. Whole chapters here and there are inserted with no connection to the main plot, except that they are on the same dirty subject. As a picture of Harlem life or of Negro life anywhere, it is, of course, nonsense. Untrue, not so much as on account of its facts, but on account of its emphasis and glaring colors. I am sorry that the author of "Harlem Shadows" stooped to this. I sincerely hope that he will some day rise above it and give us in fiction the strong, well-knit as well as beautiful theme, that it seems to me he might do.

Nella Larsen on the other hand has seized an interesting character and fitted her into a close yet delicately woven plot. There is no "happy ending" and yet the theme is not defeatist like the work of Peterkin and Green. Helga Crane sinks at last still master of her whimsical, unsatisfied soul. In the end she will be beaten down even to death but she never will utterly surrender to hypocrisy and convention. Helga is typical of the new, honest, young fighting Negro women—the one on whom "race" sits negligibly and Life is always first and its wandering path is but darkened, not obliterated by the shadow of the Veil. White folk will not like this book. It is not near nasty enough for New York columnists. It is too sincere for the South and middle West. Therefore, buy it and make Mrs. Imes write many more novels.

24.
The Press
and the Church

The church had long been one of the most influencial institutions in black society; and it was to be expected that New Negroes would attempt to modernize the traditional church. For a variety of reasons the heavy assault on the established church was relegated to the Garvey-ites and their sectarian splinter groups; while New Negroes of the left and those in the NAACP did little more than ask that the ministry become more involved in practical political and social struggle and less concerned with the hereafter.

Socialist New Negroes like Randolph and his *Messenger* crowd saw little use for things spiritual. But they did recognize the important community support they might gain from the ministry. Considering the hatred the white left spewed upon religion there was surprisingly little open hostility expressed in the *Messenger*. Instead, Randolph offered applause for those ministers willing to engage in the day-to-day struggle for a better world.

The black weeklies were generally reluctant to openly criticize the church. In many instances the leading ministers in the community were also the most wealthy black businessmen and the leaders of black society, social clubs and the like. In addition, church news sold papers, and almost every weekly had its church section, presenting homilies and announcements of Sunday picnics and musical recitals. The Baltimore *Afro-American* was one of the few papers to voice criticism of the church. Selections (a) and (b) present, from the same issue of the *Afro*, a typical church homily and a criticism of church greed written by the NAACP's William Pickens.

Garveyism was central to a shift in black religion on many counts. In selection (c) the Rev. R. R. Porter writes in the *Negro World* that

Garveyism was in itself an alternative religion in that it built a highly spiritual concept of racial unity and projected a vision of a future paradise for blacks in their homeland. The spread of Islam among blacks in the U.S. and Africa was aided by Garveyites. Numerous articles explaining the Mohammedan faith and downgrading Christianity were run in the *Negro World* and later in the *Black Man* monthly. In selection (d) from the *Negro World,* Amy J. Garvey discusses the growth of Islam in black Africa. Separatist black Christian churches spread from the Garvey movement. The most highly publicized was the African Orthodox Church of Bishop George Alexander McGuire. The beginnings of this Church as an independent branch of Episcopalians is discussed in selection (e) from the *Negro World.* (Bishop McGuire was chaplain general of the UNIA. Before World War I he had worked in Arkansas with the white communist-atheist Bishop William Montgomery Brown, who with McGuire's help had created a furor by performing integrated church services. In 1921 McGuire temporarily dropped out of the UNIA and joined the revolutionary African Blood Brotherhood. He returned to the Garvey movement in 1924 and remained one of its central figures for twenty years.)

In the Depression decade, Garveyites by the thousands dropped out of the UNIA to movements like the Black Muslims, and to follow Father Divine, Daddy Grace, and the like. In selection (f), Samuel Haynes complains bitterly in the *Negro World* that former Garveyites were finding in the likes of Father Divine "the reincarnation of Marcus Garvey."

[a]
STAND TRUE TO AMERICAN LIFE
BISHOP ROBERT E. GROSS
Baltimore Afro-American/June 9, 1922

Stand true to American life. Stand true to the Church of Christ. Stand firm until the storm blows over—and hold your people.

There never was a day when the Negro race was so dissatisfied as it is today. I have always been a conservative on race matters, but I wonder if you [know] how rapidly the church is losing hold on the race. The Negro is not looking for philanthropy, but for justice. Let this present wave of dissatisfaction move on and we shall have what Sherman once said of war.

Any man who says there is no danger does not know the situation. The task of your pastors is to hold the people up to the standards of the best that is in America. Whatever else happens do not lose your faith in God. Remember that the man who loves is far stronger than the man who hates. Strength is not always on the side of ships and armaments and ammunition. No, I am not preaching the doctrine of subserviency. I am preaching the doctrine of love—and love and forgiveness make for strength. If I thought I had a drop of subservient blood in me I would open my veins and let it out. I am simply preaching the Christian doctrine of love. And that is the doctrine you pastors must teach.

Stand true to American life. Stand true to the Church of Christ. Stand firm until the storm of dissatisfaction and its causative evils has passed—and hold your people to the realization of their highest spiritual possibilities, while striving for their intellectual and economic ones.

[b]
THE CHURCH AND THE PEOPLE
WILLIAM PICKENS
Baltimore Afro-American/June 9, 1922

In the desperate effort to make us fear the Russian democracy they are telling us and re-telling us and re-telling us about the Russian government compelling the church to give up their gold and silver and jewels and other hoarded wealth to buy food for the starving and dying people. Our reply is that any "church" that has to be "compelled" to do that ought to be torn down and its priests put into a mad-house. Why should a church have great wealth hoarded on the inside of it, while *people* die on its steps from hunger and nakedness? In the name of all the gods that ever were, *why is a church*? Is it not for the good of humanity? Any church that would not melt a golden *image* to feed a starving child, has no relation whatever to the Man of Nazareth.

The churches profess to be serving humanity and obeying God, and in the present plight of Russia, we would have much more regard for a cold, calculating business concern that had to be compelled to give, than for any church that had to be forced to give up golden wine-cups to save the lives and the souls of men. No material thing that any church can possess can be more sacred or half as sacred as the life of man. And yet, there are churches and "pastors" who think so. What a mockery they make of their pretensions. Does God think more of an image of the Virgin Mary (which, by the way, does not in the least resemble the humble and hardy mother of Jesus) than he thinks of a Russian baby? Such a God is a Moloch.

Those who let the people starve while they buy incense to burn are plain idiots or hypocrites. And when the enemies of the Russian government tell us that it is compelling such impostors to "shell out," they make us respect the Russian government.

[c]
GARVEYISM: A RELIGION
REV. R. R. PORTER
Negro World/November 22, 1920

I do not know whether or not Marcus Garvey is aware of the fact that he has given the world a new religion; nevertheless he has . . . Just as Jesus and Gautama have been misunderstood, the same holds true of the founder of Garveyism. The early Buddhists misrepresented things to win converts; the early Christians did so for the sake of sensation, the Mohammedans did likewise to outwin Judaism, Mazdaism and Christianity; and many of the present day followers of Garveyism are misrepresenting true Garveyism, simply because they do not know of its sublimity, and those who openly oppose it for no other reason than that they do not hold its founder to be a sublime person, should remember this: It is not always through sublime persons that great things come into life . . .

To me true Garveyism is a religion which is sane, practical, inspiring and satisfying; it is of God, hence a devout Garveyite cannot deny the existence of God, but sees God in you, [me] and the world. He knows God because he is part of God, and is assisting in the making of the Kingdom of God on earth. He respects all religious beliefs, yet he holds fast to that which he believes is best—Garveyism. He regards the rights of others; and obeys the laws of the land where he resides, being mindful of the fact that once he is true to himself, others, and his religion—through the right understanding of the One God, One Aim, One

Destiny—he too shall enjoy life, and live abundantly in the Kingdom of Heaven on earth, and that Africa shall once more become the land of the Good, Strong and Wise.

[d]
CHRISTIANITY IN AFRICA
AMY JACQUES GARVEY
Negro World/November 15, 1924

Christianity as taught by our Lord and Saviour Jesus Christ, is the most ethical religion in the world, but Christianity as practised by the majority of Christians is a farce and a mockery. The Divine injunction, "Love the Lord thy God with all thy heart . . . and thy Neighbor as thyself" is interpreted in terms of race and color. The fatherhood of God and the brotherhood of man is preached, but not practised.

If Christ the Reformer returned to earth today he would not recognize Christianity as the same doctrine he taught and practised in Jerusalem over nineteen hundred years ago. Christian man has fallen short of the glory of God, and has allowed this material, sordid world to rob him of his spiritual ideals and to despoil him of his moral ethics. It is therefore difficult for Christians to convert Heathens? to Christianity, for the former disregard their own teachings and imposes upon the non-Christians doctrines and religious obligations that they themselves ignore.

A Methodist missionary in Africa makes the following significant statement:

"The war has opened the eyes of the black man to some extent; he is beginning to feel himself not merely a citizen of the community in which he lives, but of a larger continent or nation of the world. Did not he or his sons go north to German East Africa, or to German Southwest Africa to help win the World War? Was he not transported overseas to France to discharge cargoes from the mighty ships, all in an effort to win the war?

"He became interested in that which is common to us all, in that he helped to win the World's War. He expects those brothers to elevate him into the light of better things. If the Christian Churches do not help the black man immediately the way to him will be blocked by Mohammedanism."

The above is an important admission of the weakness of Christianity in influencing non-Christians. The weakness lies not in the doctrine, but in its practise. Missionaries and Preachers should remember that they are regarded as the disciples of Christ on earth, and their lives should be patterned after our Lord and Saviour. Instead of practising the doctrine of love and charity, they are the fore-runners of traders; they abuse the confidence of the natives, and teach them to sing—"Take all the world, but give me Jesus." As if Jesus was a physical thing that can satisfy the wants of poor, backward peoples!

It is time the Negroes realized the hypocrisy of white missionaries, and send black missionaries to Africa instead, to teach their brothers how to live progressive lives on earth and prepare them for the Great Beyond. Africa needs new missionaries. Men of vision, self-sacrificing pioneers, who will take education and progress to satisfy the material needs of the people, and a Christianity that will satisfy their spiritual wants. Black men should teach black men.

Mohammedanism will triumph in Africa if Negro Christians are so selfish as to allow it. Islam knows no color bar, no segregation; hence the teaching of Mohammed finds a quicker response in the hearts of non-Christians, who in his awakened consciousness feels that his spirit cannot be uplifted and his physical degraded. There must be a co-ordination of the spiritual and the physical.

We appeal to the Negro Churches of all denominations to unite in this work of helping the African in Africa to know Christ and to know his own possibilities as a man. If we fail to heed the cry of awakened Africa Mohammedanism will conquer, and a further breach will be created between Africans at home and Africans abroad.

[e]
THE CHURCH ETHIOPIC
Negro World/April 2, 1921

On Tuesday . . . March 22, 1921, the Rev. Richard Hilton Tobitt, B.A., formerly a deacon in the A. M. E. Church, and recently elected [UNIA] leader of the Eastern Province of the West Indies, was ordained a presbyter of the Church of God, in the Chapel of the Good Shepherd, Independent Episcopal, of the City of New York, by "His Grace," the Most Reverend George Alexander McGuire, M.D. . . . Rev. Mr. Tobitt left next day by steamer for his field in the West Indies and bears in addition to his commission [from the UNIA] an appointment from His Grace as General Missionary for religious awakening among our people in the islands who desire to have their own religious teachers. . . . The Most Rev. George A. McGuire came from the Diocese of Antigua, B.W.I., in 1919 . . . After a brief service with one of the white Episcopal churches he became convinced that, as a disciple and convert of Garveyism, he could not longer be under the ecclesiastical government of white bishops and other clergy. He became the organizer of a new Episcopal church for his race, and believed that God called him, even as Moses and Paul were called. This religious body is known as the Independent Episcopal Church. In Greater New York there are at present three congregations . . .

Speaking for himself, Dr. McGuire said [in his Easter service at Liberty Hall] that by contact with the Hon. Marcus Garvey he had found himself. Though somewhat of a theologian, yet his (the speaker's) vision was narrow; though somewhat of a race historian his facts were limited, but sitting at the feet of his great teacher (meaning Mr. Garvey) as Paul sat at the feet of Gamaliel, he had become reanimated and his heart began to throb anew. Today he could stand foursquare to the winds and look any man in the face, whether he be white, yellow, or red, and feel himself a peer and the equal of that man. And because he was no longer a dead Negro but a resurrected Negro, he had revised his creed. . . . He had formerly known only the creed of the Apostles

Nimrod's God, in the God of Ham, in the God of Jethro. Continuing, he said: We have believed heretofore in the Caucasians' God. Now the time has come when our own teachers, receiving fresh inspiration, are not going back to the God that Moses taught his people; not to the God that Isaiah revealed to his people, nor do we believe in Mohammed's God; we believe in the God of the Negro, and we believe in Negro leadership....

Last August Dr. McGuire ... received the greatest honor of his career when he was elected Chaplain General of the Universal Negro Improvement Association, and titular Archbishop of Ethiopia, sworn to be the spiritual guide and moral adviser of the four millions of members of the association ... Archbishop McGuire feels himself truly equipped and authorized for the large work entrusted to his care and supervision, and hopes to prove himself truly an Episcopus, or overseer, of the Church for which Negroes everywhere are looking.... he believes that the time has come for church unity among Negroes; he believes that unity does not necessarily mean uniformity in worship, and that the coming African or Ethiopian Church will be big enough for all Negroes to enter, retaining their own worship as Methodists, Baptists, Episcopalians, etc. All over North, Central and South America and the West Indies ministers, catechists and lay-readers are at work under His Grace.... The Negroes of the world in convention assembled made the Most Rev. Dr. G. A. McGuire the first Prince of the Church Ethiopic. We understand that plans are under way for his enthronement at the coming convention in August next. The Negro World and its readers pray long life and successful leadership for His Grace.

[f].
THE DECLINE OF MARCUS GARVEY AND THE RISE OF THE NEW ISMS
SAMUEL HAYNES
Negro World/April 15, 1933

Since the enforced absence of the Hon. Marcus Garvey, founder and president-general of the Universal Negro Improvement Association (August 1929) of the World, from the United States, thousands of members of the organization who have labored unselfishly, devoted sacrificially for its development in their respective communities; hundreds more who have severed family ties and bonds of friendship rather than betray their allegiance to the great ideal embodied in the motto: "One God! One Aim! One Destiny!" have been driven from active participation in their respective divisions, by the treachery, disloyalty and downright dishonesty of executives delegated by Mr. Garvey to carry on in his absence. . . .

Our organization has disintegrated into a vicious network of private clubs and societies, where the principles of the movement have been subordinated to new "isms," creeds, cults, and mysticism. Former Garveyites are now enrolled in the Moorish-American Society; in various African movements, most of them founded by ex-Garveyites themselves, who had filched the constitution of the U.N.I.A. to fool the people; in new religious movements claiming to be associated with Garveyism. Former Garveyites see in Father Divine, Evangelist G. Wilson, Bishop Grace and others the reincarnation of Marcus Garvey
. . .

VI.

Toward the Future

25.
Toward the Future

To conclude this volume, two selections are chosen from the pen of Amy J. Garvey for their commentary on themes at the heart of the present liberation struggle.

When poet Langston Hughes wrote "I Am a Negro—and Beautiful," the statement was loudly applauded by Mrs. Garvey in the *Negro World* (selection [a]), because Hughes seemed to have epitomized the new-found dignity of black people.

Mrs. Garvey discusses in selection (b) the importance for the Third World of the principle of self-determination which came out of the First World War.

[a]
BLACK IS BEAUTIFUL
AMY JACQUES GARVEY
Negro World/July 10, 1926

Too much cannot be said in denouncing the class of "want-to-be-white" Negroes one finds everywhere. This race-destroying group are dissatisfied with their mothers and with their Creator. Mother is too dark "to pass" and God made a mistake when he made black people. With this fallacy uppermost in their minds, they bleach their skins and straighten their hair in mad efforts to look like their ideal type. To what end, one asks? To the end that they may be admitted to better jobs, moneyed circles, and, in short, share the blessings of the prosperous white race.

They are too lazy to help build a prosperous Negro race, but choose the easier route—crossing the racial border. It is the way of the weakling, and in their ignorance and stupidity they advise others to do like-wise. As if 400,000,000 Negroes could change their skins overnight. And if they could, would they? Seeing that the bulk of Negroes are to be found on the great continent of Africa, and they, thank Heaven, are proud of their black skins and curly hair. The would-be-white few are fast disappearing in the Western World, as the entire race, through the preachments of Marcus Garvey, has found its soul, and is out to acquire for itself and its posterity all that makes other races honored and respected.

This urge for whiteness is not just a mental gesture, it is a slavish complex, the remnant of slavery, to look like "Massa," to speak like him, even to cuss and drink like him. In last week's issue of the Nation Magazine, Langston Hughes, a poet, wrote a splendid article on the difficulties facing the Negro artist, in which he described the racial state of mind of a Philadelphia club woman, which is typical of the group under discussion. He states:

"The old subconscious 'white is best' runs through her mind. Years of study under white teachers, a lifetime of white books, pictures and papers, and white manners, morals and Puritan standards made her dislike the spirituals. And now she turns up her nose at jazz and all its manifestations—likewise almost everything else distinctly racial. She does not care for the Weinold Reiss portraits of Negroes, because they are 'too Negro.' She does not want a true picture of herself from anybody. She wants the artist to flatter her, to make the white world believe that all Negroes are as smug and as near white in soul as [she] wants to be."

We are delighted with the frank statement of Mr. Hughes in a white magazine; we do not know if he is a registered member of the Universal Negro Improvement Association; in any event his closing paragraph marks him as a keen student of Garveyism, and with stamina enough to express its ideals:

"To my mind, it is the duty of the younger Negro artist, if he accepts any duties at all from the outsiders, to change through the force of his art that old whispering, 'I want to be white,' hidden in the aspirations of his people, to 'Why should I want to be white? I am a Negro—and beautiful!' . . . We younger artists who create now intend to express our individual dark-skinned selves without fear or shame. If white people are pleased we are glad. If they are not, it doesn't matter."

Bravo, Mr. Hughes! From now on under your leadership we expect our artists to express their real souls, and give us art that is colorful, full of ecstasy, dulcent and even tragic; for has it not been admitted by those who would undervalue us that the Negro is a born artist. Then, let the canvas come to life with dark faces; let poetry charm the muses with the hopes and aspirations of our race; let the musicians drown our sorrows with the merry jazz; while a race is in the making, and steadily moving on to nationhood and to power.

Play up, boys, and let the world know "We are Negroes—and beautiful."

[b]
THE TIDAL WAVE
OF OPPRESSED PEOPLES
BEATS AGAINST THE COLOR LINE
AMY JACQUES GARVEY
Negro World/July 18, 1925

The thoughtful of the white race are alive to the fact that the darker peoples of the world are taking the much discussed war pronouncement of the late Woodrow Wilson seriously, namely, "The principle of self-determination." This phrase has been echoing and re-echoing round the globe since it was uttered, the practical application of which would usher in a new era of political and economic freedom for the darker peoples, and peace to the world; but the avaricious, selfish white man sees in it a menace to his land grabbing activities in the East, and a menace to his overlordship.

The Eastern Giant is awakened, and in his consciousness he listens to the Christian teaching of the white Missionary: "Do unto others, as ye would that they do unto you." He watches them put this into practice, and he realizes that they preach what they do not, and never intend to practice. He unmasks him, and behold he sees a common land thief, whose sole purpose is to exploit and rule. The phrase, "the principle of self-determination" coming from the lips of the white man is applicable only to members of his race; but when it is spoken to men of other races it loses its original form, and in its application resembles, "the principle of exploitation." The Eastern Giant is now exercising his muscles, and we notice a quiver in China, and an expansion in Morocco, but the day is fast approaching when he will have corralled all the strength of his scattered nerve power and stalk forth to sovereignty and to power.

The white man is too innately selfish to yield one inch of his ill-gotten power to another race. He refuses to be just and fair in his dealings with the other portion of humanity that does not look like him ... The groans and entreaties of our forebears have gone up to high Heaven, and our supplications have been heard, and in God's good time He will bring to pass that happiness on earth that all down-trodden peoples pray for. Whether we be black Mohammedans or black Christians ... our racial interests are identical. We are all struggling under the same yoke, and by the help of God, Allah, the First Cause, or the Omnipotent, we will join forces, and throw off the common oppressor, and live up to the high calling of our Creator, and in obedience to His injunction—"Ye are the lords of Creation."

Appendix

The appendix includes a listing of black American news agencies, and magazines and newspapers of general interest news and literature, and covers the period of World War I into the early 1930s. Excluded are trade journals, organs of fraternal orders, school periodicals and expressly religious publications. The appendix is compiled from listings in the issues of the *Negro Yearbook* from 1918-1919 to 1931-32, and from additional periodical listings in Robert T. Kerlin's *Voice of the Negro 1919* and Frederick G. Detweiler's *The Negro Press in the United States*. An asterisk denotes publications represented in this volume; a dagger, those appearing only in later (1925-26, 1931-32) volumes of the *Negro Yearbook*.

NEWS AGENCIES

Associated Negro Press	C. A. Barnett	Chicago
†Capitol News Service	R. Pelham	Washington, D.C.
Colored Syndicate Press Bureau	James Russell, Jr.	Washington, D.C.
Crusader News Service	Cyril V. Briggs	New York City
Hampton Institute Press Service	—	Hampton, Virginia
†Kelley Feature News Service	W. Kelley	New York City
†National Negro Publicity Bureau	—	Washington, D.C.
†Premier News Service	M. Kendrick	Washington, D.C.
Preston News Service	—	Pittsburgh
Tuskegee Institute Press Service	—	Tuskegee Institute (Alabama)

MAGAZINES

†Abbott's Monthly	Robert S. Abbott	Chicago
†Black Man	Marcus Garvey	New York City
†Bronzeman	C. W. Crews	Chicago
*Challenge	William Bridges	New York City
Champion	William H. Ferris	Chicago

Colored American	Joseph N. Hawkins	Albany, N.Y.
Commercial Journal	W. D. Allimono	Chicago
*Competitor	Robert L. Vann	Pittsburgh
*Crisis	NAACP (W. E. B. DuBois)	New York City
*Crusader	Cyril V. Briggs	New York City
Favorite	Fenton Johnson	Chicago
†Fire	Wallace Thurman	New York City
Fountain's Digest	G. E. Fountain	Parkersburg, W. Va.
Half-Century	Katherine E. Williams	Chicago
Journal of Negro History	Carter G. Woodson	Washington, D.C.
*Messenger	A. Philip Randolph and Chandler Owen	New York City
Music and Poetry	Nora Douglas Holt	Chicago
†Negro American	–	San Antonio, Tex.
New Negro	A. V. Bernier	New York City
Observer	Arthur M. Bragg	Baltimore
*Opportunity	Charles S. Johnson	Chicago
Peoples Pilot	E. D. Coffee	Richmond, Va.
Pioneer	R. E. Bevis	Waco, Tex.
Praiseworthy Muse	J. Harvey Baxter	Norfolk, Va.
Promoter	Hodge Kirnon	New York City
Searchlight	A. B. Vincent	Raleigh, N.C.
†Southern Workman	Hampton Institute	Hampton, Virginia
Up-Reach	Willis N. Huggins	Chicago
Voice	Hubert H. Harrison	New York City

NEWSPAPERS

Alabama
Anniston Observer	T. J. Jackson	Anniston
Birmingham Eagle	G. T. Buford	Birmingham
†Birmingham Mouth-Piece	J. E. Lovis	Birmingham
Birmingham Reporter	O. W. Adams	Birmingham
Times–Plain Dealer	–	Birmingham
Birmingham Truth	G. Tallifero	Birmingham
†Birmingham World	W. A. Scott	Birmingham
Mobile Advocate	James R. Knox	Mobile
Mobile Forum	J. T. Peterson	Mobile
†Mobile Sun	R. M. Perry	Mobile
Mobile Weekly Press	J. W. McConico	Mobile
Messenger	G. M. Turner	Pell City
American Star	–	Sheffield
Rural Messenger	George F. King	Tuskegee Institute

Arizona
| Phoenix Tribune | A. R. Smith | Phoenix |
| Inter-State Review | E. J. Richardson | Tucson |

Arkansas

Negro Advocate	M. L. Hampton	Fordyce
Inter-State Reporter	H. W. Holloway	Helena
Hot Springs Echo	E. S. Lockhart	Hot Springs
Arkansas Banner	L. N. Porter	Little Rock
†Arkansas Survey	P. L. Dorman	Little Rock
†Arkansas Times	J. J. Price	Little Rock
Western Review	R. M. Carver	Little Rock
Opinion-Enterprise	M. A. Clark	Marianna
Voice	–	Morrillton
White River Advocate	H. R. McMillan	Newport
Progressive Citizen	–	Texarkana
School Herald	S. W. Eichelberger, Jr.	Warren

California

Citizen Advocate	C. Alexander	Los Angeles
*Eagle	Charlotta A. Bass	Los Angeles
Liberator	Max Eastman	Los Angeles
†New Age Dispatch	F. M. Roberts	Los Angeles
†Pacific Defender	–	Los Angeles
Western Dispatch	Louis S. Tenette	Los Angeles
California Voice	E. Marshall	Oakland
†Western American	–	Oakland
Western Review	J. M. Collins	Sacramento

Colorado

Colorado Advocate	E. B. Butler	Colorado Springs
Colorado Statesman	J. D. D. Rivers	Denver
Denver Star	G. G. Ross	Denver
Rising Sun	C. H. Holmes	Pueblo

Connecticut

Hartford Herald	J. W. Youngblood	Hartford

Delaware

Wilmington Advocate	R. J. Nelson	Wilmington

District of Columbia

*Washington Bee	Lucian Skinner
Colored American	–
†Washington Daily	E. L. C. Davidson
*Washington Eagle	J. Finley Wilson
Washington Sentinel	G. H. Richardson/W. H. Davis
Washington Tribune	F. M. Murray
†Washington World	

Florida

Florida Sentinel	W. I. Lewis	Jacksonville
Western Florida Bugle	A. Purdee	Marianna
†Miami Times	–	Miami
Palatka Advocate	V. A. Hawkins	Palatka
Colored Citizen	F. E. Washington	Pensacola
Tampa Bulletin	W. D. Patten	Tampa

Georgia

Americus Chronicle	W. R. Mack	Americus
Athens Republic	–	Athens
Atlanta Independent	B. J. Davis	Atlanta
Atlanta Post	E. L. Collier	Atlanta
†Atlanta World	W. A. Scott	Atlanta
Augusta News	E. A. Lyons	Augusta
Augusta Regulator	A. M. Wimberly	Augusta
Advocate	W. J. Sapp	Brunswick
Griffin Echo	A. S. Boynton	Griffin
Rome Enterprise	A. F. Atwater	Rome
Savannah Journal	F. D. Pettie/E. W. Sherman	Savannah
Savannah Tribune	Sol C. Johnson	Savannah

Illinois

*Broad Ax	J. F. Taylor	Chicago
†Chicago Bee	E. D. Pierson	Chicago
*Chicago Defender	R. S. Abbott	Chicago
Chicago Enterprise	J. Tupper	Chicago
Chicago Plaindealer	–	Chicago
Chicago Star	Sylvester Russell	Chicago
*Chicago Whip	W. C. Linton/J. D. Bibb	Chicago
Illinois Idea	Mrs. S. B. Turner	Chicago
Peoples Advocate	R. E. Parker	Chicago
Searchlight	B. W. Fitts	Chicago
†World	J. Tipper	Chicago
Inter State Echo	C. W. Colley	Danville
Southern Illinois Press	W. E. Officer	East St. Louis
Evanston Weekly	W. H. Gill	Evanston
Weekly Star	R. Y. Webb	Mound City
Herald	–	Robbins
Advance Citizen	H. T. Bowman	Springfield
Forum	J. B. Osby	Springfield
Illinois Conservator	E. L. Rodgers	Springfield

Indiana

Gary Dispatch	I. O. Guy	Gary
National Defender & Sun	Zenobia Bagly	Gary
Freeman	George L. Knox	Indianapolis
Indianapolis Ledger	William H. Jackson	Indianapolis
Indianapolis Recorder	G. P. Stewart	Indianapolis
Indianapolis Review	William Lewis	Indianapolis
†Indianapolis Spokesman	Gabriel Stanley	Indianapolis
Indianapolis World	A. E. Manning	Indianapolis
Plaindealer	J. H. Lott	Indianapolis
Richmond Blade	R. Harris	Richmond
Terre Haute Citizen	–	Terre Haute

Iowa

Iowa State Bystander	L. C. Jones	Des Moines

Kansas

Coffeyville Globe	A. R. Ferebee	Coffeyville
Kansas City Advocate	T. Kennedy	Kansas City
Topeka Plaindealer	Nick Chiles	Topeka
Negro Star	H. T. Sims	Wichita

Kentucky

Citizen	Marshall E. Vaughn	Berea
Informer	—	Cadiz
Torchlight	J. E. Wood	Danville
Hopkinsville Times	—	Hopkinsville
New Age	M. J. Street	Hopkinsville
Saturday News	Phil H. Brown	Hopkinsville
Lexington Times	S. M. Means	Lexington
Lexington Weekly News	E. D. Willis	Lexington
Columbian Herald	P. R. Peters	Louisville
Kentucky Reporter	R. T. Berry	Louisville
Louisville Leader	I. W. Cole	Louisville
Louisville News	William Warley	Louisville
Standard	—	Louisville
Light	—	Paduca

Louisiana

Advance Messenger	J. B. Lafargue	Alexandria
National Negro Voice	R. A. Flynn	New Orleans
Negro Advocate	M. S. Hampton	New Orleans
New Orleans Bulletin	J. F. Bromes	New Orleans
News-Enterprise	A. H. Samuels/J. M. Carter	Shreveport
Shreveport Sun	M. L. Collins	Shreveport
Watchman	S. H. Ralph	Shreveport

Maryland

*Afro-American	Carl Murphy	Baltimore
Crusader	Joseph Dorsey	Baltimore
Herald & Commonwealth	W. T. Andrews	Baltimore
Maryland Voice	—	Baltimore

Massachusetts

Boston Chronicle	U. N. Murray	Boston
Guardian	W. M. Trotter	Boston

Michigan

Detroit Contender	Robert L. Poston	Detroit
†Detroit Independent	William J. Johnson	Detroit
Detroit Leader	W. P. Kemp	Detroit
†Detroit Peoples News	Beulah Young	Detroit
†Detroit Telegram	E. Adams	Detroit
New Era	—	Detroit
†Owl	H. C. Patton	Detroit
Michigan State News	G. M. Smith	Grand Rapids

Minnesota

Minneapolis Messenger	C. S. Smith/H. B. Rowe	Minneapolis
National Advocate	A. B. Montgomery	Minneapolis
†Twin City Herald	J. E. Perry	Minneapolis
†Northwest Monitor	William Helm	Minneapolis–St. Paul
Appeal	O. N. Howell	St. Paul
†St. Paul Echo	Earl Wilkins	St. Paul

Mississippi

Morning Star	W. I. Mitchell	Columbus
Weekly Times	T. S. Thigpin	Hattiesburg
New Era	T. S. Crawford	Indianola
†Southern Register	M. L. Rogers	Jackson
Central Mississippi Signal	W. A. Singleton	Lynch Kosciusko
Advance	A. A. Cosey	Mound Bayou
National News Digest	W. N. Lott	Mound Bayou
Weekly Reporter	J. A. Young, Jr.	Natchez
Cotton Farmer	A. Wimbs	Scott
Light	W. H. Rogers	Vicksburg

Missouri

Anchor	J. W. D. Mayes	Caruthersville
Missouri State Register	G. H. Wright	Hannibal
Western Messenger	J. Goins	Jefferson City
Call	C. A. Franklin	Kansas City
†Kansas City American	–	Kansas City
Kansas City Sun	N. C. Crews	Kansas City
St. Joseph Appeal	–	St. Joseph
†St. Louis American	–	St. Louis
St. Louis Argus	J. E. Mitchell	St. Louis
†St. Louis Clarion	C. K. Robinson	St. Louis
St. Louis Independent	W. Lowe	St. Louis
†United World	E. N. Bryant	St. Louis

Nebraska

Monitor	J. A. Williams	Omaha
†Omaha Guide	H. J. Ford	Omaha

New Jersey

Atlantic Advocate	J. A. Lightfoot	Atlantic City
Camden Tribune	Marcus B. Mann	Camden
Eastern Observer	J. E. Sadler, Jr.	Montclair
†Newark Herald	F. R. Clark	Newark
New Jersey Observer	R. T. Reed	Newark
Echo	W. E. Rock	Red Bank

New Mexico

†Southwest Review	S. W. Henry	Albuquerque

New York

Buffalo American	J. L. Murray	Buffalo
†Buffalo Progressive Herald	Z. A. Alexander	Buffalo
Voice	–	Buffalo
Brooklyn–L.I. Informer	William S. McKinney, Jr.	Jamaica
*Amsterdam News	J. H. Anderson	New York City
†Contender	Ulysses S. Poston	New York City
*†(Harlem) Liberator	Cyril V. Briggs	New York City
*†Interstate-Tattler	T. T. Fortune	New York City
*Negro World	Marcus Garvey	New York City
*New York Age	Fred R. Moore	New York City
*New York Dispatch	John Lyon	New York City
New York News	G. W. Harris	New York City
*Veteran	William Y. Bell	New York City

North Carolina

Charlotte Advertiser	J. T. Sanders	Charlotte
Gazette	S. B. Pride	Charlotte
Signs of the Times	H. F. Woodhouse	Elizabeth City
Gate City Argus	G. H. Mitchell	Greensboro
Colored American	C. W. Robinson	High Point
Raleigh Independent	C. Cheeks	Raleigh
Voice	H. W. Townsend	Rocky Mt.
Home News	W. H. Moore	Wilmington
Winston-Salem News	W. W. Rouork	Winston-Salem

Ohio

†Cincinnati Bulletin	C. Lindell	Cincinnati
Cincinnati Journal	H. Tolber	Cincinnati
Union	W. P. Dabney	Cincinnati
Cleveland Advocate	Ormonde A. Forte	Cleveland
†Cleveland Call	H. E. Murrell	Cleveland
Cleveland Gazette	H. C. Smith	Cleveland
†Ohio State Pioneer	A. W. Harris	Cleveland
Ohio State Monitor	F. H. Cook	Columbus
Dayton Forum	J. H. Rives	Dayton
Hamilton Enterprise	–	Hamilton
Toledo Pioneer	–	Toledo

Oklahoma

Boley Elevator	–	Boley
Boley Progress	George M. Perry	Boley
Clearview Patriarch	J. E. Thompson	Clearview
Oklahoma Guide	W. Brown	Guthrie
Muskogee Cimeter	W. H. Twine	Muskogee
Watchman Lantern	P. C. Dandridge	Muskogee
*Black Dispatch	R. Dungee	Oklahoma City
Rentiesville News	B. C. Franklin	Rentiesville
†Oklahoma Eagle	Theodore Baughman	Tulsa
Oklahoma Sun	Theodore Baughman	Tulsa

Oregon

Advocate	E. D. Canady	Portland

Pennsylvania

Advocate Verdict	F. L. Jefferson	Harrisburg
Afro-American Press	–	Philadelphia
Christian Recorder	R. R. Wright, Jr.	Philadelphia
Herald Mission	–	Philadelphia
†New Era	Charles W. Monk	Philadelphia
Philadelphia American	John W. Parks	Philadelphia
Philadelphia Courant	–	Philadelphia
†Philadelphia Independent	A. W. Lynch	Philadelphia
Philadelphia Protector	W. H. Wright	Philadelphia
Philadelphia Tribune	Bertha T. Perry	Philadelphia
Public Journal	A. W. Lynch	Philadelphia
†Spokesman	J. N. McQuingley	Philadelphia
Industrial Register	–	Pittsburgh
Pittsburgh American	R. F. Douglas	Pittsburgh
*Pittsburgh Courier	Robert L. Vann	Pittsburgh
Advocate	J. S. Williams	Wilkes-Barre

Rhode Island

Triangle	–	Newport
Advance	–	Providence

South Carolina

Charleston Messenger	Orphan Society	Charleston
New Era	R. L. Wainwright	Charleston
Informer	D. L. Witherspoon	Columbia
Light	C. J. Garrett	Columbia
Southern Indicator	J. A. Roach	Columbia
People's Recorder	J. R. Wilson	Orangeburg
Rockhill Messenger	C. P. T. White	Rockhill

Tennessee

Chattanooga Defender	J. J. J. Oldfield	Chattanooga
East Tennessee News	W. L. Porter	Knoxville
Dublin Weekly Bulletin	–	Memphis
Memphis Times	S. W. Broome	Memphis
†Memphis Triangle	T. J. Jones	Memphis
Record	–	Memphis
†Tri-State Tribune	W. A. Dunham	Memphis
Western World Reporter	J. E. Washington	Memphis
Murfreesboro Union	H. J. Bailey	Murfreesboro
Nashville Clarion	E. W. D. Isaacs	Nashville
Nashville Globe	–	Nashville

Texas

Herald	M. M. Haynes	Austin
Watchman	James H. Harrison	Austin
Beaumont Monitor	C. B. Charlton	Beaumont
Industrial Era	O. Kirkwood	Beaumont
Calvert Bugle	T. E. Tolan	Calvert

Dallas Express	J. R. Jordan	Dallas
†Dallas Gazette	–	Dallas
Colored Farmer	J. H. Owens	Denison
Gate City Bulletin	J. H. Owens	Denison
Fort Worth Hornet	J. I. Dodson	Fort Worth
†Fort Worth Light	H. M. McCoy	Fort Worth
†People's Contender	–	Fort Worth
City Times	W. H. Noble, Jr.	Galveston
Colored American	S. H. Simpson	Galveston
Galveston New Idea	D. T. Shelton	Galveston
†Houston Defender	H. P. Carter	Houston
Houston Informer	C. F. Richardson	Houston
Houston Observer	L. A. Gilmore	Houston
†Houston Sentinel	J. M. Burr	Houston
Independence Heights Record	W. R. Knox	Houston
Texas Freeman	C. N. Love	Houston
Western Star	D. S. Scott	Houston
San Antonio Inquirer	G. U. Bouldin	San Antonio
Sentinel	J. T. Walton	San Antonio
Victoria Guard	I. H. Swaizey	Victoria
Clarion	J. C. Russell	Waco

Virginia

Charlottesville Messenger	J. G. Shelton	Charlottesville
Herald	–	Newport News
Star	M. N. Lewis	Newport News
Citizens Advocate	–	Norfolk
Journal and Guide	P. B. Young	Norfolk
Colored Virginian	A. B. Mackey	Petersburg
Virginian-Messenger	–	Petersburg
Weekly Review	A. B. Mackey	Petersburg
Vigil	–	Portsmouth
Richmond Planet	J. Mitchell, Jr.	Richmond
Richmond Voice	–	Richmond
St. Luke Herald	Mrs. M. L. Walker	Richmond
Virginia Advocate	R. Deane	Roanoke

Washington

Seattle Enterprise	W. H. Wilson	Seattle
Seattle Searchlight	S. P. DeBow	Seattle

West Virginia

Advocate	J. G. Gilmer	Charleston
Charleston American	–	Charleston
Charleston Observer	–	Charleston
Mountain Leader	T. J. Nutter	Charleston
McDowell Times	–	Keystone
Pioneer Press	J. R. Clifford	Martinsburg

Wisconsin

Wisconsin Weekly Blade	J. Anthony Josey	Madison

Index

391   Index